FROMMER'S
TURKEY
ON $25 A DAY

by Tom Brosnahan
assisted by Jane Fisher

1988–1989 Edition

Published by Prentice Hall Press
A Division of Simon & Schuster, Inc.
Gulf + Western Building
One Gulf + Western Plaza
New York, NY 10023

ISBN: 0-671-62459-8

Manufactured in the United States of America

CONTENTS

MAPS

*This book is dedicated to
My Wife,
who suffered patiently its completion.*

*To travel is to discover that
everyone is wrong about other countries.
—Aldous Huxley*

INFLATION ALERT: We don't have to tell you that inflation has hit Turkey as it has everywhere else. In researching this book I have made every effort to obtain up-to-the-minute prices, but even the most conscientious researcher cannot keep up with the current pace of inflation. As we go to press, I believe I have obtained the most reliable data possible. Nonetheless, in the lifetime of this edition—particularly its second year (1989)—the wise traveler will add 15% to 20% to the prices quoted throughout these pages.

A DISCLAIMER: Although every effort was made to ensure the accuracy of the prices and travel information appearing in this book, it should be kept in mind that prices do fluctuate in the course of time, and that information does change under the impact of the varied and volatile factors that affect the travel industry.

TURKEY ON $25 A DAY

The Reason Why

WHY VISIT TURKEY? As a friend confessed, it was the only country he visited in six months of European travel that was really *different*. For if "Europe" stands for Western culture, "Asia" brings to mind vast spaces filled with civilizations reaching back through direct lines to times before history was written, all the way back to the origins of man—and Turkey lies in both.

Modern Turkey occupies a small corner of the European peninsula of Thrace and the Asian Anatolian peninsula, also called Asia Minor. A visit to the city of Istanbul will give you the chance to sail from one continent to the other on a commuter ferry—or drive right across the Bosphorus Bridge. The distance separating the two is not great, only as great as the Bosphorus is wide. There is no division as distinct as that between, say, Europe and Africa. But the division does exist because of the great cultural difference which separated these two areas until very recently.

Before 1923, when the Republic of Turkey was founded and westernization began, Turkey was the polyglot Ottoman Empire, heir to the glories of the Byzantine, Arabic, and Persian empires of the past, and the embodiment of Oriental splendor, leisure, and military tradition. The lands of the empire spread over three continents, from Algeria through Egypt to Iraq, and from Iran well into Europe, almost to the gates of Vienna. The ruler of this part of the world was the Sultan-Caliph, or "Padishah," attended in his palace by chamberlains, eunuchs, a private harem, and his chief of state, the grand vizier. The cities of his empire were adorned with kiosks and palaces of a distinctly Oriental flavor, with Turkish mosques recalling the glories of Byzantine and Arabic architecture, and with the colorful costumes, ceremonies, and customs of a myriad of peoples.

Many tourists who come to Turkey are surprised to find that names and places that are a familiar part of their own vocabulary are derived from Anatolia's past: King Midas, King Croesus, Galen, Homer, Ephesus, Troy, Angora, Constantinople, Trebizond, Cappadocia—all these people and places are parts of Anatolia's incredibly rich history as a home and trade route for a score of civilizations. The two influences, Eastern and Western, have alternated in dominating this land for thousands of years as armies and traders and migrants crossed the land bridge of Anatolia between Europe and the East. Being a Western visitor to Turkey, you're in for a surprise. Though you'll visit some of the places and be reminded of some of the people who've shaped our culture, for all its links with the modern West, Turkey can still hold for you the mystery of the Orient, a land reminiscent of the Thousand and One Nights, memories of whirling dervishes, camel caravans, pashas, and sultans.

TURKEY—A FIRST IMPRESSION: When I first arrived in Turkey, flying into the airport in Ankara, I confirmed my vague suspicions that Turkey was a hot, dusty desert of low rolling hills and sparse, scrubby vegetation. But when I got on the ground and traveled around a bit, I discovered that this relatively big country (larger than Texas) has craggy, snow-capped mountains, broad lakes, cool pine forests, miles of white beaches, snowy winters, long Indian summers —a lot to offer a tourist. At the end of summer on the Anatolian plateau, after months of straight sunshine, the land is dry and dusty. When I flew into Ankara I didn't notice that the city was pretty well deserted. Why stay in the city when there are so many nicer places to be? The Black Sea coast is relatively close and the Sea of Marmara and the beaches of the Aegean a day's bus or train ride, so Ankara's people seek out the good places and wait until the city is pleasant again. The Istanbullus leave their city for villas and cabins on the shores of the Bosphorus or for hotels and resorts on the nearby Princes' Islands in the Sea of Marmara. As the season passes and the weather cools, the places to prolong outdoor activities are the numerous spas and hot springs, especially those at Pamukkale (the old Greco-Roman spa of Hierapolis), where one can stay in a modern resort hotel for $20 double and swim in its pool of warm mineral water strewn with columns and other artifacts from the ancient past.

Turkey is a country of subtle beauties. An early-morning scene on the Anatolian plateau: a mesa in the distance with a nomad's tent at the base, his horse quietly grazing in the dewy grass as the sun creeps across the plain; the incredible blue color of the Aegean Sea; a caravan of gypsies in their picturesque wagons passing a moonscape of rock pinnacles once hollowed out and inhabited by early Christians; the palm trees lining the waterfront in İzmir moving gently in the wind, the whole town dominated by a citadel dating from the time of Alexander the Great; the sun setting into the Golden Horn of Istanbul, seeming to turn the water to gold and thus giving the river its name. Add to these the stories of a dozen civilizations, each of which has helped form the Turkey of today, and you have a place to compel your imagination and hold your interest for quite a while—especially Istanbul.

Istanbul is the city of the former Caliphate of Islam and of the Ecumenical Patriarchate of the Orthodox Church, of Turkish mosques and Byzantine churches. In the museums are beautiful Christian mosaics and ancient Turkish miniatures. The effect on a visitor is an instant fascination with the Oriental facets of the city and a comfortable familiarity with the Occidental. After a morning spent in the sultan's Seraglio, there's a lunch of wienerschnitzel and beer; or, conversely, a day in Istanbul's European quarter and a dinner of shish kebap and rakı. The city harbors an amazing variety of peoples even today, and each holds to its ancient traditions and way of life. On the Golden Horn, children crowd to Greek schools in the section called Fener. In Galata there are two synagogues, attended by people whose ancient forebears were driven from Spain by the Inquisition and who even today speak a dialect of Spanish. In the section called Beyoğlu, once the old city of Pera, little carpenters' and tailors' shops, restaurants, and coffeehouses bear Russian, Italian, German, French, and Balkan names. Near the Bosphorus in Asia is a Polish village where the best pork products in Turkey are made. And over all these different flavors added by minorities is the Turkish culture, its great mosques, delicate faïence, Turkish Delight, and tradition of the romance of the East.

The sun sets in İzmir, poised between the twin mountain peaks that dominate the harbor, said to be the place where the goddess Nemesis lived; the call to prayer drifts up from the minarets in the city of Bursa to the slopes of the Asian Mount Olympus, now Turkey's most popular ski resort; in the fast-growing vacation town of Kuşadası on the Aegean coast a Turk sits in his coffeehouse, drinking Turkish coffee and smoking a bubbling narghile; a modern cruise ship steams toward the ancient cities of Tarsus and Antioch, the sun rising on its bow. . . . This is what Turkey holds for the visitor today, and all of it at prices that equal or beat the lowest in Europe.

TOURISM IN TURKEY: The Turkish government realizes what tourism can mean for the country in terms of foreign credit and cultural exchange, and has therefore entrusted the promotion of tourism to a ministry formed expressly for this purpose. The work of restoring historical sites, encouraging the construction of new tourist facilities, supervising hotel and restaurant policies and the like has been going on for several years with gratifying results. Almost every area of interest to tourists can boast of some advance within the last few years. And yet Turkey is not in the company of slick attractions where prices are high and things are just like home, with none of the flavor of another country or culture. It still has that "edge" that keeps it in the realm of the "unspoiled" places, where the excitement of discovery has not been whittled away by too much promotion and commerciality. Right now, in all of the places that you'll want to visit in a stay of a few weeks there are good, clean accommodations at pleasantly surprising prices, from the bare but clean village hotel where two people pay $4 each, to the hotel in Istanbul with rooms for $18 double, located near the main tourist attractions and with a view of the Sea of Marmara thrown in for good measure.

ON $25 A DAY—WHAT THAT MEANS: This book operates on the theory that one can travel in Turkey spending $25 a day for lodging and three meals, broken down so that approximately $13 is for a hotel room, $2 or $3 for breakfast, $4 or $5 for lunch, and another $4 or $5 for dinner, per person. Transportation, entertainment, sightseeing, and shopping are *not* included in this basic budget. Spending $25 a day in Turkey enables one to stay in clean, comfortable, safe hotels suitable for people of all ages and both sexes. Most of the hotels mentioned in this book are moderately priced, offering double-occupancy rooms, always with bath or shower, for 7,000TL ($9.80) to 21,000TL ($29.40). For younger, more impecunious travelers, less expensive hotels, pensions, and hostels offering less comfortable accommodations at rock-bottom prices have been included. And for those with a little extra money to spend, there are a number of recommendations for establishments in the $30-a-day range. In addition to the standard, white-tablecloth restaurants in which a full three-course meal costs about $4 or $5, establishments offering simple meals or snacks at much less are described for those who want to hold their expenses below the $25-a-day level.

THE FUTURE OF THIS BOOK: This is the fifth edition of *Turkey on $25 a Day*. My own experiences and choices of hotels, restaurants, and sights have been augmented considerably by suggestions and comments from readers all over the world, for which I am very grateful. Your tips and comments on establishments mentioned in this book, or low-cost discoveries of your own, will help keep the book an extensive and up-to-date guide for budget travelers. Address your letters to Tom Brosnahan, c/o Frommer Books, Prentice Hall Press, One Gulf + Western Plaza, New York, NY 10023.

1. The $25-A-Day Travel Club—How to Save Money on All Your Travels

In this book we'll be looking at how to get your money's worth in Turkey, but there is a "device" for saving money and determining value on *all* your trips. It's the popular, international $25-A-Day Travel Club, now in its 25th successful year of operation. The Club was formed at the urging of numerous readers of the $$$-A-Day and Dollarwise Guides, who felt that such an organization could provide continuing travel information and a sense of community to value-minded travelers in all parts of the world. And so it does!

In keeping with the budget concept, the annual membership fee is low and is immediately exceeded by the value of your benefits. Upon receipt of $18 (U.S. residents), or $20 U.S. by check drawn on a U.S. bank or via international postal money order in U.S. funds (Canadian, Mexican, and other foreign residents) to cover one year's membership, we will send all new members the following items.

(1) *Any two* of the following books

Please designate in your letter which two you wish to receive:

Frommer's $-A-Day Guides
    Europe on $25 a Day
    Australia on $25 a Day
    Eastern Europe on $25 a Day
    England on $35 a Day
    Greece including Istanbul and Turkey's Aegean Coast on $25 a Day
    Hawaii on $45 a Day
    India on $15 & $25 a Day
    Ireland on $30 a Day
    Israel on $30 & $35 a Day
    Mexico on $20 a Day (plus Belize and Guatemala)
    New York on $45 a Day
    New Zealand on $35 a Day
    Scandinavia on $50 a Day
    Scotland and Wales on $35 a Day
    South America on $30 a Day
    Spain and Morocco (plus the Canary Is.) on $40 a Day
    Turkey on $25 a Day
    Washington, D.C., on $40 a Day

Frommer's Dollarwise Guides
    Dollarwise Guide to Austria and Hungary
    Dollarwise Guide to Belgium, Holland, & Luxembourg
    Dollarwise Guide to Bermuda and The Bahamas
    Dollarwise Guide to Canada
    Dollarwise Guide to the Caribbean
    Dollarwise Guide to Egypt
    Dollarwise Guide to England and Scotland
    Dollarwise Guide to France
    Dollarwise Guide to Germany

Dollarwise Guide to Italy
Dollarwise Guide to Japan and Hong Kong
Dollarwise Guide to Portugal, Madeira, and the Azores
Dollarwise Guide to the South Pacific
Dollarwise Guide to Switzerland and Liechtenstein
Dollarwise Guide to Alaska
Dollarwise Guide to California and Las Vegas
Dollarwise Guide to Florida
Dollarwise Guide to the Mid-Atlantic
Dollarwise Guide to New England
Dollarwise Guide to New York State
Dollarwise Guide to the Northwest
Dollarwise Guide to Skiing USA—East
Dollarwise Guide to Skiing USA—West
Dollarwise Guide to the Southeast and New Orleans
Dollarwise Guide to the Southwest
Dollarwise Guide to Texas
(Dollarwise Guides discuss accommodations and facilities in all price ranges, with emphasis on the medium-priced.)

Frommer's Touring Guides
Egypt
Florence
London
Paris
Venice
(These new, color illustrated guides include walking tours, cultural and historic sites, and other vital travel information.)

A Shopper's Guide to Best Buys in England, Scotland, and Wales
(Describes in detail hundreds of places to shop—department stores, factory outlets, street markets, and craft centers—for great quality British bargains.)

A Shopper's Guide to the Caribbean
(Two experienced Caribbean hands guide you through this shopper's paradise, offering witty insights and helpful tips on the wares and emporia of more than 25 islands.)

Bed & Breakfast—North America
(This guide contains a directory of over 150 organizations that offer bed & breakfast referrals and reservations throughout North America. The scenic attractions, and major schools and universities near the homes of each are also listed.)

Dollarwise Guide to Cruises
(This complete guide covers all the basics of cruising—ports of call, costs, fly-cruise package bargains, cabin selection booking, embarkation and debarkation, and describes in detail over 60 or so ships cruising the waters of Alaska, the Caribbean, Mexico, Hawaii, Panama, Canada, and the United States.)

Dollarwise Guide to Skiing Europe
(Describes top ski resorts in Austria, France, Italy, and Switzerland. Illustrated with maps of each resort area plus full-color trail maps.)

Fast 'n' Easy Phrase Book
(French, German, Spanish, and Italian—all in one convenient, easy-to-use phrase guide.)

Honeymoon Guide
(A special guide for that most romantic trip of your life, with full details on planning and choosing the destination that will be just right in the U.S. [California, New England, Hawaii, Florida, New York, South Carolina, etc.], Canada, Mexico, and the Caribbean.)

How to Beat the High Cost of Travel
(This practical guide details how to save money on absolutely all travel items— accommodations, transportation, dining, sightseeing, shopping, taxes, and more. Includes special budget information for seniors, students, singles, and families.)

Marilyn Wood's Wonderful Weekends
(This very selective guide covers the best mini-vacation destinations within a 175-mile radius of New York City. It describes special country inns and other accommodations, restaurants, picnic spots, sights, and activities—all the information needed for a two- or three-day stay.)

Motorist's Phrase Book
(A practical phrase book in French, German, and Spanish designed specifically for the English-speaking motorist touring abroad.)

Swap and Go—Home Exchanging Made Easy
(Two veteran home exchangers explain in detail all the money-saving benefits of a home exchange, and then describe precisely how to do it. Also includes information on home rentals and many tips on low-cost travel.)

The Candy Apple: New York for Kids
(A spirited guide to the wonders of the Big Apple by a savvy New York grandmother with a kid's eye view to fun. Indispensable for visitors and residents alike.)

Travel Diary and Record Book
(A 96-page diary for personal travel notes plus a section for such vital data as passport and traveler's check numbers, itinerary, postcard list, special people and places to visit, and a reference section with temperature and conversion charts, and world maps with distance zones.)

Where to Stay USA
(By the Council on International Educational Exchange, this extraordinary guide is the first to list accommodations in all 50 states that cost anywhere from $3 to $30 per night.)

(2) A one-year subscription to *The Wonderful World of Budget Travel*

This quarterly eight-page tabloid newspaper keeps you up to date on fast-breaking developments in low-cost travel in all parts of the world, bringing you the latest money-saving information—the kind of information you'd have to pay $25 a year to obtain elsewhere. This consumer-conscious publication also features columns of special interest to readers: **Hospitality Exchange** (members all over the world who are willing to provide hospitality to other members as they pass through their home cities); **Share-a-Trip** (offers and requests from members for travel companions who can share costs and help avoid the burdensome single supplement); and **Readers Ask . . . Readers Reply** (travel questions from members to which other members reply with authentic firsthand information).

(3) A copy of *Arthur Frommer's Guide to New York*

This is a pocket-size guide to hotels, restaurants, nightspots, and sightseeing attractions in all price ranges throughout the New York area.

(4) Your personal membership card

Membership entitles you to purchase through the Club all Arthur Frommer publications for a third to a half off their regular retail prices during the term of your membership.

So why not join this hardy band of international budgeteers and participate in its exchange of travel information and hospitality? Simply send your name and address, together with your annual membership fee of $18 (U.S. residents) or $20 U.S. (Canadian, Mexican, and other foreign residents), by check drawn on a U.S. bank or via international postal money order in U.S. funds to: $25-A-Day Travel Club, Inc., Frommer Books, Gulf + Western Building, One Gulf + Western Plaza, New York, NY 10023. And please remember to specify which *two* of the books in section (1) above you wish to receive in your initial package of members' benefits. Or, if you prefer, use the last page of this book, simply checking off the two books you select and enclosing $18 or $20 in U.S. currency.

Once you are a member, there is no obligation to buy additional books. No books will be mailed to you without your specific order.

TURKEY AND THE TURKS

TO THE FIRST-TIME VISITOR Turkey comes as a pleasant surprise. The exotic visions of a mysterious and unfamiliar country give way immediately to common, comprehensible scenes of people waiting for buses, dining in restaurants, and talking on the telephone. Even so, this is a different country, and many of daily life's little chores are done in different ways. This chapter will introduce you to Turkey and the Turks, their history, the way they dine, what they offer their children for amusement, what they use for money, and whether or not it's safe to drink the water.

1. A Short History

The Turkish Republic is less than a century old; Turkey's imperial history is much, much longer. A lot of the imperial glory which has been preserved goes back only to the time of the Ottoman conquest in the 15th century. But the history of the Anatolian homeland goes far back past the coming of the Turks, into eras of history which are sometimes more familiar, other times more exotic, to Western culture.

Excavations at Çatal Höyük and Hacılar show highly refined Neolithic settlements dating back to 6800 and 5500 B.C., communities as culturally sophisticated as those in the Fertile Crescent during this age. But the earliest empire to control Anatolia seems to have been that of the Hittites, formed around 2000 B.C. At its peak about 1500 B.C., it was one of the four great Eastern powers, rivaling Egypt, Syria, and Mycenae.

Near the end of their era the Hittites clashed with the powerful ruler of Egypt, Ramses II, and thus caused the first of a long line of great imperial battles which were to take place in this area. Several centuries later, while the Phrygians were building their civilization on the ruins of the Hittites, the Achaeans and Aeolians sailed across the Aegean Sea and founded colonies that were to grow to be powerful cities, the birthplaces of classical Hellenic culture. One group of Achaeans tangled with a confederation of Anatolian peoples living in Troy in the 12th century B.C.—hence the Trojan War. By the time of the first millennium B.C., the once-small Greek colonies on the Aegean coast of Anatolia had grown to be cities and formed a pact—the Ionian Confederacy—with the great cities of Ephesus and Miletus as cultural founts, spreading Hellenic science and art throughout the Aegean region and farther afield. But just as these early Greeks had come to Anatolia in pursuit of their enemies, so came the Persians, sweeping over the peninsula in the 6th century B.C. Their downfall appeared from the opposite direction in 334 B.C.: Alexander the Great crossed the Dardanelles, cut the famous Gordian Knot at Gordium (near present-day Ankara), and opened the way to Persia. Alexander died at the ripe age of 33, and his empire fell to pieces amid the quarrels of his lieutenants over the spoils.

The Roman Legions entered Anatolia a century or two before the beginning of the Christian era, conquered the powerful kingdom of Pontus, ruled by Mithridates, and the Armenian territories in the east, and made tributary states out of the cities of the Aegean, still important as trade centers. St. Paul and St. John knew Anatolia well from their missions to the Jews, Greeks, and Romans in such cities as Tarsus (Paul's birthplace), Ephesus, Antioch, and Laodicea. The first Roman emperor officially to tolerate Christianity, and later a convert to Christianity himself, was Constantine the Great, who moved the capital of the empire to a new city which he built on the Bosphorus. The move came only five years after the Council of Nicaea, held in a city to the east of Constantinople, the city now called İznik by the Turks.

In the 6th century A.D. the Emperor Justinian tried to save the old Roman Empire from being nibbled away by barbarians, but not long after his death yet another invasion swept Anatolia, this one by the Arabs, who reached the Bosphorus in 663. The Arabs retreated soon after they came, but they passed their religion on to the Seljuk Turks, who were to occupy most of Anatolia after the Arab withdrawal. The Seljuks streamed in from the East and whittled away at the Byzantine Empire, but these Turks, too, lost power after a time. The Crusades didn't help to lengthen their rule, and by the 13th century their state was weak enough to be overrun by a new wave of Turks from the East, eventually to be ruled by the House of Osman, the Ottoman Dynasty. The Ottoman power had surrounded Constantinople—all that was left of the Byzantine Empire except for a small part of Greece—long before the birth of Mehmet the Conqueror. But when Mehmet's father died, Mehmet ascended the throne, annulled the peace treaty with the Byzantine emperor which his father had honored, and took the city in 1453, putting an end to the Byzantine Empire once and for all.

The Ottoman Empire reached the height of its glory under Süleyman the Magnificent, a great law-giver and warrior who extended the boundaries of his empire far into Asia, Africa, and Europe, even threatening Vienna in 1529. The Ottoman Empire, like the old Austro-Hungarian Empire, was therefore a huge conglomeration of states and peoples. As the power of the West grew, the warlike skills of the Oriental conquerors in Turkey became more and more obsolete until the empire was little more than Anatolian Turkey, ruled by the sultan, and territories in Europe and Africa over which he reigned but did not rule. A series of Balkan wars gave the European subject peoples their freedom; the First World War saw the total defeat of the Ottoman power, and the War of Independence resulted in the establishment of the Republic of Turkey, with the country's national hero, Kemal Atatürk, as first president.

2. About Turkish Hotels

Before you start out to look for a hotel in Istanbul, or indeed in any town in Turkey, you should note the following things about Turkish hotels. There are two general categories: those that are controlled by the municipal government (usually the less expensive places), and those controlled by the national Ministry of Culture and Tourism (usually the more expensive places, with conveniences such as elevators, multilingual staff, air conditioning, and the like). Most of the new hotels being built have only double rooms with bath or shower; a "bath" in Turkish can mean a full, big bathtub *(gömme banyo)*, a short, sit-in tub, a splashbowl, a shower, or a showerhose attached to the bathroom faucet. Often you have to look at the room to know what you're getting.

Other things to look for: In summer, some cities have water-pressure and electric-current problems. Inquire about this before checking in. The hotel may have a reservoir on its roof which will eliminate any chance of pressure loss. Noise is a big problem in many hotels, for in the cities the trucks and motorcycles start early in the morning, and in the small resort towns there are sometimes scruffy little discos that blare music until late at night. A room high up in the building, or one looking onto a courtyard, will usually resolve this problem. Many of the new, moderately priced hotels have restaurants, but unless they're patronized by the public at large, they are usually suitable only for breakfast. Beware the small, empty hotel restaurant. In fact, breakfast is often tastier and cheaper in the local *pastahane* (pastry shop). Some hotels give off-season discounts of 15% to 30% in winter.

Most of the hotels in Istanbul, like small hotels in big cities everywhere, are sandwiched in between other buildings. Hence, the rooms which get plenty of sun and light are usually in the front of the building. Sometimes the hotel actually charges less for the quieter rooms in the back, realizing that they're less desirable; keep this in mind when looking for a room.

Turks are big on family accommodations while traveling, so most cheaper hotels will have a certain number of rooms with three or four beds at a price well below what you'd have to pay for a double and a single. If your needs fit it, don't forget to look at a triple room.

Some more notes: New hotels, by and large, tend to have lobbies that are much more plush than the rooms you stay in. *Don't* judge a hotel by its lobby! Because rooms with bath are often well within our budget, I've always included information on these as well as bathless rooms. Remember that during the off-season most hotel managers are gasping for customers and will give you a good discount if you simply hesitate when told the price. The discount becomes even greater if you take a look at the room, pick out its faults, tell him it would have to be a bit lower for you to stay, and move toward the door. In most cases you'll be called back; if you aren't, come back after ten minutes, tell the man you're tired of walking and that you'll take the room. Rooms with a view, especially if it's on the Bosphorus, are usually a good deal more expensive than rooms without.

Most hotels have two telephone numbers: one for the reservations clerk and another for the switchboard. The numbers given below are always the reservations numbers. Be sure to pick up the hotel's card with its name and both numbers if you think you'll have reason to call one of the rooms from outside the hotel.

Finally, every hotel is required to maintain a signed and stamped tariff giving current room rates. Ask for the *resmi fiyat listesi* and take a look at it. And each hotel has a complaints book, or *şikâyet defteri*, checked by tourism officials periodically. If you'd rather, send your complaints directly to the Ministry of Culture and Tourism, Gazi Mustafa Kemal Bul. no. 33, Demirtepe, Ankara, Turkey. The author of this book also asks to hear of any complaints.

PREPARATION FOR YOUR TRIP: Traveling in foreign countries brings you into new and strange situations, and though it's often fun to do things as the natives do, it can be irritating when simple daily habits, taken for granted at home, are upset. Over the years, readers of this book have written to tell what they found useful to have along with them while traveling in Turkey, and sharing these suggestions with you will help you to prepare better. Carry a supply of toilet paper, which is readily available in Turkey but not necessarily in the right place at the right time. If you use a washcloth daily, take one along: you'll always be given towels in a hotel, but rarely a washcloth. (If you forget yours, go into a bazaar and ask for a *banyo için kese,* a coarse-cloth mitt used for scrubbing in Turkish baths.)

3. Turkish Cuisine and Restaurants

A Turkish friend once explained that the variety and ingenuity of Turkish cooking developed during the Ottoman Empire, when Islamic religious customs required women to spend almost all their time in the house. Shish kebap, a holdover from the nomadic days when hearty meals had to be prepared quickly and pots were an extra burden, soon came to be served with countless delicious hors d'oeuvres, vegetable dishes, puddings, and desserts. Recipes were exchanged throughout the whole huge empire and among its many cultures. Turkish cuisine is now recognized as one of the world's basic cuisines, along with French and Chinese.

Islamic law forbade alcoholic beverages, so bars or pubs had no chance to grow up in the old Turkey. Instead, Turks learned to do their drinking with meals. There are many orthodox Muslims who still hold to the religious law and do their eating in *içkisiz* (drinkless) restaurants; the places which serve alcoholic drinks are called *içkili.*

Conversation is an art in Turkey. The artists go about it in coffeehouses *(kiraathane)* or teahouses *(çay evi),* a practice dating from the time of Sultan Süleyman the Magnificent; the more modern development in this field is the *pastahane* or pastry shop, where Turks talk over tea, coffee, hot milk, lemonade, or a hot, sweet tapioca-and-milk drink called *sahlep;* but instead of the water-pipe common to the coffee- and teahouses, here the beverage is accompanied by Turkish pastry. The selection of pastries seems to be endless, and though some come to you swimming in syrup or otherwise too sweet for foreign tastes, many varieties are very tasty. Finally, the Turks are inveterate strollers and munchers, and to cater to ambulatory appetites there are little shops selling all sorts of snacks and puddings, sandwiches, and drinks. Tiny stands and itinerant vendors sell *kuru yemiş*—literally, dry fruits—including chocolate, candy, cookies, dates, figs, and at least ten different kinds of nuts.

For your meals in Istanbul, and throughout Turkey, there are different places for the different times of day. An easy, cheap, delicious breakfast is best in a pastahane, where tea and croissants or pastry rarely exceeds 800TL ($1.10). The pastahanes are also good for finishing off an after-dinner stroll with dessert and coffee. For a quick lunch there are the *büfes,* from the French "buffet," and kiosks, scattered all over the city, but especially heavy on İstiklal Caddesi. At a büfe you choose your food from display cases or from a signboard, tell the cashier what you want, pay and get a *fiş* (pronounced "feesh") which you give to the person who hands you the food. Sometimes you stand and eat from a counter, but many büfes have "salons" with tables. Some even have waiter service, and, therefore, a service charge if you take advantage of it. A quick lunch of Turkish pizza *(lahmacun),* a pastry filled with chicken, sausage, or cheese *(börek)* and a soda will usually be less than 1,000TL ($1.40). At the büfes or the little sandwich kiosks, try a toasted cheese sandwich *(peynirli tost)* or one with sausage *(sosisli),* for about 250TL (35¢) or 300TL (42¢) apiece. The variety of sandwiches in these places is extensive, often including some made with stuffed vine leaves, hard-boiled eggs, Russian salad, or sheep's cheese.

For sit-down meals there are the restaurants, in three basic groupings. The first, the cheapest category, is that of the kebapçıs, köftecis, and hazır yemek restaurants. **Kebapçı** means "one who makes kebaps," and at almost any of these in Istanbul you can get a meal of soup, a meat dish, and dessert and pay anywhere from 1,000TL ($1.40) to 2,000TL ($2.80). In line with their prices, the decor in the kebapçıs ranges from very severe—bare walls, sawdust on the floor —with working-class clientele, to very comfortable with refined service. All are amazingly cheap. **Köftecis** are similar to kebapçıs in price and appearance, but they specialize in different varieties of köfte (ground meat rissoles served with spices, sauces, or charcoal-grilled, often eaten with yogurt). Finally, there are hundreds of little **hazır yemek** ("ready food") restaurants where an assortment of dishes is prepared in advance and patrons simply point to whatever they want through a glass partition separating the kitchen from the dining area, and a waiter brings the meal instantly. All of these restaurants are identifiable because the specialty is prepared in the front window; kebapçıs have a big vertical spit of döner kebap (turning kebab); köftecis have their charcoal grills, and hazır yemek restaurants their assortment of dishes. Prices are posted prominently, according to law.

For a good assortment of both Turkish and continental meals, with white tablecloths and similar service at about 2,500TL ($3.50) to 5,000TL ($7) a meal, there are many restaurants of the **Lüks,** first, and second classes. Here the Istanbul businessman takes his two-hour lunch break or lingers over dinner late into the evening. The Lüks, or luxury class, includes such places as the Hilton, but also some restaurants in which a three-course meal costs about 3,500TL ($4.90) to 6,000TL ($8.40). Cheaper meals can be found in almost any restaurant in either the first or second classes.

The third type of restaurant in Istanbul is the swank American type, catering to the jet set—mostly foreigners. Look for these in the big, fancy hotels. Check the prices and service, and you'll find that for the price of a cheeseburger and soft drink you could have a full four-course meal at a first-class restaurant where Turks eat.

4. Traveling with Children

Turks absolutely love children, and will go out of their way to solve any problems you may encounter when traveling with a child. To be completely in accord with local customs, buy a little blue-and-white glass evil-eye bead *(nazar boncuğu)* and pin it to the collar of your infant's clothes to ward off the evil eye. No well-dressed Turkish baby is without one, whether the parents believe in it or not.

Even though babies and children are honored guests in Turkey, many familiar child-care items have yet to appear in this country. Child safety seats, for instance, are not yet available from car-rental companies, and if you want this sort of protection, you will have to rig something yourself. Disposable diapers are becoming available, but cannot yet be found easily, everywhere. Restaurants do not normally offer children's menus or portions, but this presents no problem as the staff will eagerly provide simple dishes such as puréed vegetables or fried or poached eggs which do not appear on the menu. Commercial baby foods and formulas are found in the larger cities, and pure milk can be found easily everywhere.

You can save money on Turkish Airlines flights by asking for the "family fare," which grants a reduction to any adult or couple traveling with children.

Most of the better hotels can arrange babysitting services, but the arrangements will probably be ad hoc rather than normal procedure. The reason is that Turkish parents tend to take their children with them wherever they go, even to nightclubs! It's not looked upon as detrimental to keep a child out until well past midnight, and many a father carries his small son or daughter, asleep in his arms, through the quiet streets of town in the middle of the night.

As for amusements, Istanbul has its ferryboats, which provide children as well as parents with a thrill. The fortresses of Yedikule and Rumeli Hisar have enchanting turrets, crenellations, and cannons. Galata Tower is exciting for its panoramic views. The parks at Gülhane, near the Archeological Museums, and at Yıldız, on the Bosphorus, provide refreshing expanses of greenery.

In Çanakkale there is another good fortress with cannons, and a model of a minesweeper. At Troy, children can climb up into a model of the Trojan horse and peer out the windows. İzmir has ferryboats, and horse-drawn carriages for a ride around town. Its Kültür Parkı (Culture Park) has rides and amusements, including a ferris wheel and a mini-train.

Ankara's prime attraction for children is Gençlik Parkı, the Youth Park, with rowboats, a wonderfully authentic mini-train, and mechanical rides. Kids might also like to take a walk through the narrow, ancient streets of the Kale (citadel).

Cappadocia, with its labyrinths of rock-carved dwellings and churches, is a fairyland for kids. The nearby underground cities are even more impressive, and will leave a lasting impression.

5. Specific Information, from A to Z

Daily life in Turkey is somewhat like that in Europe, in other ways like that in North America, but often with a bit of the Middle East. For instance, Sunday is the day of rest, a secular one, even though Friday is the Muslim holy day. Banks keep bankers' hours as in Europe, but restaurants tend to stay open and serving all the time, as in North America. What you'll need to know about daily life in Turkey is summarized below, from A to Z.

BANKS: Banking hours are 8:30 a.m. to noon and 1:30 to 5 p.m. Monday through Friday. Outside these hours it can be difficult to change money, so plan ahead. Look for a sign on the front of the bank which reads "Kambiyo–Exchange–Change–Wechsel." Most banks post the daily exchange rates for all the major European currencies and the U.S. dollar.

Some banks charge a fee for changing traveler's checks, though not for changing cash. Try somewhere else if they say there's a *komisyon*.

If you run out of money, you can easily get a cash advance from a bank on your credit card (VISA, MasterCard, American Express), though there will be a fee of a few dollars for this service. If you don't have a credit card and you can afford to wait a month or so, send a letter home, ask them to send a check, deposit the check in a Turkish bank, and wait for the check to clear. Of course, banks can Telex or wire money in a day or two, but this will cost a lot more, perhaps $30 (sometimes the transfer fee is a percentage of the amount transferred). Still, if you're in a hurry, you may have to do it.

If you must have money in a hurry, walk into a large bank, preferably in a large town, find someone who speaks English, and explain the problem. The bank may be able to Telex your bank and request the money, or you may have to telephone your bank (remember the time difference!) and do it yourself. When the money arrives at the Turkish bank, take your passport and pick it up.

For more information on money, see "Money," below.

BUSINESS HOURS: In Turkey, **shops and markets** are open for long hours, from perhaps 6 or 7 a.m. to 7 or 8 p.m. Monday through Saturday. On Sunday most shops close, though one or two grocers will be open in each neighborhood. With only a few exceptions, **restaurants** are open and serving continuously from 11 or 11:30 a.m. to 11 p.m. or later. Many open early (6 or 7 a.m.) for breakfast. The exceptions are a few restaurants in business and financial districts which serve primarily a clientele of office workers.

Museums are open from 8:30 or 9:30 a.m. to noon or 12:30 p.m., then (in most cases) they close for lunch, reopening at 1 or 1:30 p.m. and remaining open until 5 or 5:30 p.m., perhaps later in the summer. The day of closing is Monday, with a few exceptions (most notably Topkapı Palace in Istanbul, which is closed on Tuesday).

Archeological sites are usually open from 8 or 9 a.m. to 5 or 6 p.m. every day, with no break for lunch.

Government and business **offices** may open at 8 or 9 a.m., close for lunch, and reopen around 1:30 p.m., remaining open until 4 or 5 p.m. During the hot summer months in some cities the workday begins at 7 or 8 a.m. and is finished at 2 p.m. Also, during the holy month of Ramazan the workday is shortened.

Mosques are open all the time in many cases; or, if locked, a *bekçi* (guardian) will come and open a mosque if he knows you're there. However, it's best not to visit mosques at prayertime (listen for the call of the *muezzin*) or just afterward, when the mosques will be filled with worshippers. Also, Friday, the Muslim holy day, particularly in the morning, is a busy time at mosques, and you should avoid visiting then.

CAMPING: Campgrounds are available in most tourist spots in Turkey. Most are not fancy—they're simple, with primitive but serviceable facilities. Many may fill up early in the day during the height of summer. Though some are accessible easily only by car, many are accessible by bus, or on foot. Shady campsites are difficult to find.

At many camping places you can rent a "bungalow," a very simple shelter, often an A-frame, which is actually a glorified, solid-walled tent, without furniture or plumbing. You use the common showers and toilets like other campers. This is handy if you want to travel cheaply but haven't brought any camping gear along.

Prices are very low, from 600TL (85¢) to 800TL ($1.10) per person, plus the same amount again for a tent site. Bungalows cost perhaps twice as much.

CLIMATE: Turkey is a big country of quite varied topography, and so it has many climatic zones. The winters in mountainous eastern Turkey, near the Russian border, can be savage, while the inhabitants of the Antalya coast in the south swim all winter long. Some specifics:

Istanbul tends to be hot and somewhat humid in high summer (late July, August, early September), with very little cloudy weather or rain, and temperatures in the high 70s or low 80s Fahrenheit (26° to 28° Celsius). May, June, early July, late September, and October are very moderate, with some rain but mostly clear, gorgeous days with perfect temperatures. In the winter (mid-December to mid-March) it's rainy and cold with some snow, average temperature being about 40° Fahrenheit (5° Celsius). İzmir, and indeed the Aegean coast in general, has similar weather but warmer in summer, less cold in winter. It rarely rains at all between May and October in the Aegean; the sea breezes can be delightfully cooling on warm days, though in fact the heat is fairly dry and therefore not too bothersome. But along the Mediterranean coast the summers can be quite hot—into the 90s (33° to 36° Celsius) sometimes—and too humid for my tastes. Antalya has fine weather for swimming and long evening dinners outdoors, but you must do your sightseeing before the noonday heat arrives. Ankara and the central plateau (Cappadocia, Konya) have hot and dry summers with cool evenings (cool enough for a sweater sometimes), cold and snowy winters. Spring and autumn are beautiful, spring especially for the wildflowers. On the Black Sea summers are hot but very pleasant, and all other seasons moderate and rainy. Out east the winters are usually severe (October to May), summers mild and short. The southeast is extremely hot in summer.

CLOTHING: If you tour Turkey between mid-May and mid-October you can probably do without a raincoat, but have at least a light sweater for ferryboat rides, spelunking, and so forth. You'll need a hat and sunglasses in summer. From April to mid-May and mid-October to mid-December, a raincoat will serve as a topcoat as well, and wool clothing or a hefty sweater are in order. Winter demands full raingear wherever you go, and an overcoat is not unreasonable if the winter looks to be a severe one. In a mild winter you might need your bathing suit on the south coast!

CREDIT CARDS: Turks are learning about living on plastic. Big hotels and posh shops may accept your credit card, and car-rental agencies certainly will, but ask in advance. If you have American Express, VISA, Diners Club, and MasterCard, you're probably equipped for any establishment that takes cards. Turkish Airlines may accept only MasterCard. The State Railways doesn't accept any credit cards. A shopkeeper may require you to pay the credit card fee of 5% to 7%, or charges of several dollars, for making credit-card arrangements.

CRIME: Turkey is an admirably safe place, with a fairly low level of crime compared to the United States or Europe. This does not mean you should ignore the normal, prudent precautions. Beware of pickpockets, both men and women, in any crowded place, including buses, ferryboats, and markets. Don't leave money, valuable items, or jewelry in your hotel room; if you don't want to carry such things, entrust them to the hotel safe. Don't leave luggage or other items visible in a parked car. Park your car in a guarded, or at least fenced, lot if possible to avoid thefts of parts. Don't hitchhike in lonely places, or late in the day. Avoid dark streets late at night.

CUSTOMS DUTIES AND PROCEDURES: Customs officers don't usually check tourists' baggage upon entry to the country. You're allowed to bring in two cartons of cigarettes or 50 cigars or 200 grams of pipe tobacco, and five liters of liquor, of which up to three liters may be whisky. Oddly enough, you can buy duty-free items at low prices right in the baggage-claim area at Atatürk Airport in Istanbul, right after you've passed through passport control but before you've gone through Customs!

Automobiles, motorcycles, and bicycles can be brought into Turkey for up to three months without a *carnet de passage* or *triptique*. Third-party insurance is obligatory, such as a "green card" valid for the entire country (not just for European Turkey), or a Turkish policy purchased at the border.

If a Customs officer does check your luggage, items with a high resale value in Turkey such as jewelry, electronic gizmos, or photographic equipment may be entered in your passport, which means you cannot leave the country without them, or without paying enormous amounts of Customs duty.

Speaking of leaving the country, beware of **antiquities,** which can get you into a lot of trouble. The international black market in contraband antiquities is a dirty business. Turkey has been robbed of many priceless artifacts and art objects over the years. To put a stop to the trade, the government has declared that it is illegal to buy, sell, trade, possess, or export any antiquity. If you are caught trying to get one out of the country, you will in all probability end up in prison. *This is no joke.*

DRUGS: Turkish laws concerning illegal drugs (hashish, marijuana, cocaine, opium and its derivatives, etc.) are strict, sentences are severe, and trafficking is as dirty and as dangerous as anywhere else. Though opium is grown legally in Turkey, its cultivation is now strictly controlled by the government, and sold for legitimate pharmaceutical purposes. Don't bring illegal drugs to Turkey, don't buy them here, and don't use them here.

DRUGSTORES: The Turkish word is *eczane*. They sell many drugs without prescriptions, even though the rules are that you must have a prescription. It's customary to consult a druggist (*eczacı*) instead of a doctor for minor complaints. Many drugstores sell cosmetics. In each town, drugstores take turns remaining open at night and on Sunday. For the address of the duty pharmacist, look in the front window of any eczane, where there will be a sign with *Nöbetçi* printed on it, and beneath that word, the name and address of the duty drugstore for that particular day.

ELECTRICITY: Electricity throughout Turkey is 220 volts A.C., 50 cycles, as in Europe, though sometimes it's not up to full voltage, resulting in a "brownout." Plugs are European style with two round prongs, but there are two sizes in use. Most common is the small-diameter prong. The large-diameter, grounded plug, as used in Europe, is also used here, but these won't fit the small-diameter outlets. Adapters to match the two types of round-prong plugs and sockets are not readily available. You've got to rig something up yourself unless you've brought an adapter from Europe and it happens to be the right one. Adapters for the flat-prong North American–type plugs are easily found, and are sold in many electricians' shops.

EMBASSIES AND CONSULATES: Embassies are all in Ankara, of course, but there are helpful consulates or consular agents in Istanbul, İzmir, Adana, and a few other port cities.

    Canada: Canadian Embassy, Nene Hatun Caddesi 75, Gazi Osman Paşa, Ankara (tel. 41/27-58-03).

    United Kingdom: British Embassy, Şehit Ersan Caddesi 46/A, Çankaya, Ankara (tel. 41/27-43-10); British Consulate-General, Meşrutiyet Caddesi 26, Galatasaray, Istanbul (tel. 1/149-8874); British Consulate, Necatibey Bulvarı 19/4, İzmir (tel. 51/14-54-70).

    United States of America: American Embassy, Atatürk Bulvarı 110, Kavaklıdere, Ankara (tel. 41/26-54-70); American Consulate-General, Meşrutiyet Caddesi 106, Tepebaşı, Beyoğlu, Istanbul (tel. 1/143-6200); American Consulate, Atatürk Caddesi 386, Alsancak, İzmir (tel. 51/13-21-35).

    Call before you visit any of these embassies or consulates. Diplomatic missions close on both Turkish and foreign national holidays.

ENTRY FORMALITIES: Citizens of Australia, Canada, Eire, New Zealand, the United Kingdom, the United States, and most countries of western and central Europe must have a valid passport to enter Turkey, and then can stay for three months without further formalities.

ETIQUETTE: The most important etiquette for a visitor to know is that of the mosque, but you'll also want to be acquainted with traditional Turkish hospitality customs.

At a Mosque: Dress presentably when visiting mosques. Women should not wear shorts or sleeveless dresses; a shawl covering the head and shoulders is not required, but is a thoughtful gesture. Men should not wear shorts or unusual clothing.

In front of the door of each important mosque will be a clean linoleum platform. Remove your shoes before stepping on this, and enter the mosque, stepping on the soft carpets only in stockinged feet. Don't take photographs with a flash inside a mosque unless there is no one else present. Don't make noise, and don't walk directly in front of worshippers.

Traditional Hospitality: Traditional Turkish customs of hospitality include offering refreshments to visitors, including lemon cologne, soft drinks, candy, and cigarettes. You will find that people continually ask your preference: will it be *çay, kahve,* or a cola? Do you smoke? This may happen even in a bank when you're changing money. Feel free to accept as often as you like. It is not impolite to refuse, though your host may wonder why you don't want a free drink. If you need an excuse, say *Şimdi içtim* (*sheem*-dee eech-teem), "I just drank one" (and don't need another yet).

Dolmush Customs: A note on dolmush etiquette: If you are a couple, it's customary for the man to sit next to any other man, rather than having the woman do so. Though your inclination may be to open the dolmush door and have the lady climb in first, she should do so only if she will end up sitting next to another lady, or next to the wall or door of the car. In the front seat, for example, the man gets in first, sitting next to the driver, and the woman sits between her man and the door. This protects her honor.

Meetings: It is looked upon as acceptable for a businessperson, shopkeeper, or government official to deal with several different matters and people at the same time. Don't be surprised, then, if the carpet dealer doesn't give you his undivided attention, or if the bureaucrat invites others into his office and deals with them while you're there.

GAMBLING: Gambling is illegal in Turkey, except for the lesser varieties such as the national lottery (Milli Piyango) and the sports pools run by the newspapers (Spor Toto). In a very few of the top-class hotels there are legal casinos, open only to foreigners upon presentation of a foreign passport. You must spend foreign currency for chips. The Hilton in Istanbul has such a casino.

HEALTH SERVICES: Both state-supported and private hospitals operate in Turkey, and every town of any size has at least several doctors. Fees for care are very low by American standards. Ankara has a good medical center named Hacettepe, as well as numerous other hospitals (*hastane*) and clinics. Istanbul has an American-run hospital, and also several run by Germans, French, and Italians. You can find medical care by following the standard European road sign with a large "H" on it. Clinics run by the Red Crescent (Kızılay, the Turkish equivalent of the Red Cross) are marked by signs bearing a red crescent.

Quality of medical care depends on the particular doctors and nurses involved. It's good to get a recommendation for a particular doctor from someone who lives in the city. Consulates maintain lists of doctors and dentists who have successfully treated their nationals. As a foreigner, you will probably be given the best possible treatment and the greatest consideration.

HOLIDAYS AND FESTIVALS: February and March are the best months for skiing at Uludağ, in Bursa. Competitions are held during these months. The **Festival of Manisa** (near İzmir) occurs in the second week of April. Highpoint of the festival is when a muezzin distributes a largesse of little candies to the waiting throng by strewing them from the top of a minaret. April 23 is **National Sovereignty Day**, and also **Children's Day**. Parades and speeches. May 1, May Day, is also **Spring Day**, a national holiday. During the months there are festivals at many places throughout the country, including Ephesus, Bergama, Antalya, Pamukkale, and Edirne (the Kırkpınar Greased Wrestler Matches), and Istanbul, where the **Tulip Festival** is held on the Bosphorus in Emirgan. May 19 is **Sports Day**, a national holiday. May 27 is **Constitution Day**, also a national holiday.

July 1 is **Sea Day**, when the ships in the harbor blow their whistles all together for one minute at 10 a.m. In the second week of July, there are **Sword and Shield Dances** in the festival at Bursa. The third week in August is the time for the **Festival of Troy**. August 20 is the official opening date for the İzmir **International Fair**. August 30 is **Victory Day**, a national holiday. September 9 is İzmir's **Liberation Day** (from foreign forces during the War of Independence). September is also the month for the **Festival of Cappadocia**, in Ürgüp. Istanbul's **Liberation Day** celebration falls in the first week of October, and the nation's biggest holiday, **Republic Day**, is October 29.

On **November 10**, at precisely 9:05 a.m.—the date of Atatürk's death—the entire country comes to a screeching halt for two minutes. Horns and whistles blow, bells ring, and no one moves, taking a moment to remember the national hero. Speeches and remembrances fill the rest of the day. The **Commemoration Ceremony for Mevlana**, the founder of the order of whirling dervishes, is held in Konya during the second week of December, when the dervishes whirl.

Several other important holidays are celebrated according to the Muslim lunar calendar, which means that the dates of the holidays vary by about a week each year. The biggest religious festival of the year, comparable to Christmas, comes after the month of fasting. The devout Muslim fasts throughout the lunar month of **Ramazan**, and does not eat, or drink, or even lick a stamp during the daylight hours. But after a cannon announces the close of the day, he breaks the fast with pide bread, and later has a big meal called İftar. After sleep he is awakened by drummers circulating through the town or village so that he can eat again before dawn breaks. When Ramazan occurs during the summer months, tempers can be short—working hard all day long without a sip of water in August is certainly a serious act of worship—and give rise to what's called "Ramazan kafası," which means a fellow is touchy. But after Ramazan come three days of feasting called **Şeker Bayramı** (Candy Festival), when visits, greeting cards, and gifts of sweets are exchanged. This festival is also a national holiday, and so banks and shops are closed, museums are half price, and intercity transportation is packed to capacity.

The other major holiday kept by the lunar calendar is **Kurban Bayramı** (Sacrifice Festival). The head of any household wealthy enough to afford it is obliged to buy a sheep, slaughter it, feed his family, and distribute the bulk of the meat to the poor. Kurban Bayramı is a four-day national holiday. On either of these holidays it's hard to travel, vacation resorts are reserved months in advance, and the highway from Europe is crowded with Turkish workers coming from, or returning to, Europe because of the holiday.

INFORMATION: Each Turkish town important to tourists has a **Tourism Information Office** run by the Ministry of Culture and Tourism, or by the municipal or provincial authorities, and perhaps another office operated by the local (private) tourist board. The ministry's symbol is the fan-like Hittite sun figure. Three overseas offices in English-speaking countries may be helpful:

London: Turkish Tourism and Information Office, 170-173 Piccadilly (first floor), London W1V 9DD, England (tel. 01/734-8681 or 491-0773).

New York: Office of the Culture and Information Attaché, Turkish Consulate-General, 821 United Nations Plaza, New York, NY 10017 (tel. 212/687-2194).

Washington: Culture and Tourism Office, Turkish Embassy, 2010 Massachusetts Ave. NW, Washington, DC 20036 (tel. 202/429-9844 or 833-8411).

LAUNDRY:
Though you won't see any coin-op laundromats (washaterias) in Turkey yet, laundry is a simple matter. Ask at the reception desk of your hotel and they'll arrange it, or ask a chambermaid. Agree on a price in advance, and allow at least a day to get the laundry done. In hotels, the classier they are, the more exorbitant their laundry rates. Even so, the rates are no higher than at home.

Dry cleaners (*kuru temizleme*) are found in the big cities, usually in the better residential sections or near the luxury hotels. Service is similar to that in Europe and America: fast service (an hour or two) is available if you're willing to pay 50% more; overnight or two-day service is normal. Prices are fairly low. To save money, take the clothes to the dry cleaner yourself rather than having the hotel staff do it.

MAIL:
Post and telecommunications services are the province of the "PTT," which stands for *posta, telefon, telgraf*. Every town has a PTT, usually close to the main square. Offices, mailboxes, and vehicles are marked by yellow signs with black lettering.

Here are the postal rates; check before you mail, as changes are frequent:

Postal Rates

Destination	Letter	Postcard
Turkey	20TL (3¢)	20TL (3¢)
Europe, U.K.	100TL (14¢)	70TL (10¢)
U.S.A., Canada	150TL (21¢)	120TL (17¢)
Australia, New Zealand	170TL (24¢)	140TL (20¢)

METRIC MEASURES:
Turkey uses the metric system. Here's a handy list of metric equivalents.

Weights and Liquids

U.S.	Turkey
1 ounce	28.3 grams
1 pound	454 grams
2.2 pounds	1 kilo (1,000 grams)
1 pint	0.47 liter
1 quart	0.94 liter
1 gallon	3.78 liters

Measures

U.S.	Turkey
1 inch	2.54 centimeters
1 foot	0.3 meters
1 yard	0.91 meters
1.09 yards	1 meter
1 mile	1.61 kilometer
0.62 mile	1 kilometer
1 acre	0.40 hectare

Temperatures are measured in degrees Celsius (or Centigrade). For a rough conversion from Celsius to Fahrenheit, double the Celsius figure and add 30; if you want accuracy, multiply the Celsius by 1.8 and add 32.

Zero degrees Celsius (32°F) is the freezing point; 20°C (68°F) is room temperature; 40°C (105°F) is a very hot day.

MONEY:
The unit of Turkish currency is the **Turkish lira,** abbreviated "TL," sometimes called the Turkish pound. The lira is divided into 100 kurush ("krş"), also called piastres. Inflation has reduced the kurush to worthlessness, and so all

you will encounter are liras. Coins come in denominations of 5, 10, 25, 50, and 100 liras; bills come as 20, 50, 100, 500, 1,000, 5,000, and 10,000TL. What with 30% annual inflation, you may encounter bills of higher denominations as well.

Prices in this book are quoted both in Turkish liras and in U.S. dollars under the theory that the lira prices will rise with inflation but the dollar prices will remain fairly constant. Conversion between the two currencies was done at the rate of $1 U.S. = 714TL, the rate in effect at the time of writing.

You may be happy to learn that Turks are getting used to living by those little plastic cards such as American Express, VISA, MasterCard, etc. Airlines, the fancier shops, and the more expensive hotels and restaurants will readily accept your credit card, though they may pass on certain charges to you. To rent a car, you will have to have a credit card or plunk down a very substantial cash deposit of hundreds of dollars.

Always take your passport with you when you change money.

Some banks charge a commission when changing traveler's checks. The Türkiye İş Bankası, for instance, charges about 3%, plus a fee for official stamps. To avoid such commissions, ask first, and if a commission is charged, head for another bank.

As in every country around the world, inflation has caused havoc with price tags in Turkey, and will probably continue to do so for a while. Where possible, I have included predictable rises in the prices quoted in this book. I ask the reader to bear with me for inaccuracies which may be caused by prices rising after this book has gone to press, and to remember that an establishment recommended as "the best buy for the money" will still be the best bargain, comparatively speaking, even if the price has risen somewhat.

By the way, you should try to keep some change and small bills with you at all times as many bus conductors, dolmush drivers, and shopkeepers will be unable to make change for you—there seems to be a shortage of coins and small bills.

Currency Conversion Tables

The following tables were calculated on the basis of 714 Turkish liras to $1 U.S.

TL	U.S.$	U.S.$	TL
1	.0014	.25	179
10	.014	.50	357
25	.035	1.00	714
50	.07	2.00	1,428
100	.14	5.00	3,570
250	.35	10.00	7,140
500	.70	20.00	14,280
1,000	1.40	50.00	35,700
2,500	3.50	100.00	71,400
5,000	7.00	150.00	107,100
10,000	14.00	250.00	178,500
50,000	70.00	500.00	357,000

NEWSPAPERS: English-language newspapers are sold in kiosks wherever tourists gather, and in the big hotels. You can get papers from Britain, the *International Herald Tribune,* or the *Turkish Daily News,* as well as prominent papers in other European languages. After about 7 p.m., you may be able to find the same day's papers in Istanbul's newsstands and hotels; otherwise you get them one day late.

PHOTOGRAPHY:

PHOTOGRAPHY: Turkish officialdom is wild for little photos, and you'll have to provide them for student cards and almost any other official document which might be required. These are called *vesikalık,* and many photographers advertise that they'll do *acele vesikalık,* "rush document photos." Fastest way of all is to find one of the few automatic photo machines in Turkey, the kind where you sit in a little booth, push the button, and get four poses (for 600TL, 84¢). There's one of these in Sirkeci Station.

Photocopies can be had wherever you see the sign "Fotokopi." Many stationery stores (*kırtasiye*) have copying machines.

Amateur photographers should bring their own film to Turkey, for although black-and-white and color film (both for slides and prints) is available in Turkey, it is pretty expensive. If you do buy film in Turkey, be sure to check the expiration date, and buy the brands you know. (I once returned to the U.S. having bought and taken a roll of an odd-sized East German film, and could get it developed only at a very high "special handling" price.) It's best to take your exposed film home with you to be developed, whether it be color or black-and-white.

RADIO AND TELEVISION:

RADIO AND TELEVISION: All radio and TV broadcasting in Turkey is done by an autonomous, government-supported corporation called **Türkiye Radyo ve Televizyon,** or **T.R.T.** Major cities and the more densely populated regions of the country have their own AM radio stations which play Turkish classical and popular music, and also European and American popular music. Istanbul and Ankara also have supplemental stations, broadcasting on both AM and FM, known as the **İkinci Program** ("Second Program"); this features much Western classical and popular music. As of this writing there are no broadcasts in languages other than Turkish.

Turkey has two color television stations which broadcast each evening, with news, cartoons, popular American series, and films both Turkish and foreign (the foreign ones have been dubbed in Turkish). Major sports events such as the Olympic Games and important soccer (football) matches are relayed from Europe and the rest of the world by wire or satellite, and are broadcast with Turkish commentary, but scores and playing times, etc., are superimposed on the screen, making sports events easy to follow even if you know no Turkish.

A few TV programs and, in the evening, lots of AM radio stations from Europe and the Middle East can be heard in Turkey. English-language news can be heard from the Voice of America (based in Crete), and even the BBC World Service if conditions are good.

REST ROOMS:

REST ROOMS: There are lots of public rest rooms in Turkey, but most are not up to a high standard. There is a public rest room near every mosque. The rest rooms near top tourist attractions tend to be better than most. Men will not find them as difficult to bear as women.

There is often a small fee charged for using public rest rooms, perhaps 20TL (3¢) to 50TL (7¢). If you see a sign bearing the word *Parasızdır,* use of the rest rooms is free of charge. Paper may be provided by the attendant as you enter.

Rest rooms are marked by signs that read *Tuvalet, OO,* or *WC.* The men's is *Erkek, Erkeklere,* or *Baylara;* the women's is *Kadın, Kadınlara,* or *Bayanlara.* Sometimes universal symbols are used, such as a fedora or pipe for men, or a fan for women.

In some places you will find the older, flat "elephant's feet" type of toilet on which one does not sit, but squats. It takes some getting used to, but public health experts say it is anatomically and sanitarily preferable to the Western-style commode. Whatever its benefits, you may want to search for a more familiar fixture.

TAXES: A Value Added Tax, called Katma Değer Vergisi, or KDV, in Turkish, is included in the price of many goods and services in Turkey. Notice that I said "included": it should not be added to your bill as it is already figured into the prices quoted to you.

If you buy some big-ticket item in Turkey such as a leather coat or Turkish carpet, you can recover the 15% KDV in many cases. As in other European countries with VATs, the shop where you buy the item helps you to fill out a special form, you get the form stamped by a Customs officer when you leave the country, then you take it to a Turkish bank branch in, say, the departure area of the airport or the border zone if you're leaving by car, and the bank will refund the tax amount to you; or you can have a check sent to your home, but this takes much longer.

TELECOMMUNICATIONS: Telephone, telegraph, Telex, and facsimile transmission services are operated by the post office (PTT) in Turkey.

Using the Telephone

The PTT operates two different telephone systems, the traditional operator type and an automatic direct-dial type. Use the automatic system if you can, because it's faster, cheaper, and easier. Automatic phones are yellow and have pushbuttons rather than dials.

To make a call, you'll need *jetons* (tokens), which come in three sizes. The small ones (*küçük jeton*) cost 40TL (6¢) and are for local calls. The middle-sized ones (*normal jeton*) cost 200TL (28¢) and are mostly for long-distance calls within Turkey. The large ones (*büyük jeton*) cost 400TL (56¢); these are necessary for international calls. Buy your jetons at the post office, or from a disabled person near the public telephones.

The new yellow phones have pictographs on them explaining their use; sometimes there are also instructions in English. You'll need to know the city (or area) and country codes for the place you're calling. These are on display in most PTTs and in some phone booths.

If the little square red light below the pushbuttons is lit, the phone is out of order. If it's not lit, lift the receiver and deposit a jeton. Some yellow phones have a problem accepting and holding jetons. The token may fall straight through and out the return hole. Insert the jeton and let it fall as gently as possible. Note that the fault is with the phone, not with the jeton, so trying a different jeton won't help much.

For a local call, push the buttons for the local number. For a long-distance call, look for the little round light in the last box, to the right of the pictorial instructions above the pushbuttons. When this light goes out, push "9." Then, when you hear the long-distance tone, push the buttons for the city code and the local number. If you're making an international call, push "9" again after you get the long-distance dial tone and you will get a new, international dial tone. When you hear this, push the buttons for the country code, followed by the area or city code and local number. The country code for anywhere in North America is "1." For example, a call to New York City (Manhattan) would be dialed this way: insert jeton, push "9," push "9" again, then push "1" (the country code), then "212" (the city or area code), then 555-1212 (the local number). For the United Kingdom, the country code is "44"; for Australia it's "61"; for New Zealand it's "64"; for Eire, it's "353." Turkey's code, by the way, is "90."

As you talk, watch that little round red light up top and listen for chimes on the line. Both are indications that it's time to deposit another jeton.

Sending a Telegram

To send a telegram (*telgraf*), go to any post office, write the recipient's name and address, your message, and your name on a piece of paper, and hand it to the telegraph clerk. For most foreign countries there is only one rate of service: fast and expensive. A normal telegram to North America may cost about $15.

If you're sending your wire within Turkey, you must choose the class of service: *normal* is slow, very slow; *acele* is fast, and twice as expensive; *yıldırım* costs five times as much as normal, but your message should get through in an hour or two. The address of the recipient is included in the word count.

Sending a Telex and Facsimile

Turkey's larger cities have post offices with Telex machines (*teleks*). There are Telex machines in Istanbul's main post offices; in Ankara, the most convenient Telex is the one in the little post office in Kızılay.

Write out your message, including the Telex number of the recipient, and the clerk will send the message and give you a receipt and a confirmation copy of the message.

The price for a Telex, as for a telephone call, depends on the actual time on the line. An alternative to Telex is facsimile transmission (*elektronik mektup*), which is also available in the larger PTTs.

TIME: Turkey goes by Eastern European Time, two hours ahead of Greenwich Mean Time. In the warm months from April through September, clocks are turned ahead one hour for Daylight Saving Time. The whole country is in the same time zone, so at noon in Istanbul, Ankara, or Erzurum, the time in other cities of the world is:

When It's Noon in Turkey, It's . . .

City	Winter	Summer
Paris, Rome	11 a.m.	11 a.m.
London	10 a.m.	10 a.m.
New York	5 a.m.	5 a.m.
Los Angeles	2 a.m.	2 a.m.
Perth, Hong Kong	7 p.m.	5 p.m.

TIPPING: In **restaurants,** a service charge of 10% or 15% may be added to your bill, but this is not the same thing as a tip. The service charge goes into the pocket of the owner. Leave 5% to 7% on the table for the waiter, or hand it directly to him.

If service is included, it may say so (*servis dahil*) on the bill. Still, a small tip is expected. In any situation, 5% to 10% is fine. Only in the fancy hotels will waiters expect 15% to 20% tips. In the very plain, basic restaurants you needn't tip at all, though rounding off the amount of the bill to the next larger number is common. If in doubt, the price of a soft drink will be happily accepted.

In **hotels,** tip the bellboy who shows you to your room and carries your bags about 4% or 5% of the room price. Thus if you are paying 10,000TL ($14), give about 450TL (63¢). If a bellboy does any other chores that you ask, such as getting cigarettes or a newspaper, a slightly smaller tip is expected.

For **taxi drivers,** round off the fare. If the meter says 489TL, give the driver 500TL. Taxi drivers may look for a tip from you, but that's because you're a foreigner; Turks don't tip taxi drivers unless the driver has performed some exceptional service, or has waited for them at a museum or archeological site and the waiting time was not included in the agreed price. **Dolmush drivers,** by the way, never expect tips or even rounded fares.

For **barbers and hairdressers,** pay the price for what they've done, then about 15% to the person who cut your hair, and smaller tips (5% to 7%) to those who provided other services, from the assistant barber to the one who brushes shorn locks from your clothing.

In **Turkish baths,** though you will pay for use of the baths, for a massage (if you want one), for being washed, and so forth, everyone who has had anything to do with you will expect and await a tip. After you pay your bill for the baths, pass out about 30% or 35% of the total as tips. If the attendants give you a hard time (they always expect foreigners to be more lavish than Turks), look firm and say *Yeter!*—"That's enough (tip)."

In a sleeping car on a train, the porter comes around near the end of the trip to collect an official 10% service charge. Tip him 5% of the sleeping compartment fee (not of the total amount you've paid for sleeping car and train ticket!).

TOBACCO: The most popular cigarette in Turkey is the American-made Marlboro. These and a few other American and European brands are sold legally, and they cost less in Turkey than they do at home. Locally made Turkish cigarettes are much cheaper. The standard mild filter cigarettes are **Samsun** and **Maltepe.** Though the very best Turkish tobacco is extremely mild and aromatic, it is also largely exported. The cheapest local cigarettes are strong and flavorful, though coarse.

The Turkish State Monopolies company (Tekel) makes the country's cigarettes, and imports the foreign brands. They also make pipe tobacco (*pipo tütünü*), cigars (*puro*), and cigarillos (*küçük puro*), but these are not of high quality.

Tobacco products are on sale in little snack kiosks, in grocery stores, at street vendors, and in Tekel shops.

By the way, Turkish waterpipes (hubble-bubbles) use a very strong sort of tobacco. Those who are not accustomed to it can get dizzy and nauseous from too much of it.

WATER: Pure spring water is sold in quarter-liter and 1½-liter clear-plastic bottles. The standard price for the bigger bottle, sold chilled in a grocery, is 250TL (35¢). If you order a bottle in a restaurant, there will be a markup of 100% to 300%.

Tap water is treated and is usually safe to drink, but it does not taste as good, nor is it as reliably safe, as the bottled water. Besides, even if the tap water is pure, its high limestone content may give some people loose bowels.

Other choices for water include mineral water (*maden suyu*) and mineral soda (*maden sodası*), artificially carbonated mineral water.

WOMEN TRAVELING ALONE: As in most Mediterranean countries, a foreign woman, just because she's traveling alone, is assumed to be more "free" than a local woman, and it can get to be a bore. Single guys in cars will toot at you hoping to get a better look, etc. When walking, do so purposefully and most attention and witty asides will be avoided. On trains and buses, if someone bothers you just make friends with another woman or married couple and they will see to it that you're not bothered. In effect they become your "chaperones," without which no respectable Turkish girl will travel anywhere. You, as you have none, are assumed to be unrespectable. As two young women readers of this book put it, "Females shouldn't be discouraged from traveling alone in Turkey; normal precautions rather than paranoia will suffice."

Chapter II

GETTING THERE AND GETTING AROUND

1. Getting There
2. Getting Around Turkey
3. Suggested Itineraries
4. A Stop on the Way: Edirne

TURKEY IS AT THE EASTERN tip of Europe. Years ago, visitors from North America would include a visit to Turkey in their European itineraries, but now many more North Americans are going directly to Turkey. Usually, the low prices in Turkey more than compensate for the extra mileage to Europe's eastern end. Transportation to Turkey is fast, easy, and not at all as expensive as you might at first imagine.

1. Getting There

BY AIR: The fastest, and often the cheapest, way to get to Europe or to Turkey from North America is to fly. The airlines offer a myriad of different types of tickets: full fare, excursion, APEX, budget, and charter. One form or another of air travel will fit your trip requirements and your budget. Though I will give you some guidelines and sample prices, it is important to remember that prices change from season to season, as do the restrictions on advance purchase and length of stay.

For the latest fares, and to buy your ticket, it's best to see a travel agent. As the airlines pay the agent's commission, it costs you no more to get your ticket from an agent than it does to get it from an airline.

Your Destination

With only a few exceptions, international flights arrive at **Istanbul's Atatürk Airport,** the country's biggest and busiest. The few flights that do not terminate here go to international airports in Ankara, İzmir, Adana (down near the Syrian border), Antalya, and Dalaman (on the southern coast). Antalya and Dalaman receive mostly charter flights for travelers going to the south coast.

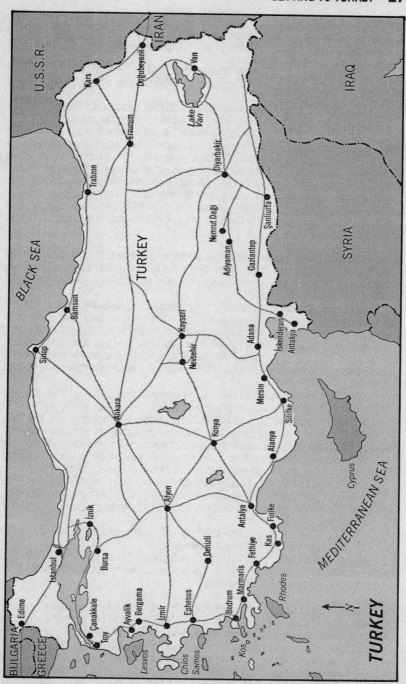

From North America

Pan American World Airways has been flying the New York–Istanbul route reliably for more than half a century, and still provides efficient and convenient daily service via Paris and Geneva.

As of this writing, **Turkish Airlines** does not fly from North America to Turkey, only from Europe; but there is talk of opening up a New York–Istanbul route.

Most of the European national airlines (KLM, Sabena, Lufthansa, Alitalia, etc.) fly from New York to their home countries, then on to Istanbul.

Among the European carriers, those from Eastern Europe often have fares worth noting. **JAT,** the Yugoslav national carrier, often has the lowest direct fare from New York to Istanbul, though you may have to stay overnight in Belgrade. Also, consider alternative routes and itineraries, such as the "open jaw," where you fly to one city (say, Vienna) and return from another (Istanbul). **Tarom,** the Romanian airline, perennially advertises a one-way standby fare of $205 from New York to Vienna, nonstop. **PIA,** Pakistan International Airlines, has one-stop service from New York to Istanbul with a low excursion fare.

Individual Fares: You can pay anywhere from $549 to $1,355 to get to Turkey and back, depending on when you go and what sort of ticket you buy. Obviously, you must be careful in buying your ticket, and purchase only what you need. Here are the details on fares.

Full Fare: A full-fare ticket is the standard of the industry. You can buy it any time you like, it's good for up to a year (and it's renewable), and you can fly any time you like as long as you make your reservation before the flight fills up. You can make as many stops en route as you like. You pay for this freedom. Round-trip New York–Istanbul fare is about $1,355 in summer high season, $100 or so less in winter. Few vacationers need the flexibility this sort of ticket provides.

Excursion Fares: Rules on these fares change frequently and from one airline to another, but here are some guidelines.

If you fly from New York to Istanbul, stay two weeks or more (but less than three weeks), and make no more than two stops en route in each direction, you qualify for an excursion fare in the range of $889 round trip in summer, slightly over $100 cheaper in winter. But if you have even more time to spend roaming the bazaars, ruins, and beaches, you can get an even cheaper fare. Read on.

Passengers who stay in Turkey over 22 days but less than 45 days, and who do not break their journey en route—no stopping off for a day or two of sightseeing in London, for instance—will pay about $851 round trip in summer, New York–Istanbul.

Can you do even better than this? Yes, by planning ahead and telling the airline your plans well in advance. Here's how:

If you purchase your ticket well in advance of your departure date and make no stopovers on your way to Turkey, you can fly round trip (only) for about $765 in summer, $675 in winter.

Group Fares: There are group fares to Istanbul sold by various tour operators during the summer months, from New York and Chicago particularly. *You do not have to be part of a group,* nor do you have to take a tour. You pay only for the flight, which is on a regularly scheduled airline, and you get your ticket at a special low group rate. There may be some restrictions. For instance, you may have to stay more than 7 nights and fewer than 180 nights. From New York, current fares are $290 to $409 one way, $549 to $969 round trip; from Chicago they are $385 one way, $639 round trip. For more information, contact a travel agent, or get hold of a copy of *JAXFAX Travel Marketing Magazine* (your travel agent will have it, or call JAXFAX at 203/655-8746 for a year's subscription at $12), or contact one of these tour operators:

Am-Jet/Amtravel, 501 Fifth Ave., Suite 2008, New York, NY 10017 (tel. 212/697-5332 or 818-0125).

Globe Travel Specialists, 507 Fifth Ave., New York, NY 10017 (tel. 212/682-8687).

Hürtürk Travel & Tours, 18 W. 56th St., Suite 501, New York, NY 10019 (tel. 212/586-2901).

Sunbeam Travel, 274 Madison Ave., Suite 904, New York, NY 10016 (tel. 212/725-8835; or toll free 800/247-6659 outside New York State).

Theresa's World Travel, 61–06 Myrtle Ave., Glendale, NY 11385 (tel. 718/381-1666).

Travel Magic, 555 Fifth Ave., New York, NY 10017 (tel. 212/972-3036, or toll free 800/543-0003 outside New York State).

Union Tours, 3175 N. Lincoln Ave., Chicago, IL 60657 (tel. 312/472-4620, or toll free 800/331-6221).

VIP Tourism Pirinçcioğlu, 20 E. 49th St., New York, NY 10017 (tel. 212/421-5400).

Charter Flights: When it comes to charter flights, you must take note: *If you take a charter flight to Greece and then go to Turkey (or any other country), the return portion of your air ticket may become invalid!* Several countries which benefit greatly from charter-flight traffic (including Greece) have enacted a regulation which prohibits charter passengers from leaving the charter destination country for the duration of their stay. So if you fly to Athens on a charter flight, and then have your passport stamped by Turkish immigration officials as you enter Turkey, the officials at the airport in Athens may not let you board the return charter flight. You will have to pay for a full-fare, one-way ticket to get home. (If you just take a day's excursion to Turkey and the Turkish immigration officials do not stamp your passport, you will have no problem boarding your return charter flight.) The regulation is enforced so that the charter destination country reaps all the benefits of the low charter fare. Bear in mind that this regulation does not apply to regular or excursion-fare flights, *only to charters.*

If you want to go by charter flight, you must go directly to Turkey. By the way, I have had no news that the Turkish officials enforce the charter regulation, which means that if you take a charter to Turkey, you can probably visit Greece then return to Turkey, and still have no trouble when you board your return charter flight.

From Europe

Pan American World Airways, Air France, and **Turkish Airlines** all fly from Paris to Istanbul. **British Airways** and Turkish Airlines fly from London to Istanbul, and Turkish Airlines offers numerous discount fares from the British capital.

Among the scheduled carriers flying to Turkey from Europe, **JAT,** the Yugoslavian airline, has the lowest fares from many European cities, via Belgrade, to Istanbul. Lots of people know this, however, and the flights are often booked solid, so reserve your seat well in advance. Also, look at the schedules and fares of other Eastern European airlines such as the Romanian **Tarom.**

Air fares in Europe are often a great deal more expensive than comparable distances traveled in North America. For instance, a normal full-fare round-trip off-season ticket between London and Istanbul is an astounding $848! When you think that the distance flown is about 1,500 miles—half the distance across the U.S. or the Atlantic—and that the normal 22- to 45-day excursion fare off-season, *New York–Istanbul round trip,* is virtually the same, then you realize how expensive it is to fly in Europe.

But before you jump to our section on taking a bus to Turkey, note that there are lots of excursion fares within Europe just as there are for transatlantic travel. You can even get on a charter flight to Turkey once you reach, say, London, and then the London–Istanbul round-trip price can be reduced by half. The lowest-ever way to do it is to take a reduced-fare flight to London and then a package tour from London to Istanbul, Kuşadası, or Antalya. The package tour can include a luxury hotel for a week and two meals a day for only about $675, but you must reserve and pay for the tour a full two months before flight date. If you don't want to have the hotel and meals, you can often get a place on the tour plane and pay for flight alone, as described above. Note that many of the lowest excursion fares cannot legally be booked or advertised outside the country in which the flight originates; that is, a flight such as the one just described could be explained to you by your travel agent in the U.S., but you would have to go to London to pick up the brochures and buy the ticket. Thus it is possible to "take pot luck" and fly off to a European city hoping to set up your onward travel when you arrive.

Flying from Athens

Olympic Airlines and **Turkish Airlines** share service on this route, with at least four daily flights in summer. Fares for the 70-minute flight are 14,920 drachmas ($111) one way, 22,170 drachmas ($165) for an excursion (round trip). If you're planning to take a charter flight to Greece and then fly on to Turkey, read the warning under "Charter Flights," above.

BY SHIP: Sad to say, air travel is probably the way you will decide to get directly to Turkey, for the more comfortable and leisurely method of going by transatlantic ship is just too expensive for most people. Fares start at $1,200 to Europe per person one way on the few scheduled lines left. Going by freighter is cheaper, much cheaper, and is an interesting experience if you can afford the weeks and weeks it may take to reach your destination.

You can, though, combine both air and sea travel, for several lines run from Mediterranean ports to İzmir or Istanbul.

From Venice

Turkish Maritime Lines (T. C. Denizyolları, or TML) operates car-ferries from Venice (Italy) to İzmir, departing Venice every Saturday evening from June through September, arriving in İzmir on Tuesday morning. The return trip from İzmir departs Wednesday afternoon, arriving in Venice on Saturday morning. One-way fares, *per person,* in modern, comfortable cabins, range from $220 to $415, breakfast and port taxes included. For starvation-budget travelers, there is a "Pullman" class in which you get a reclining seat for $185, breakfast and port tax included. Students get a 10% reduction on the fare, but not on meals. If you want lunch and dinner on board, add $30 per person. Otherwise, buy food at the market in Venice and take it aboard. The fare for a standard European-size car, by the way, is $170, port tax included; for a motorcycle it's $87. Here are the agencies to contact:

Istanbul: Türkiye Denizcilik İşletmeleri, Rıhtım Caddesi, Karaköy (tel. 11/144-0207 or 149-9222).

İzmir: Türkiye Denizcilik İşletmeleri Acenteliği, Yeniliman, Alsancak (tel. 51/21-00-94 or 21-00-77).

London: Walford Lines Ltd., World Trade Centre 1, St. Katharine's Way, London E19 UN; or Sunquest Holidays Ltd., Aldine House, 9/15 Aldine St., London W.12.

Venice: Bassani S.P.A., via 22 Marzo 2414 (tel. 32-55-86 or 31-26-68).

If you'd like to combine a Mediterranean and Aegean cruise with your trip to Turkey, there's a delightful and easy way. **Sealink British Ferries** (P.O. Box 29, London SW1V 1JX, tel. 01/834-8122; or Sealink Travel Centre, Liverpool Street Station, London EC2M 7PY) runs the car-and-passenger ship M/V *Orient Express* on a cruise route from Venice to Piraeus, Istanbul, Kuşadası, Patmos, Katakolon, and then returning to Venice. The cruise departs Venice every Saturday evening from May through October, arriving in Piraeus on Monday morning, in Istanbul on Tuesday morning, in Kuşadası, on Wednesday morning, in Patmos on Wednesday evening, in Katakolon (Olympia) on Thursday noontime, and in Venice on Saturday morning. At each port there's plenty of time to debark, see the sights, and take excursions. All meals and port taxes are included in the fares, which are $260 to $627 one way, $465 to $1,129 round trip between Venice and Istanbul or Kuşadası. The highest fares are for two persons sharing a stateroom; most of the fares are for cabins with two, three, or four beds. The fare for a car is $192 to $214 one way, $345 to $385 round trip.

From Brindisi, Italy

Libra Maritime, Plateia Loudovicou 4, Piraeus (tel. 1/411-7864), or 54 Corso Garibaldi, Brindisi (tel. 21935 or 28004), a Greek company, operates boats and buses on the route Brindisi–Patras–Piraeus–İzmir, carrying passengers from start to finish in 40 hours. Either the *Atlas III* or the *Atlas IV,* carrying both cars and passengers, departs Piraeus for İzmir three days per week in the summertime, on Monday, Wednesday, and Friday at 8 p.m.; and departs İzmir on Tuesday and Thursday at 9 p.m., and on Sunday at 2 p.m. Contact Libra in İzmir at the International Tourism Service (Enternasyonal Turizm Servis, Seyahat ve Gemicilik A. Ş.).

From the Greek Islands

It's easy to get from any Greek island along the Turkish coast over to the Turkish mainland. Buy your ticket a day in advance; you may be asked to turn in your passport the night before the trip. Before you board the boat you'll get your passport back, no problem.

From Lesbos: In Mytileni, one agent is **Dimitrios Koraka,** on Yunani Antonios Picolos Street. Greek and Turkish boats share the trade, and make daily trips in summer (late May or early June through September), departing Lesbos on weekdays at 8:30 a.m. (the Greek boat) and 1:30 p.m. (the Turkish boat). On weekends the times are different: on Saturday at 9 a.m. and on Sunday at 8 or 9 p.m. from Lesbos for the Turkish boat. Off-season, boats operate about once or twice a week, but may halt completely in bad winter weather. The fare, one way, is $15, or $25 for a round-trip ticket.

From Chios: Boats run on Thursday during the winter months, weather and customers permitting; on Sunday and Thursday in early May; on Tuesday, Thursday, and Sunday from mid-May till mid-July and from mid-September through October; in high summer there are daily boats (except Monday) from mid-July through mid-September. At other times, extra boats may run if there is enough traffic. Most of these boats depart in the morning, at 9:30 or 10 a.m., but a few depart at 4 p.m.

The one-way fare between Chios and Çeşme is $18, same-day round trip costs $20, and a round-trip ticket valid for one year costs $30. Children 4 to 12 years old get a 50% reduction. Motorcycles, cars, even small travel trailers and minibuses, can be carried on some of the ferries. The fare for an auto is between $40 and $60, depending on the size of the car.

For details, reservations, and tickets, the agent in Turkey is **Ertürk Travel Agency,** Cumhuriyet Meydanı 11/A, Çeşme (tel. 5492/6768 or 6876), in Çeşme's main square, near the fortress and across from the docks.

From Samos: Boats depart each port, Samos and Kuşadası, at 8:30 a.m. and 5 p.m. daily in high summer, about four times weekly in spring and autumn. Service is usually suspended in winter except for special excursions. The voyage costs $25 one way, $30 round trip.

From Kos: The ferries run in the morning on Monday, Wednesday, and Friday in summer, and on other days if demand warrants. Make reservations and buy tickets ($21 for the one-way fare) at least a day in advance.

From Rhodes: Boats to and from Rhodes run daily except Sunday in high summer, with Greek and Turkish boats sharing the service. If traffic is heavy they may put on a Sunday boat. Tickets cost $15 one way, $20 for a same-day round trip, and $27 for an open-date round trip.

In winter, when few of the Greek Island–Turkey services run, the boats most likely to be running are those from Rhodes to Marmaris and from Samos to Kuşadası.

From Turkish Cyprus

Turkish Maritime Lines' car-ferries operate all year between Famagusta (Magosa) and Mersin (Turkey), a ten-hour trip. From October to April departures are Tuesday and Friday evenings from Mersin, arriving in Famagusta the next morning. In summer (late April through September) departures from Mersin are on Monday, Wednesday, and Friday evenings; return trips from Cyprus depart on Tuesday, Thursday, and Sunday morning. The Friday departures from Mersin stop at Famagusta on Saturday, then go on to Lattakia, Syria.

Passenger boats and **hydrofoils** depart from Kyrenia (Girne, Turkish Republic of Northern Cyprus) for a landfall on the Turkish mainland at Taşucu, four kilometers (2½ miles) west of Silifke. The hydrofoil makes the trip in two hours. A one-way ticket costs $23, twice that amount to go and return.

For the **regular boat,** tickets cost less, but the trip is longer. The Ertürk company (tel. 7593/1033 or 1325 in Silifke; in Girne, 581/52308) operates three boats per week year round, weather permitting, on the six-hour trip, on Wednesday, Friday, and Saturday. A one-way ticket costs $18; to go and return costs $29. The Ertürk boat carries cars as well as passengers.

In Taşucu, there's a Tourism Information Office (tel. 7593/1234) right by the boat dock at Atatürk Caddesi, Gümrük Meydanı 18/A.

Note: You should be aware that relations between the Greek Cypriot *Republic of Cyprus* and the *Turkish Republic of Northern Cyprus* are virtually on a war footing. You may not be allowed to pass from one part of the island to the other. And if you intend to return to Greece, you should be aware that Greek immigration officials will not allow you into the country if your passport bears a stamp from the Turkish Republic of Northern Cyprus. It is only a stamp from the TRNC, *not* a stamp from Turkey proper, that will keep you out of Greece.

The Republic of Greece does not recognize the Turkish Republic of Northern Cyprus.

BY TRAIN: I regret to inform you that the famous *Orient Express* no longer runs between Paris and Istanbul, having been removed from the schedules in 1977. The Victorian salon cars, plush restaurants-on-wheels, and deluxe sleeping cars had long ago given way to mundane railway coaches and passable, though not luxurious, restaurants. The sleeping cars were the biggest advantage of the *Orient Express* in its later years, for only in a sleeping car could one travel comfortably and with a minimum of inconvenience in the Balkans.

But having given you the bad news, let me now give you the good: well-padded nostalgia fans can ride the *Orient Express* as it hasn't been in years, for a private firm called **Society Expeditions,** 723 Broadway East, Seattle, WA 98102 (tel. 206/324-9400, or toll free 800/426-7794), will sell you a ticket for a sleeping compartment in a 1920s-vintage Wagons-Lits coach running from Paris to Istanbul, for about $5,500 per person, one way. The trip includes meals, lectures, and excursions, and is obviously more like a "rail cruise" than mere transportation. You can get more information from any travel agent, or contact Society Expeditions directly. If you decide to do it, you're bound to have a fascinating time with a varied international group of traveling companions.

From Europe

You can still get to Turkey by regularly scheduled train, however. Marshaling point for trains to Turkey is now Munich. One train, the daily *Istanbul Express,* runs from Munich to Istanbul via Salzburg, Ljubljana, Zagreb (connections from Vienna and Graz), Belgrade, Niš, Sofia, and Edirne. You must have a reservation for this train. Couchettes (shelf-like beds six to a compartment) are available from Germany to Bulgaria and Turkey and vice-versa. The trip takes 15 hours from Munich to Belgrade, and another 25 hours from Belgrade to Istanbul (but you may want to get off in Edirne—see below). Sleeping cars only run as far as Belgrade; after that it's first- or second-class coaches, and second-class couchettes.

Prices for train travel are relatively cheap in the Balkans, as they should be considering the service provided.

Students should know that Turkey is part of the Inter-Rail youth and student ticket plan, and that you can buy an Inter-Rail card entitling you to a certain period of unlimited train travel at a refreshingly low price. It's like a EurailPass, but for students and youth only. Also, the WASTEELS reduced-rate ticket plan operates on trains to and from Istanbul.

If you travel by train, be sure to pack food, reading matter, and especially water, a commodity which is not always easily found on the train or in local stations, believe it or not. As a devotee of train travel, I hate to sound discouraging, but the trip through the Balkans can be an uncomfortable experience. Sometimes the cars are packed, there are often delays, single women can be bothered infuriatingly, the toilets defeat the nose, and there are lots and lots of border officials to treat with. You can escape these hassles in part by traveling in a first-class coach, but even this is not a guarantee of a hassle-free trip.

Transit Visas: If you go by train, you will have to get either a Yugoslavian or Bulgarian transit visa, or perhaps both.

Canadian and American passport holders need a transit visa for Yugoslavia. It's good for seven days and is obtainable at the border at no cost.

You will also need a Bulgarian transit visa (good for 48 hours), both on the trip from Europe to Turkey and on the trip back. It costs about $8 one way, $15 round trip, and *it must be obtained in advance!* You cannot get a visa at the border. Get your visa from your nearest friendly Bulgarian diplomatic representative (consulate or embassy), at home or in Europe. Americans can contact the Consular Section, Bulgarian Embassy, 1621 22nd St. NW, Washington, DC 20008. Allow a week or two if you're going to do it by mail—you will have to mail your passport.

From Greece

There is a daily train between Athens and Istanbul via Thessaloniki, but neither country seems to care much about it. According to the official schedule, the 1,400-km (868-mile) journey should take a day and a half, departing Athens or Istanbul in the evening and arriving mid-morning about 35 hours later. This is only about an hour faster than the run in 1908 when the train was run by an Ottoman company. (I'll bet the Ottoman train ran on time much more frequently than today's does.) In any case, you can still go by train (though most of your fellow travelers will be going by boat, bus, or plane), but you can't go first class: the train hauls second-class coaches only.

By the way, you can't really cut the slowness of the journey just by taking the train from Thessaloniki to Istanbul. That portion of the trip alone takes about 25 hours—if it's on time.

BY BUS: Several Turkish bus companies operate modern, comfortable buses between Istanbul and various European cities, usually working in conjunction with a European bus company. *Bosfor Turizm,* for instance, works with the German bus line "DTG" on its weekly services between Istanbul and Munich, Venice, and Vienna. Bosfor also joins services with the French firm of VIA-CIF to operate several days a week between Istanbul and Paris, Venice, Milan, Geneva, and Lyon. The various itineraries include either one night or two nights in a hotel—if it's one night, that means you spend at least one full night on the road, as the trip from Paris to Istanbul takes three full days. The fare for this marathon bus trip is about $125 one way, $160 round trip, and these sample prices include two nights in hotels plus all your meals. With only one night in a hotel, the price is about $15 cheaper. By the way, you're charged for each suitcase, knapsack, etc., you bring aboard: about $1.50 each for the first and second ones, over $2 for the third one, over $5 for the fourth one, so it pays to travel light. Students with proper identification get a 10% reduction on the cost of the ticket, journalists with Press Cards can knock off 40%; children 1 to 4 years old pay 30% of full fare, and those from 4 to 10 years old, 50%.

The **Varan Company** also runs buses between Istanbul and several points in Europe, including from Metz, Nancy, Strasbourg, Colmar, and Mulhouse (departing on Saturday); from Zürich (Saturday morning); from Bregenz, Dornbirn, and Innsbruck (Saturday); and from Salzburg and Vienna (Monday and Friday).

As with the train, those going to Turkey from Europe by bus will need to obtain a Bulgarian transit visa in advance; you can't get one at the border (see above, "By Train," for details).

Here are some addresses for the Turkish bus companies:

Geneva: Bosfor Turizm, Gare Routière Internationale, Place Dorcière, 1201 Genève (tel. 22/32-02-30).

Innsbruck: Varan Turizm, Salurnerstrasse 15 (Tourist Center) (tel. 6222/32-58-44).

Istanbul: Bosfor Turizm, Mete Caddesi, Taksim (tel. 11/143-2525); Varan Turizm, İnönü (Gümüşsuyu) Caddesi 17, Taksim (tel. 11/143-2187 or 144-8457).

Lyon: Bosfor Turizm, Aire Internationale, rue Gustave Nadaud, 69007 Lyon (tel. 858-0438).

Milan: Bosfor Turizm, Autostradale, 1 Piazza Castello, Milan (tel. 89-30-25).

Munich: Bosfor Turizm, Seidlstrasse 2, 8 München 2 (tel. 89/59-40-02 or 59-24-96).

Paris: Bosfor Turizm, Gare Routière Internationale, 8 Place de Stalingrad, 75019 Paris (tel. 01/201-7080 or 205-1210).

Salzburg: Varan Turizm, Bahnhof Vorplatz Kaiserschützenstrasse 12 (tel. 6222/75068).

Strasbourg: Varan Turizm, 18 Boulevard du Président Wilson (tel. 88/22-03-87).

Venice: Bosfor Turizm, Piazzale Roma, Venezia (tel. 41/27544).

Vienna: Bosfor Turizm, Argentinierstrasse 67, Südbahnhof, 1040 Wien (tel. 222/65-06-44; Varan Turizm, Südbahnhof Südtirolerplatz 7 (tel. 222/65-65-93).

Zurich: Varan Turizm, Klingenstrasse 9, Zürich 5 (tel. 1/44-04-77).

There are other bus companies. **Sümag Busreisen,** Hoefkade 399, 2526 BW Den Haag, in Holland (tel. 070/89-02-01), runs buses each Saturday (3 p.m. departure) from The Hague to Istanbul for $108. The trip takes about 46 hours. There is a return bus each Wednesday from Istanbul costing slightly less. In Istanbul, buy your tickets at Özsel Kollektif Şirketi, İncili Çavuş Sokak 37/1, Sultanahmet (tel. 1/526-2637), behind the Pudding Shop.

Another company, operating out of London, is **Olympic Bus,** located in Russell Square. A ticket to Istanbul via Thessaloniki costs $84 one way, twice that amount for round trip. You arrive in Thessaloniki at 4 a.m. to change buses, but note! The continuing bus may already be full, and you may have to wait for the next day's bus (which may also be full!). It may be better to take a bus headed directly for Turkey rather than for Greece. But if you do ride Olympic, the entire journey from London to Istanbul takes three or four days.

From Athens

Buses operate at least twice weekly on this route, and take 22 to 24 hours, part of that time being spent asleep in a hotel in Thessaloniki. A ticket costs about $40. Both **Bosfor Turizm** and **Varan Turizm** run this route. Other agencies are:

Athens: Rika Tours, Marni 44, Platia Vathis (tel. 1/523-2458, 523-3686, or 523-5905).

Istanbul: Ast Turizm, Beşir Fuat Caddesi 8, Tepebaşı (tel. 11/144-2006).

Thessaloniki: Simeonidis Tours, 26th October St. no. 14 (tel. 31/54-09-71 or 52-14-45).

BY CAR: Driving to Turkey, passing through half a dozen European countries, can be a very pleasant adventure. The highways are generally good, but they can be crowded, particularly with long-haul trucks on their way to Iran and the Arab countries. If you plan to take it easy, rest when you're tired, get off the beaten track for a refreshing close-up look at a village or town now and then, and you will enjoy the trip. Don't plan to rush madly along these highways, as it can be very frustrating and even dangerous.

Consider taking one of the car-ferries from Venice. Though the voyage can be fairly expensive once you add up the cost of the tickets for driver, passengers, and car, you must balance these costs against those of driving through the Balkans: hotels, fuel, visa charges, and highway tolls, not to mention the emotional costs of stress and fatigue.

If you do drive through the Balkans, remember that to pass through Bulgaria you will need to obtain a Bulgarian transit visa in advance from a Bulgarian consulate or embassy. You cannot get one at the border. If you don't want to bother with this minor hassle, plan your route around Bulgaria, through northern Greece.

Normally you cannot rent a car in Europe and include Turkey (or many other Eastern European countries) in your driving plans. If you have your own car, though, no special car documents are required for visits of up to three months. Your Green Card (insurance certificate) must be endorsed for *all* of Turkey, both European and Asiatic territories, not just for the European portion (Thrace). If it is not, you will have to buy a Turkish insurance policy at the border.

When you enter Turkey, the car will be registered in your (the driver's) passport as imported goods, and you must take it out of the country within the time allowed; the person in whose passport the car is registered must be the person to drive the car out of the country. *Do not drive someone else's car into Turkey,* as it may end up in your passport and you will then be liable for vast amounts of Customs duty when you try to leave the country without it!

If you want to leave your car in Turkey and return for it later, the car must be impounded by Customs until your return.

For information on what to do about stays longer than three months, or for putting your car in a Customs pound, contact the **Turkish Touring and Automobile Club (Türk Turing ve Otomobil Kulübü),** Halâskârgazi Caddesi 364, Şişli, Istanbul (tel. 11/140-7127).

2. Getting Around Turkey

Most vacationers returning from Turkey comment on the fantastic bus system. Big, comfortable Mercedes-Benz buses depart from modern bus stations and speed between cities with a frequency that astounds. For instance, a Mercedes coach leaves Istanbul for Ankara, an eight-hour trip, at least every 15 minutes throughout the day, and the pace of departures hardly slackens even in the middle of the night. And the cost for this journey, depending on the bus company, is an incredibly low 2,000TL ($2.80) to 3,000TL ($4.20)!

But the bus system, vast and convenient as it is, only makes up part of the picture. Turkish Airlines can save you a great deal of time if you plan to travel in eastern Turkey. Turkish Maritime Lines offers mini-cruises along Turkey's Black Sea, Aegean, and Mediterranean coasts. And the Turkish State Railways (TCDD) runs fairly modern and quite comfortable express trains between major cities, charging—if you can believe it—even less than the bus.

GETTING AROUND BY BUS: Most Turkish cities have a central bus terminal called the **Otogar** or **Santral Garaj.** An Otogar will often have its own post office, toilets, telephones with international service, restaurants, snack stands, pastry shops, tourism information booths, and baggage checkroom *(emanet).* The more expensive bus companies often have their own small, private terminals in other parts of town, to save their privileged patrons the hassle of dealing with large crowds at the main terminal.

The cost of bus travel in Turkey is about 350TL (50¢) for each 100 kms (62 miles), or less than a penny a mile! Bus fares are open to competition among companies, and even to bargaining: if a bus is about to leave and it has empty seats, you can often get a ticket at a reduced price.

Buy your bus tickets a day in advance if you can. All seats are reserved, and your ticket will bear specific seat numbers. When you buy, tell the clerk you want a *bilet* (ticket) for *yarın* (tomorrow).

Shortly after your bus begins its journey the driver's assistant will come down the aisle with a bottle of lemon cologne with which to refresh you. He'll dribble some into your cupped hands, which you should then rub together, rub on your face, dry on your hair, and sniff to refresh your nasal passages. If you ride buses much in Turkey you'll get used to this traditional sign of hospitality quickly, and you'll probably love it. One helpful hint: Try to get a sniff of the cologne before he gets to you—the good-quality ones are dry and astringent, with a real scent of lemon, but the cheap ones are overly perfumey.

The trip itself is usually a pleasant experience, except perhaps for cigarette smoke. This is the land of aromatic Turkish tobacco, though Turks, like most people, think it laudable that someone doesn't smoke or has given it up.

Your fellow passengers will be curious about where you come from, what language you speak, and how you're enjoying the country. It's polite to exchange a few sentences, even though you may find yourself saying the same things over and over.

If you want a free drink of water during the trip, just signal the assistant, ask for *su* (water), and he'll bring you a capped bottle.

The bus will stop about every 1½ hours so passengers can use the toilet, have a snack or a meal, and drink a glass of the ubiquitous *çay* (tea). At tea stops, boys sometimes rush onto the bus selling snacks, nuts, sandwiches, and the like, or a waiter from the tea house may come through with several glasses to sell. At the end of your journey the bus company may provide free minibus service from the Otogar into the center of town; save your bus ticket so you can prove that you are actually one of the company's customers.

Minibuses

Minibuses operate on many routes that are not heavily enough traveled to justify a full-size bus. In general, you'll find yourself taking minibuses from towns to villages. Often, but not always, minibuses depart from the town's Otogar; otherwise, they leave from some major intersection or from the marketplace. Sometimes you may have to wait for a minibus to fill up, or at least for a minimum number of paying passengers to appear, before the driver will depart.

BY PLANE: Turkish Airlines (THY) and several new, smaller firms, have flights operating throughout the country, with many routes beginning and ending in Istanbul, and traveling via Ankara. It's a good idea to get to the airport at least 45 minutes before flight time. THY has a policy of open seating on all domestic flights; you are not assigned a specific seat number, but may sit wherever you choose. This also means that there's not really a no-smoking section.

Turkish Airlines' safety record is good, and the security procedures at Turkish airports are quite elaborate and reassuring: each vehicle is inspected as it enters the airport grounds; bags are x-rayed as they enter the terminal; hand baggage is searched by hand, and every passenger is frisked, before boarding the flight; and on the way out to the plane, all checked baggage is arrayed on the tarmac and each passenger must indicate his luggage before it is placed in the cargo hold. Any bags not indicated by passengers are treated as suspicious (don't forget to point out your bags!).

MILEAGE BETWEEN TURKEY'S TOURISTIC CITIES
Distance in Miles

	Adana	Ankara	Antalya	Bursa	Çanakkale	Edirne	Erzurum	Istanbul	İzmir	Konya	Nevşehir	Samsun	Trabzon	Van
Adana	—	301	342	522	702	719	519	573	569	216	177	477	618	584
Adıyaman	219	513	561	725	915	910	381	764	789	435	356	517	481	928
Ankara	301	—	340	239	429	417	573	272	369	262	176	259	482	787
Antakya	118	419	459	640	820	836	516	691	687	334	295	588	615	573
Antalya	342	340	—	348	459	595	851	449	335	226	366	599	823	926
Aydın	568	375	260	309	285	428	975	451	78	352	492	634	857	1,142
Bursa	522	239	348	—	190	288	808	142	232	306	408	479	703	1,019
Çanakkale	702	429	459	190	—	143	998	209	208	486	598	669	893	1,209
Denizli	489	296	181	311	344	487	869	412	154	273	413	554	778	1,063
Diyarbakır	336	587	678	818	1,008	1,004	301	858	905	552	450	541	402	252
Edirne	719	417	595	288	143	—	937	146	350	553	593	608	832	1,205
Erzurum	519	573	851	808	998	937	—	787	942	625	485	425	202	260
Gaziantep	133	435	475	656	836	852	418	706	703	349	302	515	517	453
Istanbul	573	272	449	142	209	146	787	—	374	407	448	463	686	1,053
İzmir	569	369	335	232	208	350	942	374	—	353	487	627	851	1,137
Kayseri	207	202	431	434	624	619	420	474	552	205	65	278	401	585
Konya	216	262	226	306	486	553	625	407	353	—	140	421	606	790
Muğla	631	438	323	372	348	490	1,011	514	140	415	555	696	920	1,205
Nevşehir	177	176	366	408	598	593	485	448	487	140	—	299	466	650
Rize	655	531	872	752	942	881	159	735	900	655	515	273	49	419
Samsun	477	259	599	479	669	608	425	463	627	421	299	—	224	685
Sivas	327	275	551	515	704	693	299	547	644	326	185	212	280	552
Trabzon	618	482	823	703	893	832	202	686	851	606	466	224	—	461
Urfa*	222	523	566	745	924	941	150	795	791	438	391	615	512	362
Van	584	787	926	1,019	1,209	1,205	260	1,053	1,137	790	650	685	461	—

*May appear as Şanlıurfa, the current name.

From Istanbul, the schedule for THY looks like this:

Weekly THY Flights from Istanbul

To	No. Flights	Fare
Adana	14	40,000TL ($56)
Ankara	80	30,000TL ($42)
Antalya	16	32,000TL ($44.80)
Diyarbakır	7	30,000TL ($42)
Erzurum	8	30,000TL ($42)

There are also flights from Istanbul to Dalaman (one or two daily), Elâzığ (four weekly), İzmir (five to seven daily from Istanbul, one or two daily from Ankara), Kayseri (two weekly), Malatya (five weekly), Merzifon (three weekly), Samsun (three weekly), Sivas (twice weekly), Trabzon (daily), and Van (four flights weekly). There are nonstop flights once a week, on Sunday, between İzmir and Antalya, and twice weekly between Sivas and Malatya.

As for the smaller companies, **Istanbul Airlines** (Istanbul Hava Yolları) operates service between Istanbul and Adana, Antalya, Diyarbakır, İzmir, Trabzon, and Turkish Cyprus. **Sönmez Holding Airlines** (Sönmez Holding Hava Yolları) is a small airline owned by a large Bursa holding company; they have one small C-212 aircraft which flies from Bursa to Istanbul and back each morning, and again each evening.

BY TRAIN: Turkey is a big country, the trains are a lot slower than the buses, and for the long distances nothing can beat the convenience of flying. But certain trains constitute the most convenient, comfortable, and even luxurious method of travel, so you shouldn't rule out going by train. Train travel between Ankara, İzmir, and Istanbul is a case in point. The top trains on these lines are a pleasure to ride, by day or night.

Whenever you take an intercity train in Turkey you should take only trains classed as *ekspres* (including the super-express Mavi Trens, or Blue Trains). These are fast, comfortable, and still surprisingly cheap. Other trains, particularly those designated as *yolcu* or *posta,* move at a snail's pace. You could, quite literally, be en route for days.

The **Turkish State Railways** uses a computerized reservations system for selling tickets for reserved seats, sleeping berths, and couchettes on express and Blue Trains. Avail yourself of this useful feature, and make your reservations several days in advance of travel, if you can. Particularly on Friday and Sunday evenings, demand for space on the best trains is heavy. If you can't get space, don't despair. Often there are cancellations and you'll be able to get a seat, or a berth, when you get to the station.

Here are some fares for seats on *ekspres* trains from Istanbul to other Turkish cities:

Sample *Ekspres* Train Fares from Istanbul

To	Full Fare	Student Fare
Adana	3,500TL ($4.90)	3,200TL ($4.50)
Ankara	2,100TL ($2.95)	1,900TL ($2.65)
Denizli	2,200TL ($3.10)	2,000TL ($2.80)
Diyarbakır	4,500TL ($6.30)	4,100TL ($5.75)
Edirne	1,000TL ($1.40)	900TL ($1.25)
Erzurum	4,700TL ($6.60)	4,300TL ($6.00)

Tickets for a trip on a Blue Train service cost about 50% more than full fare on an express. You must also pay more if you take an express train and use a sleeping car, but the price is usually about the same, or less, than that for a room in a moderately good hotel. The prices below are *per person* for sleeping compartments with one, two, or three berths, from Istanbul:

Sleeping Compartment Price (Per Person) from Istanbul

To	Single	Double	Triple
Ankara	16,100TL ($22.55)	12,100TL ($16.95)	9,100TL ($12.75)
Diyarbakır	19,500TL ($27.30)	15,500TL ($21.70)	12,500TL ($17.50)
Erzurum	19,700TL ($27.60)	15,700TL ($22)	12,700TL ($17.80)
Kayseri	12,200TL ($17.10)	9,700TL ($13.60)	7,700TL ($10.80)
Tatvan	20,000TL ($28)	16,000TL ($22.40)	13,000TL ($18.20)

The Top Trains

The most popular route, by far, is the one between Istanbul (Haydarpaşa Station) and Ankara. Government officers, businessmen, families, and maiden aunts all enjoy the scenery, the comfort, the speed, and the low prices on this route. If you take only one train trip in Turkey, this is the one to take.

Here's a rundown of the country's top trains:

Blue Train: The *Mavi Tren,* with daily first-class super-express service between Ankara and Istanbul, makes the run in about 7½ hours. There are two Blue Trains per day from each city, departing at breakfast time, and just after lunch, arriving mid-afternoon and late evening.

Bosphorus Express: The *Boğaziçi Ekspresi* is a daily all-Pullman first-class express between Ankara and Istanbul, making the trip in about 9½ hours. Though a bit slower than the bus, and certainly slower than the Blue Train, it's cheaper and more comfortable than either alternative.

Aegean Express: The *Ege Ekspresi* is a daily first-class express between Ankara and İzmir, taking about 9½ hours, which is about the same time as the bus, but the train is cheaper and more comfortable.

Ankara Express: The nightly *Ankara Ekspresi* is the all-sleeping-car train between Istanbul and Ankara. The trip is longer, about 12 hours, to give you time to get a full night's rest.

Anatolia Express: The *Anadolu Ekspresi* is another nightly Ankara–Istanbul sleeping-car train, but this one hauls couchettes and first- and second-class coaches as well. It takes about 12 hours.

İzmir Express: The *İzmir Ekspresi* runs nightly in each direction between Ankara and İzmir, hauling coaches and sleeping cars, in about 12½ hours.

BY RENTAL CAR:

If you can afford it, this is the finest way to see the country. Rates are not expensive, but moderate, compared to other European countries. As for the Turkish highways, they tend to be good and not particularly crowded, except for the major truck routes (E-5, E-24). City streets are just the opposite and parking is a real problem in the large cities. Turkish drivers out on the highway tend to drive at high speed, and some are inexperienced, but they are not really nasty. In the cities, on the other hand, discourtesy and madness are the rule rather than the exception.

Some details: Your home-country driver's license will do just fine; you don't really need an International Driving Permit, but if you'd feel more secure by carrying an IDP you can get one through an automobile club at home.

You can pick up a rental car from the larger international rental firms (Hertz, Avis, National/Europcar, Budget, and Dollar/interRent), or from smaller local ones, in Adana, Alanya, Antalya, Ankara, Istanbul, İzmir, or Kuşadası. The most prominent company is Avis. The most popular rental cars are the Fiat ("Murat") 124 and 131, and the Renault 12, which are fairly fuel-efficient. The cost of fuel, for driving one kilometer, is about 23.50TL (3.3¢), or about 5.3¢ per mile.

The total cost for a week's rental of one of the aforementioned cars, with unlimited kilometers, including full insurance and tax, might be 157,000TL ($220) to 215,000TL ($301), plus the cost of gas. Keep in mind that the daily or weekly rental charge is only a small portion of what you will actually end up paying, unless it includes unlimited mileage—the charge for mileage normally ends up being far higher than the daily rental charge. Gas, as of this writing, costs about 300TL (45¢) per liter (1,136TL, $1.60, per U.S. gallon). By the way, the Value Added Tax (KDV in Turkish) should be included in all of the prices quoted to you—it should not be added to your bill as a separate item.

TAKING A MINI-CRUISE: Turkish Maritime Lines operates cruise ships on the Black Sea, Aegean, and Mediterranean coasts, but cabins are few and in great demand, so if you want to take one of these very enjoyable mini-cruises, you'll have to make reservations in advance. By the way, you don't have to ship a car in order to travel as a passenger on a car-ferry.

The popular overnight car-ferry service between Istanbul and İzmir (19 hours) sails on Friday afternoon from Istanbul, on Sunday afternoon from İzmir, all year long. In summer there are extra sailings on Monday and Wednesday from Istanbul, on Tuesday and Thursday from İzmir. Per-person fares range from $10 for a Pullman reclining seat through $40 in the most luxurious cabin. Meals are not included in the prices. The fare for a car is $30.

Another popular mini-cruise is the car-ferry service from Istanbul to Trabzon, at the eastern end of the Black Sea coast. The ferries operate year round, departing Istanbul on Monday evening, arriving in Samsun on Tuesday and in Trabzon on Wednesday morning. The return trip departs Trabzon on Wednesday evening, arriving in Samsun on Thursday morning and in Istanbul on Friday at noon. Fares between Istanbul and Trabzon, per person, are $12 for a Pullman seat, $15 to $47 for cabin berths. Cars cost $40.

Perhaps the most enjoyable cruise of all, and therefore the one most in demand, is the voyage from Istanbul to Alanya, steaming along the gorgeous Aegean and Mediterranean coasts. Eight cruises are run from early June through mid-September on a course which includes stops at Dikili (with a tour to Bergama), İzmir, Marmaris, Kekova, Alanya, Antalya, Fethiye, Bodrum, Kuşadası (for a tour to Ephesus), İzmir again, and back to Istanbul. The cruise price includes all meals, excursions to various points of interest along the way, and the entire trip from Istanbul to Istanbul. The cheapest cabin berth costs $419; the most expensive, $840.

GETTING AROUND IN THE CITIES: Every city of any size has a good municipal bus system. The **buses** operate on a ticket system: you buy one or more tickets at little booths located at the major bus stops, and then use one ticket for each trip. Tickets cost 60TL (8¢) to 100TL (14¢), depending on the city.

Minibuses and sedans also operate within cities as *dolmuş* (**dolmush, a** shared taxi), running along predetermined routes, stopping at marked stops (more or less) to take on and drop off passengers. These jitney cabs charge slightly more than the buses, but provide a good deal more comfort and convenience. You'll find them very handy.

As for **taxis,** they are everywhere, they all have meters, they use the meters, and the resulting fares are absurdly cheap. The drop rate is 250TL (35¢), 260TL (36¢) in Ankara, slightly higher everywhere at night. The average taxi ride therefore costs 400TL (56¢) to 700TL ($1) during the day and evening, not much more at night (after about 11 p.m.).

Finally, in Istanbul and İzmir you'll find **ferryboats.** White with orange trim, these sturdy craft steam up, down, and across the Bosphorus and İzmir's bay, providing cheap, convenient transportation, views of the sea, and fresh, cool breezes. Special ferry sailings on a touristic route up the Bosphorus are operated daily in Istanbul, and you should not neglect to sail on one of these. There's no better way to see the Bosphorus, and the price for a 2½-hour cruise is only 750TL ($1.05).

3. Suggested Itineraries

To sample Turkey's natural beauties and man-made wonders in detail takes the average visitor about a month; to see everything thoroughly, a summer. But few visitors can afford to spend that much time, so here are suggestions on how to plan your travel if you have less time.

ONE WEEK OR LESS: If your vacation time is very short, it makes sense to spend much of it, on your first trip to Turkey, in Istanbul with its rich concentration of architectural and historical wonders, and its plethora of good restaurants and amusement spots. You will want to get out of town for at least a day or two of excursion, though. Keep in mind, as you plan, that the Grand Bazaar is closed on Sunday, most of the city's museums are closed on Monday, but that Topkapı Palace closes on Tuesday.

Istanbul and an Excursion

Day 1: Most of your first day will be spent getting moved in, absorbing the sights and sounds of this different city, recovering from jet lag, and planning your sightseeing.

Day 2: Start your first full day of sightseeing early in the morning at Topkapı Palace, and plan to spend at least the entire morning there, and perhaps a few hours of the afternoon. You can have lunch right in the palace. After Topkapı, visit neighboring Sancta Sophia, the Blue Mosque, the Hippodrome, and the Cistern Basilica (Yerebatan Saray).

Day 3: Return to the Old City for a look at the Turkish and Islamic Arts Museum in the İbrahim Pasha Palace on the Hippodrome, and the Archeological Museums down the hill from Topkapı Palace, then stroll westward along Divan Yolu to Beyazıt Square. From Beyazıt, walk to the Süleymaniye Mosque and the Aqueduct of Valens. If time remains, take a bus or taxi to the Mosque of the Conqueror (Fatih Camii).

Day 4: Start the day with a look at the mighty city walls out by the Edirne Gate (Edirnekapı), from which it's only a few minutes' walk to the Kariye Camii (Chora Church) with its fabulous 13th-century Byzantine mosaics. The Byzantine palace of Tekfur Sarayı is also close, and should be your next stop. Spend the afternoon shopping in the Grand Bazaar.

Day 5: Today is your chance to tour the new city, on the northern shore of the Golden Horn. Visit Dolmabahçe Palace and Yıldız Park, with its various villas and mansions, especially the Yıldız Kiosk. Also take a stroll down İstiklal Caddesi from Taksim, inspecting this former Grand Rue de Pera and its huge old consulates, which were embassies under the Ottoman Empire.

Day 6: At least one day, in good weather, you must take a cruise on the Bosphorus. The special touristic ferryboats are the easiest and cheapest, and quite pleasant. You can spend the entire day cruising and sightseeing (don't miss the great fortress of Rumeli Hisar, and get to Beylerbeyi Palace if you can). Dinner on the Bosphorus is a good way to finish.

Day 7: For an excursion, choose among a flying day trip to Bursa or a ferryboat to the Princes' Islands. Better yet, plan an overnight trip and do Bursa properly, taking the ferryboat and stopping at İznik along the way. Or take a bus to Çanakkale and visit Troy and the battlefields of the Dardanelles. Or fly to İzmir and bus to Ephesus for a day at the best-preserved classical city in existence.

TWO WEEKS: With two weeks to spend, you can see a lot more, and get in some beach time as well. Here's how to spend your second week, exploring the delights of Turkey's thousands of miles of coastline.

Aegean and Mediterranean Shores

Day 1: Choose among Bursa, Çanakkale (Troy), and İzmir (Ephesus), as described above in Day 7, according to your preference and the length of your vacation time. If you have more time, do them all, starting in Bursa, continuing to Troy, and stopping at Ayvalık and Bergama on your way south to İzmir. Otherwise, fly from Istanbul to İzmir on Day 7, visit that city in the afternoon, and spend today on an outing to Bergama.

Day 2: Today must be devoted to Ephesus. Get there early, as the heat and the crowds increase as the day wears on. Have a leisurely lunch, and spend the heat of the afternoon at the beach, either Pamucak or Kuşadası.

Day 3: Using Kuşadası as a base, visit Priene, Miletus, and Didyma, and take a swim at Altınkum.

Day 4: Start early for an excursion inland to Aphrodisias and Pamukkale. You can make this a day trip, or you can plan to spend the night at Pamukkale.

Day 5: Choose between these charming small resort towns: Marmaris, the yachting capital of the Turkish Mediterranean, with the captivating village of Datça not far away; or Bodrum, also a yachting port, dominated by a craggy Crusaders' castle.

Day 6: Continue your enjoyment of the pellucid blue waters of the Mediterranean, heading eastward along the coast to Fethiye and Ölüdeniz, Kalkan, and Kaş. You can continue by chartered yacht, rented car, or bus. Spend the night in any one of these places.

Day 7: You can reach Antalya, with its half-dozen excellent archeological sites nearby, on Day 7, though you may also have lagged behind in one of the idyllic coastal towns. If you made it to this ancient city, plan visits to Aspendos, Perge, Termessos, and Side during the next few days. You may want to continue along the Mediterranean coast to Alanya.

THREE WEEKS: With this much time to spend, you can get a good look at Istanbul, the Aegean and Mediterranean coasts, and also find out about the wonders of Central Anatolia. Fly from İzmir or Antalya to Ankara, or take a bus (perhaps at night) from the coast up to the plateau. Though you may start your explorations at Konya or Nevşehir, I'll assume that most readers will see Ankara as their first glimpse of this fascinating region.

Central Anatolia

Day 1: Land in Ankara, find a hotel, and begin seeing the several sights of the capital, especially the Anatolian Civilizations Museum, the citadel, and the Anıt Kabir (Atatürk's Mausoleum).

Day 2: Start by bus or rental car for Konya. This city requires at least an overnight stay, partly because it is three or four hours' drive from anywhere else, and also because its marvelous Seljuk Turkish buildings demand to be savored. The Mevlana Museum, the former convent of the Whirling Dervishes, is your first stop. Note that Konya's buildings are mostly closed on Monday.

Day 3: Head off by bus or rental car to Cappadocia, making your base in Ürgüp. After you are settled in your hotel, you'll have time to do some exploring of the region.

Day 4: Spend the day seeing the most impressive valleys and their rock churches: Göreme and Zelve.

Day 5: Visit the underground cities at Derinkuyu and Kaymaklı, then head for Boğazkale, Kayseri, or farther east, to Nemrut Dağı.

Day 6: Those willing to drive or ride for long hours from Cappadocia can reach one of Turkey's most astounding sights, the mountaintop temples of Nemrut Dağı. Make your base at Adıyaman or Kahta. Those wanting to see the mountaintop at sunrise or sunset will have to plan on spending two nights. If you can't make it to Nemrut Dağı, head due north of Cappadocia to Yozgat for a visit to the Hittite cities at Boğazkale and Hattuşaş, then a return to Ankara.

Day 7: If you've come by bus to Nemrut Dağı, you can choose to return to Ankara or Istanbul by plane from Malatya. More time? Then use Nemrut as a starting place for a tour of eastern Turkey.

ONE MONTH: Few people have the luxury of a month's vacation all at once, but even if you are not among this lucky group, your second trip to Turkey can include a tour of the east lasting from one week to ten days. Plan this trip only for summer (late May through late September), as winter and its snows come early to this mountainous region.

Eastern Anatolia and the Black Sea

The easiest and most delightful way to tour the east is by rental car. You'll have to pick up the car in Ankara, Samsun, or Adana, as there are as yet no rental stations east of those cities.

Day 1: Assuming that you've just picked up your car, your first day will be spent driving to reach Nemrut Dağı.

Day 2: Visit Nemrut Dağı from Kahta.

Day 3: Head east to Diyarbakır. If you have time to spare, go southeast to Şanlıurfa first, make an excursion to Harran, then head due east to Mardin before turning north to Diyarbakır.

Day 4: See the sights in Diyarbakır, and take an excursion to Mardin if you haven't seen it on the way.

Day 5: Drive to Van, stopping along the way to visit the Akdamar Church on an island in Lake Van.

Day 6: After a bit of shopping for kilims in Van, drive north to Doğubeyazıt for views of Mount Ararat and a visit to the striking İshak Pasha Palace just outside of town.

Day 7: Drive to Kars for a visit to Ani, then head for Erzurum to spend the night. This may be rushed, and you may find yourself staying in Kars, unfortunately.

Day 8: After seeing the sights in Erzurum, drive north and west to Trabzon, on the Black Sea coast.

Day 9: Spend the morning visiting Sumela Monastery, and continue with Atatürk's Villa, Sancta Sophia Church, and the sights in town.

Day 10: Drive along the Black Sea coast to Samsun and stay the night here (though there's nothing to see), or press onward via Amasya to Ankara. If you must return your car to Adana, the road south via Tokat, Sivas, and Kayseri is interesting, if demanding.

4. A Stop on the Way: Edirne

If you enter Turkey by car or train from Europe, there's a good chance you'll pass through Edirne, once called Adrianople. Don't pass right through the city: there's a good reason why you should make a stop in Edirne. The first Ottoman capital was Bursa and the last was Istanbul. But while the sultan was on campaign in Europe or planning the conquest of Byzantium, he made his capital in Edirne. The monuments to this early age of Turkish conquest make the town your first important stop.

Edirne and Istanbul are the only cities in European Turkey that are of substantial size. Istanbul, of course, has Turkey's largest and most varied collection of mosques, but Edirne is second only to Istanbul. A special flavor is added to the feeling of age given by the old mosques in that almost all of the people in Edirne have moved there during or since the exchange of populations following World War I. You're liable to hear Greek and Bulgarian spoken as well as Turkish, though the speakers will all be Turks.

Because it's only four hours or less to Istanbul by bus or car, Edirne seems a good place to break a journey. But if you come by train, Istanbul will be six hours away at best, ten at worst. You might consider leaving the train at Edirne and continuing your trip by bus—it's faster, if a bit less comfortable. You must detrain at the Kapıkule (border) station, then take a dolmush (shared taxi) or a taxi into the city.

ORIENTATION: Hürriyet Meydanı (Freedom Square), at the intersection of the two main streets, Saraçlar/Saraçhane Caddesi and Talat Paşa Caddesi, is your reference point in modern Edirne; this intersection has probably been the center of town since Roman times.

Just west of the intersection is the Üçşerefeli Cami. If you head north along Talat Paşa Caddesi, you'll come to Edirne's major attraction, the **Selimiye Camii.** On the way to the Selimiye, you'll pass the Eski Cami, the city's oldest mosque.

The bus station and the train station are both on the outskirts of town. You will have to take a city bus, dolmush, or taxi to reach Hürriyet Meydanı.

USEFUL FACTS: If you come by bus or car, you can stop at the **Tourism Information Office** at the Kapıkule frontier post. Otherwise, the Tourism Information Office downtown is very near Hürriyet Meydanı, on Talat Paşa Caddesi (tel. 1811/1518).

HOTELS IN EDİRNE: The hotel situation in Edirne is not bad, offering a wide range of prices and accommodations. The most expensive places in town are quite cheap.

Edirne's old standard is the **Kervan Oteli,** Talat Paşa Caddesi, Kadınhane Sokak no. 134 (tel. 1811/1382, 1355, or 1167), on the road into the center of town from the bus and train stations. The Kervan has been caring well for travelers for over a decade, and still maintains a good standard of service. There are double rooms, each with shower or bath, which rent for 10,200TL ($14.30); single rooms (actually, a double room used as a single) are 8800TL ($12.30). The Kervan has a decent restaurant and also garage facilities.

Next choice is the **Sultan Oteli,** just out of Hürriyet Square on Talat Paşa Caddesi at no. 170 (tel. 1811/1372). It's new, has one of the most ghastly tactile lobby ceilings in the world, and offers 51 rooms (28 with bath) at the following rates: 6,900TL ($9.65) single with bath, 11,400TL ($15.95) double. The baths are an arrangement which allows one to take a Turkish "splash-bath" or a shower; they're not the full-bathtub type.

Other than these two places, there is the **Pansiyon Nil** (tel. 1811/1019), about the best of the old mansions that have been converted to hostelries. The Nil's 25 beds, most double, go for 1,500TL ($2.10) per bed; breakfast is 550TL (75¢) and a shower is about the same. To get to the Nil, from the Tourism Information Office in Hürriyet Square, walk down Maarif Caddesi, the street to the left of the office, for five short blocks. The Nil is on the right, no. 22.

If you're driving, **BP** has set up a **Mocamp** on the Edirne–Istanbul road about one kilometer (six-tenths of a mile) from town (tel. 1811/1290). It's open from the beginning of April through mid-October, can accommodate up to 600 campers, and has full services: restaurant, electricity, and water hookups, laundry, cooking facilities, and a food and supplies store, all in a fenced-in shaded site. Those without their own camping equipment can rent a bungalow. The cost at the BP-Kervansaray Mocamp is 600TL (85¢) per adult, 650TL (90¢) per tent site, 550TL (75¢) per car, or 1,050TL ($1.45) for a car-and-trailer (caravan).

There's another BP-Kervansaray Mocamp with similiar prices and facilities at İpsala (tel. 38), very near the Greek-Turkish border, three kilometers (two miles) along the road from İpsala toward Istanbul.

RESTAURANTS IN EDİRNE: The restaurants in town, except for one in the Kervan Hotel, are fairly modest. A meal for $2.50 is something that comes naturally; in the kebab and köfte places, it's difficult to spend even that much. For a restaurant, try the **Üçler Lokantası** on the street out of the bus terminal. Walk down Saraçlar Caddesi to the post office ("PTT") and turn left onto the street on its side. Walk down this street, following the signs to the Üçler, and turn left again. The Üçler is on this street—Saraçlar Camii Sokak—at no. 12, few doors up on the right. A meal of shish kebap, buttered spinach, a salad, and melon for dessert, with a soft drink comes to 1,000TL ($1.40). For comparable prices in a restaurant with a little more elbow room, go to the **Kırkpınar Lokantası,** at no. 67 on the next street over.

Perhaps the finest and tastiest food to be found downtown is served up in the **Aile Kebap Restaurant,** overlooking Saraçlar Caddesi a short distance out of Hürriyet Square. Follow signs to the post office ("PTT"), which is on Saraçlar; right next to it, above a bank ("Yapı ve Kredi Bankası") is the bright, clean, spacious room of the Aile. You enter by the side street which runs between the restaurant and the PTT. Potted palms dot the room here and there, and waiters in white shirts and black trousers whisk plates of steaming kebap or hearty vegetable dishes to your table in very little time at all. Perhaps the only thing to compare with the Aile is the restaurant of the **Kervan Hotel,** which is more expensive, and a bit out of the way. A meal with beverage and service included should cost no more than 2,500TL ($3.50) at the Aile; you can have a light lunch for less.

Other than restaurants, Edirne exhibits a good number of tiny kebap and köfte places, especially on Saraçlar Caddesi. All of the köftecis on the street look about the same, and charge 900TL ($1.25) for a plate of köfte (charcoal-grilled rissoles), a salad, a pudding for dessert, bread, plus some mineral water (*maden sodası*) to drink.

THE SIGHTS: I said that Edirne has an amazing variety of mosques. Here's proof.

Just out of Hürriyet Square is the **Üçserefeli Cami** (built 1447), or "Mosque with Three Galleries." The "galleries" are the tiny balconies on one of the minarets. The different parts of this mosque—the minarets, the doorways, the court-yard, the sanctuary itself—all seem as though they were built at slightly different times. The architecture is a blend of many styles, with a great deal of the old Seljuk Turkish artistry worked in. There are some fine blue tiles with white Ara-bic lettering over the doorways in the courtyard. Before entering the mosque, be sure to take your shoes off. The sanctuary is hexagonal, with an arch forming each side, a style you won't find in Istanbul.

One of the outbuildings on the mosque grounds is an old religious school which has been restored and is now used as a student dormitory. Take a peek in if you're interested in what student life was like in the Turkey of 500 years ago.

Across the street from the mosque is a **hamam,** or Turkish bath, built by Turkey's most famous architect, Sinan, in the 1500s. It's been restored, and you can take a Turkish steambath there, wash off with cool water, and take a nap in one of the bed cubicles, all for 700TL ($1).

From Hürriyet Square, walk up Talat Paşa Caddesi to get to the **Eski Cami** (finished in 1414), the oldest Ottoman mosque in Edirne. This one is in the an-cient style introduced by the Arabs. The mosque has 13 domes altogether. As you enter the mosque your eyes will be hit by the inscriptions: huge Arabic let-ters decorating every wall quoting from the Koran or naming the prophets and caliphs. On the left wall is a *tuğra,* the personal seal of the Ottoman emperors, which takes up the whole wall as it gracefully sweeps out of one corner to curl into intricate lettering. The painted ceiling follows no particular style. The mosque, like the group of people in it, seems to be a catch-all. You might tiptoe into a Friday "Sunday school" lesson (the Muslim sabbath is Friday), with rows of women sitting cross-legged on the floor watching a *hoca* (pronounced *ho*-jah) in a long flowing robe and immaculate white turban as he quotes from the Koran and explains the passage, adding a lesson of his own to the reading. You'll see women who seem to be fairly rich next to the poor beggar-woman you gave a coin to in the street. It seems that the people of Edirne hold this mosque in even higher esteem, because of its age, than they do the magnificent **Selimiye Camii** which dominates the city from its hilltop perch not far from the Eski Mosque.

The Selimiye (1575) is Edirne's most famous mosque, even if it is not the favorite of the city's Muslims. Walk up Mimar Sinan Caddesi, starting just out-side the Eski Mosque, to get to the Selimiye. Make sure you're on this street, as you should approach the mosque from the front to really feel its full effect.

As a Turkish friend said, the Selimiye is the architect Sinan's masterpiece, in the old sense of the word, meaning the work he submitted to other masters for acceptance into the guild. He seems to have passed the test, for this was not the last mosque he built. Compared to the other two mosques you've looked at, this one is very symmetrical. It's a lot smaller than some of the ones in Istanbul, but seems to be more in proportion here than a really big mosque would be. After the first and second gates, you're in the courtyard with a marble ablutions foun-tain. The courtyard and the arcade around it are used for prayer during the sum-mer when the weather's good, though it's usually cooler inside. The interior is famous for several things: its Turkish tiles, which you can see close up in the mihrab, or prayer niche, section of the mosque. The mimber (pulpit) is made of marble carved into a delicate open net design. Many mimbers have this design on the supporting walls, but it's usually carved in superficially, not open as this one is. The dome of the mosque is supported by eight columns, but they've been set into the walls so that they don't break the span of the interior—the sort of construction used in Sancta Sophia in Istanbul. Put all of these together and you get a touching effect of peacefulness and beauty. The little fountain in the center of the floor is for drinking (there's usually a cup by it) but also to give the sound of running water to the inside of the mosque, a trick learned from the earlier

Seljuk Turks, who liked the pleasant, peaceful sound in their buildings. If you happen to be in the mosque on the hour, a deep vibration will spread to you as it fills the mosque—the low, mysterious chime of the big old grandfather clock to the right of the prayer niche. The acoustics of the walls and the ceiling, when the carpeted floor is taken into account, are just right.

As you walk around the interior enjoying the workmanship, notice the old muezzin (in charge of giving the call to prayer five times a day, and also the overseer of the mosque) who sits in a corner near the doorway, reading from a Koran resting on a special stand intricately carved and worked in mother-of-pearl. Some muezzins memorize the entire book, and are often called upon to chant passages at special services. If you happen to notice the locked metal box on a stand as you go out the door, you drop a coin in for the upkeep of the mosque, and as you pass him, the muezzin thanks you, says good-bye, and wishes God to give you abundance.

For a building that seems so young (compared to the town's other mosques), the Selimiye has seen a lot of history. You probably noticed the sultan's loge to the far left of the prayer niche, which allowed the monarch to pray with his people without being among them. There is a story that some of the mosque's precious tiles, the ones with inscriptions, were removed and taken home by a Russian general who brought his triumphant troops into Edirne during the Ottoman-Russian war in 1778.

A mosque tour of Edirne isn't complete without a walk to the **Beyazıt Camii complex** (1488), a 20-minute walk from Hürriyet Square. Walk down Saraçhane Caddesi beside the Üçserefeli Cami, and turn left just after the Turkish bath built by Sinan. Walk one block and bear right at the little old fountain onto Horozlu Bayır Caddesi. The street changes names to become İmaret Caddesi just as it crosses the Tunca River. The bridge over the Tunca was built in connection with the mosque complex, in 1488.

Sultan Beyazıt II did a lot for the city in the way of public works by building a mosque with a full complement of other buildings. Within the same enclosure are two religious schools, a mental institution, a soup kitchen for the poor, and other buildings used for humane activities. These are all being restored to their original form, very slowly, by a team of two or three stonemasons who chip away monotonously at blocks of new stone, copying to the last detail the workmanship in the crumbling old blocks before them. If there are no other people around this can be an eerie place, even in the middle of the day. The forest of domes covering the many buildings seems to betoken great activity, numbers of people working, sleeping, talking, or performing their religious duties. Instead it's quiet, except for the tap, tap, tap of the stonemasons' hammers; the wind hums through the empty stone halls, pigeons coo in the rafters of the mosque's courtyard. Inside the mosque itself these noises are left out, but the simple round shape, the empty sultan's box, make it a very lonely place. Though the mosque is still used for prayer, few people walk this far out of town when there are so many mosques more handy.

The sultans had several palaces in this one-time capital, as you might imagine. Though they once rivaled Istanbul's great Topkapı Palace in richness and size, there's not much left of them today. For a glance at the ruins, walk up the road on top of the river dike which runs next to the Beyazıt II mosque. You'll probably notice a lot of soldiers in the area around the ruins. In a city so near the borders of two other countries, there's liable to be a sizable military contingent.

Near the ruined palaces, on the island between the two branches of the river, the famous **Kırklareli Wrestling Matches** are held every year in late May or early June. These are the ones in which brawny giants of men wearing only tight leather trousers grease themselves from head to foot with olive oil, circle in a mysterious, almost dance-like ceremony while they size one another up, then tackle, slip, fall, grip again, and strain against their opponent until one gives in—usually from exhaustion. The matches take place near the end of May each year. Check with the Tourism Information Office downtown for times and ticket information.

If you take Saraçlar Caddesi south out of Hürriyet Square, you'll go over the two old bridges on the Tunca and Meriç (Maritsa) Rivers, each an old arched structure with a *mescid* (small prayer space) built right into the bridge. For a picnic, walk on Saraçlar Caddesi and cross one of the bridges to get to the woods and a good picnic spot, or else turn left just before the first bridge and go a few kilometers down the riverbank to the **Söğütlük Forest Park** for your lunch and—if you like muddy water—a swim in the river.

A walk around the restored covered markets in the town yields another find, Edirne's famous bars of **scented soap** carved in the shape of fruits and vegetables, or imprinted with the design of the Selimiye mosque. Pick up a simit (sesame seed roll, circle shape) from a vendor.

ONWARD TO ISTANBUL: To reach Edirne's Otogar, take a city bus or dolmush from the Eski Cami. Buses run very frequently from Edirne, departing about every 20 minutes or so throughout the day for Istanbul's Topkapı bus station. At the garage, a ticket seller will come up to you and want to lead you to the office to buy a ticket. Ask him to see the bus first, just in case he's selling seats on one of the few old clunkers left on this run. If the bus looks all right, buy your ticket for 1,200TL ($1.70).

The trip to Istanbul takes four hours, with a ten-minute rest stop in either Çorlu, where there's not much to see, or in **Lüleburgaz,** a town with some nice old Ottoman buildings (a Turkish bath, a mosque, etc.) right near the bus stop and worth a walk around. Along the railroad tracks one can see ruined World War I gun emplacements, but from the bus the trip is a comfortable run through patchwork fields and towns with a few thatched houses. The Edirne–Istanbul road is also famous for it's traffic accidents, being one of the busiest roads in the country, and the one that the weary, all-night drivers from Europe hit just when they're at their weariest. Luckily, the bus drivers on this route see accidents all the time, and they seem to get the message. They don't seem to relax until they see the grand City Walls of Istanbul.

If you go by bus, you'll end up at a garage just outside the city walls near the famous Topkapı, or Cannon, Gate (not to be confused with the palace of the same name, in another section of the city). Ignore the taxi drivers who will insist you need a cab (they climb onto the bus looking for passengers while it's still moving), walk the half block to the Topkapı and enter the city. Just inside the walls is a stop for municipal buses. Several come by here; all go through Aksaray Square, where you can transfer for another part of the city if that's where you're going. If you're tired, though, and simply can't take more bus travel, a taxi to Aksaray should cost about 1,100TL ($1.55); to Taksim Square, 2,000TL ($2.80).

Chapter III

ISTANBUL: CITY ON THE BOSPHORUS

1. A First Impression
2. Orientation
3. Arrival and Transportation
4. Useful Facts
5. Tourism Information

THE GREAT BRITISH HISTORIAN Edward Gibbon once described the site of Istanbul as "formed by nature for the center and capital of a great monarchy." The monarchy is gone, the capital of the new republic is Ankara, but the city built during almost 2,000 years of imperial rule remains.

The site was the choice of Constantine the Great, who decided at the beginning of the 4th century that the Roman Empire needed a new capital in the East. From this Roman beginning the city and empire evolved into the blend of Roman, Greek, and Oriental cultures that came to be called "Byzantine." After a thousand years of Byzantine rule, the Turkish hordes which had swept over all of Anatolia succeeded in capturing the greatest prize of all, and the Byzantine emperor's capital became the city of the Ottoman sultan. There are numerous reminders of the city's Byzantine past, but many of the best places to see were built after the Conquest—since 1453—and gave the city its reputation as an Oriental imperial capital of unrivaled splendor.

1. A First Impression

Undoubtedly the best way to enter Istanbul is by sea. As your ship cruises through the Sea of Marmara toward the mouth of the Bosphorus, the world-famous skyline of Istanbul spreads before you. The grand mosques with their minarets, situated on the seven principal hills of the city, stand above the neighboring buildings and form a pattern stretching the full length of the city. Then, as you enter the Bosphorus, two of the world's greatest religious monuments are laid out on view: the Blue Mosque of Sultan Ahmet I and the Church of the Holy Wisdom, or Sancta Sophia, built by Justinian. As you round Seraglio Point and head toward the dock at the foot of the Galata Bridge, the sultans' palaces are on display: to your left the Seraglio, or Topkapı Palace, to your right Dolmabahçe Palace, the residence of the last Ottoman sultans, built in the 1800s to symbolize the grandeur of the empire. You dock in the mouth of the Golden Horn and debark into a city of contrasts: Eastern and Western, new and old, beautiful and ugly, a city like no other in the world. If you can possibly arrange it, come to Istanbul by sea!

Even if you find it impossible to come by sea, whichever way you come you'll get the flavor of the city instantly. Trains from Europe come in across a rolling plain, then through the quaint little stations of the suburbs, past factories and big apartment blocks, finally rounding Seraglio Point itself, the railroad tracks running right next to the palace walls. (If you saw the movie *Topkapi,* this is the railroad line shown far below the palace roof where the action was taking place.) Or if you fly into Atatürk Airport, 15 miles out of the city, your airport bus will take you along a four-lane highway which suddenly narrows after a time in order to penetrate the old city walls at the famous Cannon Gate (or through the gate called "Christ's Postern," on the Sea of Marmara), built during the Byzantine Empire and still standing. Later the bus will roar through an underpass within view of the modern municipal government buildings and then immediately afterward pass under an aqueduct built by the Emperor Valens in the 4th century.

The first thing that hits you about Istanbul is that it is teeming constantly. During all but the summer months, the city's sidewalks are jammed with shoppers, workers, strollers; its streets are packed with every conceivable kind of vehicle, from the horse cart to the Cadillac. Just within the last few years the traffic problem has reached monumental proportions, and the "five o'clock rush hour" has almost become a full-day affair. Luckily for tourists, many of the people who live in the city seek peace and quiet for their vacations outside the city limits, leaving the sidewalks and streets more open to visitors. The next most notable characteristic is the noise level—everything is louder than in other cities.

As for the physical side of Istanbul, it might best be described by Dylan Thomas's phrase as an "ugly, lovely town." Turkey's biggest port and the halfway house between Europe and the East might be expected to have its seamy sides, which Istanbul does. For contrast, there are the city's countless monuments to its great past, almost all of which are kept in careful repair or have undergone restoration. Constantinople was the Middle Ages' most glorious city; the Turks still call Istanbul the "Earth's Pearl," and their poets never tire of describing it. Orhan Veli Kanık, a pioneer of modern Turkish poetry, describes it this way:

> I listen to Istanbul, with my eyes closed:
> First a light breeze blows
> And sets to swaying slowly
> Leaves on trees;
> From a far way comes
> The ceaseless tinkle of water-sellers' bells;
> I listen to Istanbul with my eyes closed.
>
> I listen to Istanbul, with my eyes closed:
> Just now birds pass in droves
> Far above, calling, crying.
> Nets are drawn from fishing weirs;
> A woman's feet touch the water;
> I listen to Istanbul with my eyes closed.

I listen to Istanbul, with my eyes closed:
The deep coolness of the Covered Bazaar;
Chatter of crowds in Mahmutpasha;
Mosque courtyards filled with doves;
Sounds from the docks of hammers pounding;
Smells of sweat on the fine spring wind;
I listen to Istanbul with my eyes closed.
—*Bütün Şiirleri (trans. by T. Brosnahan)*

2. Orientation

Istanbul is made up of equal parts of water and land: three parts of each. Once you get this formula down, you will have little trouble finding your way among the different parts of the city. The most modern part of the city, including the airline terminal and some of the best hotels and tourist facilities, is called **Beyoğlu.** From the hub of **Taksim Square,** avenues radiate to all sections of the new city. **Cumhuriyet Caddesi,** a wide, tree-lined, four-lane road, leads up past the Istanbul Hilton, the Sheraton, and most of the ritzy nightclubs and restaurants to the newest sections of the city, thence on toward the Black Sea coast. **İnönü Caddesi,** once called Gümüşsuyu Caddesi, begins in front of the big new Cultural Center in Taksim and leads down the hill to the shores of the Bosphorous next to Dolmabahçe Palace, where it connects with the shore road. **İstiklal Caddesi,** or Independence Avenue, the main thoroughfare in Beyoğlu, begins near the Galata Tower and wanders through the part of the new city once known as Pera, the city where most of the Europeans residing in the Ottoman capital lived and worked. The countless side streets and passages leading off of İstiklal Caddesi are filled with the intriguing sights that have made Istanbul a city of fascination.

Across the **Golden Horn,** a freshwater outlet dividing the two European parts of the city, three bridges lead into the **Old City.** This peninsula is the site chosen by Constantine the Great for his capital, and holds most of the great and famous sights of Istanbul. From the foot of the **Galata Bridge** (officially called the **Karaköy-Eminönü** bridge) in **Eminönü Square,** near the large Yeni Cami (New Mosque), narrow streets lead past the European railroad terminal at **Sirkeci** to connect with **Divan Yolu,** the wide street through Istanbul's most historical districts. From the first hill of the city, on which you'll find Topkapı Palace, Sancta Sophia, and the Blue Mosque, Divan Yolu leads up to the second hill past the Hippodrome to the Grand Bazaar (**Kapalı Çarşı**) and the University. At the municipal bus terminal of **Hürriyet Square** (also called **Beyazıt Square**) the road changes names and continues as **Yeniçeriler Caddesi,** the "Avenue of the Janissaries." The avenue passes the main gates of the University and approaches **Aksaray Square,** and changes its name again, this time becoming **Ordu Caddesi.** From Aksaray Square, roads lead to the various gates in the city walls and to the **Atatürk Bridge** over the Golden Horn.

Finally, across the **Bosphorus,** the straits which connect the Black Sea and the Sea of Marmara, is the Asian suburb of **Üsküdar,** once called Scutari. The **Bosphorus Bridge** is Istanbul's pride and joy, but the commuter ferryboats which ply the waters between Üsküdar and the Galata Bridge are a much more enjoyable way to cross, and at 14¢ a ticket, it's got to be the cheapest intercontinental cruise operating! The main points of reference in Üsküdar are the car-ferry dock, the dock and railroad station for all Asian trains at **Haydarpaşa,** and the commuter-ferry dock at **Kadıköy,** the ancient city of Chalcedon. There is an intercity bus station at Harem.

Something to keep in mind while you're strolling through Istanbul—or anywhere in Turkey, for that matter—is that sidewalk standards are not up to those you may be used to. Hazards range from the minor surprise of a pothole through things like bits of pipe which can trip you to real hazards like uncovered manholes. It's wise to give a wide berth to wrecking or construction sites in the city to avoid falling masonry or plaster. And when entering the bazaars watch for the posts, only 3½ feet high, put in the doorways to keep vehicles out. They'll be hidden by the throng and can be very painful.

3. Arrival and Transportation

Anyone approaching a foreign city of six million people needs a little advice on how to get around. First I'll get you from where you land to where you'll be sleeping, and then I'll tell you how to make your way to points of interest.

ARRIVAL BY AIR: The fastest way into town is by **taxi.** As your driver may well see himself as a Grand Prix racer, it may be faster than you'd like. In any case, the cost will be about 5,000TL ($7), or slightly more depending on what part of the city you're headed for.

A cheap alternative is the **USAŞ airport bus,** which costs only 550TL (75¢). It departs from the domestic terminal and goes into town, stopping in Aksaray (near Laleli) before ending its journey at the Turkish Airlines terminal in Şişhane Square. Free shuttle buses will take you from the international terminal to the domestic terminal every ten minutes throughout the day. Buses into town leave every 20 or 30 minutes between 5:30 and 9 a.m., every hour between 9 a.m. and 2 p.m., and again every 20 or 30 minutes from 2 p.m. to just past midnight. The trip takes 25 to 45 minutes.

ARRIVAL BY TRAIN: All trains coming from Europe end up at **Sirkeci Station,** next to Eminönü Square, beneath Topkapı Palace.

To catch a bus or dolmush going to Sultanahmet, Beyazıt, Laleli, and Aksaray, go out the station door and cross over Ankara Caddesi using the pedestrian overpass.

For Taksim, go out the station door, turn right, and walk to the little refreshments stand, where you'll find the dolmush to Taksim. It runs in the morning and early afternoon only. If there is no dolmush, walk toward the sea and catch a bus to Taksim from Eminönü.

ARRIVAL BY BUS: The bus will stop at **Topkapı Bus Station,** right outside the city walls next to the Topkapı or Cannon Gate. **Taxi** is the easiest way to get to your hotel, and considering that a cab should cost perhaps 1,500TL ($2.10), and no more than 2,500TL ($3.50) to any hotel in the city, this is not an extravagance. Otherwise, there is a municipal **bus** stop just inside the Cannon Gate from which you can catch a bus or dolmush to Aksaray and Laleli; change in Aksaray for a bus or dolmush to Sultanahmet or Taksim.

There is also a bus station on the Asian side of the Bosphorus at a place called **Harem.** Some buses make a stop at Harem, but virtually all begin and end their journeys at Topkapı.

You don't have to drag yourself all the way out to Topkapı Bus Station to buy your onward tickets. Bus company **ticket offices** are clustered in Laleli on Ordu Caddesi, near Sirkeci Station on Muradiye Caddesi, in Taksim on Mete Caddesi very near the opera house (Atatürk Cultural Center), and to the right (south) of the opera house down the hill a block along İnönü Caddesi, on the left-hand side. **Varan** is at İnönü Caddesi 29/B (tel. 149-1903 or 144-8457); **Arama Turizm** is at İnönü Caddesi 31 (tel. 145-2795).

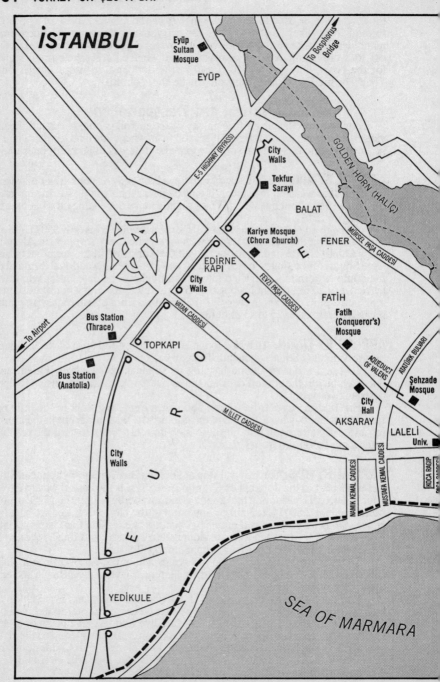

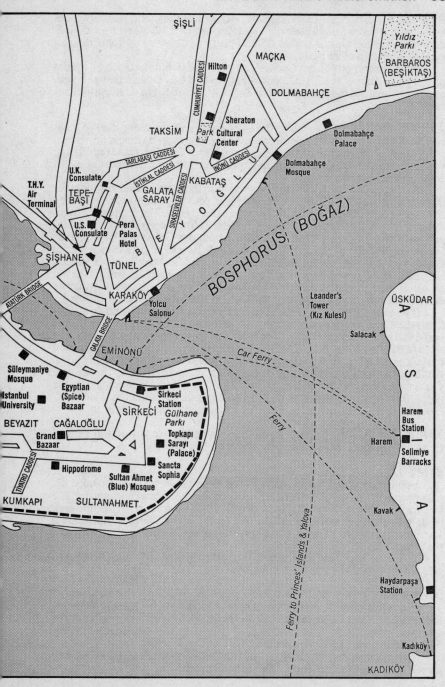

ARRIVAL BY SHIP: Passenger vessels dock at **Karaköy**, and passengers debark into the Yolcu Salonu (International Passenger Terminal) on Rıhtım Caddesi very near the Galata Bridge. The Ministry of Culture and Tourism has a small information office here.

Taxis abound on Rıhtım Caddesi, and bus and dolmush routes to Taksim pass right in front of the Yolcu Salonu. For the Old City (Sultanahmet, Laleli, and Aksaray) go to the western side of Karaköy Square to the dolmush and bus stops.

ARRIVAL BY CAR: Approaching the city from the airport along the E-5 highway, you have a choice of routes into the center. The most exciting is the coastal road; the one via the Cannon Gate (Topkapı) is the most direct; the expressway which loops around to the north of the city, later crossing the Bosphorus Bridge, is the least attractive.

For the coastal road, leave the expressway at the airport, following signs for the seaside towns of Yeşilköy or Ataköy. Make your way to the shore of the Sea of Marmara and drive into the city along the water's edge. The road passes Yedikule, the Fortress of the Seven Towers, and the Marble Tower. The city's southern walls will be on your left. The view across the Bosphorus to Üsküdar, Haydarpaşa Station, and Kadıköy is wonderful. Turn left onto Mustafa Kemal Caddesi for Aksaray and Laleli, or continue around Seraglio Point for Sirkeci, Eminönü, the Galata Bridge, and Beyoğlu. (Note that as of this writing the old Galata Bridge is being replaced with a new structure, and the roadway may be closed. You may have to detour up the Golden Horn to the Atatürk Bridge.)

If you head straight toward the city from the airport, you'll end up at Topkapı, the Cannon Gate. Go through the gate and along Millet Caddesi, and you'll end up in Aksaray Square. For Laleli and its inexpensive hotels, continue straight through Aksaray and turn left just before the big university buildings on the left. For Taksim, use the flyover in Aksaray Square to turn left and head up Atatürk Bulvarı. Cross the bridge over the Golden Horn, head up the hill, and you'll pass through Şişhane Square with its Turkish Airlines terminal (on the right). Bear right after the terminal, loop around to the left, and you'll join İstiklal Caddesi at Tünel Square. İstiklal Caddesi ends in Taksim Square.

TRANSPORTATION: Though transportation details are covered in general terms in Chapter II, here are some specifics for this vast city.

Buses

Istanbul's red-and-beige city buses run everywhere, and I've included details on which bus to take whenever necessary in the following chapters. The fare for a single ride is 100TL (14¢), or 60TL (8¢) for students. The blue-and-white buses are privately owned but city regulated, and fares on these are a sometimes a few liras cheaper. On the private buses you can buy a ticket right on the bus.

The route name and number appear on the front of each bus. On the curb side is a signboard with the bus's itinerary.

Dolmushes

You'll find these dolmush departure points to be of use: Taksim, Karaköy, Eminönü, Sirkeci, and Beyazıt. You can find the dolmush ranks most easily by asking any passerby, . . . *dolmuş nerede?* ("Where's the dolmush to . . . ?"), filling in the name of your destination.

Sultanahmet, near the majority of Istanbul's important sights, is not well served by dolmush except from Aksaray and Beyazıt.

To be sure of where a dolmush is headed, look in the car's front window, or ask just by saying the name of your destination.

Ferryboats

The mouth of the Golden Horn by the Galata Bridge is always busy with white ferries, and now with hydrofoils as well. Though the ferries are not convenient for short distances, as are Venice's little vaporetti, they provide an extremely pleasant, cheap, and efficient means by which to cross the Bosphorus and the Sea of Marmara, and to cruise up the Bosphorus.

Take a ride around Seraglio Point, good for photos of Topkapı, Sancta Sophia, and the Blue Mosque, by boarding any boat from Dock 7 or 8 in Karaköy. The trip over to Haydarpaşa or Kadıköy and back will take about an hour and will cost a mere 90TL (13¢). Ferries for cruising the Bosphorus, to the Princes' Islands, and across the Sea of Marmara to Yalova, are covered in the appropriate sections below.

The Subway

Istanbul's little two-station subway is called the **Tünel,** and it runs between Karaköy and the southern end of İstiklal Caddesi. It was built by French engineers over a century ago for European merchants who wanted to get from their offices in Galata to their homes in Pera without having to walk up the steep hill. The fare is 80TL (11¢); trains run every five or ten minutes from early morning until about 10 p.m.

4. Useful Facts

The information below is for when you are having problems or are looking for possibilities. Having facts right at hand will help you deal with this vast and sometimes confusing metropolis.

AIRLINES/AIRPORTS: Istanbul has just one airport, **Atatürk Hava Limanı,** near the town of Yeşilköy about 15 miles west of the city on shore of the Sea of Marmara. It's the country's foremost international airport, and receives flights from around the world.

Most international airlines and travel agencies have **downtown offices** near Taksim Square, on Cumhuriyet Caddesi going north from Taksim to the Hilton hotel. Pan Am's office (tel. 147-4530) is right in the Hilton arcade. British Airways, Swissair, Alitalia, and Air France are all on Cumhuriyet. Turkish Airlines has several ticket offices, including one in the Hilton arcade (tel. 147-0121), another near the PTT on Cumhuriyet at Taksim (tel. 145-2454), yet another across the street from Sirkeci railway station (tel. 522-8888), and also one in its ticket office in its air terminal in Şişhane Square (tel. 145-4208), near the Galata Tower and the upper station of the Tünel subway.

The only regular **airport bus service** runs from the Turkish Airlines' Şişhane terminal out to the airport, from 5:30 a.m. until 12:30 a.m., for 550TL (75¢).

ART GALLERIES: Most of Istanbul's galleries have periodic shows, not permanent collections. The **Taksim Belediye Galerisi** is in the same row of modern shops as the Taksim Post Office, down at the far end. The **Painting and Sculpture Museum** is not a museum but a gallery. It has the best of Istanbul's foreign shows, and is open from 10 a.m. to 5 p.m. every day but Monday and Tuesday. Take a dolmush from Taksim or Eminönü to Beşiktaş. The museum is on the right, past Dolmabahçe Palace just before Beşiktaş Square.

Finally, Istanbul's best free Turkish shows are given by the **Yapı ve Kredi**

Bankası in its big Galatasaray branch office, in Galatasaray Square. Exhibits change frequently and include ancient Anatolian treasures, Turkish folk art, clothing, musical instruments, and others. Be sure to stop in to the bank in Galatasaray for a look at what's currently being shown. Admission is free.

AUTO REPAIRS: The people to contact in the first instance are at the **Türkiye Turing ve Otomobil Kulübü** ("Turkish Touring and Automobile Club"), head office in Şişli Square, no. 364 (tel. 148-3747). Şişli is a mile or so north of Taksim Square along Cumhuriyet Caddesi; many dolmushes and buses go directly to it from Taksim. Besides helping you with Customs problems related to your car, insurance, etc., they publish a quarterly pamphlet called *Istanbul: A Handbook for Tourists,* free for the asking at the headquarters. It includes a list of auto-repair shops currently recommended as well as much other useful information.

BARBERSHOPS: Istanbul's best is in the **Divan Oteli,** on Cumhuriyet Caddesi near Taksim. A cut costs 4,000TL ($5.60) and is very good indeed; that money goes to the shop, so tip the barber and the brush boy. In more plebeian shops cuts go for about 1,800TL ($2.50); shaves, for 900TL ($1.25). Tips are expected.

BATHS: The Turkish bath, or hamam, can be found in every neighborhood in the city. These tend to be ancient places where you can use the steamroom and wash yourself for 1,200TL ($1.70) or less. If you want a scrubbing by one of the attendants, add 50% more, plus the attendant's tip.

BEAUTY PARLORS: Same applies as to barbershops. The **Hilton, Divan, Sheraton,** and **Intercontinental** are the best, and most expensive, with English-speaking staff.

BOOKSTORES: İstiklal between Galatasaray and Tünel has the biggest concentration. In Galatasaray, at 178 İstiklal, is the **Sander Kitabevi,** with French, German, Turkish, and English books; the **Alman (German) Kitabevi** is at 481 İstiklal; **Haşet (Hachette),** the French firm, has a branch with some English books at 469 İstiklal, and another each in the Park and Hilton Hotels; the **French-American Kitabevi,** 513 İstiklal, is similar. There are also several shops on Cumhuriyet Caddesi near the Hilton.

CAMPING PLACES: The **London Highway (Londra Asfaltı),** Rte. E-5, has several of these. The **BP Mocamp** is in Bakırköy, on the highway near the airport. The **Kartaltepe** (tel. 71-56-75) and **Londra** mocamps are right on the highway near the Coca-Cola plant.

CAR RENTALS: The major car-rental firms have offices or desks at the airport, and downtown, near Taksim Square.

Avis has offices at Atatürk Airport in both the international (tel. 573-6445) and domestic (tel. 573-1452) terminals. The downtown office is just off of Cumhuriyet Caddesi, across that street from the Divan Hotel, at Yedikuyular Caddesi 4/A, Elmadağ (tel. 141-2917).

Budget is at the airport's domestic terminal (tel. 573-2920), and downtown near Taksim at İnönü Caddesi, Kunt Apartımanı 33/1, Gümüşsuyu (tel. 149-5714).

Europcar (National, Tilden) is in the international terminal (tel. 573-7024) at the airport, and downtown near Taksim at Cumhuriyet Caddesi 47/2 (tel. 150-8888).

Hertz is in the international terminal (tel. 573-5987), and in the Istanbul Sheraton Hotel (tel. 148-9000), as well as at Cumhuriyet Caddesi 295, north of Taksim in the district called Harbiye (tel. 141-5323).

InterRent has a downtown office at Recep Paşa Caddesi 23/2, Taksim (tel. 155-0690).

CHURCHES (See also "Synagogues"): Protestant, nonsectarian—**The Union Church of Istanbul,** sometimes called the Dutch Chapel (tel. 144-5212), is on the grounds of the Netherlands Consulate-General, at 415 İstiklal Caddesi (there's also an entrance on Postacılar Sokak, a nearby side street); services are in English. Catholic—**St. Antonio di Padova,** on İstiklal just past Galatasaray when going toward Tünel (tel. 144-0935), with services in French and Italian. Anglican—in the **British Consulate,** on Meşrutiyet Caddesi just out of Galatasaray (tel. 144-4228). Istanbul being the seat of the **Orthodox Patriarchate,** churches of this rite are scattered throughout the city, with principal ones in Taksim Square (visible from the monument in the traffic circle); near the Yeni Rejans restaurant off İstiklal Caddesi near Galatasaray; and, of course, at the Patriarchate in the Fener section of the city on the Golden Horn.

CLIMATE AND CLOTHING: Normal weather for Istanbul from May to October is sunny and warm with occasional showers. In July and August it can get quite hot (up to 90°F, 32°C) and is often very humid. November to April one experiences more rain, and in January and February some snow and freezing weather. The climate, overall, might be compared to that of Washington, D.C. In summer, a shirt and skirt or trousers; in spring and fall a sweater for the evenings and for ferryboat rides; and in winter a warm suit or sweater and raingear.

CONSULATES: U.S.A.—Meşrutiyet Caddesi 106, Tepebaşı (tel. 1/143-6200). **United Kingdom**—Meşrutiyet Caddesi 26, just out of Galatasaray Square (tel. 1/149-8874). The **French, Scandinavian,** and **Netherlands** consulates are on İstiklal Caddesi; the **Belgian,** on Sıraselviler Caddesi, a block out of Taksim; the **West German** and **Japanese** consulates are on İnönü Caddesi, a few blocks from Taksim on the hill down to Dolmabahçe.

DOCTORS: The **Amiral Bristol Hastanesi** (tel. 1/148-6030), also called the **Amerikan Hastanesi (American Hospital)** has an outpatient clinic. Take a dolmush from Taksim to Nişantaş, then ask for the hospital; it's a short walk to the address on Güzelbahçe Sokak. A taxi to the hospital from Taksim costs 750TL ($1.05); from Eminönü or Aksaray, about 1,600TL ($2.25). There are also German, Italian, and French hospitals in Istanbul; doctors and nurses at each institution are Turkish, but often have been trained abroad and usually speak the foreign language in question. Istanbul also has several doctors in the various specialties who speak foreign languages and have had excellent preparation, although they are not connected with any hospital. Ask at the consulate for a list of recommended physicians.

HASHISH: Istanbul is no longer the mecca for hash users it once was. The times when hash was available cheaply and safely are past. The police are out to make their arrest and conviction statistics look good; the pushers are willing to help them by selling out purchasers who they believe may not purchase again. The minimum sentence is three years—maximum is death. The consulate can do al-

most nothing to help except try to see that you get a fair trial. Some years ago a young American smuggling hash killed several Turkish policemen before he was machine-gunned to death, and the bad feeling from this incident still remains. In short: don't.

LIBRARIES: The USIS Library (tel. 1/143-6200) is in a building connected to the American Consulate, 106 Meşrutiyet Caddesi. The **Library of the British Council** is in the grand ballroom of the British Consulate in Galatasaray Square. **Bosphorus University,** in Bebek on the Bosphorus, has the largest English-language collection in Istanbul. Take a dolmush for Emirgan from Taksim, or take a no. 40 bus—"Taksim-Sarıyer" or "Taksim-Emirgan" (Sahil Yolu)—and get off at the "Üniversite" stop. It's a long walk up the hill.

PARKING: The Cultural Center in Taksim has indoor and outdoor parking lots, for which you pay by the hour or the day. Attendants with official caps help you to park on the streets and lots open to parking in other areas of the city. Tip them. Drivers in Istanbul are forced to park on sidewalks, medians, on anything available. If there's an attendant there, it's legal.

PARKS: Gülhane Parkı, next to Topkapı Sarayı (Palace), is the old palace park, now open to the public. The **Promenade** in Taksim, stretching from the square to the Divan Hotel, is free; likewise the Hippodrome. Yıldız Parkı, one of the old imperial parks, is up the Bosphorus on the way to Ortaköy (dolmush from Taksim). The **Belgrade Forest** is north of Istanbul. To get to the heart of it, take an Orman Fakültesi bus (no. 42) from Taksim to the last stop. There's a small **Luna Park** (amusement park) near Dolmabahçe Palace, in the valley below the Hilton.

POLICE: The Tourism Police office (tel. 166-6666) is the Emniyet police office, called the **5. Şube** ("besh-*in*-jee shoo-bay"), in the Passenger Terminal (Yolcu Salonu) on the docks in Karaköy. There is another office in Sultanahmet Square.

POST OFFICE: The Central Post Office is the huge pseudo-Oriental palace on Yeni Postahane Sokak (no. 25), near Sirkeci Station—ask for the **Büyük Post-ahane.** It's open from 8 a.m. to 9 p.m. every day, including Sunday. Go here for *poste restante* (general delivery), but only from 9 a.m. to 5 p.m. Monday through Friday, and Saturday mornings. The Galatasaray post office is open during the same hours. In Taksim, it's 8 a.m. to 7 p.m. The tiny post office in the Grand Bazaar (follow the "PTT" signs) is open whenever the Bazaar is. Special Delivery is called *"ekspres";* registered mail is *"kayıtlı."*

SHOESHINE: Standard price is about 300TL (40¢), but the men with the splendid boxes in Taksim get away with asking more. The shine they give is said to be the best in the world.

SHOPPING HOURS: For most shops, 9 a.m. to noon and 1:30 or 2:30 to 6 or 7 p.m. Shops are usually open all day Saturday, closed Sunday. The Grand Bazaar is open from 8 a.m. to 6:30 p.m. every day except Sunday.

SYNAGOGUES: The most convenient is the **Neve Shalom** (tel. 44-15-76), on Büyük Hendek Sokak, the street between Şişhane Square and the Galata Tower. From the square, walk a few blocks down the street to the synagogue, on your right. **Beth Israel** is in Şişli Square (tel. 48-64-99).

TOILETS: There are public ones under the Galata Bridge, in the Karaköy pedestrian underpass, in the Hippodrome, next to the high school in Galatasaray, and in Taksim behind the French Consulate. They usually charge 20TL (3¢) but it couldn't be for cleaning. All mosques have toilets, usually as ancient as the mosques themselves.

TRAINS: All trains to and from Europe meet at **Sirkeci Station,** in the Old City near the Galata Bridge. All Asian trains leave from **Haydarpaşa Station** across the Bosphorus (get a ferry to Haydarpaşa from Dock 7 or 8 in Karaköy). Tickets are sold at both stations, and at **Arama Turizm,** İnönü Caddesi no. 31, near Taksim Square. Look for the "Devlet Demiryolları," "TCDD," or "D.D.Y." sign.

TRAVEL AGENCIES: Most have offices along Cumhuriyet Caddesi, near Taksim, but there are a few in Aksaray and Sultanahmet as well. Travel agents, like most things, range from excellent to pretty awful.

WEATHER REPORT: During the summer it's almost always sunny. If you're in doubt, keep an eye on the lights atop the Beyazıt Tower on the grounds of Istanbul University, visible from all over the city; or on the lights from Büyük Çamlıca hill in Asia, visible half the length of the Bosphorus. The lights are coded: blue means fair weather, green means rain, yellow is for fog, and red for snow.

5. Tourism Information

There are Tourism Information Offices at frontier posts where you might enter Turkey by bus or car. There's also one at **Atatürk Airport** in the International Arrivals area (tel. 573-7399 or 573-4136), in the Yolcu Salonu near **Karaköy Square** for those who arrive by ship, and also in **Sirkeci Station** for those who come by train.

In **Sultanahmet Square,** the office is at the northern end of the Hippodrome (tel. 522-4903) in a low brick-and-glass building which can be difficult to spot.

There are two offices in the **new city.** The nearest to Taksim is two long blocks north along Cumhuriyet Caddesi, in the Hilton Hotel arcade (tel. 140-6300 or 140-6864). The other is very near Galatasaray Square and the British Consulate, in the İstanbul Bölge Müdürlüğü building on Meşrutiyet Caddesi.

Chapter IV

ISTANBUL'S HOTELS

1. Choosing a Hotel Location
2. Hotels Near Taksim Square
3. Hotels in Tepebaşı
4. Hotels Near Aksaray
5. Hotels in Sultanahmet
6. Hotels Near Topkapı Bus Station
7. Special Places

NO MATTER WHAT YOUR BUDGET, Istanbul has the hotel for you. It is one of those marvelous cities in which there is everything for everyone, as far as hotels are concerned. Want to stay in a clean, presentable, convenient hotel room with bath for 10,000TL ($14) double? No problem. Are you traveling on a few dollars a day and you want a clean but safe, and very cheap, bed for the night? You'll find it, and it may cost only 2,500TL ($3.50). Do you normally stay at one of the best places, yet you'd like a luxury room for $50 to $75 double, half the normal luxury price? You've got it. Is this a special trip, on which you'd like to stay the night in a former palace, whatever the cost? It's here, and the price is actually moderate for what you get.

Having said that, let me add that there are good rooms and bad rooms, rooms worth the price and those that are overpriced. You should inspect the hotel room before you register as the quality of the room may have nothing to do with your general impression of the hotel; the particular room you are renting may be better or worse than the hotel's lobby or façade, and one room may be better or worse than another. If you don't like what you see, ask to look at something else.

1. Choosing a Hotel Location

What most travelers are looking for when they visit Istanbul is a clean, comfortable small hotel of some 25 to 50 rooms with hot water, elevator, restaurant, and at least a few staff members who speak English. Istanbul has them, newer buildings constructed within the past 10 or 15 years. Prices of 7,000TL ($10) to 21,000TL ($30) for a double room with bath are the norm. These hotels can be found in Taksim Square and nearby Tepebaşı, near Aksaray in the district called Laleli, and near the Topkapı Bus Station. Generally speaking, the low-priced hotels and hostels are in Sultanahmet. The center of the posh hotel district is certainly Taksim Square, but there are several important exceptions covered below under "Special Places."

TAKSİM SQUARE: As the area where European-style living first established itself in the Ottoman dominions, the north bank of the Golden Horn remains the locus of the luxury life. Most international airline offices, travel agencies, nightclubs, and consulates are in either Taksim or Tepebaşı. The Etap Marmara Hotel, formerly the Istanbul Inter-Continental, is right in Taksim, the Istanbul Sheraton is a block away, and the Hilton is just two blocks beyond the Sheraton.

There are also several smaller hotels near Taksim which charge more moderate rates, and Taksim-area hotels tend to have hotter water, more English-speaking staff, and little things like notepaper in the rooms, things which moderately priced hotels in other areas may not have. Some of the moderately priced hotels have rooms with views of the Bosphorus, and you definitely pay a premium for these, but that view may make your stay particularly memorable.

TEPEBAŞI: İstiklal Caddesi runs southwest from Taksim Square, taking a dog-leg bend at Galatasaray Square, and ending at Tünel Square. West of İstiklal Caddesi between Galatasaray and Tünel is the district called Tepebaşı, which was the first real European-style hotel district in the city. The main street of the district is Meşrutiyet Caddesi, where you'll find the British and American Consulates, the romantic old Pera Palas Hotel, and right next to it the modern tower of the Etap Istanbul Hotel. If you stay here you'll be in good company.

AKSARAY (LALELİ): In the Old City, a mile or so to the west of the major attractions such as Topkapı Palace, Sancta Sophia, and the Grand Bazaar, is bustling Aksaray Square. The "square" itself is not much to look at. Auto traffic roars through in a constant flood, and the modern buildings are drab and characterless. A frilly 19th-century Ottoman mosque is virtually hidden by a highway flyover. But only a few steps from the square is the quiet, shady district known as **Laleli,** positively crowded with little hotels, many of them modern, most with 20 to 40 rooms. Prices here range from the starvation-budget at 5,000TL ($7) double, and go over the top of our daily budget at 21,000TL ($29.40). So you should be able to find a room at a moderate price, whatever your interpretation of that term is. What Laleli does not hold are rock-bottom cheap hotels and luxury palaces. The bonus of the location is that here you are within walking distance of the Grand Bazaar, and a short ride from the eastern tip of the Old City, with its crowd of ancient buildings.

SULTANAHMET: This is the city's low-budget haven, and the location speaks for itself. Though the very basic, often noisy, sometimes shabby hotels here were the throbbing heart of "hippy" Istanbul several decades ago, these unglamorous hostelries share the neighborhood with the Blue Mosque, Sancta Sophia, and Topkapı Palace. The location couldn't possibly be better for a tourist. The hotels, however, are for those to whom budget is more important than comfort. The graceful old exception to this rule is described below under "Special Places."

SPECIAL PLACES: For these few exceptional hotels, location must be a secondary consideration, giving primacy to the character of the hotel itself. These special places are located in Sultanahmet, in Tepebaşı, and on the shores of the Bosphorus.

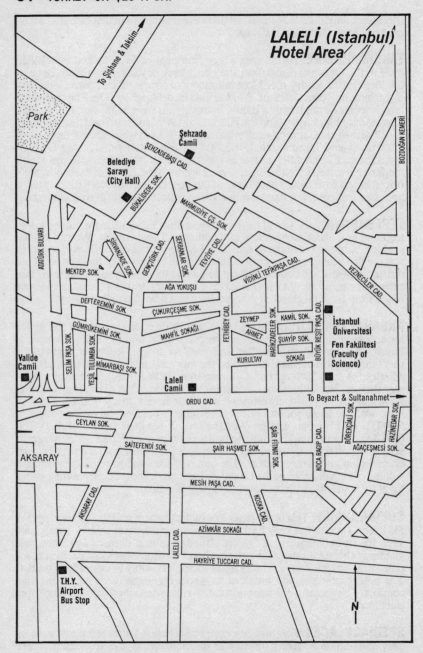

LALELİ (Istanbul) *Hotel Area*

2. Hotels Near Taksim Square

Assuming that you want to enjoy the pleasures of lodging in Taksim to the full extent of your budget, I'll start with a moderately priced place, then mention some cheaper spots, and finally cover the luxury line-up.

MODERATELY PRICED HOTELS: Just out of Taksim Square along the western side of Cumhuriyet Caddesi is the large and prominent office of Air France, and to the left of the office is the beginning of Şehit Muhtar Caddesi. Walk along Şehit Muhtar to Topçu Caddesi, and you'll see the **Otel Eresin,** Topçu Caddesi 34 (tel. 1/150-3367 or 150-4476), a new and quite modern seven-floor, 60-room hotel. Its very comfortable guest rooms are equipped with bathtubs, television sets, and little refrigerators. The price is 35,000TL ($50) double. Topçu Caddesi is a quiet street, yet if you stay here you're only a minute's stroll from the bustling square.

North along Cumhuriyet Caddesi, on a side street not far from the Hilton, is the **Hotel Konak,** Nisbet Sokak 9 (tel. 1/148-4744), a hotel several decades old which has to its advantage an experienced staff and a status location near the big hotels, though Nisbet Sokak itself is nothing to brag about. Single rooms with bath are priced at 22,000TL ($30.80) single, 28,000TL ($39.20) double, 33,000TL ($46.20) triple, breakfast included.

LESS EXPENSIVE PLACES: As you face İstiklal Caddesi, standing in Taksim, the street to the left of İstiklal is called Sıralsviler Caddesi. There are two hotels that are worth your consideration just a short walk down this street. The **Hotel Keban,** Sıralseviler Caddesi 51 (tel. 1/143-3310), is just out of Taksim Square near İstiklal Caddesi (look for the Maksim Theater, and the hotel is just a few doors down). The Keban has 87 air-conditioned rooms with bath or shower, elevators, a barbershop, and a restaurant; some of the guest rooms have little refrigerators in them. For all this you pay 12,000TL ($16.80) single, 14,700TL ($20.60) double.

The **Dilson Hotel,** Sıraselviler Caddesi 49 (tel. 1/143-2032), just a few steps along Sıraselviler from the Keban, is similar, with 90 rooms priced at 13,500TL ($18.90) single, 18,800TL ($26.30) double; some larger, multibedded family rooms are available here as well.

Continuing along Sıraselviler Caddesi out of Taksim, turn left at a sign reading **Plaza Hotel,** Aslanyatağı Sokak 19/21 (tel. 1/145-3273), just before the Alman Hastanesi (German Hospital). This little hotel is hidden away on a quiet street which bears the curious name "Street of the Lion's Bed." I doubt that lions ever slept here, but if they did, it would have been for the marvellous views of the Bosphorus. The older rooms and facilities here are kept clean and priced at 8,000TL ($11.20) single, 12,000TL ($16.80) double for a room with bath, or 1,000TL ($1.40) to 1,500TL ($2.10) less for a room without private bath.

THE BIG SPLURGE: You can pay so-called international rates for a luxury hotel room in this city, and you will get a delightful world-class hotel. But you needn't pay that much for an extra touch of comfort. The **Divan Oteli,** on Askerocağı Caddesi at Cumhuriyet Caddesi, Elmadağ (tel. 1/146-4020), more or less across from the Sheraton and two blocks from the Hilton, was founded by Vehbi Koç, Turkey's millionaire industrialist, and was meant as a suitable place for his business associates before the Hilton and Sheraton were built. The Divan's dining room has a reputation as being among the city's finest places to eat, and the hotel's rooms and public spaces are very comfortable, but the hotel is smaller (96 rooms) than the 400-plus Hilton and Sheraton. All the comforts and services of a luxury hotel are here, including friendly, English-speaking staff. Room prices are quoted in dollars, and are $60 single, $75 double, taxes and service included.

The **Etap Marmara Hotel,** right in Taksim Square (tel. 1/144-8850), was built as the Istanbul Inter-Continental, but was later taken over by the French chain. Many rooms have fabulous Bosphorus views; the rest overlook Taksim, its park, and the city. The location is surely the most convenient in the city, and the hotel itself is beautiful, with all the amenities, including a bank branch and pastry shop. Room prices, quoted in U.S. dollars, are $90 to $110 single, $100 to $135 double, plus 15% service.

The **Istanbul Sheraton,** at the northern end of Taksim Park (tel. 1/148-9000), shares with its high-style neighbors the wonderful views of the Bosphorus and the Old City, and also has a good location, for slightly higher prices. Among the large luxury hotels, the Sheraton is looked upon as the best of the bunch. What you pay here depends a great deal on what you enjoy. If you have a room with a sea view and twin beds, the price is $135; for a room with that same Bosphorus view, a queen-size bed, and a mini-bar, it's $145.

A bit farther from Taksim along Cumhuriyet Caddesi, the **Istanbul Hilton,** Cumhuriyet Caddesi, Elmadağ (tel. 1/146-7050), is set in its own spacious park, with tennis courts and a swimming pool, and gives you the feeling of staying at a private club, albeit a very large club. Though the oldest luxury hotel in the city, the Hilton has been carefully kept up-to-date. To accommodate the increased luxury traffic arriving in Istanbul these days, the Hilton is putting the finishing touches on a large addition of ultramodern guest rooms, which may be ready for occupancy by the time you arrive. Prices are $96, $116, and $145 for double rooms with bath.

3. Hotels in Tepebaşı

Should you decide to stay in Tepebaşı, the quickest and easiest way to get there is by taxi, or you can take a dolmush from Taksim; it departs from a street corner to the left (west) of the Air France office. You may have to take a dolmush that goes past Tepebaşı to Aksaray and pay the full fare, even though you will get out midway. If you prefer, you can catch a bus along Tarlabaşı Caddesi near the dolmush departure point.

Coming from Karaköy, take the Tünel to the upper station and walk the several blocks to the hotels.

Points of reference here are the British Consulate, very near Galatasaray, and the American Consulate, right next door to the Pera Palas Hotel. With one exception, all the other hotels mentioned here are in the two blocks between these two consulates.

For a description of the Pera Palas Hotel, see the section on "Special Places," below.

BUDGET CHOICES: Right down the hill behind the American Consulate is the modern and comfortable **Otel Bale,** on Refik Saydam Caddesi (tel. 1/150-4912), the most modern hotel in the area except for the luxurious Etap Istanbul. Some of the Bale's rooms have views of the Golden Horn, all have baths or showers, and prices are 12,000TL ($16.80) single, 15,500TL ($21.70) double. Though the busy street out front detracts from the hotel somewhat, it also provides quick and easy transportation to various parts of the city.

The **Büyük Londra Oteli,** Meşrutiyet Caddesi 117 (tel. 1/149-1025 or 145-0670), the "Grand London Hotel," dates from the late 19th century, as does the Pera Palas. Though it shares a common heritage with its larger sister establishment, the Büyük Londra has much smaller and more modest rooms with bath or shower, and has seen a good deal of use, but it does preserve some of the *fin de siècle* glory at a very moderate price. A room with shower costs 8,800TL ($12.30) with one double bed, 17,500TL ($24.50) with twin beds.

Facing the entrance to the Pera Palas Hotel is the **Hotel Sedir,** Meşrutiyet Caddesi 189 (tel. 1/149-9589), which has a problem. Meşrutiyet Caddesi is so heavily trafficked that the front-facing rooms do not afford much opportunity to sleep at night, particularly if it's summer and the windows must be left open for ventilation. But if you can get a quiet back room you'll be fine, and you can just skip across the street in the evening for a drink in the Pera's marvelous old bar. The Sedir's rooms with bath go for 9,800TL ($13.70) double. The hotel has an elevator.

Right beside the Etap Istanbul is the modest **Yenişehir Palas Oteli,** Meşrutiyet Caddesi, Tepebaşı (tel. 1/149-8810), an older hotel with eight floors of suitable though hardly luxurious rooms with showers, little in the way of views in any direction, and moderate prices of 10,000TL ($14) single, 13,000TL ($18.20) double. It's a good choice mostly for price and location.

THE BIG SPLURGE: What about a modern tower of a hotel with absolutely fabulous views of the Golden Horn and the Old City from some of its air-conditioned rooms, a swimming pool on the roof, a nightclub, and all the other luxury-hotel services, right in the heart of old Pera? That's the **Etap Istanbul Oteli,** Meşrutiyet Caddesi, Tepebaşı (tel. 1/144-8880), almost across the street from the Pera Palas. (Don't confuse the Etap Istanbul with its sister hotel, the Etap Marmara, in Taksim Square.) The Etap Istanbul has all the modern conveniences, a good enough location, and prices of $60 single, $75 double, for the best rooms. If you take a room with a less spectacular view the price is a bit lower. But this is among the most popular hotels in the city and it's often completely filled (sometimes by groups), so reserve early if you can.

4. Hotels Near Aksaray

The district of Laleli is to the north and east of the Laleli Camii ("Mosque with Tulips") on Ordu Caddesi, just east of Aksaray Square. Coming from the Grand Bazaar and Beyazıt Square, you will pass some large university buildings on your right, and at the end of them is Büyük Reşit Paşa Caddesi, the eastern limit of Laleli. Walk one block past Büyük Reşit Paşa to Harikzadeler Sokak, and begin your explorations here.

ON HARİKZADELER SOKAK: Of the narrow streets in this district, Harikzadeler Sokak is virtually lined with hotels on both sides. (You may see the name of this street as Hakikzadeler, or Harikzedeler.) I'll describe the many hotels on this street, then go on to the ones on neighboring streets. Use the handy map in this book to find your way around the streets, and choose your lodging from among these:

The **Hotel Ayda,** Harikzadeler Sokak 11 (tel. 1/526-7867), is among the less expensive places on the street, and also among the plainest. Double rooms with shower here cost 6,000TL ($8.40), and the prices are the hotel's biggest attraction.

The **Hotel Eyfel,** Kurultay Sokak 19 (tel. 1/520-9788 or 520-9789), is just off Harikzadeler Sokak. Though the hotel is not as old as its Parisian namesake (the Eiffel Tower), it has been here for quite a while, though periodic renovations have kept the guest rooms presentable and the bathrooms attractive. Over the years modern services have been added, and now the Eyfel can boast elevators, a restaurant and cocktail lounge, and a popularity with some tour groups. Rooms are priced at 8,200TL ($11.50) single, 10,250TL ($14.35) double, with shower; you pay 2,100TL ($2.95) for an extra bed in a room. These prices include breakfast.

The **Hotel Neşet,** Harikzadeler Sokak 23 (tel. 1/526-7412 or 522-4474), is a modern and nice enough, if small, hotel with rooms costing 4,200TL ($6) single, 7,000TL ($10) double, and a friendly staff willing to help out with any problems you may have.

The **Hotel Oran,** Harikzadeler Sokak 40 (tel. 528-5813 or 527-0572), facing the aforementioned Hotel Neşet, has 22 rooms with shower for 4,200TL ($6) single, 7,000TL ($10) double. It's a popular caravan stop for tour groups and may be full up during the high summer months.

Several hotels are just a few steps off Harikzadeler Sokak on Zeynep Kamil Sokak, a short street running over to Büyük Reşit Paşa Caddesi.

The **Ömür Hotel,** Büyük Reşit Paşa Caddesi, Zeynep Kamil Sokak, Vezneciler (tel. 1/526-3030 or 520-9728), is, despite its imposing address, at the corner of Zeynep Kamil Sokak and Harikzadeler Sokak. Though it's among this area's more modest lodgings, it has a good and long-standing reputation for pleasing dollar-conscious travelers. Its very suitable rooms go for 4,250TL ($5.95) single, 6,250TL ($8.75) double, with private shower.

The **Hotel Sırmalı,** Zeynep Kamil Sokak 45 (tel. 1/520-7642), just off Harikzadeler Sokak, is only two steps from the Hotel Ömür. The Sırmalı is among the low-budget stars on the street, and if money is more important to you than comfort, check it out. Prices are 4,000TL ($5.60) single, 6,000TL ($8.40) double, for a room with shower.

Back on Harikzadeler Sokak itself, the **Hotel Zürih,** Harikzadeler Sokak 37 (tel. 1/520-1067 or 520-1359), is at the northern end of the street, near the corner with Vidinli Tevfik Paşa Caddesi. The Zürih is among the newer places in Laleli, and tries to live up to its Swiss name in terms of cleanliness and efficiency. Prices are higher than most of the aforementioned places, but so is the quality of what you get. Rooms with bath for 10,000TL ($14) single, 14,000TL ($19.60) double, breakfast included.

ON AĞA YOKUŞU: Another little street lined with hotels is called Ağa Yokuşu. It's a short east-west street which runs between the larger streets of Fethi Bey Caddesi and Yeşil Tulumba Sokak. Hotels along this street tend to be a cut above those on Harikzadeler Sokak.

Among the nicest hotels in this area is the **Hotel Barın,** Fevziye Caddesi 25, Şehzadebaşı (tel. 1/522-8426 or 526-4440), just off Ağa Yokuşu near its eastern end. The Barın is one of the newer places on the street, with 30 fairly luxurious rooms, all of which have showers, some of which have bathtubs as well. Prices are 9,250TL ($12.95) single, 13,000TL ($18.20) double, bath and breakfast included.

The **Hotel Burak,** Ağa Yokuşu 1 (tel. 1/522-7904 or 523-7521), is a standard modern small hotel, perhaps the most typical in Laleli, charging 7,200TL ($10.10) single, 10,200TL ($14.30) double. Breakfast is included in the room price.

Facing the Hotel Burak across the street is the **Hotel Diana,** Ağa Yokuşu 2 (tel. 1/528-0760 or 526-6921), among the newest and choicest places in Laleli, charging 12,000TL ($16.80) for a double with bath, breakfast included.

The dowager tourist hotel of Laleli is undoubtedly the **Hotel Washington,** Ağa Yokuşu 12, Laleli (tel. 1/520-5990), which has been here for decades. Because of its fame and its comforts, because the staff is used to foreigners, and because tour operators love this hotel, the Washington charges 9,700TL ($13.60) single, 15,000TL ($21) double, with bath and breakfast.

More or less next door to the Hotel Washington is the **Hotel Burç,** Ağa

Yokuşu 18 (tel. 1/520-7667), which, though not as comfortable, is just as well located, and charges far less: 7,200TL ($10.10) single, 9,800TL ($13.70) double, breakfast included.

With a name like **Hotel La Miraj,** Fethi Bey Caddesi 28 (tel. 1/511-2445), half a block off Ağa Yokuşu, one might think the hotel difficult to lay hands on, but in fact it has been here serving travelers for years. It's an older building, well restored, charging 7,000TL ($10) single, 11,000TL ($15.40) double, for largish rooms with bath, breakfast included.

Finally, the **Hotel Doru,** Gençtürk Caddesi 44, Laleli (tel. 1/526-5905 or 527-6928), just a few steps south off Ağa Yokuşu, is yet another small, modern, presentable place to stay, with 25 rooms with bath priced at 7,500TL ($10.50) single, 10,000TL ($14) double.

5. Hotels in Sultanahmet

Sultanahmet is the backpackers' domain, an area of very inexpensive hotels and hostels located cheek by jowl with some of the world's most magnificent buildings. The one exception to this rule is the luxurious restored Ottoman mansion hotel named the Yeşil Ev, which is covered below under "Special Places."

The old favorite of the student set in this area is the **Yücelt Y. Hostel,** Caferiye Sokak 6, Sultanahmet (tel. 1/522-4790), literally across the street from Sancta Sophia. The Yücelt began its life many years ago as a YMCA hostel, but it has not been so affiliated for several years. Even so, it keeps a "Y" in its name to reassure clientele. The Yücelt has all the things a good hostel should have: double rooms without baths for 4,400TL ($6.15), with bath for 5,500TL ($7.70), three-bedded rooms for 1,750TL ($2.45) per person, and dormitory beds for 1,250TL ($1.75) each. It has an inexpensive cafeteria, a laundry room, a bulletin board, public showers, and a Turkish bath. The location speaks for itself.

Other than the Yücelt, you will notice several hotels right on Divan Yolu facing the Hippodrome, among them the Hotel Güngör, the Hotel Stop, and the Sultan Turist Oteli. While these do have low-priced rooms, they are liable to be extremely noisy. A far better choice is the faded but comfortable **Hotel Klodfarer,** Klodfarer Caddesi 22 (tel. 1/528-4850 or 528-4851), a block off Divan Yolu, facing the vacant lot which has beneath it the Binbirdirek Cistern. Old-fashioned and dark but friendly, the Klodfarer has been hosting thrifty foreign travelers for years. It has a cheap restaurant and rooms with bath for 5,000TL ($7) single, 7,000TL ($10) double, 10,500TL ($14.70) triple.

6. Hotels Near Topkapı Bus Station

Entering Istanbul for the first time, with luggage, after an exhausting trip, is a daunting prospect. After pouring yourself off a bus at Istanbul's chaotic Topkapı Bus Station, you may just want to make your way to the nearest decent hotel. To do this, go through the Cannon Gate on Millet Caddesi, the main boulevard. You'll pass a Military Police post on the right-hand side a hundred yards down, and shortly thereafter you'll come to the **Hotel Olcay,** Millet Caddesi 187 (tel. 1/585-3220), a bright and modern place with polished service, a large restaurant, and very comfortable bath-equipped guest rooms priced at 17,000TL ($23.80) double.

By the time you arrive, you may have a choice of comfortable lodgings, because the **Otel Şehrazat** is presently under construction right next door to the Olcay.

If the aforementioned hotels seem to be too expensive for your budget, consider the **Hotel Ulubat,** Kalburcu Çeşme Sokak 10 (tel. 1/585-4694), a simple but comfy old place directly behind the Hotel Olcay in which rooms with bath cost 5,000TL ($7) single, 7,250TL ($10.15) double. The hotel has a small restaurant and its own parking lot. Still too expensive? The **Hotel Emir Sultan,** right next door to the Ulubat, is even cheaper.

7. Special Places

Those travelers for whom price is no object will find some truly exceptional lodgings available in Istanbul. Though a double room at any one of the establishments described below will break our budget, I'm aware that many faithful $$$-a-Day readers are happy to put aside their thrifty habits now and then to enjoy a Big Splurge. If you decide to do it here, take comfort in the fact that a Turkish-style splurge is probably more exciting, and less expensive, than in most other countries.

There are many plans for new, special luxury hotels in Istanbul, including the conversion of a palatial Ottoman stone barracks into a Holiday Inn Crowne Plaza Hotel, and the restoration of the ruined imperial palace of Çırağan into a small, exclusive hotel. But for now, Istanbul's exceptional hotels are these:

THE YEŞIL EV: Formerly named the Konak, this is the first of the several hotels and other historic buildings to be beautifully restored under the auspices of the Turkish Touring and Automobile Club. The **Yeşil Ev,** Kabasakal Caddesi, Sultanahmet (tel. 1/528-6764 or 511-1150), is actually a *konak,* or Ottoman town house, but as this name caused confusion with the Hotel Konak in the new city near the Hilton, it became the Yeşil Ev (Green House). The Yeşil Ev is quite lovely, a graceful old Ottoman home virtually rebuilt from scratch and furnished with antiques in exquisite taste. Each room in the house is different, of course, but all give the feeling of living among the Ottoman nobility in the 19th century. The only bad aspect of the Yeşil Ev is its instant and continuing success, which is enormous. It's very difficult to find a vacant room here, but if you do, you'll pay $35 single, $48 to $52 double, $84 triple, or $125 for the best, the Pasha's Room. Breakfast, service, and tax are included in these rates.

Relief is in sight from the demand for rooms in the Yeşil Ev. Not far from the house, behind Sancta Sophia, clinging to the walls of Topkapı Palace, is a row of Ottoman houses which have also been rebuilt and refitted by the Touring Club as lodgings for travelers very similar to those at the Yeşil Ev in both furnishings and price. For information, ask at the Yeşil Ev.

HIDIV KASRI: From the time of its founding until our own century, Istanbul was the Imperial City, the Second Rome, the center of the world for anyone in the eastern Mediterranean. Every king and potentate came here to breathe in the glories of empire. The Egyptian royal family, who looked upon themselves as Turkish and spoke Turkish rather than Arabic at home, often spent their summers here in a traditional wooden mansion on the Bosphorus. However, in 1906 Khedive Abbas Hilmi built himself a palatial villa on the most dramatic promontory overlooking the Bosphorus.

The **Hidiv Kasrı** (Khedive's Villa), near the village of Çubuklu (tel. 1/331-2651), can accommodate 50 guests, and is set in its own large park above the town. You'll need a taxi to reach the hotel as Çubuklu is a 30-minute drive north of the city.

The villa is in a marvelous art nouveau style, with a circular entry hall complete with fountain and a semicircular façade looking toward the sunset across the Bosphorus. On the ground floor the west-facing room is now the restaurant; on the upper floor it's the master bedroom.

Rooms with bath cost from $42 to $62 for a small double room on the top floor, through $100 for one of the large bedrooms once used by the royal family.

The royal suite, which in this case truly deserves the name as it was the king's quarters, costs $200 per night double. Ask for the Hidiv'in Dairesi.

By way of background, you might like to know something about the Egyptian royal family. The Ottomans lost control of the province of Egypt early in the 19th century to a military adventurer named Muhammed Ali, who took over the government of Egypt by force, slaughtering by treachery the Mameluke ruling class (of Turkish extraction) which had governed Egypt for centuries. The sultan, unable to conquer Muhammed Ali, granted him a great degree of independence in exchange for tribute and allegiance. The sultan reigned over Egypt, but Muhammed Ali and his heirs ruled, and spent the province's considerable revenues.

To preserve the fiction of Ottoman sovereignty, the ruler of Egypt was not called "king," but rather "khedive" *(hidiv),* an obscure old title revived specifically for this situation to protect the sultan's feelings and his honor.

Late in the 19th century the British took control of Egypt in effect, though not in law. They needed to control the Suez Canal, and the quasi-independent status of the khedive suited their purposes perfectly. Muhammed Ali's line sat on the throne of Egypt until King Faruk was overthrown by Gamal Abdel Nasser in the 1950s.

THE PERA PALACE HOTEL: The huge old **Pera Palas Hotel,** at Meşrutiyet Caddesi 98–100, Tepebaşı (tel. 1/145-2230), is the prime luxury hotel out of the 19th-century glories of Ottoman Constantinople. When Georges Nagelmackers, founder of the renowned Compagnie Internationale des Wagons-Lits et Grands Express Européens, began his luxury train service between Paris and Constantinople in the 1880s, he had a problem. His pampered passengers, among them dukes and dastards, counts and concubines, descended from his plush coaches into Constantinople only to discover that there was no suitable place in the city for them to stay. So Nagelmackers was forced to build them one. He built a palatial hotel among the vineyards of Pera, and called it the Pera Palace (in Turkish, Pera Palas).

The Pera Palas has 120 rooms with high ceilings, period (more or less) furnishings, and bathrooms to match. Some rooms have views of the Golden Horn. The hotel opened in the 1890s and was advertised at that plague-ridden time as having "a thoroughly healthy situation, being high up and isolated on all four sides" and "overlooking the Golden Horn and the whole panorama of Stamboul." The Hilton or Sheraton of its time, it was the favorite lodging place of kings and prime ministers, and stars of stage and society. Atatürk stayed here in a suite (now a museum) when he wasn't using Dolmabahçe Palace as his base, and Room 411 was Agatha Christie's favorite.

Well, the hotel is no longer "isolated on all four sides," having been hemmed in by modern buildings long ago; but the hotel is still right next door to the American Consulate, and is still open for business. Besides catering to tourists in search of the faded glories of old Constantinople, it's a favorite venue for Turkish wedding receptions and business conferences.

As for price, it used to be fairly cheap to stay here, but the management has discovered that foreigners will pay quite a lot for nostalgia, and has raised the prices to unconscionable heights. Now you pay luxury-class prices, but you do not get luxury services such as air conditioning, soundproofing, and television. Rooms with bath and a fairly mediocre buffet breakfast are currently priced at $75 to $95 single, $85 to $115 double. Rooms on the lower floors are quite noisy, and west-facing rooms which catch the late afternoon sun can get very hot and stuffy in summer. If you plan to stay here, the rule is to choose your room with great care.

ISTANBUL'S RESTAURANTS

TURKISH CUISINE IS FAR MORE than shish kebap, Turkish coffee, and Turkish Delight. The local cuisine, developed over a thousand years, has been compared to French and Chinese in its finesse and in its passion for fresh ingredients and careful preparation. Though it shares many of its characteristics with the more familiar Greek cuisine, lots of unbiased observers give Turkish cooks higher marks.

Not only is Turkish cooking good, it's unbelievably cheap, even in the big city. You can dine with the best of them and easily stay within our daily budget. A delicious meal of savory kebap, with a salad, drink, and dessert, need cost only 2,500TL ($3.50), and many times it will cost less. If you add the relative luxuries of wine or beer with a meal, the price might just rise to 3,500TL ($4.90).

Here are Istanbul's better restaurants, described by area.

1. In and Around Taksim Square

As Taksim Square and İstiklal Caddesi are among the main business and shopping places in the city, this area is well provided with places to eat both large and small, plain and fancy. To help you orient yourself, I'll describe the square's dining possibilities by area.

İSTİKLAL AND SIRASELVİLER: Heading south out of the square are two busy streets which hold literally dozens of restaurants, kebapçıs, cafeterias, beerhalls, and snack stands. I'll describe some full-service, white-tableclothed restaurants first, and then some cafeterias.

Full-Service Restaurants

Among the most dependable and pleasant restaurants near Taksim is the **Hacı Baba,** İstiklal 49 (tel. 144-1886), entered through this unimpressive doorway, or around the corner on Meşelik Sokak. This is a big restaurant with several rooms, and a small terrace in the back next to the Aya Triada church—a fine place to dine in good weather. A meal of chicken-noodle soup, stuffed cabbage, orman kebap (meat and potatoes in sauce), and a soft drink, tip included, will cost about 3,500TL ($5.10). There are menus in English and a waiter or two who speak it. The restaurant is open every day from 11 a.m. to midnight, but try to get there before the rush hours (noon to 1 p.m. and 7 to 8 p.m.) if you want to get a table on the terrace.

Between Taksim Square and the entrance to Hacı Baba is a smaller place, without the pretty terrace, but with attentive waiter service and a quiet upstairs dining room. It's the **Fıçı Restaurant,** and you might try it if the Hacı Baba is packed.

Slightly farther along İstiklal Caddesi, toward Galatasaray, is the **Piknik Restaurant,** İstiklal 40, a modern, attractive if simply decorated place with welcoming signs in several languages, including English. The interior is air-conditioned, the waiters are English-speaking and eager to please, and a full meal of a starter, grilled kebap, side dish, and dessert may cost only 3,000TL ($4.20).

Self-Service Cafeterias

Standing in Taksim Square and looking toward İstiklal Caddesi, the street to the left of İstiklal is called Sıraselviler Caddesi. At no. 40 on this street, half a block out of Taksim, is the **Selvi Kafeterya,** a modern dining place with the distinct advantage of having all its dishes on view. Eat lightly or eat heartily—there is no waiter to intimidate you into ordering more than you want, and no service charge to pay (although it's customary to leave a few coins or small bills for the person who collects the trays and wipes the tables). Stews, kebaps, salads, and desserts are all here for you to enjoy. A meal of soup, main course, and salad or dessert here, plus a beverage, will cost in the range of 1,350TL ($1.95) to 1,700TL ($2.45).

Walk down İstiklal Caddesi for a good selection of self-service eating places of all types. The **Antep Restaurant,** at İstiklal 3, has a cafeteria line along its heavily laden steam tables, right at the front by the entrance. This place is nothing fancy, but the food is good and the price can't be beat: a full Turkish chowdown might set you back 1,500TL ($2.20), or 2,000TL ($2.80) if you're really hungry. The **Pehlivan Restaurant,** at İstiklal 5, is very similar in food, ambience, and price.

CUMHURİYET CADDESİ: This busy boulevard has many dining possibilities. My own feeling is that the ones near Taksim are somewhat pretentious and overpriced. If the view were good they'd be worth patronizing, but the view is of buses roaring by. Walk up Cumhuriyet to the first cross street, however, and to the right, by the entrance to the Divan Oteli, is the **Divan Pub.** You could spend 10,000TL ($14) dining at the restaurant in the hotel, but in the Pub, the bill might amount to 4,000TL ($5.60) and the food will still be very good. The Pub, which is not an English-style pub but a bright, modern, informal restaurant, is famous for its döner kebap. Beer and wine are available. The Divan Pub is actually the "coffeeshop" of the plush Divan Oteli, and is thus open every day.

Speaking of the Divan Oteli, you should know that its pastry shop, the **Divan Pastanesi,** to the left of the hotel's main entrance, is considered the best in the city. While it's not particularly cheap, it is particularly good, and the delicious treats so prohibitively priced at home are quite moderately priced here. The pastry shop has a branch in the Etap Marmara Hotel right in Taksim Square, as well.

OFF-THE-BEATEN-TRACK WITH A VIEW: There are a number of restaurants in Istanbul which, though off the beaten track, are worth the trouble to find because of the views they offer. The most cordial of these, combining both a restaurant and a tea garden, is the **Cennet Bahçesi,** from which you get a truly panoramic view of the Old City with Topkapı Palace, the mosques, the mouth of the Golden Horn, the Bosphorus, Asia, the Islands—one of the best views from inside the new city. Prices for a meal here are in the 4,000TL ($5.60) to 5,000TL ($7) range, but well worth it, considering the quality of the service, the food, and the view. If you want just the view and a bit of relaxation, have a soft drink in the terrace below the restaurant for 350TL (50¢). To get to the Cennet, from Taksim Square walk down the hill on İnönü (Gümüşsuyu) Caddesi (beginning in front of the Cultural Center) and turn right just before the big German Consulate. The street turns right after a block and splits into three streets, one of which goes along the side of a little flat-iron mosque, to the left. This is Ayazpaşa Camii Sokak; follow it to a T-crossing on Saray Arkası Sokak, turn right and follow this street. You'll have to turn left just past a French church to follow the road. After the turn, the Cennet is at the end of the slight incline, right in front of you. The restaurant is open Sunday and late every evening, during the warm months only.

2. In Galatasaray and Tepebaşı

Between Galatasaray Square and Tünel Square are several interesting and different places to dine. A few are very convenient to the hotels of Tepebaşı; others are well worth searching out because of their special excellence and appeal.

NEAR THE PERA PALAS: Those staying at the Otel Bale, Büyük Londra, Yenişehir Palas, Pera Palas, or Etap Istanbul Hotels will want to know of two convenient and very serviceable restaurants on Meşrutiyet Caddesi between the Büyük Londra and the Etap Istanbul. First is the **Restaurant Tuncel,** Meşrutiyet 129 (tel. 145-5566), a small but pleasant place with formal-looking waiters, polite service, but surprisingly moderate prices. A full meal based on shish kebap or lamb chops, including an appetizer and dessert, and the price will be only 2,000TL ($2.80) to 3,000TL ($4.20).

A few steps down the street toward the Etap Istanbul Hotel brings you to the **İrfan Restaurant** (tel. 144-2597), which matches the aforementioned Tuncel in convenience, pleasurable ambience, and price.

A RUSSIAN RESTAURANT: At the end of a dark, dingy passageway at İstiklal 244 (official address: Olivo Çıkmazı 17) is a former dance hall run by Russians who emigrated to Istanbul during and after the Russian Revolution. This section of the city of Pera was full of Russian nobles after the Revolution, holding revels and dances late into the night. The last vestiges are to be found at the **Yeni Rejans** (tel. 144-1610), a restaurant where several little old ladies who fled the war—one was a ballerina in Kiev—came to make their living. Dark-wood paneling, the orchestra balcony—these are all that's left of the dance-hall atmosphere. The place has an authenticity which makes up for a lack of glitter, plus some of the best food in town at reasonable prices. Delicious borscht is the way to start (order it with pirochkys, little dumplings eaten on the side), breaded veal cutlet a good way to continue. For dessert, take your pick of apple strudel or meringue Madeleine, puffy meringue covered with thick chocolate sauce. I usually splurge when I go here, and end up paying about 5,000TL ($7) for a soup-to-coffee meal with wine, although I could just as easily have a meal for under 3,750TL ($5.25). Although the chicken Kievsky is delicious, other high-priced specialties tend to be disappointing. You're better off sticking to the standard items with lower prices.

The Rejans is hard to find, but well worth the trouble, for it's a true scene out of the old Istanbul. Walk to the end of the Olivo Çıkmazı and up the stairs at no. 17 to the brick entryway—a very unlikely place for a restaurant. The waiters speak a bit of English, but are never allowed to do anything but carry plates. The Russian ladies handle everything else, from taking your order to adding up the bill. They speak Russian, Turkish, French, and English.

The tipping system at the Rejans deserves a special note. Although there is a standard 10% service charge, none of this ever sees the waiters' pockets. The ladies who wait on you will expect a tip, and the waiters don't receive any of this either. Therefore you're asked to pay *three times* for service! Here's how I usually do it: pay the bill (and the service charge), decide what I'd like to leave as a tip, leave less than half of the tip on the plate, and hand the rest to the white-jacketed waiter, who will be waiting to say good-bye at the door. The Rejans is open for lunch every day from noon to 2:30 p.m., for dinner from 6:30 to about 11 p.m.; closed Sunday.

THE FLOWER PASSAGE: When you're ready for some fun, head for the Çiçek Pasajı (Flower Passage) at İstiklal 172. The arcades and inner court of the old Pera City Hall are stuffed with little fish-and-beer places, usually of the second class, where meals of hors d'oeuvres, a fish plate, a huge glass of beer, a salad, bread, and service are about 3,000TL ($4.20) to 3,800TL ($5.30). The cheapest of these are the ones in which you eat at long narrow tables in brightly lit rooms, or even from a slab of marble perched on a barrelhead in the courtyard itself. These restaurants are not for the fastidious, but very agreeable to the adventurous. The more sedate places are suitable, obviously, for more sedate tastes: here you sit inside and get restaurant service, even though the place is called a "beerhall." Try the **Pasaj Birahanesi**, on the left just past the nut stand as you enter the passage; there is a ground-floor room usually filled with men, and upstairs an *aile salonu* (family room) where women feel more at home. My favorite of these places, though, is the one on the corner by the other entrance to the Pasaj, at 7/8–15/10 Pasaj, the **Kimene İçkili Lokantası.** Go inside and downstairs to the vaulted, wine-cellar-like rooms where Turks will be toasting one another with big glasses of draft beer, singing Oriental drinking songs in minor keys. On the walls are signs with mottoes such as "Silence Is the Epitome of Gentlemanly Behavior," and "The Polite Man Is an Example to All His Peers." Though the clientele is mostly male, women are certainly not shunned. This is one of the few restaurants in its class to have authentic "atmosphere." This is also one of the few places in Istanbul where you can get good fish meals at reasonable prices—highly recommended for a great deal of fun and camaraderie.

IN TÜNEL SQUARE: One of the best of Istanbul's fine restaurants has surprisingly moderate prices. It's the **Four Seasons Restaurant,** İstiklal 509 (tel. 145-8941), on İstiklal Caddesi just out of Tünel Square, very near the Swedish Consulate. The Four Seasons is the pride and joy of headwaiter Musa Hiçdönmez and his English wife, Gay, who decided to open a place of their own in Istanbul after years of service in such places as the Strand Palace Hotel and the

London Hilton. You dine in a large, high-ceilinged room with a bar in one corner; Gay sees to the bar while Musa, a tall, dignified, and serious man, makes sure that preparation and service are impeccable. After a very fine dinner of chopped liver pâté, Bosphorus sea bass amandine, a delicate salad, and dessert, I mentioned to Musa and to his able assistant, Remzi Coşkun, that they seemed to be perfectionists. The reply was, "We know what perfect service is, though we have yet to reach it!" You can take your choice of a decent assortment of main dishes including the several fish in season, tournedos Rossini, roast leg of lamb, entrecôte bordelaise, or a variety of grilled meats. Dessert features (of course) crêpes Suzette, banana flambé, or a pastry from the trolley.

If you throw caution to the winds and order what you want, excepting only lobster thermidor, and if you drink wine, you may spend $15 per person; but there is no need to do this as the restaurant features a "set lunch" and "set dinner" every day priced at 3,750TL ($5.25) for lunch, 4,250TL ($5.95) for dinner for five courses. The restaurant is open noon to 3 p.m. for lunch and 6 p.m. to midnight for dinner every day except Sunday.

3. In Karaköy

Though there are many little snack shops around Karaköy Square, there are only two good, special restaurants, and they are both open only for lunch.

FOR SEAFOOD: Seafood is the specialty at the **Liman Lokantası** (tel. 144-1033) and the **Liman Cafeteria,** above the Yolcu Salonu (International Passenger Terminal) 100 yards east of Karaköy Square itself. Be sure to take a look on the dock side of the building to see if there's a ship in port at the time. If no ship blocks the view, the Liman's panorama of the Old City and the Golden Horn is the finest around. The decor, though formal, is spare, and nothing special.

In the cafeteria, you pay a set price of about 4,000TL ($5.60), then you help yourself to the various dishes from the steam tables set up near the entrance. The Lokanta, upstairs, is much more formal and somewhat more expensive. Many of the available fish are set out on ice on a display table—you can choose the very fish you want. A full, elegant, delicious lunch with wine costs 6,000TL ($8.40) to 9,000TL ($12.60). Note that I said "lunch." Both the cafeteria and the Lokanta are open *only for lunch,* from noon to 4 p.m.; closed Sunday.

Though you can have a good dessert at the cafeteria or Lokanta, you might want to step across the street to the baklava shop called **Güllüoğlu,** on the street level of the large parking garage. Most customers here buy their baklava by the kilo to take home with them, and prices are posted on the trays of baklava by the kilo. The baklava comes in various flavors: *cevizli* (with crushed-walnut stuffing), *Şam fıstıklı* (with pistachio nuts), *kaymaklı* (with sweet clotted cream), and even *çıkolatalı* (with chocolate stuffing). You can also order *kuru baklava* (dry baklava), which is made with less of the honey-and-sugar syrup. Try a 100-gram portion *(yüz gram)* for starters, and you can compute the price merely by dropping a zero from the kilo price. It should be in the neighborhood of 500TL (70¢) to 800TL ($1.10), depending on the flavor. Güllüoğlu is open long hours, from morning till early evening; closed Sunday.

UNDER GALATA BRIDGE: You may have heard of the little fish restaurants located right beneath the roadway on Galata Bridge, the floating pontoon span across the mouth of the Golden Horn. Well, at this writing the bridge is being replaced with a new, modern structure, and so I can't say anything certain about the fate of these little places. When the new bridge is in place, no doubt they will creep back to their accustomed positions and again offer good, fresh fish at moderate prices, and a taste of Old İstanbul in the bargain.

4. In Eminönü

Right at the mouth of the Golden Horn in a district which has been filled with markets since Byzantine times, Eminönü has surprisingly few restaurants of any type. But the dining possibilities, though scarce, are unique in the city, and shouldn't be missed. Since business activity here dies down toward dinnertime, the meal to have in Eminönü is lunch.

IN THE EGYPTIAN BAZAAR: Until the restaurant's master chef died a few years ago, **Pandeli** (tel. 522-5534) was one of the best restaurants in all of Europe. The food and service are still of very high caliber, though the master's gift is lost. Pandeli is located in the Mısır Çarşısı (Egyptian Bazaar), in Eminönü Square at the foot of the Galata Bridge. Walk in the front door of the bazaar, and as you step over the big stone threshold, look to your left. A little door opens into a tiled staircase, which leads to the restaurant. Pandeli is a Lüks-class place with three tiny rooms with small windows looking out onto the Golden Horn, the bridge, the Bosphorus, and Beyoğlu; and one larger, central room with several windows looking down into the bazaar itself. Service is quite refined, the food is delicious, and as long as you don't order fish you can eat for 5,500TL ($7.70) or slightly more. Fish is the specialty of the house and is superb, but runs about 8,500TL ($11.90) for a full meal. If you just want to enjoy the restaurant's atmosphere and a simple but good meal, order soup and a vegetables-with-meat plate (*etli sebze*). But this is one of the city's best restaurants, so a more expensive meal is still a good value. Lunch is the only meal served, but you can have it any time from 11:30 a.m. to 3:30 p.m.

A SEAFOOD SNACK: Too expensive? The area around the Galata Bridge, on both sides, is the center of the city, so it has very few neighborhood eateries charging low prices. But you can eat well for almost nothing. Here's how: during the afternoon and evening, boats tie up at the ends of the bridge and fry up their own fish steaks (usually turbot), serving them tucked into a quarter loaf of fresh bread; sliced onions and salt are in boxes tied to the guard rail, and you add them to taste after the boatman hands your sandwich up to you. The *balık-ekmek* (fish-and-bread) sandwich costs only 800TL ($1.10), and is delicious. The boat's "kitchen" has hardly been inspected by the health authorities, but I'm addicted to these treats and have never had any stomach trouble from them. To chase it, have a glass of *ayran* (the yogurt drink) from one of the little stands on the lower walkway of the bridge. Prices are posted on the stand. Finish off with 50 grams (*elli gram*) of nuts from a nearby vendor, and you'll have had a filling lunch for 1,100TL ($1.55).

BIRTHPLACE OF TURKISH DELIGHT: That soft, chewy, sweetish confection which we call Turkish Delight, but which the Turks call *rahat lokum,* or just *lokum* for short, was invented in Istanbul at the shop of **Ali Muhiddin Hacı Bekir** in the year 1777. Innovation was not a quality prized by the stodgy Ottomans, but even the sultan and his court took to this new, soft confection with enthusiasm. It was, as its Turkish name translates, "comfortable in the throat," and a welcome change from hard candy.

Ali Muhiddin Hacı Bekir was a confectioner from the remote mountain town of Kastamonu, and his descendants have owned and run the shop ever since he opened it. Though the family has several other shops in the city (most notably on İstiklal Caddesi near Taksim), and even one in Cairo, you can drop by the original shop on Hamidiye Street, near the corner with Şeyhülislam Hayri Efendi Caddesi, more or less behind the Yeni Cami (New Mosque), and pick up a kilo box of Turkish Delight for about 1,400TL ($1.95). Ask for an assortment *(çeşitli),* or order it *cevizli* (with walnuts), *Şam fıstıklı* (with pistachios), *port-akkallı* (orange flavored), or *bademli* (with almonds). Don't be afraid to ask for a (free) sample first. Just say *Denelim* ("Let's try it"). In the cooler months they also make the city's best *helva* (halvah). Ali Muhiddin Hacı Bekir is open daily except Sunday.

5. In and Around Sultanahmet

The center of Istanbul's greatest concentration of historical and architectural monuments has surprisingly few good restaurants. But there are several quite serviceable places which will provide well for the appetite you whetted with a morning's vigorous sightseeing.

IN TOPKAPI PALACE: Inside the confines of **Topkapı Palace** is a restaurant operated by the famous Konyalı firm, whose original establishment across from Sirkeci Station dates from 1897. Tables are set out under awnings at the very northern end of the palace, underneath the Yeni Köşk, and the view of the Bosphorus and of Üsküdar is very fine. The situation is ideal, the service is polite (though often slow because of the great numbers of diners who crowd in for lunch), but the prices are a bit steep—expect to pay around 3,000TL ($4.20) to 4,500TL ($6.30) for a good, full-course lunch. You can, if you're not ravished by hunger, order just a sandwich and a beverage at one of the little café tables on the terrace below the restaurant, but this may end up costing half of what a good lunch does and is thus not really value-for-money. Perhaps the way to do it is to rationalize: splurge on a good lunch in the imperial palace, and eat lightly in the evening to save money. Above all, try to avoid the noon to 1 p.m. crush of diners here; but don't come too long after lunchtime, or the excellent döner kebap will be all gone.

ALONG DİVAN YOLU: The first place you should consider on Divan Yolu is the **Vitamin Restaurant,** Divan Yolu 16 (tel. 526-5086), facing the Hippodrome, a bright and modern place with the standard steam tables in the front windows, and those delightfully low Turkish prices. It's possible to choose three or even four plates from the ready food, order a beverage as well, and still keep the cost of lunch below 1,600TL ($2.25), though you can spend up to 2,500TL ($3.50) if you order grilled meat and go all out. The restaurant is open every day, for all three meals.

The **Çınar Lokantası,** an unpretentious little restaurant on Divan Yolu (three blocks up the hill from the Sultanahmet bus stop, on the right), has been a favorite with readers of this book for years. For a full restaurant, it constitutes the best buy in the square. Besides the street-level room there's an upstairs dining room with a view of sorts, and an added bonus: on the way upstairs you pass the open kitchen, and you can take a look at the day's selection of "ready food." If nothing suits your fancy, feel free to order a grilled-meat dish. Lunch or dinner here will cost about 2,500TL ($3.50) for a full meal; there's a 10% service charge added to the bill.

The **Lale Restaurant,** right by the bus stop in Sultanahmet Square (tel. 522-2990), started out as a pastry shop, and as it served inexpensive and delicious puddings as well, soon came to be known as the best place for a cheap snack among the hippies who flocked to Istanbul over a decade ago. Soon it was so crowded with customers that breakfasts of sausages and eggs were offered for people who camped in vans in the square; then came light lunches and dinners. Though hippies are now a dying breed, the young, adventurous, and unorthodox still gather at the Lale to see and be seen, exchange travel tips and information on rides and riders, and warn one another not to mess with drugs here anymore. The self-service fare tends to suit the heavily foreign clientele, with a good number of familiar American and European offerings filled out with traditional Turkish dishes, and prices are moderate: a decent meal can be had for 2,500TL ($3.50) to 3,500TL ($4.90). Don't expect to pamper your tastebuds at the Lale, but what the food lacks in delicacy is hardly noticed as the clientele is so interesting. Open every day.

Even cheaper than these places, but still with very tasty food, are the köftecis at nos. 58 and 98 Divan Yolu. For a full, nourishing meal, they can't be beat: charcoal-grilled köfte (mildly spiced meat rissoles) is about 650TL (90¢) a portion, salads are even less, yogurt the same; and if you have the standard workingman's lunch of köfte, salad, yogurt, bread, and water, the total, with 10% service, will be less than 1,300TL ($1.80). If you're really hungry you can order a double portion of köfte, or a slightly more expensive plate of shish kebap.

6. In Beyazıt and the Grand Bazaar

You will be happy to know that the all-inclusive Grand Bazaar harbors half a dozen dining places. Like any good shopping mall or department store anywhere, you needn't leave the premises in order to refuel yourself for continuation of a shopping spree.

WITHIN THE GRAND BAZAAR: Plan to get to the Grand Bazaar around lunchtime because then the big tour-group buses take off for their own lunches somewhere else and leave you several very good, cheap restaurants to choose from in the bazaar itself. In the bazaar, the best restaurant is the **Havuzlu Lokantası,** right next to the post office. Entering the bazaar from the Nuruosmaniye Gate, walk along the bazaar's main street. Kalpakçılar Caddesi, until you see a little fountain on a corner on the right. Above it will be a sign pointing the way to the PTT (post office). The restaurant is actually part of a bazaar street that's been walled off and dressed up a bit. In summer, if the furniture shops nearby haven't been filling the air with paint, you can have a pleasant lunch in the little court outside the restaurant's front door, where tables will be set up around a marble fountain. Take a peek in the kitchen if you wish, or order from the English menu. Entrees range from köfte for 700TL ($1) to bonfile at 2,500TL ($3.50). The service is polite, if a bit slow.

The favorite place of people who work in the bazaar, and of shoppers who know the area inside and out, is the tiny **Sevim Lokantası,** a collection of several former shops converted into cramped but congenial dining rooms, and a number of tables set out in the bazaar's narrow streets. At 11:30 a.m. the staff will be bustling around, setting tables, and slicing bread in preparation for the noon-time rush, and by 12:15 p.m. every table will be full, so go early or late. Though the dining rooms are quaint, with primitive paintings done on the walls, the streetside tables are less claustrophobic. Meals of three courses here will cost 1,800TL ($2.50) to 2,800TL ($3.90). To find the Sevim, go to Sipahi Sokak and then turn onto Koltuk Kazazlar Sokak. The Sevim is bounded by (and occupies parts of) Terpuşçular Sokak, Koltuk Kazazlar Sokak, and Kahvehane Sokak.

A similarly cheap place is the **Rumeli 2 Restaurant,** Perdahçılar Sokak 60, at the corner of Takkeciler Sokak.

AN OUTDOOR CAFÉ: For rest and refreshment in good weather, make your way to the **patio café** next to the Beyazıt Camii (Mosque of Beyazıt), between the bazaar and Beyazıt Square; the easiest way to get there is by walking through the Old Book Bazaar. Students from neighboring Istanbul University are among the most frequent gatherers at the café, so prices are not high, people-watching is interesting, and the quiet, shady spot is a great place to rest weary feet.

7. In Aksaray

The square itself and side streets in Aksaray are packed with little eateries of all types, so finding a suitable place for any meal is not difficult at all. It's a good area for exploring on your own, but to start you off, here are a few suggestions.

By far the most sought-out eatery near Aksaray is one with a long menu and an even longer name. It's the **Hacıbozanoğulları Kebapçı and Baklavacı,** at the corner of Laleli Caddesi and Ordu Caddesi (tel. 528-4492), across the street from the Laleli Cami. The decor is modern and the big room is crowded with tables and chairs to handle the enthusiastic lunchtime crowds which come for a meal of kebap, served many ways, from 400TL (56¢) for a small portion; yufka, the paper-thin flat bread of the Anatolian peasant; and iced ayran, a drink made from mixing drained yogurt with fresh spring water. Pide, a leavened flat bread, is served as well, and all these breads are baked right in the restaurant's own bakery in the rear. For dessert you must have baklava, of course, for about 700TL ($1) per serving: *cevizli* means it's made with walnuts. *Şam fıstıklı* is with pistachios, *kaymaklı* is with clotted cream. Go the whole way and have their Spesyal Kebap (a mixed assortment), flat bread, ayran, a salad, and baklava, and the bill will be 4,500TL ($6.30). Take it easy and you can eat for half that.

For a restaurant with lots of ready food, not just kebaps, try the **Kardeşler Restaurant,** Ordu Caddesi 202, at the corner of Büyük Reşit Paşa Caddesi. You'd expect an eatery in which you can have a full meal for under 2,000TL ($2.80) to be somewhat rundown, but this one is just the opposite, with its brass and marble accents, bright lights, and a hungry but not wealthy student clientele. It's convenient to most Laleli hotels, and is open for all three meals, every day of the week.

8. The Seafood Restaurants of Kumkapı

The district of Kumkapı (Sand Gate), about half a mile due south of Beyazıt Square, is filled with fishermen who enjoy living in one of Istanbul's most colorful and interesting neighborhoods. Where there are fishermen, you'll find fish restaurants. As a fish dinner, even in a modest restaurant, has become something of a luxury for Turks, you can expect to pay more for a dinner here than at a kebapçı or even in a nice restaurant. But the fish here is fresh and delicious, and if you're willing to spend 5,500TL ($7.70) to 7,000TL ($10) per person for a full dinner with wine or beer, by all means come.

Among the best things to order in a Kumkapı restaurant is kılıç şiş (swordfish shish kebap), skewered chunks of fresh swordfish, charcoal-grilled. Another good choice is fish poached with vegetables (buğlama), but you can get simple pan-fried fish, and as an appetizer, pickled fish, if you'd rather. The price for your dinner will depend on how much you eat, which fish you order, and whether or not that fish is in season. For the least expensive fish, ask for the *mevsimli* (seasonal) ones, and choose from among them.

To get to Kumkapı, start from the Beyazıt Camii in Beyazıt Square, cross Yeniçeriler Caddesi, and walk down Tiyatro Caddesi ten short blocks. If you come by cab, figure to pay 1,200TL ($1.75) from Sultanahmet. Or you can take a *banliyö* train from Sirkeci Station around Seraglio Point, getting off at Kumkapı, the second stop. The fare is a mere 70TL (10¢).

Kumkapı has several dozen seafood restaurants, many ranged along Ördekli Bakkal Sokak, the street between the train station and the main square, and others in the narrow streets radiating from the square. Among the best of the restaurants is the one named **Kemal.** Another good choice is **Minas,** Samsa Sokak 7 (tel. 522-9646), right on the main square. An informal establishment despite its lace curtains and white tablecloths, it gives you a good view of the activity in the square.

9. Along the Bosphorus Shores

If you have the time, you must have at least one meal, lunch or dinner, at a restaurant on the shores of the Bosphorus. To sit in a restaurant and dine on fish or a freshly grilled kebap, sip cool white wine or cold beer, and watch the ship traffic on the aquatic highway is one of this city's greatest pleasures. To do it right can be cheap or expensive, as you wish, but even the most lavish places charge refreshingly moderate prices.

A FERRY RIDE: You can make a special trip one evening to have dinner, or you can combine a ferry cruise on the Bosphorus with lunch at a shore restaurant. For instance, take a morning ferry cruise up the Bosphorus as far as **Yeniköy,** on the European shore. Debark at Yeniköy, and right next to the ferry dock are several small restaurants where you can have an inexpensive lunch before heading south by bus and dolmush to see the fortress of Rumeli Hisar.

TARABYA: For dinner, a good suggestion is to take a bus, cab, or ferry as far north as **Tarabya,** a town which has served as a "let's get out of the city" summer resort for Istanbullus since Byzantine times. Today the small cove here is lined with nothing but restaurants, most serving seafood, many offering live entertainment (which you may or may not want), and all charging moderate prices in the range of 5,000TL ($7) to 8,000TL ($11.20) for a full meal, with wine.

THE TRADITIONAL FAVORITE: Perhaps the most famous and respected of Bosphorus restaurants is not on the shore, but overlooking the Bosphorus from a perch among the hills above the town of Emirgan. The **Abdullah Lokantası,** Koru Caddesi 11 (tel. 163-6406), was founded about a century ago but has been at this idyllic location, in the midst of the gardens whence come most of the vegetables served here, for less than half that time.

The dining room is a modernish, stylized chalet which you must reach by taxi. From Taksim, allow 30 to 45 minutes for the ride. The restaurant is open for lunch (noon to 3 p.m.) and dinner (8 p.m. to midnight) every day. Call for reservations before setting out on this expedition.

The cuisine is Turkish with continental accents: the menu offers grilled lamb and sturgeon, börek, and caviar. Try some of the Turkish dishes not often found on restaurant menus, such as mantı, a lamb ravioli in a light yogurt sauce. You can expect to pay 8,000TL ($11.20) to 10,000TL ($14) per person for lunch or dinner here, all included.

THE KHEDIVE'S VILLA: Matching, even exceeding, the location and service of Abdullah (if not the food), is the dining room in the **Hidiv Kasrı,** perched on a hilltop above the village of Çubuklu (tel. 331-2651), on the Asian shore. For a description of the Khedive's Villa, see above in Chapter IV, then call and make reservations before getting a taxi for the 40-minute, 5,500TL ($7.70) ride.

A string trio playing graceful '30s ditties entertains diners in the semicircular dining room on most evenings. The menu here sticks to traditional Turkish dishes such as kebaps, lamb chops, small beef steaks, and those inventive vegetable plates. The food is good and the service attentive; the villa itself, the view, and the grounds are unforgettable. You can expect to pay about 7,500TL

($10.50) per person for a meal. Don't forget to add in the round-trip taxi fare to your calculations. You may want to make a deal with the driver and have him wait to take you back after dinner. This is not as extravagant as it sounds, and it's very convenient.

CHEAPER AND CLOSER: For a cheaper, less formal, more conveniently located place, try the **Kaptan Restaurant,** Birinci Caddesi 53 (tel. 165-8487), on the shore road in the village of Arnavutköy. This is a small, simple place with indoor tables and a terrace with a Bosphorus view. As you enter from the street, choose from the salads and hors d'oeuvres in the refrigerator cases by the kitchen; select a fish to be grilled, fried, or poached; order a bottle of cold white wine (try Doluca, particularly the Riesling, or a Kavaklıdere)—then settle in to enjoy the view and some good conversation. A full meal of fish, fried potatoes, eggplant salad, white sheep's-milk cheese, puffy böreks, and fruit for dessert, should cost no more than 4,500TL ($6.30) per person. Note that the Kaptan is popular, and thus is crowded by 7:30 p.m. every evening of the week. Plan to arrive before 7 p.m. if you want one of the seaside tables.

Chapter VI

SEEING THE SIGHTS IN ISTANBUL

ISTANBUL IS PACKED with curious sights, people, and situations. Those at the ends of dark passageways or in forgotten corners you'll certainly find for yourself. As for the "big" sights—well, the city seems as though it was designed for sightseeing. Spend your first few days in the area around Sultanahmet Square in the Old City, and you'll find Topkapı Palace, Sancta Sophia, the Blue Mosque, the Hippodrome, Yerebatan Saray (the "Cistern Basilica"), the Turkish and Islamic Arts Museum, the Archeological Museum, and Gülhane Park—in short, most of the major sights in Istanbul, all within a few minutes' walk from the bus stop in the square.

If you plan to see the sights on your own, one of the best buses is the T-4, which, like the T-1, runs a circle route around the old and new cities from Taksim to Dolmabahçe. Karaköy, Eminönü, Sultanahmet, and Hürriyet (Beyazıt) Square. After the bus station at Hürriyet, the trip continues through Aksaray, Unkapanı, across the Atatürk Bridge to Şişhane, Tünel, Galatasaray, and then back to Taksim. The T-4 bus runs in this direction, the T-1 in the opposite direction.

Istanbul's tour companies operate numerous tours of the city's sights, and prices are low to moderate. Most companies offer good value-for-the-money. If you are daunted by the thought of getting acquainted with this vast and bustling city on your own, you might want the help of a guided tour. If not, then head out on your own. The best way to start is with two once-over-lightly walking tours, described below.

1. Two Walking Tours

No method of exploration better acquaints you with a city than strolling along its streets. The first tour below takes you through the newer part of the city, from Taksim Square to Karaköy and the Galata Bridge. The second one continues where the first leaves off, and takes you from the southern foot of the Galata Bridge in Eminönü Square up past the major sights of old Istanbul, by the Grand Bazaar, and to the modern nexus of Aksaray Square.

Whether you take a tour, hire a guide, or do it all alone, you might want to pick up a copy of *Strolling Through Istanbul*, by Hilary Sumner-Boyd and John Freely, an excellent and very detailed guide to the archeological and architectural treasures of the city. Published by the Redhouse Press in Istanbul, it is on sale in every bookstore, many hotels, and in postcard stalls in Topkapı Palace, Sancta Sophia, and similar places.

FROM TAKSİM TO KARAKÖY: The center of modern Istanbul is Taksim Square. Besides being a good area for restaurants and some hotels, as we've seen, Taksim is also the best starting point for orientation walks around this part of the city. Leave Taksim, gamble with your life crossing the traffic circle (the spirit for both drivers and pedestrians in Turkey is that of a grand free-for-all) and walk down İstiklal Caddesi. Though this street was once the main street in Pera, it's now called upon to be one of İstanbul's most important thoroughfares —like a Fifth Avenue—although it's woefully narrow for such a big job. On your right is a former French hospital now used as the French Consulate; behind the shops on your left is a huge Orthodox church, and next to it an Armenian school. Strolling along, you pass rows of little eateries: restaurants, places specializing in kebaps or işkembe çorbası (tripe soup), a favorite dish among Turks, said to cure a hangover. Some places advertise kuru yemiş (dried fruits); they are the lifeblood of İstiklal, for it's a favorite place for a stroll, and Turks don't stroll without something to munch on. All sorts of nuts (even shelled pistachios), apricot paste pressed into sheets and dried (pestil), dates, figs, chocolate, and Turkish Delight (lokum) are on sale. A hundred grams of nuts, plenty for a walk, will cost anywhere from 20¢ (peanuts) to 70¢ (pistachios). Buying and selling prices are always displayed (prices are by the kilo).

Soon you'll come to a small mosque on your right. The **Ağa Camii,** or "Noble's Mosque." Although no loudspeaker burdens its minaret, there is one— alas!—in the nearby tree. (I once saw a muezzin stand out on a minaret, microphone in hand, and give the call as if recording a ballad.)

Just before coming to the bend in the road at **Galatasaray Square,** walk on the right side of the street and turn into a passageway at no. 172, immediately before the little open-air market street. This is the **Çiçek Pasajı,** or Flower Passage, crowded with beerhalls, taxi drivers, boys selling American cigarettes at inflated prices, and—at the end of the passage, in the market—flowers. Some of the best inexpensive fish restaurants in Istanbul are here in the Pasaj, and most have rooms downstairs (or upstairs), out of the constant brouhaha. In summer, if the crowds aren't too great, sit outside at a barrel covered with a slab of marble and see what fish is in season. For a snack, try mussels fried on a stick from one of the numerous stands, and a glass of beer, either dark (siyah) or light (beyaz). Raw mussels, fried fish, grilled lamb's intestines (called kokereç) are also on sale, if you're hungry enough. Turn the corner in the Pasaj and leave, but look at the inscription over the doorway: "Cité de Pera." This building was once the city hall of the European community in Constantinople.

Walk up through the market. Flowers are considered by the Turks as one of God's greatest gifts to man, and are bought, worn, or displayed on the slightest pretext. In fact, Holland's famous tulips came from Turkey in the 1500s. A short distance from the doorway into the Çiçek Pasajı, on the same side, another huge doorway leads into a hidden square and a big Armenian church, typical of the surprises to be found in the dark corners of the city. Walk back down toward İstiklal, but turn right before you come to it, into the **Aynalı Çarşı,** or **Avrupa Pasajı,** a marble-paved passage with walls lined with statuary and small shops. The shops sell mostly dressmakers' goods, flowers, perfumes, and so forth. At the end of the passage, a turn to the right will take you past the British Consulate, one of the huge old embassy compounds built a century or more ago. Follow **Meşrutiyet Caddesi** around the corner to the left to go to **Tepebası,** the one-time hotel center of Istanbul, the Pera Palas Hotel, the American Consulate, and a fine view of the Golden Horn. Or from the passage entrance, turn left to get back to İstiklal at Galatasaray Square.

In Galatasaray Square, the road turns in front of massive gates sealing off a proportionately massive building. When I first saw this place all sorts of questions passed through my mind: Whose palace was it? What was his (or her) relationship to the sultan? I discovered from a Turkish friend that **Galata Sarayı,** or Galata Palace, has always been what it is today: a Turkish- and French-language high school.

On the lower part of İstiklal there are similar surprises. An Orthodox church at the end of a passageway, a quaint old square hidden back among Greek tailors' shops (enter at no. 222), an Italian basilica, a Spanish chapel hidden down a flight of stairs, a tiny church nestled at the foot of a modern office building. On the left side of the street are three more of the huge consulates that were built in the 1800s not simply as consulates, but as estates to house the embassies from the capitals of Europe to the Ottoman sultan. Since the capital was moved to Ankara, they're kept up as consulates and cultural centers. I've heard that many foreign governments which own such big old places wouldn't mind getting rid of them, mostly because of large upkeep costs. But since they were originally presented to them by the sultan, no one's sure who owns them now, or how they should be sold. For a good look at the best of these, turn left down **Postacılar Sokak,** which brings you into a square between the Palace of France and the Palace of Venice (the Italian Consulate), little changed since the middle of the last century. Walk back up the hill to **İstiklal.**

At the end of the avenue the surprises continue, for if you keep going straight rather than turning with the street, you'll pass the **Tekke,** or whirling dervish monastery, on your left. Dervishes were banned at the beginning of the republic, and now perform only once a year, in December, in Konya. This tekke is now a museum. Past the Tekke are old bookshops and silversmiths' shops run by French-speaking proprietors, and part of the way down the hill the road passes the **Galata Tower.**

The Galata Tower was built by the Genoese in the Middle Ages to be part of the city wall system. It's been rebuilt and refurbished many times since then, and has been used as a prison and fire lookout. Several decades ago it was completely redone, fitted out with an elevator, restaurant, nightclub, souvenir shops, and so on, and you now pay 700TL ($1) for a look at the view.

To get back to Taksim Square, walk to İstiklal Caddesi, and catch any bus in front of the subway station in **Tünel Square.**

If you're going to continue your walk, here's your chance to try Istanbul's **Tünel,** a small two-station subway which takes people between Karaköy, at the foot of the Galata Bridge, and Tünel Square, at the end of İstiklal Caddesi. The subway was built in 1873 by a French company, and until a few years ago still had the beautiful old lacquered wooden cars, kept in amazingly good repair. But the craze for modernization hit the Tünel; the cars are now rubber-tired copies of the Paris Métro, and the Karaköy station, once a quaint Swiss chalet, is now a big concrete box. The Tünel is still the quickest way up or down the hill, and in summer the coolest as well. It operates from 7 a.m. to 9 p.m. weekdays, 7:30 a.m. to 10 p.m. on Sunday.

At the bottom of the hill, down from the Galata Tower, is the section of the city formerly known as Galata, now called **Karaköy.** The Galata Bridge running across the Golden Horn from Karaköy to Eminönü is one of the busiest places in town, except at 4:15 a.m., when the center section of the bridge is removed to let ships enter and leave the Horn. Don't be alarmed if you feel a bit unsteady while walking across the bridge, because it's moving just as much as you are. The entire bridge floats on huge pontoons, and rocks like a ship whenever it's hit by waves. The new bridge, now under construction, will be more solid. The view from the bridge is one of the best in Istanbul, especially at sunset or dusk. Looking toward Asia, the lights in the city across the Bosphorus twinkle under the flood of light from a full moon, the gleaming white ferries ply back and forth, swinging their powerful spotlights across the water, now on a fisherman in a tiny boat, now on the docks or the bridge, and the pleasure kiosks of the sultans, lit up on the hill of the Seraglio, serve as a backdrop. As if this weren't enough to make you want to stay for weeks, turn around and look up the Golden Horn. The Golden Horn was once lined with palaces, kiosks, and pleasure gardens; then both its banks were covered with dingy docks, marine repair shops, and such things. But now it has been cleaned up, and at sunset, during the proper time of the year, the sun sinks into the end of the Horn and spreads its light over the length of the water, turning it to gold. Above the water on the left, dominating the scene from its hilltop is the grandest mosque in all of Istanbul, the one built by and named for Sultan Süleyman the Magnificent.

FROM EMİNÖNÜ TO AKSARAY: On the other side of the Galata Bridge is the Old City, the part in which the sultan and his government lived and worked. Eminönü Square, a major stop for municipal buses, is dominated by the New Mosque (**Yeni Cami**), a scant 300 years old. Beside it is the Egyptian Bazaar (**Mısır Çarşısı**), also called the Spice Bazaar because the shops used to sell only spices and condiments. Now other things are sold as well, but the predominance is still in the condiment line, and you can still get frankincense (**Çam sakızı**) for about $8 a pound. Outside the market in the little park are the public scribes who type letters and official documents for those who cannot write or those who know only the Arabic alphabet (Turkish script was changed from the Arabic to the Latin alphabet in 1928). When the document is finished, it will be "signed" with a metal seal by the person who commissioned it. Seals are on sale here too.

Go back to Eminönü Square and walk along the ferry docks until the road curves, passing Sirkeci Station. Behind the station, a rather dingy street called **Muradiye-Hüdavendigar Caddesi** leads to a road beside the Seraglio walls, **Alemdar Caddesi.** You can take a trolleybus through this section if you don't feel like walking. Catch any trolleybus running past the station away from the water. They all pass Sultanahmet Square.

Soon you come in to the **Alay Kiosk** on the left, an imperial parlor built right into the walls so the sultan could review *alays,* the festive carnival-like processions of trade guilds that took place on holidays or after military victories. The sultan's sentries also kept an eye on the comings and goings of government leaders, for right across the street is the famous **Sublime Porte,** the gateway which gave its name to the Ottoman government. The central government buildings and the Grand Vizier's offices and residence were behind it. A few steps more bring you to the entrance of **Gülhane Park,** once the Topkapı Palace park, now open to the public, complete with a little zoo, an aquarium, and a picnic area.

If you have time, try this detour: Walk through the wall into the Gülhane Park area, but instead of paying and entering the park by the gate on the left, walk up the road on the right. Halfway up the hill is one of Istanbul's biggest concentrations of museums, including the **Tiled Kiosk (Çinili Köşk),** the **Museum of Oriental Antiquities,** and the **Archeological Museum.** Continuing up the hill on the same road, you'll come to the first courtyard of **Topkapı Palace** (no entrance fee for this courtyard). There's a good view of the Bosphorus and the Sea of Marmara from here. The city's oldest church, Aya İrini, is in this courtyard. Walk through the large gate through the palace walls to get to Sancta Sophia and the charming little Fountain of Sultan Ahmet III. Just outside this gate, look to your right at the Sultan's Gate to Sancta Sophia, built while the building was serving as a mosque.

Covering the First Hill of the city are some of Istanbul's biggest tourist attractions. Sultanahmet Square is the center of this area, and used to be the center of the city's largest hippie colony. All of the big sights are grouped around the one-time center of power, the area in which the Byzantine and Ottoman emperors lived. Spread across the end of the peninsula are the Big Three that you must see first: **Topkapı Palace, Sancta Sophia,** and the **Blue Mosque.** In front of the last two is the wide promenade still called the **Hippodrome,** after its use during imperial times. **Divan Yolu** is the main avenue going past the Hippodrome and up the Second Hill.

Walk up Divan Yolu to the **Çemberlitaş** (or Burnt Column), a monumental column built by Constantine the Great in A.D. 325, and one of the oldest structures in the city. During the time of the Ottoman Empire there was a legend which went that Turkish sovereignty in Europe would come to an end when this column toppled. The column, apparently, was not in on the legend, and failed to keep the appointment. Turn right just before the column and walk down the street to the entrance to the grounds of the **Nuruosmaniye Mosque.** Walk through the grounds to get to the **Grand Bazaar (Kapalı Çarşı).**

Divan Yolu changes names to **Yeniçeriler Caddesi,** then to **Ordu Caddesi,** as it makes its way toward Aksaray Square. In the section called **Laleli,** on the right side of the street, is the **Laleli Cami,** or Tulip Mosque. Shortly after passing the mosque, you enter Aksaray Square.

2. Topkapı Palace

First stop on any visitor's sightseeing list is where the Ottoman sultans, their dozens of women, and their hundreds of servants lived and worked. Find the nearest stop for a dolmush or for the T-1 and T-4 circle-route buses, and head first for Topkapı Palace, the ancient Seraglio, one of the most romantic palaces in the world. Keep in mind that there is a gate in the city walls called Topkapı, and that any bus, minibus, or dolmush bearing the legend "Topkapı" will be going there, which is miles from the palace. You want to find a bus or dolmush to Sultanahmet Square.

TOPKAPI—AN INTRODUCTION: Part of the Turkish heritage is a love of fresh air, and Topkapı Palace, the official residence of the Turkish sultans for centuries, is a very open-air sort of place. The extensive system of walls and gates makes it a veritable fortress, the kind of fortified enclosure the Turks built at Rumeli Hisar on the Bosphorus and Yedikule on the Sea of Marmara, then camped inside under the stars. As for the sultan, he kept the outdoors as a daytime activity and found better things to do at night. The palace is therefore a collection of smaller buildings: service buildings, quarters for the thousands of people who lived there and served the sultan. There was a special building for each purpose: for meeting with the Divan (cabinet), for receiving foreign diplomats, for relaxation, and, of course, the Harem—all of these rooms scattered among open courtyards and gardens. From Sultanahmet Square, walk around to the right of Sancta Sophia and behind it, past the charming fountain of Sultan Ahmet III, to get to the first of the palace gates.

Topkapı Palace is open every day except Tuesday from 9:30 a.m. to 5 p.m. (to 7 p.m. in July and August). Entrance is 1,000TL ($1.40); separate entrance fee to the Harem, 500TL (70¢). Admission costs only half as much on Sunday and holidays.

THE FIRST COURTYARD: The first, or **Imperial Gate,** separated the outside world from the special world of the palace. Inside the first gate a large courtyard used to be a scene busy with Janissaries, woodcutters, and companies of guards. The ancient **Church of Aya İrini,** to the left of the roadway, has foundations dating from the time of Byzance, that is, before the founding of Constantinople. It's been repaired and rebuilt many times. In 381 the Second Ecumenical Council met here to reaffirm the Nicene Creed. After the conquest and the construction of Topkapı Palace, it was used for storage of weapons needed by the palace.

The church is now almost devoid of ornament, the glittering mosaics and colorful patterned marble slabs having been removed for use elsewhere. But the bareness of the interior makes the visitor more aware of the design and acoustics of the church, and seems to add to, rather than detract from, the sacred atmosphere. It's one of the most peaceful, cool places in the city, except when the Istanbul Festival is in progress and recitals are held in the ancient building.

THE SECOND COURTYARD: The **Gate of Salvation,** or middle gate, leads into the palace proper, but before buying your ticket, take a look at the little fountain to the right of the gate, where the executioner washed his equipment after doing his duty to condemned prisoners. Through the gate, on the wall to the right, is a fine map of the palace and grounds.

Head toward the old **palace kitchens,** where the museum's fabulous collection of Oriental porcelain is displayed. The range goes from ancient Chinese ware, through pieces obtained as booty or as gifts from the crowned heads of Europe, to Istanbul porcelain and glass made around the turn of the century. One of the rooms of the old kitchen has been left with the original implements so you can see how the servants' food was prepared. (The sultan didn't eat this institutional food, but had his prepared in a small kitchen elsewhere.) The palace kitchens prepared food for an average of 2,500 people a day, all of whom worked or lived in the palace, and on festival days the cooks might have to satisfy 5,000. By the way, the only person allowed to be on horseback in this second court was the sultan himself, and on a few special occasions, his mother. Everyone else had to walk.

The **Kübbealtı,** or Council Chamber, was the official meeting place of the Divan, or State Council, and the sultan would listen to the debates through a little grilled window. A road going downhill to the right near the middle gate leads to an exhibition of the imperial carriages.

THE HAREM: Perhaps the most famous part of the palace is the **Harem,** now open after years and years of restoration work. Only a fraction of the Harem's 400 rooms are on display, but these give a good picture of what life was like for the women and imperial children who lived there. The entrance is near the Council Chamber, tours are in groups led by a guide only, and there's an additional charge of 500TL (70¢) for those who wish the visit.

The guides vary in quality from very good to pretty awful, so to help you understand the things you'll see, here's a short synopsis. The first room you enter was a guard room, as the gate you've just passed through was a "tradesmen's entrance" to which women selling luxury goods would come in hopes of having the sultan's ladies buy their wares.

In the second room you enter (don't speed right through), notice the wonderful tiles with rarely seen greens and whites. The beautiful tiles from the kilns of İznik (Nicaea) are one of the triumphs of Ottoman art, and are spread liberally throughout the palace. The black eunuchs' quarters is a small suite of rooms (all so tiny!) where these "guardians of the sultan's greatest treasure" lived. Those in training lived at the top, while the comparatively larger and more beautifully furnished rooms on the ground floor were reserved for the bigwigs. The chief black eunuch was a high minister of state ranking in importance with the Grand Vizier.

The guide's fourth stop is in the chief wives' apartments (there were four), the fifth stop in the Valide Sultan's ("Queen Mother") apartment. The sixth stop is the sultan's Turkish bath, the next an 18th-century reception room complete with Dutch tiles (to fit the decor) and a fantastically horrible armchair with lion's-paw legs and an eagle back that was given to the sultan by Kaiser Wilhelm II. The guide's eighth speech is delivered in a lovely room with a fountain decorated by Murad III and used as his "privy chamber." The fountain's soothing sound would blot out any conversation between the sultan and a confidant to a potential eavesdropper. (It's a wonder modern politicians, concerned with "leaks," haven't thought of this!) The next stop is the library-study and the dining room, decorated by Ahmed I in the 17th century. (Note the appetizing fruit-bowl paintings on the walls.) Following this you will visit the suite of rooms often referred to as "the Cage," where the heir to the throne was raised in luxurious imprisonment, far from the outside world where he might pose a threat to the ruling monarch. The dome of this room, the Veliaht Dairesi, is made of leather, and the windows have quaint little fountains in them. The tour of the Harem is over soon after you leave this room.

THE THIRD COURTYARD: The third gate, the **Gate of Felicity,** leads into the part of the palace reserved for the sultan, his harem, and his immediate attendants. Other than these few, only the highest officials were allowed to enter, and very few of these were allowed past the **Arz Odası** (Audience Chamber), the rich, ornate little kiosk just inside the gate. Upon the death of a sultan, his successor would sit before the Gate of Felicity on a golden throne (now in the Treasury) to receive the congratulations and pledges of fealty from the high and low of the empire (mostly high). For receiving foreign ambassadors, the sultan used the Arz Odası. He sat on a divan covered with seed pearls (someone has estimated there are at least 15,000) while the ambassador was led up to him held by two attendants. Meanwhile the presents the ambassador had brought would be paraded by a small doorway to the left so that the sultan could judge whether he was worthy of good favor. All conversation was through an interpreter, even if the ambassador spoke Turkish or the sultan spoke French—no need to soil the Imperial Ears with common talk! It was traditional for the sultan to arrange audiences for days when the Janissaries were to be paid so that the ambassador could be suitably impressed by these fierce soldiers dressed in cloth of gold and silver and paid out of tremendous sacks of coins dragged in for the purpose.

This is my favorite part of the palace, and best shows what it was like to live a sultan's life. To the right of the Arz Odası are the exhibits of costumes, ranging from the early Oriental caftans to 19th-century gold-and-braid uniforms, and the world-famous **Treasury.** About the Treasury I needn't say much—you'll see. Thrones with thousands of jewels, mother-of-pearl, and tortoise shell; emeralds weighed in pounds; medals, fabulous jewelry of every description, and the famous dagger shown in the film *Topkapi* (which is not stored in the palace tower, as in the film, but in a display case in the Treasury like every other valuable item). Don't miss the Spoonmaker's Diamond, 84 karats of stone that put on a fine light show.

A favorite exhibit of mine in this section of the palace is the **Sâyebân,** the sultan's pavilion, a sort of tent of tremendous proportions, heavily embroidered and designed to make the monarch look as imposing as possible. The tent was carried on the yearly military campaign into the Balkans, and would be set up whenever the sultan had need of an audience chamber.

At the far end of the palace is the place where the greatest and richest rulers built their own pleasure kiosks, calling on their vast empire's best artists to do the work. In these rich miniature palaces they would while away the cool summer evenings on a sofa, smoking a water pipe and watching girls from the Harem dance or listening to them play, with the imperial city spread out below them, its vulgar noises drowned by the sounds of nearby fountains. The views from this part of the palace, especially from the little gold-topped shelter called the **Arbor of İftar** and from the promenade behind the **Yeni Köşk** (Abdul Mecid's Kiosk) are the best in the palace. Don't miss the beautiful tiles on the walls in parts of this area, nor the old, curious grandfather clock built into an outside wall—like the ones seen in mosques to tell people the time for prayer.

Below the Yeni Köşk (enter through the front door of the köşk) is a fairly expensive—but not unreasonable—restaurant run by the management of the Konyalı Restaurant. (See Chapter V for details.)

On your way back through the palace, you'll see exhibits of embroidery, weapons, ceramics, seals, and the priceless **Relics of the Prophet Mohammed** (his robe, a tooth, a hair from his beard, a letter) kept in one of the prettiest suites of rooms in the palace.

3. Sancta Sophia and the Blue Mosque

Bordering the Hippodrome are two of the grandest religious edifices in the world, competing for your attention. Coming from Topkapı Palace, stop at Sancta Sophia first.

SANCTA SOPHIA: Dominating the area of the Hippodrome is the massive pale-yellow Church of Sancta Sophia (in Turkish, Aya Sofya), built in the 6th century as the grandest cathedral in Christendom, later converted to a mosque. In 1935 all religious character was removed and it became a museum.

The original construction was the work of the Emperor Justinian, one of Byzantium's most famous rulers for three reasons: the reconquest of much of the Roman Empire that had been lost to barbarians, the building of Sancta Sophia, and the bankrupting of the empire. The cathedral was one of his grandest construction projects and contributed greatly to the latter. Construction was finished in 548, and the emperor inaugurated the church as the "Eye of the Universe" by entering and exclaiming, "Oh Solomon, I have outdone thee!" Since then the building has changed considerably. The dome, reaching a height of 180 feet from the ground, has no visible support but the walls. Even though it was originally built of extra-light bricks manufactured in Rhodes specifically for the purpose, the dome has fallen several times. In fact, the original shape of the building is hard to see because of the buttresses, foundations, and supports that have been added on the outside during the last 1,400 years in order to support the dome.

At the gate, admission tickets are on sale for 1,000TL ($1.40), half price on Sunday and holidays. Hours are 9:30 a.m. to 4:30 p.m. (to 7 p.m. in July and August) every day except Monday.

Once you're inside, don't miss the mosaic over the first doorway you come to, one of the best-preserved mosaics in the museum (even better than those in the gallery). As you enter the narthex, there are rows of doors on either side. On the left are the doors to the outside—these were the original front doors to the church. On your right, the doors into the sanctuary include a huge central one for the exclusive use of the emperor. Note the holes made by the feet of his guards, standing by the doors over the centuries, just inside the threshold. Again, don't miss the mosaics over these doors.

To appreciate the architects' genius, enter the great church slowly, looking through the emperor's Imperial Door into the sanctuary. Walk slowly and notice the first semi-dome open above, then another semi-dome, then the great dome held, as it were, "by a great chain suspended from heaven." St. Peter's in Rome is the only church which comes to mind for comparison, but remember that Sancta Sophia is 1,000 years older.

The feeling of great age and history is all around. Mosaics of saints look down from high above; there's a special loge for the sultan which he could enter and leave without being seen; the mihrab (prayer niche) is not centered in the apse because it must point directly toward Mecca; imagine what it must have been like with all of the cup-like glass oil lamps lit, in the chandeliers, on the walls, around the dome; clap your hands and listen to the sound echo through the room for minutes.

Upstairs in the gallery are a few more mosaics, some of which are mere fragments of the originals. The best of these are along the gallery on the right side of the building as you face the altar. Most of the restoration work done to the mosaics was sponsored by the American Association for the Preservation of Byzantine Monuments, to which I offer profound thanks. The most interesting mosaics are the ones right at the end of the gallery, against the front walls of the building. Here you see the Empress Zoë on one side, her husband on the other. Look closely and you'll see that the husband's picture does not look like the original one. Zoë had a number of husbands, and had the mosaic changed every time she married, just to keep things in order.

In the courtyard outside of the buildings are signs pointing to the **Tombs of Selim II and Murad III,** pretty tiled mausolea reputedly built by the great architect Sinan about 1577. The little coffins are of the sultan's progeny, laid to rest with him as they followed.

THE BLUE MOSQUE: Literally a stone's throw away from Sancta Sophia is the magnificent Blue Mosque, the **Mosque of Sultan Ahmet I,** built during ten years of work at the beginning of the 17th century. The sultan wanted his mosque to rival, if not surpass, the glory of Sancta Sophia, so he built it where all could compare the two. The Blue Mosque wins by a mile, but only because the comparison is grossly unfair. The 350-year-old mosque is a young upstart compared to its ancient neighbor.

From the outside the mosque is a delight to look at. Get the full effect by entering through the front gates, just off the Hippodrome by the Egyptian obelisk. The rich geometric designs are the work of Muslim artists, who were forbidden to portray animals of any kind. Go through the courtyard with the fountain where Muslims are obliged to wash hands and feet before prayer, and then take off your shoes before stepping on the mosque's precious carpets. For women whose clothing doesn't meet strict standards (long skirts, sleeves, scarfs, etc.) there are robes available at the entrance, free of charge.

Inside you'll see that the Blue Mosque gets its name from over 21,000 pieces of faïence with which the walls are covered. The many windows, the painting on the ceiling, and the color of the tiles give the mosque an airy quality that's ruined only partially by the massive pillars the architect found necessary to hold up the dome (compare the architecture of Sancta Sophia). Also notice the grandfather clock against one of the pillars. There's not a mosque in Turkey that doesn't have a clock of some kind in it; most have the tall old grandfather clocks, their faces still dotted with the old Arabic characters. The original stained-glass windows have long since gone, along with the knowledge of how they were made, but the modern replacements do not lose the colorful effect altogether.

On the way out, notice the ramp to the right of the "tourists' entrance." There's a story that Sultan Ahmet had a ramp rather than steps built here so he could ride his horse all the way up to the door of the Imperial Box in the mosque. The six minarets of the Blue Mosque caused some consternation in the Muslim world for a while, especially in Mecca, where local Muslims forced the sultan to add another minaret to the six of the Elharam Mosque's collection so that this very holy place would not be outdone.

4. In and Around the Hippodrome

To appreciate the historical and cultural importance of the Hippodrome (At Meydanı in Turkish), take a short walking tour, starting from the Cistern Basilica, then heading south almost to the Sea of Marmara's shore.

THE CISTERN BASILICA: Across the street from Sancta Sophia, under a little park on Divan Yolu, is the Cistern Basilica (**Yerebatan Saray** in Turkish—the Sunken Palace). The entrance is through a little stone building on Yerebatan Caddesi just where it joins Divan Yolu. For 250TL (35¢) you can walk downstairs and out onto a platform built above the water. Try to remember the scene from the film *From Russia With Love,* where the action is in a boat floating toward a periscope through an underground body of water. Filming for that part of the movie was done here, though there's no longer any periscope and the Russian Consulate is in Beyoğlu. The view of this cistern, built by Justinian, with its 336 columns, is well worth the small amount you must pay to get in. Open from 9:30 a.m. to 4:30 p.m. every day except Tuesday.

THE HIPPODROME: Outside again, walk across Divan Yolu and down the street which separates the Blue Mosque from the obelisks on the mall. The mall is really the old Hippodrome, one of the oldest constructions in the city, dating from before the time of Constantine. The first object you pass is a fountain presented by Kaiser Wilhelm II of Germany to Sultan Abdul Hamid II. Next, one of the most interesting decorations in the Hippodrome, an **obelisk** dating from the 15th century B.C., originally in Egypt, brought to Constantinople by the Emperor Theodosius—his figure is carved on the pedestal which supports the obelisk—and erected in A.D. 390. The obelisk is thought to have been much taller than it now is, even three times as tall. It was commissioned by Thutmose III to commemorate his conquest of Syria.

Beside the obelisk is the **Serpentine Column,** another of the city's oldest monuments, also pilfered from a temple, this time from Delphi, where it had stood since the 5th century B.C. until Constantine brought it to the city. Originally it was higher, and had three snakes' heads at the top.

The last monument in the Hippodrome is the **Obelisk of Constantine,** a rough stone column once covered with bronze plates. The bronze disappeared a long time ago, probably going the way of all valuable metals in a declining empire: made into cannons and coins. Another story goes that the Crusaders, when they captured the city in 1204, thought that the obelisk was covered in gold, and fell over one another trying to get at it.

At any of these three monuments it is easy to see the original level of the Hippodrome, a few feet below the present surface. The filling-in took place during the reign of the sultans, who did not use it for the tournaments and races popular during the Byzantine era. But in both empires it was a popular place for political gatherings, especially those which ended with the deposition of the monarch.

THE TEXTILE MUSEUM: At the back of the Blue Mosque is the city's **Museum of Kilims and Flat-Woven Rugs** (Kilim ve Düz Dokuma Yaygılar Müzesi), open from 9:30 a.m. to 4:30 p.m. for a 200TL (28¢) admission; closed Monday. On the way in you may see a woven nomad's tent, fully furnished, the setting in which many of the kilims were made and used.

These stone-vaulted rooms beneath the great mosque are now filled with displays of Turkish nomad women's supreme expressions of folk art. Around the corner and up the ramp by the Blue Mosque is another section of the Textile Museum, the **Carpet Museum** (Halı Müzesi), with displays of napped carpets.

MUSEUM OF TURKISH AND ISLAMIC ARTS: Facing the Blue Mosque across the Hippodrome is the **Palace of İbrahim Pasha,** built in 1524 and considered at the time to be the most sumptuous private residence in the empire. İbrahim Pasha, its builder and occupant, was Süleyman the Magnificent's Grand Vizier, and also his son-in-law and confidant. The palace now houses the Türk ve İslam Eserleri Müzesi, the Museum of Turkish and Islamic Arts, open from 10 a.m. to 5 p.m. daily except Monday. Admission costs 300TL (42¢).

The historical exhibits on the upper floor date from the time just after the founding of Islam (A.D. 700s), and continue through the Ottoman Empire, which ended in 1923. You'll see here the most beautiful examples of Ottoman decorated wooden Koran holders and Koran stands, exhibits of calligraphy (one of the finest arts in Islam), Turkish miniatures, illuminated manuscripts, and fine antique Turkish carpets.

On the lower floor are ethnographic exhibits, including a black camel-hair nomadic tent, furnished with a nomad family's normal daily needs, and also with an explanation of the nomadic lifestyle, in English. This theme of direct observation is continued inside, where real-life displays show you all about carpet and kilim weaving in village homes, and the plants and materials used to make the natural dyes. There are furnished rooms from other homes as well: from a Central Asian felt hut, from a Turkish village house, and an Ottoman living room from a house in the city of Bursa.

SOKOLLU MEHMET PASHA MOSQUE: If you continue on past the Obelisk of Constantine, you'll go down the street called Mehmet Pasha Yokuşu; on the left is a mustard-colored building of the Industrial School. Bear right and two blocks down the hill on the left is the Sokollu Mehmet Pasha Mosque, surrounded on all sides by a wall. There are several entrances; the main one is on the southwest corner and can be reached by turning left when you enter the small square at the bottom of the hill. Walk up a flight of stairs to reach the courtyard and medrese. There will probably be no one around, in which case just remove your shoes (slippers are provided for your use) and have a look around. This is one of Sinan's smaller mosques and, I think, one of his more beautiful. It was built for the daughter of Selim II in 1571 and has a definitely feminine beauty, which is not seen in Sinan's other mosques. The wall around the mihrab is all of İznik tiles of very good quality; and with the flower-motif stained-glass windows against stark-white walls the whole effect is very light and gay.

The area around the mosque is small-town-like, and you will be able to see a bit of Turkish life: women crocheting, children playing, the milkman calling. All in all the atmosphere is very pleasant, dominated, it seems, by the cool presence of the mosque.

THE "LITTLE SANCTA SOPHIA" MOSQUE: From behind the Sokollu Mehmet Pasha Mosque, follow Kadırga Limanı Caddesi for a few short blocks to reach the Küçük Aya Sofya Camii, or **"Little Sancta Sophia" Mosque.** It started life as a small Byzantine church built by the Emperor Justinian and Empress Theodora, sometime between A.D. 527 and 536. The interior plan is typical of an early Byzantine church, though this building was repaired and modified during the Ottoman period. It was converted at the time of the Conquest in 1453, and later enlarged with the financial assistance of the sultan's chief white eunuch around the year 1500. The eunuch's tomb is to the left as you enter.

5. The Archeological Museums and Gülhane Park

To the west of Topkapı Palace, down the hill, is the palace park, named **Gülhane.** On your way to the museums, take a stroll in this shady refuge to escape the roaring buses and constant traffic on Alemdar Caddesi.

To reach Istanbul's group of archeological museums, leave the park but don't go outside the enclosing walls. Rather, turn left just before the gate in the walls, and walk up the cobbled slope toward Topkapı. The entrance to the museum complex is on the left. It's open from 9:30 a.m. to 5 p.m. daily (closed Monday off-season). At a booth to the right of the entrance you buy a ticket for 500TL (70¢), half price on weekends and holidays, which admits you to all three museums. As of this writing, the Çinili Kiosk is undergoing restoration and is open only on Tuesday. Also, the Oriental Antiquities Museum closes for lunch between noon and 1 p.m.

In the courtyard of the complex is a little café serving hot and cold drinks and snacks at tables among ancient columns, capitals, and statuary.

THE ARCHEOLOGICAL MUSEUM: The Archeological Museum houses a huge collection of statuary, inscription stones, sarcophagi, mosaics, and so forth, much of it displayed to advantage. Upon entering, go to your left and in the center of the first room notice the sarcophagus once thought to be that of Alexander the Great. It's in astoundingly good shape after being around for more than 2,000 years. In fact, some of the original paint is still on its figures. A diagram on the wall near the other doorway will show you how carefully the sarcophagus was buried, the reason for its fine preservation. In the other wing on the ground floor don't miss the sarcophagus of Tabnit, King of Sidon, with the king himself beside it. The sarcophagus looks almost brand-new. The king, after almost 3,000 years, does not. The king liked the sarcophagus so much that he dumped its former occupant out and had himself interred, and this is where he's been since the 6th century B.C.

ÇİNİLİ KIOSK: Across the courtyard from the Archeological Museum is the Çinili Kiosk, one of the first buildings to be built by the Turkish conquerors after they took the city. The whole building was once covered in the beautiful tiles that are now only on the front. Inside is an exhibition of Turkish tilework from the earliest İznik (Nicaea) tiles, in my opinion the best ever made in Turkey, to the contemporary ones made in Kütahya and on sale in the Grand Bazaar. It's a very nice little museum, the building as well as the collection.

ORIENTAL ANTIQUITIES MUSEUM: The third museum in this group is that of Oriental Antiquities (**Eski Şark Eserleri Müzesi**), a truly fascinating place filled with some of the most striking works of art and most important artifacts ever brought to light. For instance, the marvelous high-relief tiles of lions which graced the "Street Procession" scene and the Ishtar Gate in the Babylon of Neb-uchadnezzar II (604–562 B.C.) are here; you can inspect "working copies" of Hammurabi's Code, one of the ancient world's greatest advances in law (even though it stipulates "an eye for an eye"); there are Egyptian mummies, beautiful scarabs and "usbeti," statuettes, jewelry, engraved tablets, articles from Islamic South Arabia (Yemen), and from Assyria and the Hittite Empire. All of these items are attractively displayed in a completely remodeled museum.

6. Istanbul's Bazaars

Bazaars are to be found in every town of any size in Turkey. All are ar-ranged on the department-store plan with separate areas for clothing, jewelry, carpets, and so forth. The main difference is that, unlike department stores, ba-zaars are usually outside affairs. A number of city streets are set aside for the bazaar, and vines and canopies are put up to shade buyers and products from the sun and rain.

THE GRAND BAZAAR: The Grand Bazaar in Istanbul is like any bazaar except that, as its Turkish name **Kapalı Çarşı** (Covered Market) explains, it is all within one huge building. Depending on how you measure it, the covered market here could be the largest shopping center in the world, numbering over 4,000 individ-ual shops.

Though built at the time of the Conquest, the bazaar is by no means simply a quaint old tourist attraction. The great majority of shops cater to both Turks and tourists, especially those dealing in jewelry and clothing. The exception to this rule is the area known as the **Old Bazaar** (in English!). This separate little enclosure in the center of the bazaar specializes in copper, old guns and coins, antiques of all varieties, old Oriental clothing, rugs, tiles, and high prices. It's not unusual for merchants in this area to earn a 300% profit on a single item. Unfortunately, some of the best souvenirs to be found in Turkey are here, so you should by all means take a look. If intrigued, you should price similar items in several shops (preferably not neighboring ones), then you should go outside the Old Bazaar and look for similar shops, or go outside the Grand Bazaar alto-gether, to an area I'll describe below, and look for the same items for much less. Shopping tips and information on restaurants in the bazaar are given in other chapters of this book. The bazaar is a phenomenon that must be seen, and de-spite my scare tactics on the subject of prices, you should not give up the idea of going to the bazaar to shop. Useful words while you're strolling through the ba-zaar's maze of streets are *"Dokunma"* (doh-*koon*-mah: "Hands off!") and *"İs-temez"* (iss-teh-*mehz:* "I don't want to buy it").

Best times to visit the bazaar are the first hours of the morning, lunchtime, and late afternoon when the big tour groups aren't stuffing the narrow streets and raising prices even further. By the way, there are several public toilets in and around the bazaar; the cleanest is near the Nuruosmaniye Mosque entrance (in the mosque courtyard). There is another in the Havuzlu Restaurant (see Chapter V).

GRAND BAZAAR (Kapalı Çarşı)

Nuruosmaniye Mosque

Çuhacı Han

NURUOSMANİYE CADDESİ

ÇUHACI HAN SOKAĞI

Sandal Bedesteni (Municipal Auction)

SIRA ODALAR SOKAĞI

AYNACILAR SOKAĞI

AĞA SOKAĞI

MUHAFAZACILAR SOKAĞI

Zincirli Han

VARAKÇI SOKAĞI

KALCILAR SOKAĞI

Kürkçüler Çarşısı (Leather Market)

UNCUOĞLU SOKAĞI

SANDAL BEDESTENİ SOKAĞI

REİSOĞLU SOKAĞI

KARAMANLI SOKAĞI

TERZİLER SOKAĞI

ACIÇEŞME SOKAĞI

KUYUMCULAR CADDESİ

Old

Old

Bazaar

Bazaar

KOLANCILAR SOKAĞI

SAĞHAFLAR SOKAĞI

KESECİLER CADDESİ

DİVRİKLİ SOKAĞI

KALPAKÇILARBAŞI CADDESİ

PERDAHÇILAR SOKAĞI

TERLİKÇİLER SOKAĞI

KAVAFLAR SOKAĞI

SAĞHAFLAR CADDESİ

ZENNECİLER SOKAĞI

TAKKECİLER SOKAĞI

ORTA KAZASLAR SOKAĞI

KAZASLAR SOKAĞI

RESSAM BASMACILAR SOKAĞI

YAĞCILAR CADDESİ

Şark Kahvesi

FERDADECİLER SOKAĞI

KOLTUK KAZASLAR SOKAĞI

Sİ PAHİ SOKAĞI

YORGANCILAR CADDESİ

PÜSKÜLCÜLER SOKAĞI

TERPUŞÇULAR SOKAĞI

Hatipemin Han

GAZİ ÇELEBİ SOKAĞI

FESÇİLER CADDESİ

TUĞCULAR SOKAĞI

Havuzlu Lokantası

YARIMTAŞ HAN SOKAĞI

İSHAKLI İKTİSADLI SOKAĞI

MEKTEP SOKAĞI

BODRUM HAN SOKAĞI

HACI HÜSNÜ SOKAĞI

Beyazıt Square

Ali Paşa Han

ÇADIRCILAR CADDESİ

Sahaflar Çarşısı (Old Book Bazaar)

Beyazıt Mosque

The Grand Bazaar is open every day except Sunday from 8 a.m. to 6:30 p.m.

Outside the Bazaar

Even more picturesque than the bazaar, and a great deal cheaper in price, are the shops to be found huddled around the bazaar on little side streets. Here items identical to those in the Old Bazaar are offered at a good cut in price. The owners know they can't charge as much as the bazaar shops because they don't have the status location. One street, specializing in copper but having one or two antique shops, is **Çadırcılar Caddesi,** running down the left side of the bazaar as you face it from the bus stops in Hürriyet Square.

Don't neglect the more pedestrian-looking but valuable iron-mongers' shops loaded with thousands of old keys, hinges, bits and scraps of iron, and curious rusted utensils. If you buy a piece of copper which is unpolished, the shopkeeper will usually have it polished for you at no extra charge, though you may have to come the next day to pick it up.

There are two entrances to the bazaar on Çadırcılar Caddesi, and across the street from them, an entrance to the **Old Book Market (Sahaflar).** The Sahaflar specializes in such finds as ten-year-old editions of American college catalogues and Serbo-Croatian-to-Turkish dictionaries, but also sells religious books and old hand-illuminated Korans as well.

THE EGYPTIAN BAZAAR: The Egyptian Bazaar (Mısır Çarşısı), or Spice Bazaar, at the foot of the Galata Bridge in Eminönü, is a smaller version of the Grand Bazaar, once devoted exclusively to herbs and spices. Today it has expanded to include food, record players, stoves, and kitchen items—things of only slight interest to the casual stroller. The streets around the Egyptian Bazaar are very interesting; try to do some wandering in this area.

Like the Grand Bazaar, it's open daily except Sunday from 8 a.m. to 6:30 p.m.

7. Süleymaniye and Rüstem Paşa Mosques

Though the Blue Mosque is the most famous and accessible of Istanbul's 500 mosques, several others vie for your attention. The Mosque of Süleyman the Magnificent is the city's largest and grandest. The Rüstem Paşa Mosque, built by Süleyman's Grand Vizier, is very small, but is among the city's most beautiful because of its gorgeous interior tilework.

THE SÜLEYMANİYE MOSQUE: The biggest mosque in Istanbul, dominating the Golden Horn from its hilltop perch, is the Süleymaniye Mosque, or Mosque of Sultan Süleyman the Magnificent. Besides the sheer size of the mosque, it's interesting for the stained-glass windows inside and for the carved mihrab and mimber. The mosque is the work of the great Ottoman architect Sinan, who also built the Selimiye Mosque in Edirne and the smaller Şehzade Mosque in another part of Istanbul. His grave is in the area of the mosque, as are those of Sultan Süleyman himself, his wife, Roxelana, and other members of the imperial family.

When this mosque was built (1550), the Ottoman Empire was at the height of its glory. The custom then was to build whole communities within the grounds of a mosque: hospitals, schools, homes for the poor, workshops, and so forth were all included in the masterplan.

To get to the Süleymaniye Mosque, go to the entrance of the University near Beyazıt Square, walk through the University garden past the Beyazıt Tower and out the rear gate which leads directly to the mosque. If the university gates are closed, walk to your left around the walls; this route is a bit longer and not so pretty as walking through the grounds of the university, but gets you there just as well.

MOSQUE OF RÜSTEM PAŞA: Though small and in a dingy area of the city, the Mosque of Rüstem Paşa ranks with the city's finest because of the beautiful tiles which cover its walls inside. Rüstem Paşa, the son-in-law and Grand Vizier of Süleyman the Magnificent, had the mosque built in 1550 by the architect Sinan. The Grand Vizier's story is a sad one. He could never keep his monarch completely happy and was continually falling from favor, only to be restored soon afterward when the great sultan realized his worth.

The tiles in this mosque are some of the finest produced at the famous tile ovens of İznik, and are easier to see at close range, because of this mosque's size, than are those in the Blue Mosque. Don't miss taking a look at this little gem. To get to it, from Eminönü Square, walk along the right side of the Egyptian Bazaar and take the second street on the right (opposite a door into the market). Follow this for several blocks through the market, past shops selling coffee, spices, and dried fruit in large sacks, suitcases piled along walls, and woodwork and clothing shops, until you get to the mosque, on the right side of the street. Go up a stairway to enter. It's best to visit the mosque in the afternoon, when it's more likely to be open.

8. Kariye Camii (Chora Church) and City Walls

Of the vestiges from Byzantium, none is more impressive than the massive city walls, nor more beautiful than the glittering 13th-century mosaics in the Kariye Camii, built as a church, converted into a mosque, and now a museum.

The trip to the Kariye Museum, the walls, and the palace starts in Eminönü (or along Divan Yolu) with a no. 86 trolleybus (Edirnekapı). You take it to the end of the line, then follow the little street that the bus stops on into the residential district for a few blocks. You may have to ask where the museum is, though usually all of the smiling residents anticipate your question and point the way. The bus ride takes the better part of a half hour; the walk, a few minutes.

KARİYE CAMİİ (MUSEUM): The best Byzantine mosaics to be seen this side of Ravenna, and in fact some of the best mosaics in the world, are in the Kariye Museum, once a mosque, but originally built as the Church of the Holy Savior in Chora, out near the city walls. This church, like Sancta Sophia, dates originally from the time of Justinian, though most of what you will see is from the 14th century. Inside, the ceiling and cupolas are covered with dazzling mosaics depicting biblical scenes including the birth of Christ, the feeding of the 5,000, and the Wise Men going to Bethlehem. On the walls in the narthex are portraits; the shading of the colors shows an artistic skill that must have been at its height when these works were done. The sanctuary itself has only one mosaic, over the door, depicting the death of the Virgin Mary. The marble paneling of the walls is a lot like that in Sancta Sophia. Also as in Sancta Sophia, the mihrab is off center so that it points directly toward Mecca. In a side arcade are frescos done much later than the mosaics, which seem pale when compared to the rich gold and colors of the mosaics. The museum is open from 9 a.m. to 5:30 p.m. every day except Tuesday; admission costs 400TL (55¢). Take binoculars for a close look at the workmanship if you happen to have them along; no loss if you don't.

TEKFUR SARAYI: From the museum, walk up toward the city walls, then to the right along the walls until you come to Tekfur Saray, the **Palace of Constantine Porphyrogenetus.** This palace (ruins, partially restored) is the only Byzantine palace left standing in Istanbul. For a tip of a few coins the guard will let you walk around at your leisure. (The palace is officially closed on Monday, but you can usually get in; official admission is 200TL, 28¢.) When I was there, a boy dragged out a rickety ladder and had me climb the walls of the palace, where there was a splendid view of the city, the walls, and the Golden Horn. Try to pick out the big red-brick Greek school near the residence of the patriarch of Constantinople, home of the leader of the Orthodox church, as well as the usual landmarks: the Galata Tower, the chief mosques, and the bridges on the Golden Horn. Anyplace along the walls that you can climb to would serve well for a picnic spot.

THE FORTRESS OF THE SEVEN TOWERS (YEDİKULE): Another of the
sights of Istanbul that sounds as though it's been taken straight from the *Thousand and One Nights* is the Fortress of the Seven Towers, where prestigious prisoners of the sultan's government were imprisoned until their families or countries paid a big ransom, or, as often happened, until they were beheaded.

The fortress, really a fortified enclosure, dates from before the Conquest. The Turks made extensive repairs and changes to the Byzantine structure, which had only four towers. To the left as you enter is the Tower of Inscription where various graffiti left by European ambassadors, ship captains, and adventurers have been found. The inscriptions have been removed, but the view from the top of this prison tower is worth the climb up the dark, narrow stairway. On the other side of the enclosure is the Golden Gate, a monumental portal through which the Byzantine emperors would enter the city after triumphant wars abroad. The main doorways were bricked up against the invasion of the Turks, and have remained that way.

The view from the Tower of Sultan Ahmet III (near the gate in the city wall) is the best in the fortress. From here you get a good perspective of the entire fortress, its moat, and the huge walls of the city trailing off to the Golden Horn.

Take a no. 80 bus (Yedikule) from Eminönü Square or Divan Yolu to the end of the line, about a 25-minute ride. Walk up the hill from the bus stop through the gate in the city wall and turn right at the first street to get to the fortress entrance. Yedikule is open every day from 9:30 a.m. to 5 p.m. Admission is 250TL (35¢).

9. The Golden Horn and Eyüp

THE GOLDEN HORN: A century or two ago a boat trip up the Golden Horn revealed palaces, pleasure kiosks, and imperial gardens on the sides of the city's seven hills. But in this century the romance was swept away as Turkey industrialized. The pleasure gardens were replaced by a motley, ugly collection of coal heaps, shipyards, factories, and workshops.

A few years ago a young and activist mayor of Istanbul named Bedrettin Dalan accelerated clean-up efforts, and today the Golden Horn is lined for much of its length by parks and esplanades. Clean-up of the estuary's waters continues, and a boat trip along the Golden Horn is once again a pleasure.

From near the Galata Bridge, you can catch a ferry for the 30-minute ride to Eyüp, near where the city walls join the waterway. Boats depart every hour or two, and charge 100TL (14¢) for the ride. For the return trip, consult the schedule posted on the ferry. "Haliç" is the Turkish name of the Golden Horn. Plan to be gone two hours, from start to finish. The trip to Eyüp can be made by bus also, leaving from Eminönü on a no. 99 ("Eyüp") bus. Less comfortable, more expensive, longer ride.

EYÜP: The **Grand Mosque of Eyüp** is one of Istanbul's most attractive places of worship, famed for its relics of Mohammed's standard-bearer, Eyüp, and the footprint of the Prophet himself. The mosque was completely rebuilt in the 1800s in a style that can only be described as Islamic baroque. The marvelous tiles are the finest things to be seen at Eyüp.

Because of its famous relics, the mosque of Eyüp is a place of pilgrimage. All during the day people approach a little grilled window surrounded by fine tiles, say a prayer, and wipe their hand on the grill in order to take some of the blessing with them as they go. In the Arab raids on Constantinople in 670, Eyüp, a friend of the Prophet's, was killed. Some 800 years after his death the bones of the standard-bearer were miraculously located on the site of the mosque, which was subsequently built by Mehmet the Conqueror as a fit place to store the relics.

As you come out of the mosque enclosure, turn to the right and follow the walls to a path leading up a hill into a cemetery. Don't let the taxi drivers fool you—it's only a short walk up the hill to the café where Pierre Loti, the Turcophile French novelist, used to sit and view the city. The café has thus been immortalized and so have its prices: Turkish coffee or soft drinks are outrageously priced—about three times the normal price. But if you sit in their café, you buy one of their drinks. I found the view worth the price.

10. The Imperial Palaces of Dolmabahçe and Yıldız

North of Beyoğlu on the Bosphorus's western shore is the vast imperial palace of Dolmabahçe, the last official residence of the Ottoman *padishah* (sultan). A mile or two to the north is the large park of Yıldız, once an imperial pleasure ground dotted with kiosks, small palaces, and barracks for the imperial guard, but now a public park. Between these two is the district of Barbaros Hayrettin Pasha, formerly (and still usually) called Beşiktaş. In Beşiktaş is the Naval Museum (Deniz Müzesi), housing mementos of Turkey's long and formidable naval history. Seeing these sights is perhaps the best way to grasp the grandeur and glitter of the Ottoman Empire.

TRANSPORTATION: Dolmush and bus lines descend the hill from Taksim Square along İnönü Caddesi to deposit you at Dolmabahçe Palace. Many lines also run north along the shore from Dolmabahçe to Barbaros (about a mile), and from Barbaros to Yıldız (half a mile). You can walk to all of these sights, but I suggest the following instead: plan your trip carefully to avoid days and hours when the sights are closed, and then start early in the morning with a taxi ride to the Chalet Kiosk (Şale Köşkü) in Yıldız Park. The taxi will take you from Taksim to the park and up the steep slope to the top for about 1,700TL ($2.40). Visit the sights in the park, walk down the hill to the shore road, turn right, and walk to Barbaros and the Naval Museum. You can have a bite of lunch in the Malta Kiosk in the park, or in the market area across the shore road from the Naval Museum. Take a dolmush or bus south from here along the shore road to Dolmabahçe, planning to get to the palace when it opens for the afternoon at 1 p.m.

YILDIZ PARK AND CHALET KIOSK: As though Istanbul didn't have enough palaces, Sultan Abdülhamid II (1876–1909) built one as a little guesthouse for the German emperor to use during a state visit. The sultan called it a chalet. Some chalet! It has 64 rooms. The imperial park of Yıldız already had several smaller kiosks good for resting the Imperial Feet or having a refreshing cup of tea. Today all of these kiosks, several greenhouses, and the park itself have been beautifully restored under the auspices of the Turkish Touring and Automobile Club.

The park is open from 9 a.m. to 6 p.m. every day; admission costs 20TL (3¢) for pedestrians, 200TL (28¢) for cars (including taxis).

The Chalet Kiosk

At the top of the hill, enclosed by a wall, is the Chalet Kiosk (Sale Köşkü), built in 1882 and later (1898) enlarged. Kaiser Wilhelm II of Germany was the chalet's intended occupant, and in fact the sultan's friend and ally did stay here several times during visits. But it was Abdülhamid himself who fell in love with the chalet and decided to live here rather than in Dolmabahçe. Actually, security had a lot to do with it. Many people wanted Abdülhamid out of the way, and the high walls and relative isolation of the Chalet Kiosk no doubt appealed to the sultan as a safe haven. Not that all this caution did him much good. He was ultimately deposed, and left the Chalet Kiosk for Sirkeci Station in April 1909. A special train took him to internal exile in Ottoman Salonica, though he was later allowed to return to the capital, kept under close guard.

The Chalet Kiosk was also the last Istanbul home of the last Ottoman sultan, Mehmet V (Vahideddin), who departed for exile on November 11, 1922. This time the vehicle was a British man-o'-war.

Since the fall of the empire, the republican government has used the Chalet Kiosk as a guesthouse for visiting heads of state. Such luminaries as Charles de Gaulle, Pope Paul VI, Nikolai Ceauşescu, and the Empress Soraya of Iran have enjoyed stays here.

Admission to the kiosk and its grounds costs 500TL (70¢); hours are 9:30 a.m. to 4 p.m. daily except Monday.

You enter the grounds along gravel walks said to have been built by Abdülhamid as a security measure: the noisy gravel warns guards of any intruder's movements. At the kiosk door, a guide will approach you to begin the guided tour, which you must take if you want to see the place.

The first section, where you enter, was the original chalet, built in 1882. The first suite of rooms was used by Abdülhamid's mother for her religious devotions, for receiving guests, and for "resting." In the tea room, the furniture has gold stars on a blue background ("star" in Turkish is *Yıldız*).

The second section of the kiosk was constructed in 1898, and at that time the original part was converted to the harem and thick steel doors were installed. One of the reception rooms in this newer section is furnished in pieces made by Sultan Abdülhamid himself, who was a skilled woodworker. This was more than a hobby—Ottoman tradition held that "being sultan" was not enough of a "job" to justify one's existence in the eyes of Islam. Each man should be master of a skill useful to society, and should practice that skill. Past sultans had been calligraphers, musicians, poets, or artists of other types. Abdülhamid liked making furniture.

The most striking room in the new section is the Great Hall, its floor covered by a carpet woven especially for the room in the imperial factory at Hereke. The carpet weighs 7½ tons, and had to be brought in and laid before construction on the room was complete: it is so big there would have been no way for it to enter the building otherwise.

The Tent Kiosk

This pretty, ornate little kiosk (Çadır Köşkü) at the top of the hill, not far from the Chalet Kiosk entrance, was built between 1865 and 1870 as a place for the sultan to enjoy the view, rest from a walk, and have a cup of tea or coffee. You can enjoy the same imperial-class pleasures today, and drinks are served (no food) as long as the park is open. The marble terrace overlooking the Bosphorus is the best place to sit.

The Malta Kiosk

Across the valley from the Tent Kiosk is a larger, though similar, kiosk called the **Malta Kiosk** (Malta Köşkü; tel. 160-2752). This also is a fine place for refreshments, but the Malta Kiosk serves snacks and even light meals as well as beverages during park hours. You might end up spending 2,500TL ($3.50) for a lunch of shish kebap here.

Below the Malta Kiosk, in the valley, are two greenhouses, the **Winter Garden** (Kış Bahçesi) and the **Green Nursery** (Yeşil Sera). After passing these two lovely buildings, you descend through the park to the entrance and the shore road. Under Sultan Abdülhamid's care the park was filled with exotic flowering plants and trees from around his vast empire, and many still flourish.

The Ceremonial Kiosk

Also at Yıldız is a large complex of stone buildings on Barbaros Bulvarı, not accessible from inside the park (go to Beşiktaş and walk up the hill on Barbaros Bulvarı). The large stone 19th-century barracks complex is used by Istanbul University, but a part of it has been restored and now holds art shows.

THE NAVAL MUSEUM: The Naval, or Maritime, Museum (Deniz Müzesi) is near the main intersection in Beşiktaş, next to the ferryboat dock. In the little park here is the tomb of the famous Ottoman admiral, Barbaros Hayrettin Pasha.

The museum has two sections. The one with an entrance on the street holds general exhibits of naval memorabilia; another, with an entrance facing the Bosphorus, holds the sultans' barges. It costs 250TL (35¢) to enter either section, which you can do from 9:30 a.m. to 4:45 p.m. every day except Monday or Tuesday. To reach one section from the other, you must leave the museum and pay a second entrance fee.

The most exciting exhibit in the museum is the display of sultans' barges. These sleek boats, some with 13 banks of oars, sliced through the Bosphorus waters like arrows, speeding the sultan, a chosen servant, or in later times even one of his wives, to an appointment or a picnic. The imperial wives were protected from the prying eyes of outsiders by a little latticework cabin, while the sultan, who wished to be seen, would have a red velvet, gold-tasseled canopy to shield him from the sun. The typical boat was close to 35 yards long, but only 2½ yards wide, accounting for its swiftness. The fighting galley on display had 24 pairs of oars with three men to each oar, and was obviously made for power rather than speed. Make sure you don't miss the displays on the second floor (balcony), nor the view you get of the ground-floor exhibits from above. The famous "Piri Reis" map of North America, said to have been drawn from a now-lost map by Columbus, is the pride of Ottoman geography, and you can buy a well-done colored reproduction of it at the ticket window.

DOLMABAHÇE PALACE: Istanbul is often associated with the decadent grandeur of the later Ottoman Empire, a city of intrigue, mystery, squalor, and unparalleled showy magnificence. Dolmabahçe Palace alone, without the other palaces and relics of the empire, would be enough to give Istanbul its reputation for luxury. Unlike ancient Topkapı, built courtyard style to please outdoorsmen, Dolmabahçe was built European style and stuffed with wealth to refute rumors of the empire's poverty—which it helped to create.

The palace is open from 9 a.m. to noon and 1:30 to 4:30 p.m.; closed Monday and Thursday. Admission and the obligatory guided tour costs 1,000TL ($1.40). Check your camera at the door. Though you're allowed to photograph (without flash) upon payment of an exorbitant fee, it's too dark inside to do so.

An English-speaking guide will show you around on the one-hour tour through the family quarters, reception rooms, the sultan's bath and the baths of the Harem, and the Harem itself (with steel doors). You can see the enormous bed of the enormous sultan, Abdul Aziz; the secret windows through which the Harem girls watched official goings-on in the throne room; a myriad of Bohemian crystal chandeliers, including the 4½-ton giant in the throne room; Sèvres vases; and the usual monarch-to-monarch gifts. The throne room comes complete with dazzling gold throne and an enormous heating problem.

A main attraction of the palace for Turks is the small room where Kemal Atatürk died in 1938 while on a visit to Istanbul. All the clocks in the palace are stopped at the moment of his death: 9:05 a.m. The date, November 10th, is commemorated with memorial services every year.

11. A Visit to a Turkish Bath

The hamam, or Turkish bath, is one of the Turks' most ancient institutions. The complicated procedure of steamrooms, massages, scrubbing, sudsing, dousing with hot and cold water, and finally resting on a couch for a half hour is designed not so much to clean you as to put you back into action to face the world again. It's a guaranteed cure for hangover and general tiredness. Turks who stay out too late at night have been known to go straight to a hamam from the party and, after a bath of an hour or two, on to the office.

The most satisfactory baths for your first visit are at the **Cağaloğlu Hamamı** (tel. 522-2424), a recently refurbished 16th-century structure in the Old City. The hamam has separate men's and women's sections, open every day from 7 a.m. to 8 p.m. (women's section), and 7 a.m. to midnight (men's section). An attendant will present you with a price list to inspect before you bathe: 1,000TL ($1.40) for the basic charge (you wash yourself), 2,000TL ($2.80) total if an attendant washes you (he or she does a much better job than you could do yourself). Top price is 5,000TL ($7), which includes attendant washing plus a massage. Tea, coffee, and shoeshines are a few hundred liras more. The hamam is located not far from Sultanahmet Square on Hilaliahmer Caddesi (same street as Yerebatan Caddesi, near where it meets Ankara Caddesi).

The **Galatasaray Hamamı** (tel. 144-1412) is at the end of Suterazi Sokak (no. 24), a street running left off İstiklal Caddesi as you walk toward Galatasaray Square from Taksim.

A real Turkish bath is an unforgettable experience. Here's the way it goes: You enter the baths, remove your shoes and exchange them for a pair of clogs or slippers at the bottom of the stairway (tell the shoeshine boy whether or not you want your shoes shined; if you don't say anything, chances are he'll shine them). An attendant will show you to your cubicle, where you undress and put on the cloth he's given you. Go back down to the main floor and into the baths. I should mention that here Turkish custom demands that you always kep the cloth wrapped around you. It's considered very impolite to be seen totally naked in the all-male baths, though this stricture does not always apply in the women's baths. Stay in the first room of the baths for a few minutes to get accustomed to the temperature, then move on toward the hottest room, making sure you've adapted to the heat. In the steamroom are marble platforms—very hot—with wooden palettes on top where you can stretch out and relax while the steam works on you. An attendant will come around and ask if you want a massage. A full massage is a fascinating thing to watch: the attendant kneads, thumps, rubs, and even walks on all parts of the body until it's so loose it can hardly move.

When you think the steam's worked into you, head for the medium-hot room and find a washbasin for the washing. You can do this yourself to save money, as I've mentioned, but if you have an attendant do it you'll come out a lot cleaner. He'll use a coarse cloth mitten and rub every bit of dirt off, then douse you in warm water, swash you with a horse-tail pulled out of a bucket of suds, then more water a bit cooler this time to finish it off. After this, you're done in the baths proper. Walk to the door and an attendant will swathe you in fresh towels to prevent a chill, and let you out of the bathing rooms. Back up the steps to your cubicle; order a tea or Turkish coffee if you want on your way up, and the attendant will bring it.

Stay in the cubicle as long as you want to; you can even take a nap, which is what most Turks do.

12. Istanbul's Nightlife

As the sun goes down, the lights come on in Istanbul: Topkapı Palace, Sancta Sophia, the Blue Mosque, and the Süleymaniye are flooded in golden light until after midnight, making a wonderful spectacle. You'll find lots to do at night in this enchanting city.

TOURS: Almost every tour organizer in the city offers an "Istanbul by Night" tour which typically includes a bus ride along the Bosphorus to a waterside fish restaurant for dinner (included in the tour price), then back to town to a nightclub for the bellydance and folk dances; one drink and a chance to dance to an orchestra are usually thrown in, and the price is about 10,000TL ($14).

THE ISTANBUL FESTIVAL: For several years now Istanbul has played host to an international arts festival each summer in July. Artists of worldwide reputation and lesser-known young artists perform drama, opera, chamber music, recitals, folk dancing, and symphony concerts. In addition, shows of the plastic and graphic arts are arranged at various places in the city. If you visit the city during the festival, get tickets (sold at the ticket windows of the Cultural Palace —the Opera House—in Taksim) to a concert or recital in the Church of St. Irene for a real treat. The most exciting event of the annual festival, though, is the performance of Mozart's *The Abduction from the Seraglio,* performed right inside Topkapı Palace! Open-air stands are erected in front of the Middle Gate, which is used as part of the set. Prices for tickets for this and other festival happenings vary with the event and the placement of the seat, but the cheapest seats are usually around $2, the most expensive rarely more than $10. If you're in town when the festival's on, don't miss it!

SOUND AND LIGHT: Performances during the warm summer months take place in Sultanahmet (where else?). You sit on benches set up between the Blue Mosque and the little formal garden-with-pool to the north of it. Even without the commentary, the sight of the mosque floodlit is a brave scene indeed. Commentary is in French, German, English, and Turkish, one language per night. Check at the Tourism Information Office for schedules of English-language nights. The show is free.

OPERA, SYMPHONY, RECITALS: Istanbul's opera house, the **Atatürk Kültür Merkezi** (Atatürk Cultural Center) in Taksim Square, is the venue for performances of opera, symphony, chamber music, and solo recitals, and special events. Istanbul has a resident opera company and ballet, and what they lack in world-league vocal and dramatic qualities, they make up for in panache. At the opera, costumes and sets are surprisingly good, lead singers quite adequate or very good (with guest artists from Europe—particularly Italy—appearing frequently), and prices for seats are subsidized and thus are very inexpensive by European or American standards. The opera and ballet have a full season of the great classics beginning each autumn; don't be surprised to hear the chorus and Turkish leads singing in Turkish, the European guest artists singing in Italian, French, or German, all in the same opera.

The city also has a symphony orchestra, and the Presidential Symphony Orchestra, based in Ankara, comes here frequently on tour. Recitals by Turkish musicians (particularly Turkey's several excellent young pianists) are also held in the Cultural Center, and foreign musicians of universal reputation make frequent visits as well. Programs are published each month of the fall, winter, and spring (and in summer for the Istanbul Festival); for full information and tickets, drop in at the box offices right in the Cultural Center in Taksim.

MOVIES:

The city has a good number of movie theaters, some that play European and American flicks in the original language versions. Most of these are located on İstiklal Caddesi between Taksim and Galatasaray, though there are a few on Cumhuriyet Caddesi too. The ones on Cumhuriyet include the **As Sineması** at no. 229 and the **Şan** at no. 69. In Taksim, you'll find the **Venüs** at the beginning of Sıraselviler Caddesi. On İstiklal, look for the **Dünya** and the **Fitaş,** both at no. 24, the **Saray** at no. 112, the **Emek** at no. 126, the **Rüya** at the same address, and the **Atlas** at no. 209. The **Yeni Melek,** at the end of Hava Sokak, displays its currently running film on İstiklal, as does the **Yeni Ar,** at the end of Yeşil Çam Sokak.

When choosing a film, look over the billboard ads for the words "İngilizce" (English) or "Orijinal" (Original) to see if you'll be able to understand the film or not. If all you find is the word "Türkçe," the film's been dubbed in Turkish. Every theater sets one day of the week aside as Halk Günü (People's Day) and offers reductions on all seats for that day. Prices per seat are 400TL (55¢) or under, depending on where you sit. The *Balkon* (balcony) is considered the best section and is therefore the most expensive; *Birinci* means on the floor near the screen, and *Koltuk* means on the floor near the middle or in the back of the house. All seats are reserved, and it's a good idea to buy your tickets a few hours in advance. Ushers expect a hundred liras' tip.

NIGHTCLUBS AND SHOWS:

Those clubs which are at all interesting are also expensive, but if you do it right, you'll be able to afford a night on the town.

The nightclub and disco district is on Cumhuriyet Caddesi. The clientele, mostly middle-class business types, make an enthusiastic, fun-loving audience, a welcome change from the somber mood of most places.

Walking along Cumhuriyet, you cross the street, pass the Divan Hotel, and then, on your right, little alleyways begin to appear between the buildings. Most of the clubs are stashed in one or another of these alleys. The first you come to is the **Module,** a discothèque which requires that a man be a member to enter single, but will sell him a "guest ticket" if he has a date. The rule requiring you to come with a date was made to keep the clientele from being overpoweringly male, a big problem in these places.

After the Module comes the **Régine,** a favorite hangout for the young single set in Istanbul, including a number of European (especially Scandinavian) and American girls who live and work in the city. The disco is downstairs, and again you're required to buy a "membership." In the same building as the Régine is **Gülizar,** a classy version of what is called, in Turkish, a *pavyon,* denoting a club with low lights, lots of B-girls, and a strip show. The show here is considered by some to be the city's best; there are certainly a lot worse. The prices, however, are a bit high: 6,000TL ($8.40) for the first drink even if it's tea. Second drinks are less, however. You sit in a sunken area to listen to the band

and watch the show, or at a bar raised above the tables in order to see everything. There are three shows: at 9 p.m., 11 p.m., and 1 a.m.

The **Casino d'Istanbul,** once located in a wondrous old 19th-century villa on the Bosphorus, was moved to the Hilton basement, where the money is. It's open only to holders of foreign passports (bring yours along for proof), from 9 p.m. until the wee hours, and offers the usual array of machines and games for lira coins and bills.

There are many clubs and *gazinos,* outdoor restaurants sometimes featuring entertainment, which have summer quarters on the shores of the Bosphorus, changing place from season to season.

The rooftop nightclubs in the **Sheraton** and **Etap Marmara** hotels have shows nightly, and you can take them in for the substantial price of one drink— about 4,000TL ($5.60), depending on the drink and the day of the week; prices are higher on weekends. A bellydancer and folkdance teams are regular entertainers at these shows, but my experience has been that the shows, like the food served in the hotel restaurants, is more likely to be bland than spicy. You can hardly come away disappointed, however, because the view of the city at night is itself worth the price of the drink.

FOLK DANCING: The **Turkish Folklore Association** sponsors dancing during the summer months at a convenient location. Dancing begins at 9 p.m. The building which houses the performance, the **Hacı Beşir Medresesi,** a medieval muslim religious school, is as interesting as the dancing and can be found by walking down the hill from Sancta Sophia toward Gülhane Park, and turning right onto Hükümet Konağı Sokak; or by going to the Vilayet (Istanbul Provincial Government Building) and turning right onto this same street in front of it. Starting from either end of Hükümet Konağı Sokak, the Hacı Beşir is midway on the street. Look for signs for the Türk Foklor Kurumu.

There are different groups of dancers and types of dances every night, but here's a sketch of the ones I saw: The first group of men and women come on carrying candles stuck to plates, sliding along in graceful, whirling dances with candles lighting their movements, later setting the candles down in front of them for other dances. The music is the piercing wail of a wooden village flute and a Turkish drum, sometimes softened by a clarinet or accordion. Other dancers, from Erzurum in eastern Turkey—an all-male group dressed in black trousers, white shirts, black vests, and red cummerbunds—go through dances that are slower and more dignified, at times almost strutting. Among the groups from eastern Turkey, there were some from districts near the Russian border, dressed in Georgian outfits—like Cossacks in movies—with fur-trimmed hats and high black boots. The fast Cossack dances, including the famous "jump" step, make the crowd yell *Yasha!* ("Bravo!") as they build up to fever pitch. The women in the group, dressed in long satin gowns, can't be so quick but add a bit of grace to the dance.

If you go to the dances on a night when the majority of the audience is Turkish, you're in luck. The onlookers have almost as much fun as the dancers, clapping to the music, singing along, and cheering for a particularly good step.

In addition to the performances at Hacı Beşir, dance exhibitions are held from time to time in the **Açık Hava Tiyatrosu** (Open-air Theater) next to the Hilton. Check with the Tourism Information Office in the Hilton arcade for the latest news on what's happening there.

CAFÉS: The narrow, winding streets of Istanbul don't lend themselves to sidewalk-café life, but still there are several places to sit and watch the parade of evening strollers. The **Lale Restaurant,** in Sultanahmet Square, was once just a pastahane that gained some fame as the first hippie hangout in Istanbul; it was called the "Pudding Shop," at least by its long-haired clientele. It's still a favorite haunt of hippies and traveling types who sit there in the evening and sip coffee or tea and talk, except when the traffic on the street gets so loud they can't hear one another. Another favorite on this side of the city is the tea house across the street from the entrance to the university, on Yeniçeriler Caddesi.

In the new city most of the best places are relatively expensive, charging almost 1,500TL ($2.10) for pastry and coffee. These are all along Cumhuriyet Caddesi, out of Taksim. The one that's worth the money is the **Divan Pastanesi,** in the Divan Hotel, where the service is polished and the pastry is always fresh—a statement that can be made of few pastane in Istanbul. The Pastanesi is actually inside the hotel proper, but in summer tables are set out in front of the door.

LOW LIFE: Istanbul used to have one of the world's most interesting "low lifes," with cheap strip and bellydance joints, bars full of sailors and women of the streets, and Greek-type bouzouki joints full of the city's non-Turkish citizens. There is little of this left anymore. The Cyprus crisis closed most of the bouzouki joints; the bars and bellydancers—the good ones, at least—have all moved on to greener pastures. If you want to browse through what's left, take a stroll through the **Çiçek Pasajı** at about 8 or 9 in the evening. Not far inside the gate of the passage, a narrow stairway on the right leads down into a strange little joint with entertainment you have to see to believe. The **Kimene Lokantası,** discussed earlier, is not only a restaurant but a beerhall, and therefore has itinerant clarinet-and-drum duos which stroll in every now and then for a little entertainment. Life in the passage pretty well closes up by 11 or 11:30 p.m., so get there early.

THE BOSPHORUS BY NIGHT: You might want to consider one more suggestion for a night's entertainment: a boat ride up the Bosphorus. The Hilton and Sheraton Hotels operate cruise boats, as do various tour companies, but you can have almost the same experience by taking a ferry. The ferries run until past midnight, as do the city buses along the shore. In several hours you could see most of the Bosphorus lights and be back in the center of town. For instance, a 7:45 p.m. boat from the Eminönü docks goes all the way to Yeniköy, arriving there at 9:35 p.m. If you took a bus to İstinye, on the European coast below Büyükdere and Sarıyer, you might hop on the 8:20 p.m. ferry and cruise down to the Galata Bridge, arriving at 9:40 p.m. Check these times to be sure; they modify the schedules slightly twice a year. Take a sweater or jacket as it will be chilly on the water.

Chapter VII

THE WATERS
AROUND ISTANBUL

1. About Ferryboats
2. Bosphorus: The European Shore
3. Bosphorus: The Asian Shore
4. The Marmara Beaches
5. The Princes' Islands

BECAUSE OF ISTANBUL'S location on an isthmus, there are few places of interest that are so far away they can't be visited in a one-day trip from the city. In this chapter are the hints required for seeing the Bosphorus, the suburbs in Asia, the Marmara beaches, and the Princes' Islands on the lowest possible budget.

1. About Ferryboats

For your trips out of the city you'll be using Istanbul's extensive ferryboat system. You might want to pick up the TML timetable that applies to the Istanbul ferries. It's called a *tarife (tah*-ree-feh) and is on sale at all ferry ticket offices. Maps of the ferry dock area are included in the booklet. Schedules for the ferries are also posted in all boats and at all docks. You'll need some help in reading them, so here goes:

Boğaz, Boğaziçi	Bosphorus
Köprü	Galata Bridge
. . .'dan . . . 'a	From . . . to . . . (as in Köprü'dan Boğaz'a, "From Galata Bridge to the Bosphorus")
Kalkış, *or* (K.)	Departure
Varış, *or* (V.)	Arrival
Hat, Hattı	Route
Araba Vapuru	Car-ferry
. . . günleri yapılır/yapılmaz	Operated/not operated on . . . (days; see Appendix I for days of the week and months)
Hergün	Daily

Traditionally, names and stopping times of docks on the European side of the Bosphorus are printed on the timetables in black, and names and times for the docks on the Asian side are in red.

Make an effort to plan your Bosphorus trip a day ahead of time. Pass by a ferry dock and find a boat that suits your needs, and then arrive the next day at the docks about 20 minutes or more ahead of time so you won't be rushed in buying your ticket or in finding a good seat (the boats with good schedules for tourists tend to fill up quickly in summer). Boats leave from docks 1, 2, 3, and 4 in Eminönü; ask at a ticket window for the destination you want, and the ticket seller will direct you to the proper dock for your boat. Passers-by will also be helpful in this regard (Turks generally anticipate a visitor's every need and courteously help him or her along—it's part of their culture); but every now and then some rotten egg will "help" by offering to buy your tickets, and will then rip you off—perhaps in collaboration with an unscrupulous ticket seller. If you get to the docks early, buy your own tickets and count your change before you leave the ticket window—as you should anywhere in the world—there can be no problems. Be sure to keep your ticket, as you must show it to an inspector on the boat and must turn it in when you reach your destination.

Tickets range in price from 100TL (14¢) to 750TL ($1.05), depending on length of journey and whether you buy a *gidiş* (one-way) or *gidiş-geliş* (round-trip) ticket. Prices are printed on all tickets.

2. Bosphorus: The European Shore

For the trip up the European coast, you have several choices. If you've just come over from Asia, hopping buses and dolmushes for the short trips up and down the coast is probably your best plan. But if you're beginning the day with this trip, you have a treat in store. Several times a day ferries leave docks 2 and 3 in Eminönü on special "touristic" runs which zigzag between the European and Asian coasts on the way up the Bosphorus. These are ideal for seeing the Bosphorus, for no matter how much or how little time you have to spend, a trip can be planned to suit it. For example, the trip from Eminönü to the dock at Yeniköy takes only 80 minutes, in which time you see the most interesting parts of the Bosphorus shores. After a visit to the fortress at Rumeli Hisar, the return trip to the city can be made by bus (slightly faster). If you want to spend a full day, take the ferry all the way to **Sarıyer** (about 1⅓ hours). The entire trip is only 750TL ($1.05)! From this town you can start back down the coast by dolmush and bus, exploring more closely the sights you saw from the ferry, or you can head for the beaches at **Kilyos** on the Black Sea. Be sure to get to boat dock no. 3 about 30 minutes before it's scheduled to leave, for these boats fill up early.

RUMELI HISAR: On your cruise, you can't miss Rumeli Hisar, the **Fortress of Europe.** When Mehmet the Conqueror came to power over the Ottoman Empire in 1451, he ruled over an area stretching from eastern Anatolia to Hungary. Right in the middle of his empire, however, was an alien state—the remnant of the Byzantine Empire that still existed at that time. All that was left was the city of Constantinople and a few lands in what is today Greece, but the Byzantine capital was a prize that Mehmet wanted badly. Accordingly, he built the two fortresses still standing at the narrowest part of the Bosphorus in order to control this entrance to the city. He put thousands of workmen on the job and had it completed in only three months. The power of this fortress, and a few other tricks, won him the conquest of the city in 1453, only a year after the fortress was built.

Mehmet was a leader with dramatic plans. Rumeli Hisar is one of the best proofs of this, but there were others he used in conquering the Byzantine capital. To gain control of the Golden Horn, closed off during the war by a huge chain stretched across its mouth, he transported a flotilla of boats overland from Dolmabahçe to Kasımpaşa, a port on the Golden Horn. All this was done by night so that the next morning the Turks took the Byzantine navy by surprise, finishing it off with little difficulty.

Another of Mehmet's schemes deals with the guns used to batter in the mighty city walls. A gunmaker had offered his services to the Byzantine emperor, but the emperor, low on funds, couldn't pay him. Mehmet found out about the gunmaker's plans to cast several mammoth siege guns and set him to work right away for a good wage. The guns proved to be instrumental in breaking the stubborn Byzantine resistance.

The castle is open every day but Monday from 9:30 a.m. to 5 p.m.; admission costs 200TL (28¢), half price on weekends. Like Topkapı Palace, this is a very open-air place. The garrison of 400 Janissaries probably had tents or wooden shelters for quarters; the ruins of their mosque are still visible. An elevator allows you to get to the top of one of the towers painlessly (but for a small fee); the top of this tower is a good place to begin a tour of the walls. The funny shape of the fortress seems to indicate that it was built to defensive requirements, but there's also a story that Mehmet had it built in the shape of his personal monogram (in the old Turkish script, of course). Whether good for defense or not, it was admirably designed for the offensive work it was built to carry out. Right down by the road which skirts the walls of the fortress, in the outer wall, are some gun ports and guns. By firing just above water level across the Bosphorus narrows, the garrison of the castle had full control over everything moving up or down the Bosphorus. No wonder the fortification of these straits and those at Gallipoli (the Dardanelles) has been so bitterly disputed for centuries—especially by Russia.

The **Bosphorus University (Boğaziçi University)** was, until a few years ago, Robert College, an American-administered liberal arts college straight out of the New England tradition. The college has moved to a different campus, down the Bosphorus in Arnavutköy, but the architecture of the university belies its ancestry.

TARABYA: Tarabya, farther up the Bosphorus, is the site of one of Istanbul's plushest hotels, the **Grand Tarabya** (you can't miss it). The inlet here is surrounded by restaurants, hotels, and swimming areas, as it has been for centuries. This is the famous old resort of **Therapia,** once sought out by the Byzantines as a haven of rest and relaxation.

For a swim in these rather expensive waters, try the public swimming pier on the opposite edge of the inlet from the one dominated by the hotel. The bus stop next to it is called "Banyo." There's a small fee for swimming here and for using the various facilities.

SARIYER: Sarıyer might be called a typical Bosphorus fishing town. Tourists coming through the town have upset its sleepy way of life somewhat, but the wizened men in their knit caps still row out to net fish in the fast currents of the Bosphorus and afterward can be seen carefully hanging out the nets to dry or mending tears in them. Because the currents are so strong here, fishermen can also use the system of tying stationary nets to posts placed in the course of a current; the fish swim straight in.

It used to be that fish was the cheapest protein-rich food to be had in Istanbul, but intense exploitation of the Bosphorus, Marmara, and Black Sea fishing grounds by the fleets of half a dozen nations have depleted the waters a great

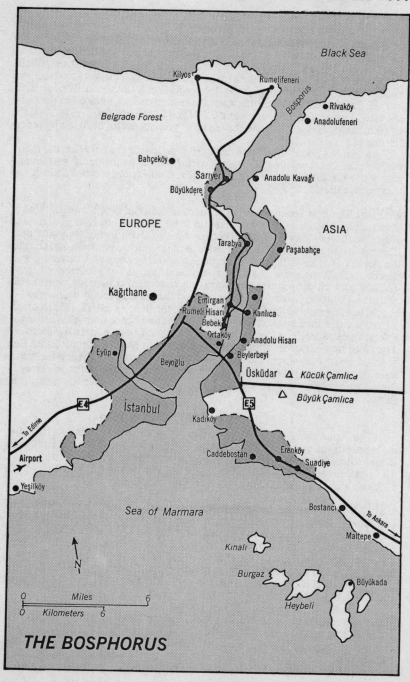

Black Sea

Kilyos

Rumelifeneri

Bosporus

Rivaköy

Anadolufeneri

Belgrade Forest

Bahçeköy

Sarıyer

Anadolu Kavağı

Büyükdere

EUROPE

ASIA

Tarabya

Paşabahçe

Kağıthane

Emirgan

Rumeli Hisarı

Kanlıca

Bebek

Ortaköy

Anadolu Hisarı

Eyüp

Beylerbeyi

Beyoğlu

Üsküdar △ *Küçük Çamlıca*

△ *Büyük Çamlıca*

E4

İstanbul

E5

Kadıköy

To Edirne

Airport

Erenköy

Caddebostan

Suadiye

Yeşilköy

Bostancı

To Ankara

Sea of Marmara

Maltepe

N

Kınalı

Burgaz

Büyükada

0 *Miles* 6

0 *Kilometers* 6

Heybeli

THE BOSPHORUS

deal. The lone fisherman, out in his tiny skiff, still makes a living here in Sarıyer, but he's forced to charge more for his catch.

Sarıyer has many fish restaurants to choose from, most fairly expensive, but a few are within our range. From the dock, turn right and walk along the town's main street until you get to the town mosque. Just past it is a tiny street, on the right, with fish sellers behind their makeshift stands. Walk down this street and bear to the left, straight through the door of the **Balık Lokantası.** Though without the fancy decor of the more expensive restaurants, this place has the same sea view. Fish entrees here are about 2,500TL ($3.50) to 3,500TL ($4.90) if the fish is in season. If you just want the sea view, you can eat for even less by ordering one of the meat entrees.

Sarıyer has gone "mod" now, and fish is no longer the only dish its restaurants serve. The town now has a pizza parlor (on the main street), and several pastry shops *(pastane)* serving cakes and börek, which can serve as a filling and inexpensive snack.

KİLYOS: The best beach within easy reach of Istanbul is undoubtedly that at Kilyos on the Black Sea. Dolmushes run from near the bus stop in Sarıyer to Kilyos as soon as they fill up, and charge 325TL (45¢) for the 20-minute ride. Climb into one of these, liable to be twice as old as you are yourself, and chug up the slopes of the low hills, passing through colorful fields, past little restaurants perched on hilltops, through a military area and finally into the village of Kilyos. The dolmush will drop you at the town's only important crossroads, next to a tea house and a grocery store. Take the road on the left and follow it down to the beach, bearing right at the fork. Admission to the beach is 200TL (28¢), including the use of a little straw changing hut; cabins and beach umbrellas are available at an extra fee. The long, sandy beach is open from 8 a.m. to 6 p.m. every day. Note that Kilyos is famous for its *undertow,* a feature of most Black Sea beaches. Swim only where indicated; don't swim if told not to. If you feel yourself being pulled out to sea, swim without panic *parallel* to the beach, *not* directly toward it. You'll make it unless you panic and try to fight your way straight to shore.

3. Bosphorus: The Asian Shore

The Asian shore of the Bosphorus is not quite so easy of access from the main part of the city, but it holds just as much to see and do as the European shore. Allow a bit more time for transportation on your Asian excursion.

Besides the familiar ferryboats, there are also dolmushes and buses from Üsküdar and other Asian shore points to Taksim Square.

ÜSKÜDAR: In the days of the Byzantine and early Ottoman Empires, **Scutari** (Üsküdar in Turkish) was the first night's stop on the warriors' route into Anatolia. The emperor would always encamp here for the night, after having left the Seraglio that very same morning. The reason is clear: it took the army a whole day and part of the night to be transported across the Bosphorus. This first stop had its advantages, of course. Urgent messages could catch up with the emperor in no time at all if dispatched from the capital by fast boat, and the emperor could always send home for the few things he had inevitably forgotten.

From the ferry dock in Üsküdar you can start on walks around the town. There are several mosques worth a look, but the main attractions are the old Istanbul houses, the romantic wooden structures that gave the city a lot of its charm a century ago. Though most of these in the European sections of the city have tumbled down from sheer dilapidation or have given way to modern slabs of apartments, a few good examples of this type of house have survived here.

A good object for your walk through the town is the **Çinili Cami,** or Tiled Mosque, a little gem filled with İznik tiles, similar to the Rüstem Paşa Camii in Eminönü. From the ferry dock, walk straight up the big street in front of you (Hakimiyeti Milliye Caddesi) and through the shopping district to another fork. On the left will be a small side street called Tavukçu Bakkal Sok, which you take to Çavuşdere Caddesi. Turn right onto Çavuşdere and walk along this street and up the hillside about half a mile until you come to the mosque.

Üsküdar is famous for its cemeteries as well. The **Büyük Mezaristan** is one of the holiest Muslim cemeteries, and one of the largest in the East. You'll be able to spot it by the tall cypresses which are scattered all through it, towering over the surrounding buildings. This is a characteristic of Turkish cemeteries, these tall trees. One Turkish poet referred to the cemetery as the "country of the cypresses."

ÇAMLICA: One of the favorite picnic places for the people of Istanbul is the hilltop forest called **Büyük Çamlıca,** reached by bus or dolmush from Üsküdar. Take an Ümraniye bus (no. 11) or dolmush from the ferry dock to the stop called **Kısıklı.** From here it's a short taxi ride to the top, or a cheap dolmush ride if there are dolmushes running. If you're a hiker, take Büyük Çamlıca Caddesi out of the square (it's the one by the bus shelters) and walk to the path to the top, which turns left off the road a few hundred feet from the square.

The view from the top is Istanbul's best. The panorama includes the entire city, the Islands, the Sea of Marmara, the Bosphorus, and the hinterland of Asia on the opposite side of the hill. If you haven't brought your own lunch, you can buy a snack here, or a cold drink and sip it under the pine trees. The lookout tower near the grove is for fires, and also contains the bright signal lights which broadcast the weather forecast over a large area, due to the tower's visibility. A blue light means tomorrow will be fair, green means rain, yellow is for fog, and red means you're in for some snow.

The smaller hill next to Büyük Çamlıca (Big Çamlıca) is called **Küçük Çamlıca** (Little Çamlıca). Walk out of Kısıklı Square in the opposite direction to get to this lookout, less crowded than its bigger neighbor. There's a fine big park on the way, always loaded with picknickers and other sights native to such areas: women in bright baggy shalvar pants, a girl's voice singing a minor-key Oriental song, and a pair of small, dark eyes peering over a windowsill at the action in the street.

UP THE COAST OF ASIA: From the bus stop next to the dock in Üsküdar, bus no. 15 begins its long journey up the Asian coast of the Bosphorus to **Beykoz,** the last big town before the Black Sea. Hop on and off this bus along its route to see the things I'll mention below. For the short hops, a passing dolmush will do as well.

Beylerberi Palace

Take the bus to **Çayırbaşı,** a short ride from the dock through little villages with tiny ferry docks and waterfront restaurants (surprisingly expensive). Just before Çayırbaşı, the bus passes through a tunnel. Walk from the bus stop back to the tunnel and along the narrow sidewalk running the length of the tunnel, where you'll find the entrance to Beylerbeyi Palace. (Ferries from dock 3 in Eminönü make the 45-minute run to Beylerbeyi about every two hours; tickets cost the same as to Üsküdar.)

This small palace was built in 1865 by Sultan Abdülaziz. He used to get away from the busy life in the city by coming here, where the view of the Bosphorus and the surrounding forests creates a very restful atmosphere. You have to take a tour through the building, rather than just wandering alone. The staff of guides here is not multilingual as at Dolmabahçe, so you might get a guided tour in Turkish—lots of help. But a guide is really not necessary. Most of the palace speaks for itself. Though the majority of rooms are decorated in the thickest of Ottoman baroque, some parts of the palace are appealing, such as the huge central fountain and pool, which must have given a cool, peaceful effect to the large central room which it dominates. Your guide will point out Sultan Abdülaziz's official reception room and the furniture he used, encrusted with pounds of gold ornament in proportion to the sultan's massive bulk. Another room, the guide says, is the one used by Empress Eugénie of France when she visited the Ottoman capital in 1869. This was during a period when the Ottoman and French emperors were trying to better their relations with one another. Eugénie's visit was in exchange for one made by the sultan to Paris. The French emperor, Napoléon III, didn't accompany his wife on her trip to the East, which, the guide mentions slyly, was all the better for her romantically inclined host. Another room, lined with wood paneling, was said to have been furnished by the sultan himself, who did woodworking in his spare time.

In the grounds of the palace on the Bosphorus shore are two graceful little kiosks, not open to the public right now, where it's easy to picture the sultan or his family having tea, right over the water. For a good view of the Bosphorus at this point, take a peek through the gates of the fence built along the dock. There's always a ceremonial soldier on duty here, complete with rifle, and though you're not supposed to picnic on the dock, he won't mind if you take a peek at the view.

Beylerbeyi is open from 9:30 a.m. to 4:30 p.m.; closed Monday and Thursday. Admission costs 500TL (70¢).

Küçük Su Kiosk

If Beylerbeyi is a retreat from the city, the Küçük Su Kiosk (tel. 332-0237) must be a retreat from a retreat. From Çayırbası bus stop, take the bus to the **Plaj** stop and walk across the creek (the "Little Sky-Blue Water") to the kiosk. It's actually a tiny white palace, now being completely restored. This looks like a perfect place for an evening party with a small group of friends—exclusive, of course. Actually, the meadow behind the kiosk was a favorite picnic spot for the Ottoman upper classes during the 19th century. It is said they came up from the city in sleek gilded boats, moored in the Büyük Gök Su (across the meadow), and socialized on the weekend. People from Istanbul still find this one of Asia's best picnic spots.

The kiosk is open from 9:30 a.m. to 4 p.m.; closed Monday and Thursday. Admission costs 300TL (42¢).

Anadolu Hisar

From the kiosk it's a short walk to Anadolu Hisar, or the **Fortress of Anatolia,** right on the banks of the Büyük Gök Su. By now you've noticed the big fortress called **Rumeli Hisar** (Fortress of Europe), Istanbul's most famous castle, across the Bosphorus. Whereas Rumeli Hisar is in very good condition (after restoration, of course), only one tower remains of Anadolu Hisar. What's left has been restored and the area around the castle has been made into a park. Though the castle today could hardly perform its original function as a guard tower governing traffic through the Bosphorus, it forms a good background for the tiny homes, shops, and tea houses built at its base on the banks of the stream. Gaily painted fishing smacks and the low-bellied cargo boats, called caiques, take the place of the gilded barges of former royalty.

. . . And Back to Europe

The rest of the sights on the Asian side you may want to explore on your own, though for the remainder of the most interesting things to see on the Bosphorus, it's necessary to cross to Europe. Several ferryboats run on "ring" routes to get you across the water. Runs leave every hour or two for a 20-minute voyage. There's a ring boat operating from Anadolu Kavağı in Asia to Rumeli Kavağı and Sarıyer in Europe, and another operating from Paşabahçe and Beykoz in Asia to Yeniköy in Europe.

Some towns also have *dolmuş motor* (private motorboats), and these will ferry you across much as a dolmush car does on land.

If you miss the boat and don't want to try for a dolmush (car) across the Bosphorus Bridge, hire a fishing smack to take you across—it costs about 1,800TL ($2.50), and worth it for the excitement.

No matter which route you take from Asia, you'll arrive in Europe at some point along the Sahil Yolu, the coast road. Buses run north and south along this road all day long between Taksim and Eminönü in the south and such points as Bebek, Emirgan, Yeniköy, Sarıyer, and Rumeli Kavağı to the north. Dolmushes are the best way to go short distances.

4. The Marmara Beaches

Although I still hold that your best bet for swimming in Istanbul is Kilyos Beach on the Black Sea, Istanbul has a good selection of other beaches which you might want to try out. First among these is the big beach at **Florya,** a suburb of Istanbul on the European coast of the Sea of Marmara. Trains for Florya leave from the **Banliyö** platforms of Sirkeci Station every half hour or less for the 30-minute ride to Florya. You can take any train; they all pass Florya. A bus runs this route beginning in Taksim Square and passing through Aksaray; it's bus "F," "Florya," and the trip might last an hour.

The beach is directly opposite the train station, just a few steps down the road from the bus stop. Privately run beaches line parts of the shore here, but the beach you're interested in is the **Florya Büyük Belediye Plajı.** Entrance to the beach is 100TL (14¢), changing room included. For slightly more you can have safe-deposit service for your clothes. Right next to the beach is a modern cafeteria overlooking the water, and it *is* a cafeteria, where you take your food through a line and pay no service charge. The beach and its facilities are open from 7 a.m. to 7 p.m. every day.

5. The Princes' Islands

The islands in the Sea of Marmara right at the mouth of the Bosphorus have been used through the ages as a hunting ground for Byzantine royalty, a prison or place of exile for those who met with the emperor's displeasure, a refuge for Orthodox and Armenian monks and nuns, and finally as a resort for Istanbul people tired of the bustle and noise of the city. The name Princes' seems to have been tacked on by foreigners who associated the islands with the adventures of Byzantine royalty. The Turks simply say **Adalar**—the Islands—when referring to them.

TRANSPORTATION: Ferries to the islands depart from both Sirkeci (Dock 5) and Kabataş (Dock B, near Dolmabahçe Mosque), but the **express ferries** are the ones you want, and they depart only from Kabataş. The trip from Kabataş to Heybeli, the first express ferry stop, takes 50 minutes, whereas by normal boat from Sirkeci the trip is almost twice as long. Büyükada, the largest and most interesting island, is another 15-minute trip past Heybeli. I'd recommend that you take the express boat all the way to Büyükada, see that island, then take a later boat for the short hop over to Heybeli, and after you're done there, catch a returning ferry to Kabataş. The express trip from Kabataş to Büyükada costs 450TL (63¢).

Here are some convenient departure times (subject to change): from Kabataş, the one morning express ferry departs at 9:45 a.m.; from Sirkeci, normal ferries depart at 6:50 and 10:50 a.m. and 12:50 and 2:50 p.m. The few morning boats from the city to the islands fill up quickly, and though you'll almost certainly get aboard, you may have to stand the whole way unless you get aboard and claim a seat more than 30 minutes before departure. There are many afternoon and evening boats, but these don't leave you much time for sightseeing on the islands.

Return trips depart Büyükada for Kabataş at 1:40, 2:40, and 6:40 p.m.; the slower boats to Sirkeci depart Büyükada at 4, 6, and 7:30 p.m., and there are three even later boats. Departures from Heybeli are 15 minutes after the aforementioned times. Ferries shuttle between Büyükada and Heybeli throughout the day.

Besides the ferries, there is now **hydrofoil,** or *deniz otobüsü,* service from Kabataş to Büyükada. The trip takes only 22 minutes, and costs 1,000TL ($1.40).

BÜYÜKADA: The small islands of Kınalı and Burgaz are passed on the trip to the bigger two called Heybeli and Büyükada. The big ones hold the most interest for you, the smaller ones have less to see and do. Büyükada, the biggest island of them all, is the best place to begin your tour. Walk off the ferry dock and you're back in the last century. Up the main street are a clock tower and small monuments set in little grass plots; along the waterfront, couples sip tea or cold drinks and watch the boats pass; the sleepy little streets hold rows of shops with awnings shading their fronts from the burning sun. And best of all, there are no cars! Except for a few police Jeeps, town service trucks, and the telegram delivery boy's motorbike, no motor-driven vehicles are permitted on the islands. Instead, loads are transported and people get around in horse-drawn carriages or on bicycles.

Outside the town, by the dock, the island holds a few more settlements and lots of forested hills good for a picnic or a walk. On the edges of the forests are huge old mansions with picturesque gardens in front, many of them still manicured daily by the house gardener. The houses are great sights, with Victorian ornamentation and peculiar "observation tower" cupolas on the roofs.

There are no really good beaches on Büyükada; activities are limited to walking and relaxation unless you know someone with a boat and a set of waterskis. But it's a good change from the city, and you'll want to experience it at least once. Here are some hints: walking from the dock, the market and business sections of the town, along with the fairly expensive seaside restaurants, lie to the left; for a walk through the old houses up to the pine trees on the hilltop, walk to the clock tower and bear right. You can get a carriage from the stop on the left of the clock tower square. Bargain with the driver for a tour around the island, about an hour trip, for about 4,000TL ($5.60).

Büyükada seems a dream from the 19th century. It's strange to a 20th-century person to be able to hear the sound of people walking, of muffled horses' hooves, of bicycle bells, and nothing more. Graceful old hotels with dowagers on the verandas, dark wood-paneled restaurants with white tablecloths and gleaming crystal, and rooms with tranquil views of the sea bring the tableau to life. There are plants everywhere. All in all, after even the briefest look around, it becomes obvious to the modern-day visitor that the islands found their proper place a century ago, and stayed there. For those who have the wherewithal to make the dream a reality, a night in the old **Splandit (Splendid) Hotel** (tel. 351-6950) will cost 17,000TL ($23.80) per person, all meals included.

HEYBELİ ADA: The trip to Heybeli Ada, the neighboring island, takes ten minutes. On the left of the dock is the big naval college, while on the right, tea houses and cafés extend the length of the waterfront, broken now and then by patches of color where fishermen are drying their nets. Activities here are much the same as on Büyükada, with these additions: tea or a cold drink is available in any of the tea houses on the waterfront; a carriage ride to the other side of the island will bring you to some small strips of sand for swimming.

Just down the road from where the carriage drops you off is a pay beach, but if you can do without the facilities (and the crowds), walk to your left just before the entrance to the pay beach, through the forest, past the naval college's installations, to a small point extending into the water from a corner of the island. The beach (at the bottom of the bluff) is thin and pebbly, but the swimming area is sandy and warm. A good idea for those who really want to swim is to rent a rowboat (2,000TL, $2.80, an hour) from next to the pay beach and row down here to swim; you might take a row out to the private little island just off shore.

A grand tour of Heybeli by horse-drawn carriage will cost about 5,000TL ($7). There's a lively nightlife on the island, but it's mostly private goings-on among people from the city who own houses on the islands. The islands are really a place for a daytime visit, preferably on a weekday.

Chapter VIII

ACROSS THE SEA
OF MARMARA

1. Getting There
2. Yalova and Termal
3. İznik (Nicaea)
4. Bursa
5. Uludağ

IN THE LATE 13TH CENTURY, a small settlement of Turkish tribesmen under the capable leadership of their chieftain, Osman, began to expand their control over nearby areas. Nicaea, capital of an empire only a half century before, soon came under their influence; not long after, they captured the Byzantine town of Bursa (Brusa) and made it the first capital of the Ottoman state. Osman, for whom the empire was later named, is considered its founder. When he died he was succeeded by his son, Orhan, and the succession of capable and talented rulers after him continued well into the 16th century.

Further conquest moved the capital to Edirne, then to Istanbul, but the first Ottoman capital was here in Bursa, on the slopes of Uludağ, or "Great Mountain," the one the Greeks called the Mount Olympus of the province of Bithynia. As the culture of the young empire emerged, it spread over and changed the old city, adding new buildings to the beauty of the setting. The Turks still call it Yeşil Bursa—Green Bursa—and though the greenery abounds on the mountain and in the plain below the city, modernization has taken a lot of greenery from the city itself. Still, there's a lot to see and do here—it's a "must" destination on your Turkish itinerary, and the major destination in this chapter. But neither must we miss İznik, the ancient city of Nicaea. You might also want to make a detour and take the waters at an attractive thermal spa which has been popular since Roman times.

1. Getting There

You have your choice of going by air, direct bus, or ferryboat. But virtually everyone agrees that the cheapest and most interesting way to get from Istanbul to Yalova, Termal, İznik, and Bursa is by ferryboat and bus or dolmush. In case you miss the passenger ferry, I'll give you information on how to climb aboard the car-ferry, which also goes to Yalova.

THE PASSENGER FERRYBOAT: Express ferries steam away from the Istanbul dock at Kabataş, near Dolmabahçe, several times daily on the two-hour trip to Yalova, a town on the Asian Marmara coast. From Yalova it's a 20-minute bus or minibus ride to the baths and hotels at Termal, or a 75-minute ride by bus to Bursa, longer if you take in İznik on the way.

In summertime express ferries depart Kabataş at 9 a.m. (nonstop), 9:45 a.m. (two stops), and at 2:15, 6:30, and 7:40 p.m. Monday through Saturday; on Sunday and holidays departures are at 8:30 a.m. (two stops), 9:30 a.m. and noon (nonstop), 2:15 p.m. (two stops), 5:45 p.m. (nonstop), and 9 p.m. (two stops). A one-way ticket on a nonstop boat costs 1,300TL ($1.80), half that much on a two-stop voyage (stops are at Heybeli and Büyükada in the Princes' Islands). There is less service, about three boats daily in each direction, in the winter. By the time you read this the city may have taken delivery of its new hydrofoils. If they go into service on this route, look for drastic schedule changes and faster, more expensive service.

Departures from Yalova for the return trip to Kabataş are at 6, 8:30 (except Saturday), and 11:30 a.m., and 1:30, 5, and 8:50 p.m. Monday through Saturday. On Sunday and holidays boats leave Yalova for Istanbul at 6:20 and 11:15 a.m. (two stops), 1 p.m. (nonstop), and 8:20 p.m. (two stops); this last boat docks at Sirkeci, near the Galata Bridge, rather than at Kabataş.

Be careful! Two of the boats on Sunday, at 3 and 6:15 p.m., go only to Büyükada, not all the way to Kabataş.

Board the boat at least 30 minutes before departure time; 45 minutes or an hour is not too early in summer, as the boat will fill up quickly.

THE CAR-FERRY: The passenger boats from Kabataş are definitely the most pleasant and convenient way to go. But if you miss the boat, don't despair. You can go by car-ferry (whether or not you have a car), and you'll save a bit of money in the bargain.

Car-ferries depart from the special dock at Kartal, a town east of Üsküdar on the Marmara shore, every hour on the hour (except at 2 a.m. and 4 a.m.). The voyage takes 75 minutes and lands you in Yalova, right next to the passenger-ferry dock. A one-way passenger ticket on the car-ferry costs 400TL (55¢).

But before you can board the car-ferry you must get from Istanbul to Kartal. Take a passenger ferry from Karaköy to Haydarpaşa Station (90TL, 13¢), then take any *banliyö* (suburban) train (50TL, 7¢). Trains begin running at 6 a.m. and make the trip from Haydarpaşa eastward along the coast every 20 minutes; the journey from Haydarpaşa to Kartal takes about 40 minutes. After leaving the train at the Kartal Station, walk downhill to the shore and left to the car-ferry dock. Return car-ferry voyages from Yalova are at the same times and prices as those from Kartal. The coastal trains to and from Haydarpaşa operate until around midnight.

FLYING TO BURSA: It's possible to fly from Istanbul's Atatürk Airport to Bursa. A company called **Sönmez Holding Hava Yolları** operates two daily flights (except on Sunday) between Istanbul and Bursa. The little planes ferry the company's executives back and forth between their Bursa factories and Istanbul offices. For reservations, contact the airline at the airport's domestic terminal (tel. 1/573-9323 or 573-7240), or buy your ticket downtown from the **Moris Seyahat Acentesi,** Tünel Pasajı 11, Beyoğlu, just opposite the Tünel Station (tel. 1/149-8510), or at **Anadol Turizm,** Cumhuriyet Caddesi 261 (tel. 1/146-8084), not far from the Hilton.

To get to the airport, take the airport bus from the Turkish Airlines terminal in Şişhane Square.

BY BUS: Though there are several daily buses from Topkapı Bus Station to Yalova and Bursa, this is the least convenient way to go. The trip takes something like six hours because you must loop all the way around the Sea of Marmara. And the price is about that of an express ferry, which gets you there in two hours.

2. Yalova and Termal

Whether you arrive by ferryboat or by bus, you will step down in Yalova in the main square, right at the center of town, and you'll be faced with a large and dramatic statue of Atatürk.

Yalova is a farming town which also makes part of its living as a transportation point. Though it has all the services you might want, there's no reason to stay unless an emergency arises.

TERMAL: The hot, mineral-rich waters that spring from the earth here were first exploited in Roman times, but the Ottomans also used the baths ever since they first arrived in this area over six centuries ago. Atatürk also enjoyed coming here, and he ordered the construction of a cottage for himself, and a hotel for other visitors.

Getting There

The Yalova municipal bus named "Taşköprü–Termal," the no. 4, will take you the 7½ miles (12 km) to Termal for 90TL (13¢), or you can take a minibus for 150TL (21¢). To find the bus and minibus departure area, do this: as you debark from the ferry in Yalova, walk toward the statue of Atatürk and turn right on the first street. The stop for both buses and minibuses is a block down on the left-hand side.

The road winds west and south of Yalova and passes down lanes of lofty plane trees planted for the express purpose of shading the road and welcoming the visitor. As you reach your destination, you will enter a verdant valley, cool with shade and the sound of a brook. Walk up the slope from the parking lot into a garden setting. Patio cafés, restaurants, a few hotels, and the baths themselves are only a few steps from where the bus drops you.

Hotels

The hotels in Termal are basically resorts, not just lodgings, and so prices are somewhat higher than what you might expect. The hotels are quite nice, though, and well worth the money. Both are operated by the government's Tourism Bank, and both have restaurants that serve delicious meals at moderate prices.

The **Turban Yalova Termal Çamlık Oteli,** Termal, Yalova (tel. 1931/4905), and the **Turban Yalova Termal Çınar Oteli** (same address and telephone number), are priced at 17,200TL ($24.10) to 19,825TL ($27.75) single, 22,500TL ($31.50) to 26,200TL ($36.70) double, the price depending on whether the room is in the front or the back of the hotel; breakfast is included in these prices, which are for the high summer season. Off-season rates are 25% to 30% lower, but they do not include breakfast.

Taking the Waters

The hotels at Termal have their own bathing facilities for those serious about hydrotherapy. But if you stay here you must at least try out the three other baths. The **Valide Banyo,** charging 550TL (75¢) for a 90-minute session, is an Ottoman institution, recently refurbished and quite a sight to behold. The

Sultan Banyo is even grander, and also costs a bit more, at 1,750TL ($2.45) for one person, 2,200TL ($3.10) for two. The **Kurşunlu Banyo,** or "Lead-roofed Bath," has a large open-air swimming pool which you can use for 850TL ($1.20); also an enclosed pool and sauna, for 1,000TL ($1.40), beneath the lead roof, and small private cubicles for individuals and couples, charging 850TL ($1.20) single, 1,150TL ($1.60) double.

When you're done at the baths, and have taken a stroll in the gardens, visit Atatürk's cottage, which is open now as a museum.

ONWARD TO İZNİK: After Termal, return to the main square in Yalova. At the end of the dock in Yalova is the usual confusion of porters, men selling *simits* (sesame-seed rolls), and bus hawkers. For the trip to Bursa, pick a comfortable-looking bus, hop aboard, and in a few minutes you'll be off on the 1¼-hour trip. Buy your ticket right on the bus: 650TL (90¢). Taxis operating as dolmushes also run from the Yalova docks to Bursa. It'll cost you over twice as much as the bus, but it's faster and more comfortable. But before speeding off to Bursa, you might want to consider a detour to İznik (Nicaea). For details of that side trip, read on.

Among the buses waiting at the Yalova dock will be one going to İznik, ancient Nicaea, famous as the site of the first Ecumenical Council in 325 and a later one in 787, and also as the center of the Turkish tile industry at the height of its artistic achievement. The tiles in most of Istanbul's great mosques were made here. If you take the morning boat from Istanbul, you can see İznik on your way to Bursa, and still arrive in Bursa in time to find a hotel for the night. A bus hawker will be looking for passengers to İznik at the docks. Don't confuse İznik with İzmit, another town nearby. The 90-minute trip costs 600TL (85¢). The road runs along the shore of the İznik Lake for much of the trip. The lake is a vast expanse of water with hardly any settlements along the shore; a house here and there is about all. Finally the bus rattles through the Istanbul Gate in the old city walls of İznik, turns left at the main crossroads in the town, right next to the ruins of the Sancta Sophia Church, and rolls the block or two to the town's bus station.

The old city walls have four gates; the two main streets of the town run between pairs of gates, north to south and east to west, meeting next to Sancta Sophia.

3. İznik (Nicaea)

Nicaea was a pretty important town in the Byzantine Empire. In fact, when Constantinople was captured by the Crusaders in 1204, it became the capital of the short-lived Empire of Nicaea, actually those remnants of the Byzantine Empire which the Crusaders had not taken. As soon as Constantinople was retaken by the Byzantines, Nicaea ceased to be a capital, but retained its importance through the rest of the Middle Ages.

ORIENTATION AND INFORMATION: İznik was founded as a Roman town, and therefore has two main streets, from north to south and from east to west, which cross at the center. Right at the central intersection is the Sancta Sophia Church. The **Tourism Information Office** (tel. 2527/1933) is east of the church several blocks, on the main commercial street of Kılıçaslan Caddesi. Working hours here are 8:30 a.m. to noon and 2 to 5:30 p.m. every day in summer, shorter hours off-season. A block or so beyond the Tourism Office is the **museum** and the **Green Mosque.** In the opposite direction is the lake.

HOTELS: If you're stranded in İznik, or want to spend a day on the shores of the lake, there are several suitable hotels you can try. In the center of town near the bus garage, just across the street from the Belediye Sarayı (Town Hall), the **Hotel Babacan,** Kılıçaslan Caddesi 104 (tel. 2527/1211), with 42 double rooms (12 with private shower), charges 2,750TL ($3.85) single and 3,850TL ($5.40) double without bath, 3,300TL ($4.60) single and 4,950TL ($6.95) double with bath.

The **Motel Burcum** (tel. 2527/1011), a 25-room place right on the shore of the lake, has comparable facilities, and charges 7,020TL ($9.85) double, breakfast included.

Similarly well situated, and with identical prices, is the **Çamlık Motel** (tel. 2527/1631), at the southern end of the lakefront road.

RESTAURANTS: A light meal of white cheese (*beyaz peynir*), bread, and a bottle of beer will cost less than 650TL (90¢) at one of the places on the shore, such as the **Dostlar** (tel. 1585), near the Motel Burcum. Even cheaper are the little restaurants along Kılıçaslan Caddesi near the Town Hall and the Hotel Babacan. Look for the **Köşk Lokantası** (tel. 1843) and the **Çiçek Restaurant,** facing one another. At either place, a full lunch or dinner will not cost more than 1,800TL ($2.50), but note that the Çiçek serves no alcohol and that the Köşk has a slightly more attractive decor.

THE SIGHTS OF İZNİK: To get an idea of what it was like in Roman and Byzantine times, take a walk on the walls of the city. At any of the city's gates you can get an idea of its size—big for the time, compared to the quiet Turkish town it is today. Nowadays there's lots of room for the red-tiled houses scattered throughout the city, with little beehive ovens behind them and pumpkins and squashes in the gardens. The commerce (and importance) of the town is limited mostly to grape growing. The big refrigerated trucks from Yugoslavia, Bulgaria, and Austria that come to load up with grapes are a familiar sight in the town.

Walking around İznik, the place where I most felt the real charm of the town was at the **Lefke Gate** (the eastern one, at the end of the street passing near the museum). The Lefke Gate is actually three gates passing from a chute next to the first gate. Walking through the gates you see old inscriptions, friezes, decoration, and several Muslim graves. The road out of town runs beside an old aqueduct, still in working order, which brings water to the chute next to the first gate, and from there into the town. The road is charming, with a nearby saint's tomb, oxcarts, and country views enhancing its beauty.

For Byzantine monuments, look at the **Sancta Sophia Church,** fairly well ruined now, but with some good frescoes and a fine mosaic floor. To get the key, walk up the street past the bus garage following the signs to the museum. A man will come back with you from the museum and will open the door anytime from 9 a.m. to noon or 2 to 5 p.m.; admission costs 200TL (28¢).

The city's Muslim inheritance includes one of Turkey's finest mosques, a real gem of Islamic architecture and of the tilework which made İznik famous. The **Yeşil (Green) Mosque** is right across the street from the museum. The museum itself (open from 9 a.m. to noon and 1:30 to 5 p.m., closed Monday; 200TL, 28¢ admission) has the same collection of relics as most small-town museums, but the building is interesting. It's an old *imaret,* or soup kitchen. These were often built by benevolent rulers near great mosques as an example of Muslim charity, and they dispensed food to the poor for free. There are some examples of İznik tilework in the museum, but not as good as those in the Çinili Kiosk in Istanbul, or in the great mosques. In one glass case is a collection of ornate mascara bottles used by Ottoman women.

Next to the museum is a minaret which had its top shaken off in an earthquake. You can climb to the top for a look at the town, but be warned! You've never seen steps so narrow and dark; and at the top, you find yourself in a stork's nest.

Only a few ruins down by the shore of the lake mark the site of Constantine's palace, the place where the First Ecumenical Council was held. In order to solve the problem of Arianism, Constantine called the council, which upheld the position of Athanasius and condemned Arius, formulating its decision in the Nicene Creed. The Seventh Council, however, was held in the Sancta Sophia Church. It was at this council that the iconoclastic controversy, the one involving the question of religious images, was solved; iconoclasm, or the "breaking of images," was rejected, opening the way to progress in the development of Byzantine art forms.

While you're at the museum, ask a staff member to take you to see İznik's most fascinating sight, discovered only a few years ago: the **Yeraltı Mezar,** or **Katakom,** as some people call it. It's a Byzantine family tomb uncovered by workmen during construction of a road. Except for one intrusion by graverobbers, the tomb had been undisturbed until its discovery. The paintings decorating the walls and ceiling are almost perfectly preserved: geometrical designs, flowers, and the ubiquitous Byzantine peacocks. The man with the key will take you to the bus garage where you can rent a minibus to take you the few kilometers out of town to the site. If you get to İznik, don't miss this. (Note: Another tomb, nearby, is *not* worth the trouble. Don't let the guard talk you into going there.)

ONWARD TO BURSA: Buses depart İznik's little bus station for Bursa about every hour through the day, with the last bus at 6 or 7 p.m. The 90-minute trip costs 650TL (90¢). If you've seen what there is to see in İznik, head for the big city, where the hotel selection is broader and the restaurants are better, more numerous, and yet just as cheap. The countryside between İznik and Bursa is one of rolling hills dotted with small villages with white minarets. On the way, the bus passes a roadside scene: a gypsy caravan, one of the wagons covered in plastic; later on, a marble mill, piled high with slabs of stone to be used for everything from kitchen counters to gravestones.

By traveling along the borders of the big İznik Lake, over the hilly countryside and across the wide flat plain, you will find yourself at the base of the towering mountain and in Bursa . . . you can't miss it!

4. Bursa

Because of its heritage as the first Ottoman capital, Bursa is particularly rich in religious monuments: great mosques (which also, in early times, served as living quarters), baths, and *türbes* (tombs) of the wealthy and powerful. Besides its beautiful buildings and its greenery, Bursa is also famous for its knives, fruit juices, and for Turkish towels, which were invented here to be used at the many baths.

ORIENTATION: The center of the town is **Cumhuriyet Alanı** ("Republic Plaza"), referred to locally as **Heykel** (statue) because of the equestrian statue of Atatürk erected there. From this square, the big boulevard called **Atatürk Caddesi** runs through the new part of the city, past the Tourism Information Office, bears right and becomes **Cemal Nadir Caddesi,** then bears left and changes to **Altıparmak Caddesi.** This street continues as the main thoroughfare all the way to Çekirge, and is called **Çekirge Caddesi.** In the other direction out of Cumhuriyet Square, going east into an old part of the city, several streets lead to some of the city's most famous monuments. **Yeşil Caddesi** passes the Yeşil (Green)

Mosque and the Yeşil Türbe (Green Mausoleum), and the Emir Sultan Mosque. When the bus brings you into town, you'll stop at the **City Garage** on **Mahmudiye Caddesi** (called **Ulu Caddesi** by local people). Ulu Caddesi is connected to Cumhuriyet Square by **İnönü Caddesi**, also called **Yeni Yol.** The city is spread along the foothills near the mountain's base, and extends from the easternmost section of the city to the mineral baths of Çekirge, a suburb several kilometers to the west.

GETTING AROUND: If you fly to Bursa, the airport bus will drop you near the center of town; if you arrive by bus, leave the bus station and cross Uluyol to the dolmush stop on the opposite side. From this point dolmushes will take you to Heykel, where you transfer for dolmushes and buses to other parts of town. To identify dolmushes and their routes in Bursa, look in the car's windshield for a small plastic sign hung on suction-cup hooks. The sign will tell you the car's destination; or it may say "Taxi," indicating that it's not operating as a dolmush for now.

From Heykel, dolmushes and buses leave for Emir Sultan, and it is these cars you should take for many of the major sights to see. Cars and buses also leave here for Çekirge, the mineral baths center, and for Kültür Parkı and Sigorta, intermediate points along the road to Çekirge.

USEFUL FACTS: Many of Bursa's **banks** are located along Atatürk Caddesi in the center of town, between the Ulu Cami and Heykel. The **main post office** (Merkez PTT) is on Atatürk Caddesi across from the Ulu Cami. The **Tourism Information Office** is at Atatürk Caddesi 82 (tel. 241/12-359) near the Ulu Cami. The staff is friendly, English-speaking, and very helpful. The bus station has its own little Tourism Information Desk as well.

WHERE TO STAY: You have your choice of several areas when you stay the night in Bursa. You can stay in the center of the city, which is convenient but noisy, or in Çekirge, which is less convenient but very quiet, with the bonus of free mineral baths. There are also hotels atop Uludağ (covered in the last section of this chapter), but you would want to stay up there to get away from the city, not as a base for sightseeing.

Downtown Hotels

Traffic noise is minimized at the **Hotel Dikmen,** Fevzi Çakmak Caddesi 78 (tel. 241/14-995), about 150 feet up the hill on the street (also sometimes called Maksem Caddesi) which begins beside the main post office. The Dikmen plays host to tour groups, but if rooms are available you'll pay 9,622TL ($13.45) single with shower, 12,585TL ($17.60) double with shower, 13,325TL ($18.65) double with bath.

Across Fevzi Çakmak Caddesi from the main post office stands the **Hotel Artıç,** Postane Yanı, Ulucami Karşısı 123 (tel. 241/19-500), in a very convenient but also very busy location. Choose a room carefully with noise in mind, and you can stay right here for 6,600TL ($9.25) single, 9,350TL ($13.10) double, with private shower.

For Budgeteers: A much more modest lodging is the well-used **Otel Çamlıbel,** İnebey Caddesi 71 (tel. 241/12-565 or 25-565), in a quiet location. To find the hotel, walk one block west from the main post office, past the Türkiye Emlak Kredi Bankası, and turn left onto İnebey Caddesi. The Çamlıbel is two blocks up the hill. The hotel has an elevator, dependable hot water, good cross ventilation, and private parking for a few cars. Rooms go for 3,300TL ($4.60) single, 4,700TL ($6.60) double, 6,000TL ($8.40) triple without private shower; or 4,500TL ($6.30) single, 6,200TL ($8.70) double, and 7,500TL ($10.50) triple with private shower. Breakfast is served in the hotel, but is not included in the aforementioned prices.

Near the Bus Station: Gazcılar Caddesi, a block south of the bus station, has a hotel which, though very modest, will do if you arrive in the middle of the night and don't want to hunt for something farther afield. It's the **Gazcılar Oteli**, Gazcılar Caddesi 156 (tel. 241/49-477), neat and clean if simple, with central heating and rooms priced at 3,300TL ($4.60) single, 4,700TL ($6.60) double without shower, or 4,500TL ($6.30) single, 6,200TL ($8.70) with shower.

Hotels in Çekirge

The hotels in Çekirge, aimed at the hydrotherapy market looking for a cure or a spa holiday, are a cut above the downtown places. If you don't mind taking ten-minute bus, dolmush, or taxi rides to get between your hotel and the sights, and you are looking for comforts, by all means stay in Çekirge.

The **Yıldız Oteli**, on the main street at the upper end of the village (tel. 241/66-605), is deluxe as far as Çekirge goes, with all the comforts, and prices of 21,450TL ($30.05) double, with breakfast. The only thing missing is the view of the valley, but that's available at its sister establishment, the **Büyük Yıldız Oteli** (same phone), less than half a mile farther up the hill, on the outskirts of town. Besides modern rooms and furnishings, and the best possible views, the Büyük Yıldız is quiet. Rooms rent for 30,650TL ($42.90) double, breakfast included.

At the center of the village is the **Termal Hotel Gönlü Ferah,** Çekirge Caddesi (tel. 241/62-700), with wonderful views of the valley, comfortable accommodations, and smooth service. Though you can get all the comforts on the street side of the hotel, convince yourself that it's time to splurge so you can enjoy the marvelous view. Room prices are 26,860TL ($37.60) double on the street side, 30,500TL ($42.70) double on the view side, and breakfast is included.

Right next door to the Gönlü Ferah is the **Hotel Dilmen** (tel. 241/21-701), with very similar accommodations at the same prices.

Rooms at the **Yeşil Yayla Oteli**, behind the Yıldız Oteli (tel. 241/68-026), up at the far end of the village past the military hospital, are much simpler and also very much cheaper. For a simple bathless room here one person pays 3,250TL ($4.55) single, 4,400TL ($6.15) double. As with most Çekirge hotels, daily use of the hotel's mineral bath facilities is included in the room price.

RESTAURANTS IN BURSA: Many places have lent their names to various

dishes in the realm of Turkish cuisine, but no name is more widely known than that of *Bursa kebap,* which is thin slices of grilled döner kebap spread on a bed of flat pide bread and topped with melted butter and a savory tomato sauce. Bursa kebap is synonymous with İskender kebap, for it was a Bursa chef named İskender (Alexander) who invented the dish. Though Bursa kebap is made and served all over Turkey now, it is still a specialty here, and two of our recommended places to dine excel in its preparation. By the way, Bursa is also renowned for its fruits and vegetables, which, in season, are easily the best for hundreds of miles around. Don't leave without tasting a Bursa peach *(şeftali)* if you visit during the season.

For Bursa Kebap

The talk of Bursa these days is a place called **Hacı Bey**, on Ünlü Cadde (tel. 16-440), a Bursa kebap restaurant just off the square at Heykel. Go to Hacı Bey for the best döner of your life: thin slices of the succulent, grilled meat on a bed of flat pide bread, topped with savory tomato sauce, browned butter, and parsley, with yogurt on the side. The sauce and butter are poured on right at your table after the plate is brought, so wait for them. The decor in the restaurant is nothing to brag about, just plain and simple. But you go there for a real culinary experience, not for atmosphere. A portion of Bursa kebap with yogurt, a salad, mineral soda, and coffee, with tip, will be 1,500TL ($2.10). Highly recommended—in fact, a must when you're in Bursa.

Another good place for döner kebap is the **Kebabci İskenderoğlu,** at Atatürk Caddesi 60, which serves this kebab, and almost nothing else, to crowds of hungry Bursalıs at lunchtime for 550TL (75¢) a portion. If you're hungry, order a *duble* (double) portion. Remember not to start in on your kebap until the waiter brings the tomato sauce and butter to pour on your plate.

For "Ready Food"

For a quick, good, cheap meal of cafeteria-style food, head for the **Şehir Lokantası,** İnebey Caddesi 85 (tel. 26-203), near the Çamlıbel Hotel, only half a block off Atatürk Caddesi. Though not a fancy place by any means, it is clean and airy, and the steam table is always filled with hearty dishes which can make a full meal for less than 1,300TL ($1.80).

In the Kültür Parkı

Bursa is fortunate to have a vast swath of greenery in its midst. Besides the Archeological Museum and other amusements, the Kültür Parkı, north of the road to Çekirge, has half a dozen small restaurants. Each restaurant has an indoor dining room and also a summer patio dining area shaded by trees. Having lunch at one of the outdoor places here is among Bursa's greater pleasures, especially following a busy morning's sightseeing. The **Selçuk Restaurant** is typical of them all, with friendly service, good food, and low prices. I paid 1,900TL ($2.65) for a full lunch, beverage and tip included.

For İnegöl Köfte

Lowly köfte has an honored place on the dinner tables of Bursa, and lots of back-street restaurants specialize in the dish. A modern köfteci, in the main square, is the **İnegöl Köftecisi,** down a side street at Atatürk Caddesi 48. It's a clean, bright place with speedy service, and has the added advantage of staying open later in the evening than a lot of other eating places. Plain köfte is 400TL (55¢); made with onions or with cheese it's 650TL (90¢); side dishes such as a salad, cacik (yogurt with shredded cucumber and garlic), or piyaz (white beans, onions, and peppers in oil and vinegar, served cold), are 250TL (35¢) a plate; desserts are the same.

Another köfteci, the **Özömür Köftecisi,** is located in part of the restored Covered Market complex, and offers köfte and about the same side dishes as the İnegöl at the same prices, but with the charming atmosphere of an old bedesten. It's a very small place, no bigger than one of the old market shops, and very popular with Bursa people, so get there early to avoid the rush. The Özömür is located right next to the Ulu Mosque, which is on Atatürk Caddesi, on the far side as you come from Cumhuriyet Square. A whole lunch should come to about 1,400TL ($1.95).

If you stay a few days in Bursa and try both of these places, for the sake of variety I suggest that you launch out on your own into the winding little streets in the market area or off Atatürk Caddesi, and find yourself a little köfteci of your own. Prices will invariably be lower than at the two places I've mentioned, and who knows? You might find a blue-ribbon chef.

In Çekirge

The **Çardak Restaurant** is the restaurant of the Ada Palas Hotel, but in summer it moves from the hotel dining room across the street to a rustic building with a fine view over the plain. This restaurant might be crowded, especially on weekends, but if you get there early enough you'll be able to find a table. Here, too, there's an English translation of the menu. The Çardak now has competition in the form of the **Papağan Restaurant,** right next door and sharing the view of the valley in Çekirge. A meal at either place will be in the range of 4,000TL ($5.60), and I recommend that you choose whichever one looks to be busier, meaning that the chef of that particular place is trying extra-hard just then.

Breakfast alla Turca

Hot soup, eggs, bread and jam, white cheese, and black olives are all regulars on Turkish breakfast tables, but undoubtedly one of the best, cheapest, and most savory breakfasts served in this country is börek. Several pastry and pudding shops on Atatürk Caddesi will have a large, flat rectangle of steaming *su böreği* in their windows from 7 to about 9 a.m. Enter, point to the börek, and the chef will cut you a portion and chop it into manageable pieces. Take it to a table, order a glass of hot milk-and-sugar, and you've got the quintessential Turkish breakfast for 600TL (85¢) or less. The börek is made of wheat flour and sunflower-seed oil and stuffed with white cheese and chopped parsley—with the milk-and-sugar a good start to the day: hearty, quick, and inexpensive.

THE SIGHTS OF BURSA: The main sights in Bursa are those left from the city's days as an imperial capital. Some of the earliest and greatest of the Ottoman rulers were born and lived here, and left monuments which still give some idea of what life must have been like then.

The Green Mosque and Tomb

To start, take a bus (no. 1 or 2) or an Emir Sultan dolmush to the **Yeşil Cami,** (Green Mosque) from Atatürk Caddesi. The mosque is open most of the day. The carved marblework on the doorway is some of the best you'll see in Anatolia. Take a look inside and you'll soon see that it was built as far more than a place of worship. On the sides of the building are rooms with shelves and fireplaces, meant to be quarters for important government officers such as the high judges and ministers of state. The sultan himself had sumptuous quarters in rooms above the front door, decorated with fine tilework trimmed in gold. Rooms to either side of the sultan's loge were furnished for servants, advisors, and girls of the harem. The mihrab of the mosque is almost 50 feet high and echoes the work of the front door, with the addition of tiles in the intricate carvings near the top of the inset. Mehmet I was reigning when the mosque was completed in 1419. Instead of the Byzantine influence, which predominates in Istanbul, the Yeşil Mosque and the other mosques of Bursa lean toward the old Turkish styles as found in Samarkand and parts of Iran.

The **Yeşil Türbe** (Green Tomb), across the street from the mosque, is the burial place of the mosque's builder, Mehmet I. Take a walk through the tomb, the walls of which are decorated with fine tiles. This is one of the prettiest of many tombs in Bursa built on the same plan: small buildings, round or hexagonal, with some tile decorations on the outside, but the best workmanship around the walls of the interior. Visit any day from 8:30 a.m. to noon and 1 to 5:30 p.m., for free.

From the tea garden next to the mosque you can get a good view of the city, and take a rest.

The Ethnographic Museum

The **Turkish Islamic Art Museum (Türk İslam Eserleri Müzesi),** also called the Ethnographic Museum, is just down the street a short way from the Yeşil Cami toward the center of town. Here is kept this city's heritage from its Ottoman past: tilework, inlaid wood, costumes, pictures, articles of jewelry, and a strange circular wooden compass with a full map of the world painted on its face and the compass needle pivoting on Mecca. The museum is open from 8:30 a.m. to noon and from 1 to 5:30 p.m. every day except Monday. Admission is 200TL (28¢), half price on Saturday afternoons, Sundays, and holidays.

Emir Sultan and Beyazıt Mosques

A short dolmush ride farther along the same street which passes the Yeşil Mosque brings you to the **Emir Sultan Camii,** another of Bursa's collection of mosques. Walk around behind the mosque (following the road), and continue past the bus stop straight down the hill into the residential section. Eventually you'll come to the **Yıldırım Beyazıt Camii,** down in the valley, the big mosque visible from the top of the hill. The road passes through the busy section housing Bursa's silk industry, with little factories on every side weaving and dying material for handkerchiefs and scarfs. This is an older section of Bursa, and one of the more interesting ones: dark-eyed children with bright smiles, horsecarts painted with delicate flower motifs, and an outside market stretching down the street from the big mosque in the valley. The mosque is one of Bursa's earliest, a model for many of the city's other mosques, including the Yeşil Mosque.

To get back to the main square, walk down the road which turns left from the road you came on, then walk down the hill to Kurtuluş Caddesi, where you can get a bus or dolmush back to Cumhuriyet Square.

The Bat Pazarı

Bursa has an interesting market and small-industry area, called the Bat Pazarı (as opposed to the covered market, *kapalı çarşı* or *bedesten*—see below). No, they do not sell bats (either baseball or flying) in the Bat Pazarı—*bat* is the Turkish word for goose, and this must at one time have been where geese were brought to be sold. Now it's a warren of little streets alive with the clanking of hammers, the huffing of bellows on forges, the racket of tinsmiths at work, the intense quiet of the inside of a tiny cloth shop. Here you can see blacksmiths making the famous Bursa knives (not a particular type of knife, but rather all types of knives with Bursa steel blades), *baltas* (Turkish hand axes), or *sobas* (sheet-metal stoves). In a tiny square is a huge old tree which serves as focus for the market. Old men sit here to watch the activity, peddlers lay out their wares on a cloth, buying and selling of a horse or a goat takes place at this spot. An old man may come through the center of the throng dragging a ganglion of ropes which he has made by hand, and is now willing to sell for a small amount. The Bat Pazarı is to me one of the more delightful things to see in this delightful city. To find it, walk down the hill on İnönü Caddesi (Yeni Yol) out of Cumhuriyet Square (Heykel) almost to the small mosque set out in the street. Turn right onto one of the little streets before you come to the mosque and the Bat Pazarı is yours.

Ulu Cami and Bedesten

Near the main square, the sights to see include two of the city's biggest: the **Ulu Cami,** or Great Mosque, and the maze of restored buildings making up the

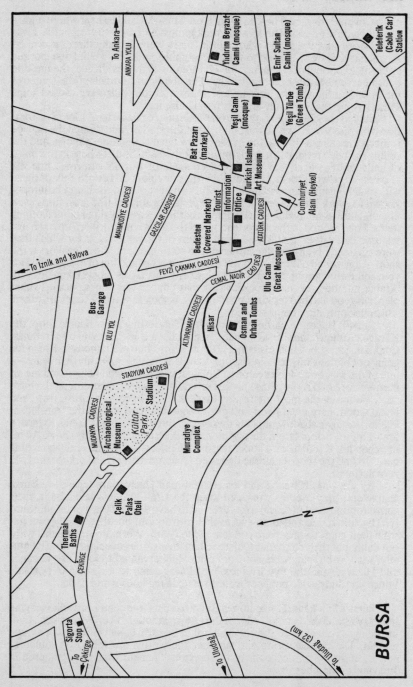

To Ankara

ANKARA YOLU

Yıldırım Beyazit Camii (mosque)

Emir Sultan Camii (mosque)

Teleferik (Cable Car) Station

Yeşil Cami (mosque)

Yeşil Türbe (Green Tomb)

Bat Pazarı (market)

Turkish Islamic Art Museum

MAHMUDİYE CADDESİ

GAZCILAR CADDESİ

Tourist Information Office

To İznik and Yalova

Bedesten (Covered Market)

ATATÜRK CADDESİ

Cumhuriyet Alanı (Heykel)

FEVZİ ÇAKMAK CADDESİ

CEMAL NADİR CADDESİ

ULU CAMİ CADDESİ

Ulu Cami (Great Mosque)

Bus Garage

ULU YOL

ALTIPARMAK CADDESİ

Hisar

Osman and Orhan Tombs

STADYUM CADDESİ

Stadium

Kültür Parkı

MUDANYA CADDESİ

Archaeological Museum

Muradiye Complex

N

Çelik Palas Oteli

Thermal Baths

ÇEKİRGE

Sigorta Stop

To Çekirge

To Uludağ

To Uludağ (32 km)

BURSA

city's Covered Market. The Ulu Cami is on Atatürk Caddesi near where it joins Cemal Nadir Caddesi. The mosque took almost half a century to build. I was told a story that the sultan who built it (there were actually three) promised Allah that if he were allowed to win an upcoming battle, he'd build one mosque as big as 20 normal ones—hence the Ulu Cami's 20 domes. Inside, the mosque doesn't resemble any other in Turkey. The ablutions fountain in the center of the floor is a fine touch, and the inscriptions on the walls have caused some Turks to quip that it's really an inscription museum.

Behind the Ulu Cami is the **Covered Market,** or **Bedesten.** A lot of restoration work has been done on the buildings of the market, and though the outside is much the same as it was, the inside is now lined with modern shops, and the ceiling has been redone in a modernistic wood design. Still, it's here in this maze of halls and passages that you'll turn up some of Bursa's surprises: fine silk scarves; huge wool socks knitted in the riotous colors of Turkish folk designs, with matching knit caps and mittens; "Turkish towels" and the heavy bathrobes known to every Turk as one of Bursa's specialties. In fact, the local firms even manufacture as many different designs of bathrobes as they do of other clothing items. Poke around in the alleys leading off the main streets to turn up old hans, restored caravanserais still used by members of the same guilds for which they were originally built. In one corner of the section reserved for jewelers is the shop of a wizened old man who will spread out his collection of old watches for you, somewhat grumpily, but with loving care: tiny ladies' pocket watches with Arabic numbers, a thick pocketwatch that chimes the hours, various other pieces in good and bad repair, some working as soon as you pick them up, others which tick only after being shaken.

Bursa's Bedesten harbors a particularly interesting and valuable shop, the **Karagöz Antique Shop,** Eski Aynalı Çarşı İçi 12 (tel. 18-727), run by Mr. Şinasi Çelikkol. Şinasi Bey and his father, Rafet, before him are famous in Bursa for going out of their way to help visitors, as well as being known for their wares—one of the first times I ever came to Bursa, it was Rafet who helped find me an inexpensive hotel room. Since his father's death, Şinasi has continued the business, gathering the most interesting carpets, items in copper, brass, iron, and inlaid wood, garments, hand-knit gloves, etc. It's hard to find the translucent leather *Karagöz* shadow puppets these days, but Şinasi always seems to have a few of these "actors" from the traditional Turkish Punch and Judy show. All his merchandise is sold at very good, reasonable prices—you can't really go wrong here. To find the shop, enter the Bedesten (covered market) and ask for the Eski Aynalı Çarşı.

By the way, Karagöz and his straight-man Hacivat are legendary Bursa characters. Employed as workmen when the Ulu Cami was being built, their comic routines and practical jokes are said to have delayed the work significantly. The sultan demanded an end to their disruption, but they simply couldn't stifle their gags, so they were condemned to death. Work proceeded well without them, but their comrades took to telling their stories over and over. Eventually, shadow puppets were cut from camel hide, painted to look like Karagöz and Hacivat, and the two irrepressible clowns came to life again in portable Punch and Judy–style puppet theaters set up in tea houses and parks.

Bursa's Silk Trade: For centuries Bursa has been the center of a silk-weaving industry established on the order of the Ottoman sultan. People from surrounding villages converge on the city in April to buy the baby worms at an annual market. During the spring and summer the worms are raised on mulberry leaves, and they spin cocoons of the precious filament which are gathered in June and September.

Should you happen to be in Bursa during one of these important "silk trade months," head for the eastern end of the Bedesten and find the **Koza Han,** a caravanserai named for the silk cocoon (*koza*). The Koza Han, an attractive building recently restored with the aid of a multi-million-dollar grant from the Aga Khan, is the throbbing heart of the silk trade. Another traditional silk market is the one in the **Emir Han,** in the southwestern part of the Bedesten. Both are locales for silk brokers' offices and warehouses. As for the silken cloth, it's sold by the meter or the bolt in the bazaar, but you may prefer a souvenir such as a blouse, scarf, or handkerchief.

Hisar

Bursa is still sometimes talked about as a charming old Ottoman town, and it is just this in some sections, though modernization has destroyed a great deal of its charm. For a look at an old section with big trees here and there, some of them gutted at one time during their centuries of life but still full of leaves; with old, white-bearded men with canes and black prayer caps, sitting in the sun and drinking tea, waiting for the muezzin to call them to prayer; of old gravemarkers topped with carved turbans (which denote the dead man's rank) scattered in picturesque confusion through green cemeteries dotted with cypresses, head for the Hisar section of town, where there is still some of this old Bursa. Hisar was once the citadel of the town. Some of the walls are still intact, though they, like the old town itself, have suffered much from modernization. From the Ulu Cami, walk down Atatürk Caddesi, but instead of bearing right down the hill as the main road does, turn left a bit farther on and head up into an old market section, finally coming out on Pınarbaşı Caddesi. Use this street as a starting point for your wanderings in the old town.

If you're interested in seeing the tombs of the two first great Ottoman leaders, Osman and Orhan, work your way to the corner of the fortress walls overlooking, and closest to, Atatürk Caddesi. The tombs are here in a little park above the city and the plain.

Muradiye

One of the city's nicest spots is that near the **Muradiye Mosque** (take a dolmush from Cumhuriyet Square to Muradiye; or bus 2, which runs from the Yeşil Mosque through the main square and past the Muradiye on its way to Çekirge). Besides the mosque, built by Sultan Murat II, there are a number of tombs here decorated in the finest Turkish tiles, an old hospital that's been renovated and is again being used, and most interesting of all, the **Old Ottoman House** (17. Y.Y. Evi), an ancient Bursa house said to have been lived in by a 14th-century sultan (though it was probably built a few centuries after he lived). The house itself is interesting, but even more so is what's inside. It's now a museum, but not the standard glass-case-and-fragment-of-something type that's such a bore to go through. The old house has been refurnished—as a house!—with things found in the Bursa area. There are three rooms restored as of this writing, with more to be redone in the future. The sitting room has comfortable, low Oriental sofas along two walls, a fireplace at one end, and a complex of cupboards and shelves at the other, carved and painted in traditional designs. The dining room has cushions placed on the floor around a single big soup dish and spoons for several people, made of a dark and light ivory. Outside these two rooms, open to the stairway, is the servants' waiting room, furnished with rows of pillows, each with its own hand mirror so that the servant could check on his presentability before attending his master. If you're interested in getting a glimpse of what Turkish life was like, don't miss a visit to this museum. It's open every day but Monday from 8:30 a.m. to noon and 1 to 5 p.m.; 100TL (14¢) for admission.

Cultural Park

Not too far from the Muradiye complex is **Bursa Kültür Parkı**, or **Cultural Park**, a large area of greenery equipped with a sports stadium, restaurants, nightclubs, amusements, tea and beer gardens, and also Bursa's **Archeological Museum (Arkeoloji Müzesi)**. Broussa, or Prusa, was an important town under the Romans and the Byzantines, but its history goes even farther back to the time of Hannibal (200 B.C.). The artifacts from this rich history are preserved in the Arkeoloji Müzesi, open every day but Monday from 8:30 to noon and 1 to 5:30 p.m., for 500TL (70¢) admission. There is a bus stop on Cemal Nadir Caddesi (the road between Bursa and Çekirge) called "Arkeoloji Müzesi," and this is where to get off; enter the park through the gate nearby.

The Baths

Most of the buses and dolmushes going to Çekirge pass near the famous baths of Bursa, just off Çekirge Caddesi. For adventurous types, I recommend a ride to the Çelik Palas or Kükürtlü stop, and a walk down the hill. The most famous of the Bursa baths are the sulfur baths of **Kükürtlü**, now inside the hotel of the same name, and the **Yeni Kaplıca**, a Turkish bath on the site of a bath complex originally built by Justinian. The Yeni Kaplıca is a standard Turkish bath, with the three-room system: one cool, one warm, and one hot; in the middle of the hot room is a pool big enough for a plunge. The baths I describe here are reserved for men, the women having a separate, less elaborate establishment nearby. The basic charge for steam and washing yourself is 700TL ($1). The atmosphere is that of a huge, busy locker room—little privacy. It's especially crowded all day Friday.

For a sulfur bath, the Kükürtlü Hotel has several rooms in which to take one, varying in privacy from one big room in which everybody washes, to individual steamrooms of the type found in Çekirge's hotels. The baths are as rickety as the hotel, but if you're in the mood for an adventure, go to the hotel and tell them you want to try either the *sıra banyo,* a system where you wash in a first room, then enter a second room, tall and vaulted, lined with marble bathtubs in which you sit and soak; or the *aile banyo,* the family bath, where you get a steamroom all to yourself, unless you want to bring your family (there's a sign over the door to this potentially sinful place notifying bathers that a marriage license must be produced on demand!).

LEAVING BURSA: If you plan to fly back to Istanbul, contact Sönmez Holding Airlines at **Ottomantur,** Kızılay Pasajı, Çakırhamam (tel. 10-099 or 22-097), for tickets, or call the airport at 64-623 or 64-477. Flights leave Monday through Friday at 8:30 a.m. and 5 p.m., on Saturday at 9 a.m.

Those going to Istanbul by land have two ways to proceed: by getting a place in a taxi-dolmush going to Yalova, or by taking a bus from the central garage, the **Şehir Otobüs Garajı,** down on Uluyol. Sign up for dolmushes at the offices along Atatürk Caddesi which advertize "Yalova Dolmuş," or take a dolmush from Heykel (Cumhuriyet Alanı) to the "Garaj" stop. At the central garage, just tell one of the hawkers you want to go to Yalova and he'll direct you to the proper ticket window for the next bus. You should catch a bus 90 minutes before the ferry is due to leave Yalova for Istanbul if you want to be sure to be on that boat. If you go by dolmush, start at least 75 minutes before boat time.

The central garage is the place to go for any other land transportation out of Bursa. Buses leave frequently for Ankara (seven hours; 2,800TL, $3.90), İzmir (7% hours; 2,200TL, $3.10), and Çanakkale (six hours; 2,400TL, $3.35). You can also, if you wish, catch a bus directly to Istanbul and go all the way by land, bypassing the ferry ride (but who'd want to?). Unless you check times the day before, you may have to wait up to an hour for a bus to any given place. To avoid this delay, go by the garage the day before you plan to leave, or have your hotel call and ask for departure times.

5. Uludağ

If the weather is good when you visit Bursa, consider taking the cable-car ride to the top of Uludağ for the view and the cool, fresh air. For those who want to get away from it all completely, there are hotels and restaurants on top of the mountain, and though they're a bit more expensive than those in town, some are still within our budget range.

Getting to the top is half the fun. Dolmushes go up the side of the mountain, but a cheaper and better way is by cable car, called the **teleferik.**

GOING BY CABLE CAR: Get a dolmush or a bus (no. 8) from Cumhuriyet Square for the 15-minute ride to the teleferik station (tel. 13-635) at the foot of the Uludağ. Except in very bad weather or heavy winds, the teleferik runs about every 40 minutes. The cars hold 35 people maximum and leave as soon as full if this happens before the scheduled departure time. A round trip, all the way to the last station and back, costs 1,800TL ($2.50) and takes about 30 minutes each way. If you only want a short ride, buy a ticket only for the trip from the base station to the halfway house: 15 minutes each way.

The base station is called **Teleferuç;** the halfway house is **Kadıyayla.** The summit station of the teleferik is called **Sarıalan.** To the right of the corridor as you come out of the cars in the station is a little snackbar with a view of the valley. The area around the station has some restaurants with tables outside under pine trees, a number of A-frame bungalows rented by the National Parks Service for specified periods of 25 days, a smaller chair lift running to the section called **Cennetkaya,** and a stop for dolmushes to take you to **Oteller,** the main hotel section, near the mountain's highest peak.

DRIVING UP THE MOUNTAIN: Those with rental cars can drive almost to the top of Uludağ by taking the auto road which starts from beside the main post office, or the road west from Çekirge. Otherwise, there are dolmushes from the bus station, charging somewhat more than for the trip by cable car.

About halfway up the mountain you'll come to the entrance to the national park, where each car must stop and pay an admission fee to the park of 200TL (28¢) per person, 500TL (70¢) for a car and driver. After passing the park boundary, the hotel zone (Oteller Mevkii) is about 7 miles (11 km) along the very winding road of rough granite-block pavement.

HOTELS ON ULUDAĞ: When you plan your stay on top of Uludağ, several points are important to remember. First, it's chilly up here, even in summer, so bring a sweater and windbreaker even if you feel foolish about carrying them in summer. Next, have hotel reservations during the winter ski season, as these hotels are primarily for skiers and can be fully booked at peak ski periods. Also, you should know that only a few of the hotels are open in summer, and that these hotels often require some sort of board arrangement (two or three meals per day) no matter what the season. This is just as well, as there aren't really any restaurants up here.

The best moderately priced place to stay is the **Otel Beceren,** Oteller Mevkii, Uludağ, Bursa (tel. 2418/1111), an establishment which is actually two separate buildings, one of which closes in summer. For 15,000TL ($21) you can get a double room with bath and television with six channels of video programming; breakfast is included in the price. For 25,000TL ($35) two people can have that same room and all three meals.

As for the other hotels, the **Büyük Otel,** Oteller Mevkii, Uludağ, Bursa (tel. 2418/1216), is the old standard, having been here for decades. It has fairly small rooms, shower or bath equipped, which rent for 20,000TL ($28) double, breakfast and dinner included.

Largest and grandest of the mountaintop hotels is the **Grand Hotel Yazıcı,** Oteller Mevkii, Uludağ, Bursa (tel. 2418/1050). Prices here are the highest on the mountain, and though the comforts are in place, the price for a room still seems high, considering that it includes a shower, but no meals and no TV set: 19,000TL ($26.60) single, 30,000TL ($42) double.

EXCELSIOR: Besides the view and the fresh air, the Oteller area is not much different from Sarıalan, except that the highest point on the mountain is visible from here. With the proper shoes and the will to do it, it's about a three-hour hike to the shelter right on the peak, where you'll find a place to sit and a visitor's book to sign.

Chapter IX

THE NORTH AEGEAN

1. Çanakkale and Gallipoli
2. Troy (Truva)
3. Assos (Behramkale)
4. Ayvalık
5. Bergama (Pergamum)

THE DARDANELLES, the famous Hellespont of antiquity, are the straits dividing European and Asiatic Turkey, and the Aegean and Marmara Seas. The modern name comes from the name of the legendary founder of Troy, Dardanus. It was between these two shores that Leander swam to visit his lover, Hero—until one stormy night he failed to make it. Xerxes and Alexander the Great found the straits only a small hindrance. They both built bridges of boats and continued their marches. In World War I it was the key to Constantinople, but British and ANZAC troops failed to capture the straits during the bitterly fought Battle of Gallipoli.

Even today, people come here to "swim the Hellespont," ever since Lord Byron revived the fad. The American Ambassador to Turkey, Mr. Mac-Comber, swam the turbulent waters in 1975. But to cross from Europe to Asia less strenuously, catch one of the ferries that run between Gelibolu and Lapseki, or Eceabat and Çanakkale. The boats operate around the clock.

1. Çanakkale and Gallipoli

Çanakkale was one of the most crucial points of defense to the Central Powers in World War I. Huge guns guarded the straits against the intrusion of Allied warships, and their gun crews went to their work of range-finding with all the zeal of soldiers in a holy war.

Today Çanakkale is a sleepy little town that gets its only excitement from the travelers coming across the Dardanelles and going on to Troy. But there are memorials to Çanakkale's heroic past. On the hillside above the opposite shore are emblazoned in huge letters the words "Dur, Yolcu!" meaning "Traveler, stop a moment!" to remember the events which took place here. You can get a close look at **Kilitbahir Fortress** (the name means "Lock on the Sea") from the ferry which runs to the European shore. In fact, besides visiting the **Archeological Museum,** the ferry ride is about the only purposive activity you can partake of here. But the very Turkish activities of waterfront-strolling, eating long evening meals, tea-house-sitting and playing "tavla" (backgammon) are extremely popular in Çanakkale. In short, it's an easygoing and very pleasant little place.

GETTING THERE: There are 13 daily buses from Bursa to Çanakkale (5½ hours; 2,400TL, $3.35), dozens from Istanbul (5½ hours; 2,400TL, $3.35), and at least 15 buses a day from İzmir (1,500TL, $2.10) via Bergama, Ayvalık, and Ayvacık (the turnoff for Assos/Behramkale). From Edirne there are two direct buses per day.

Çanakkale's bus station is about half a mile inland from the center of town. When the time comes to leave Çanakkale, you can buy bus tickets at the bus company offices on the main street near the ferry docks.

If you're driving a rental car, or if you plan to visit the battlefields at Gallipoli, you will want to know about the **ferries** that cross the Dardanelles. There are two car-ferry services running at different points close to Çanakkale.

The more convenient southern car-ferry service runs between Çanakkale and Eceabat, near the battlefields of Gallipoli. Between 6 a.m. and 11 p.m. ferries depart each town every hour on the hour; there are also boats at midnight and at 2 a.m. from Eceabat, and at 1 and 3 a.m. from Çanakkale. The crossing from Çanakkale to Eceabat takes about 25 minutes in good weather. Because of the schedules, a round trip thus takes 90 minutes.

The slightly less frequent northern service runs between Gelibolu and Lapseki, departing Gelibolu at 1, 6, 7, 8, 9, and 10 a.m., noon, and 2, 4, 5, 6, 7, 8, 9, 10, and 11 p.m. From Lapseki, departures are at 2, 6, 7, 8, 9, 10, and 11 a.m., and at 1, 3, 5, 6, 7, 8, 9, and 10 p.m. and midnight.

You don't have to be driving a car to travel on one of these ferries. Passengers without cars are carried at a fare of 90TL (13¢) per person; for those with cars, fares are 1,200TL ($1.70) and up for a car and driver.

ORIENTATION: The center of town is a big open square stretching back from the docks to the Belediye, or Town Hall, building. The town's **Tourism Information Office** (tel. 1961/1187) is at the dock end of the square, only a few steps from the water. The office features a large display board with the name of every hotel in town and current prices, and the clerk watching the office usually knows some English and will be glad to help you find a room or a bus.

HOTELS AND MOTELS: The prominent new **Otel Anafartalar,** İskele Meydanı (Dock Square) (tel. 1961/4454), a few steps to the north of the ferry docks, is the most comfortable place in town. The front rooms in this seven-floor building have views of the straits, and there's a nice restaurant with a similarly good view on the hotel's roof. Prices are 11,300TL ($15.80) single, 13,000TL ($18.20) double, for a room with private bath.

Just off the main square, behind the clock tower, is the 35-room **Hotel Bakır,** Rıhtım (or Yalı) Caddesi 12 (tel. 1961/2908 or 4088). Modern double rooms here, many with excellent views of the water, go for 8,750TL ($12.25) single, 13,650TL ($19.10) double, 17,300TL ($24.20) triple, breakfast included.

The 66-room **Hotel Büyük Truva,** Kayserili Ahmet Paşa Caddesi (tel. 1961/1024), is six blocks north of the docks and the square. The hotel is actually part of the Hotel and Restaurant Workers' Union School, which means that service, by the school's students, is especially careful and considerate. A terrace in front of the hotel serves as a restaurant and tea garden on summer evenings. Rooms are a bit small but adequate, and cost 9,000TL ($12.60) single, 14,000TL ($19.60) double, bath and breakfast included.

A block inland from the Otel Anafartalar is the bright, clean, and new **Otel Yıldız,** Kızılay Sokak 20 (tel. 1961/1793 or 1069), on a quiet little street, renting

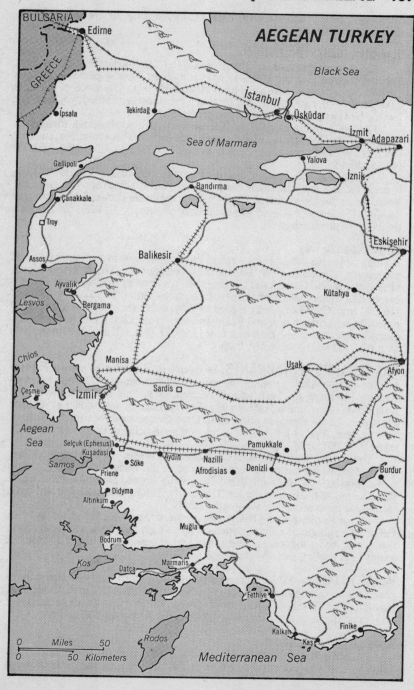

rooms with private shower for 6,000TL ($8.40) with a double bed, 9,000TL ($12.60) with twin beds.

Starvation-Budget Hostelries

The **Avrupa Pansiyon,** Matbaa Sokak 8 (tel. 1961/4084), behind the clock tower and down past the Hotel Konak, is a quiet, friendly pension run by a Turkish family, who make sure all is clean and neat. The price of a bed is 2,000TL ($2.80), or 5,000TL ($7) for two if breakfast is included; you can rent just the bed (without breakfast) if you prefer.

The odd-looking brick **Hotel Kervansaray,** behind the clock tower (tel. 1961/1187), has behind its weird façade a nice garden with a fountain, cooking facilities for guests, and rooms which rent for 1,000TL ($1.40) single, 1,600TL ($2.25) double.

The **Hotel Konak,** across the street from the Kervansaray (tel. 1961/1150), is quite modest and somewhat old-fashioned, but it advertises "constant hot water" in its double rooms, some of which have private showers. Here you pay 3,080TL ($4.30) for a double without private shower, or 4,840TL ($6.80) for a double with private shower.

On the Road to Troy

If you have a car and you want to stay comfortably in a tranquil grove of evergreens overlooking the Dardanelles, consider the **Tusan Truva Motel,** Güzelyalı Mevkii, Çanakkale (tel. 1961/4987), a hostelry that has more the ambience of a small, quiet retreat than of a highway motel. The Truva is 10 miles (16 km) from Çanakkale, off the road to Troy; turn right at a point just under 9 miles (14 km) from town, and follow the signs a mile and a half to the motel. Comfortable rooms with bath here cost 13,300TL ($18.60) double with shower, 14,800TL ($20.70) double with bath.

ÇANAKKALE'S RESTAURANTS: Without a doubt the most enjoyable place to dine in Çanakkale is along the waterfront promenade. The town is well equipped to serve you here, as half a dozen restaurants desert their cramped little dining rooms and set tables out to the left of the car-ferry docks as you face the water. All are similar in price, and a three-course meal consisting of soup or an appetizer, fried or grilled fish, salad, and a soft drink or bottle of beer might come to 2,200TL ($3.10), all in.

You can choose from among the **Restaurant Boğaz,** which is big and lively; the **Rıhtım,** which has been here for decades; the **Bizim Entellektuel,** whose name translates as "Our Intellectuals"; or the **Çanakkale Restaurant,** which some regard as the best of the lot. The nearby **Yalova Liman Restaurant** has a third-floor patio with a fine view of the straits.

As you sit dining in the balmy evening air, you may get to witness, as I did, the unsettling sight of a tiny wooden caique, which runs back and forth across the straits, being loaded up with innumerable passengers, about 50 cases of empty beer bottles, and a Volkswagen.

WHAT TO DO: Çanakkale has two museums of interest, and you may want to plan a trip across the Dardanelles to visit the battlefields at Gallipoli. Otherwise, it's off to Troy, 20 miles (32 km) south of town. But first take a walk to the Army and Navy Museum, and a dolmush or bus to the Archeology Museum.

Army and Navy Museum

From the Tourism Information Booth right next to the ferry docks, walk south along the waterfront until you reach the military zone and the entrance to the Army and Navy Museum (Askeri ve Deniz Müzesi), open from 9 a.m. to noon and 1:30 to 5 p.m., for free. Though the museums are officially closed on Monday and Thursday, you may in fact find them open. The museum grounds, actually the grounds and fortress of Çanakkale, are open to visitors every day until 10 p.m.

As you enter the grounds, you will see the mighty Çanak Kale, or **Fortress of Çanak,** built by Mehmet the Conqueror in the 15th century, and still armed and manned in the defense of the straits. Within its walls are dozens of cannons, ancient and modern, Turkish and European. The castle keep is now a gallery for various exhibits.

Outside the fortress near the shore is a replica of the minelaying ship *Nusrat,* which frustrated the Allied plan to force the straits and to race for Constantinople during the Gallipoli campaign of World War I.

Near the *Nusrat* is the entrance to a small museum with memorabilia of Atatürk, who became a military hero during the battles of Gallipoli.

The Archeology Museum

Çanakkale has a new Archeology Museum (Arkeoloji Müzesi) less than a mile from the clock tower on the road to Troy. Hop any municipal bus or dolmush marked "İntepe" or "Güzelyalı" and it will drop you at the museum, or you can walk to it in about 15 minutes. The museum is open from 10 a.m. to 5 p.m., closed Monday; admission costs 500TL (70¢), half price on Sunday and holidays. Signs in the museum are in both Turkish and English.

Exhibits in the attractive new building are arranged chronologically, from prehistoric fossils and Bronze Age artifacts up to and through those of the Roman period. The most interesting exhibits are those from Troy, labeled according to the excavation level at which they were found.

A Visit to Gallipoli

Called Gelibolu in Turkish, the narrow, mountainous peninsula on the northwestern side of the Dardanelles has seen more than its share of history. It was here that the Ottoman armies first set foot in Europe in the 1300s, headed for Christendom and bent on conquest. And it was here that the ultimately victorious Allied powers in World War I lost one of their most important battles.

The best way to see the battlefields, which are spread over a large area, is with a tour. **Troy-Anzac Tours,** near the clock tower in Çanakkale (tel. 1961/1200), organizes three-hour tours of the battlefields at a cost of 11,500TL ($16.10) per person; this includes car, driver, and guide.

The first thing you notice when arriving by ferryboat from Çanakkale is the fortress, called **Kilitbahir,** or "Lock on the Sea." Like the Çanak Kale on the opposite shore, Kilitbahir was built by Mehmet the Conqueror as an aid to cutting off supplies and reinforcements to Constantinople during the conquest of that city in the early 1450s. But the most famous fight for Gallipoli was to come 4½ centuries after Mehmet's conquest of the great city.

Under the direction of the young Winston Churchill, then civilian head of the British navy, a combined naval and land campaign was planned to capture positions on Gallipoli, force the straits with heavily armored ships, and sail across the Sea of Marmara to seize Constantinople. Had the plan been successful, the Ottoman capital would have fallen to the Allied enemy, and the immensely important water route from the Mediterranean through the Aegean and the Marmara to the Black Sea would have fallen into Allied hands.

Churchill's campaign, set in motion in March 1915, was unsuccessful, not due to lack of bravery on the part of the British, Australian, New Zealander, and French troops who fought here, but because of bungled tactics, missed opportunities, and bad luck. A significant portion of the Allies' bad luck came from the fact that they were facing an utterly fearless and marvelously competent young Ottoman lieutenant-colonel of infantry: Mustafa Kemal, later known as Atatürk. Because he correctly guessed the Allied battle plan when his superiors did not, Kemal was able to stall the Allied advance, and ultimately to turn it around, though his signal victory wiped out his unit and almost resulted in his own death from shrapnel. The battles at Gallipoli raged on and off for nine months. The Allied ships took their survivors on board in January 1916 and steamed away.

Today the battlefields on the hills of Gallipoli are covered with military cemeteries—Turkish, British, French, and ANZAC (Australian and New Zealander)—somber reminders of tumultuous events that affected the course of world history.

2. Troy (Truva)

The legends surrounding Troy—hard to separate from its history—involve some of the most romantic names of antiquity and mythology. The Trojan War was supposedly fought around 1200 B.C. The general staff on the Greek side included Agamemnon, Achilles, Odysseus (Ulysses), Patroclus, and Nestor. On the Trojan side the heroes were Hector and his brother, Paris, who had kidnapped Helen from her husband, Menelaos, the King of Sparta, thereby causing the whole affair. The battle is said to have raged, on and off, for ten years. Hector killed Patroclus, thus enraging Achilles, who succeeded in killing Hector. Achilles's enemy, try as he might, was unable to wound his assailant, because Achilles had been dipped in the River Styx by his mother when he was still a baby and was therefore invulnerable in all those parts of his body which the water had touched. Paris had to avenge the death of his brother, however, and knew that Achilles's only vulnerable spot was the heel by which his mother had held him during the dipping. Paris, a true hero, shot Achilles right in the heel.

The war was dragging on. The Greeks might have given up except for an idea from Odysseus. The wooden horse he requested was built, the armies left in their ships one morning, the soldier-filled horse was dragged into the city, and while the city was drunk with celebration the smuggled soldiers opened the gates (the ships had returned under cover of darkness) and started on the slaughter of the populace.

This, at least, is the version given by Homer in the *Iliad*. Some modern historians differ, contending that the probable cause of the war was a rivalry over control of the trade which passed through the Dardanelles. So much for romance.

GETTING THERE: Minibuses fill up at Çanakkale's Otogar (bus station) every 30 to 60 minutes in summer, and head off to Truva (Troy), less than an hour away. One-way fare for the trip is 300TL (85¢). Off-season, dolmushes may not run all the way to Troy, but they will certainly go as far as Tevfikiye, a village less than half a mile from the ruins.

When you're done at Troy, you can hitch a ride out to the highway from Troy and hope a bus with an empty seat will come by. Once on this route I caught a soft-drink truck, and when we got to our destination I offered to pay the driver dolmush fare, as is customary, but it turned out I had no change. The driver said, "Forget it!" and leaped from the cab, plucked two (warm) bottles of pop from a case on the back of the truck, opened them, and we toasted the end of a successful, if short, journey!

TEVFİKİYE: This little village, just outside the archeological zone, is where you can buy soft drinks and snacks, and even find a barebones place to sleep (or camp) for the night. As the flow of visitors to Troy increases, Tevfikiye takes on more and more the aspect of a Turkish Disneyland, with things like "fragments of the wood from the original Trojan horse" and "replicas of the original treasure" on sale or on view.

THE RUINS OF TROY: Troy is open to visitors from 8:30 a.m. to 8 p.m. every day in summer, till 5 p.m. in winter, for 200TL (28¢).

If you've heard anything about Troy, it's probably that there's nothing to see here. Well, there is something to see, but it's really interesting only if you have a detailed archeological guidebook to the site, or a personal guide who knows both the history of the cities and of the excavations. What you can get out of a visit to the ruins if you don't have these things is the feeling of the area, a view to the Aegean Sea over the Plain of Troy, and some sense of what went on here. Imagine living in this small (for our times) city on a lonely plain as a Greek armada was disgorging troops nearby for an assault and siege. It's worth the trip just to stand on a fragment of wall in the city and look over the landscape around you, and let your imagination go.

Among the ruins are a few private houses, a temple or two, the Bouleterion, or Senate, built around Homer's time (8th century B.C.?), several gates, including one with a ramp up which the Trojan Horse was supposedly dragged. The gate here was not big enough, so the story goes, and had to be partially dismantled so that the horse could be brought in. The reconstruction of the gate after the horse had entered is still identifiable.

The city was a going concern until the 4th century A.D., so there are some Roman vestiges as well: a theater, the Temple of Athena (rebuilt by the Romans), various columns and inscriptions. The different levels of the city are marked by signs, Troy VII being the one extant at the time of the war. The construction of the various walls tells you a lot about the city's progress through the centuries. As the city and its civilization grew, the stones in the walls were carved more neatly; the walls were built more strongly, sometimes at a slant.

About in the middle of the tour (following the signs) is a sacrificial altar near two wells, one of which was supposedly used for storage of the blood of the slain animals.

Through the centuries since the *Iliad* was written, scholars had come to accept the whole story as a fabrication made from whole cloth by Homer. There had been expeditions to find the lost city, based on descriptions of the Troad (the vicinity of Troy) in the poem. After all had given up, an amateur archeologist named Heinrich Schliemann decided to try again. Born in Germany, he had struck it rich in the California goldrush. With plenty of money and a team of workmen, he came to this area and told the workers where to dig. It took a few years, during which the entire scholarly world laughed at him, but Schliemann finally uncovered an ancient city—no, nine ancient cities, one on the top of another! Vindicated at last, Schliemann was feted throughout the scholarly world, and expeditions followed him in his work, notably that of Professor Blegen of the University of Cincinnati, who discovered yet another two cities, and completed the excavations.

3. Assos (Behramkale)

Assos is difficult to get to, but impressive when you reach it. The ancient town was founded in the 700s B.C. by colonists from Lesbos, the Greek island which is visible across the Gulf of Edremit. Once founded, it flourished and became a center for scholars and philosophers. Aristotle paid a visit and stayed three years, and St. Paul visited briefly.

The town made its living as a port and as an agricultural center, and though it is no longer used as a port (except by the occasional yacht), it's still a farm town. The main part of the village is on top of a lofty hill surrounded by a massive wall, large fragments of which remain intact. At the very foot of the hill, almost in the water, is the old port, now a tiny hamlet of a dozen buildings which cling precariously to a narrow beachhead right up against sheer rock.

The situation of the town is very impressive, and the panoramic view a marvel, but at the moment there is little else to see or do. The famous Temple of Athena is going to be rebuilt, but until it is, visitors will have to be satisfied with a visit to the Murad Hüdavendigar Mosque atop the hill, a look at the great walls, a meal, and perhaps a night's sleep, in one of the simple pensions down by the harbor.

GETTING THERE: Those with their own cars will find Assos easily accessible; those without will have to plan carefully, as public transportation is not convenient.

South of Çanakkale 45 miles (73 km; two hours) is the town of Ayvacık (*not* Ayvalık!), the turnoff for Behramkale, which is then 12 miles (19 km) to the south along a narrow, winding but paved road. If you come by bus, start early in the day, and then ask in Ayvacık for dolmushes to Behramkale, or hitch a ride with another tourist.

As you approach Behramkale, take the right fork and you'll come to the impressive city walls, and also the necropolis. A mile and a half past the fork, on a stone-block road which winds down the steep cliff, is the port.

HOTELS: There are three small hotels and a few little camping places in the port section. The **Hotel Behram** (tel. 16) rents very tidy, comfortable rooms for 17,000TL ($23.80) double, breakfast and dinner included; you're required to take the meals, and you might as well do so as dining choices are limited. Cheaper places are the **Hotel Yıldız** (tel. 18) and the **Motel Assos** (no phone), where double rooms with shower rent for 6,000TL ($8.40), no meals included.

RESTAURANTS: The three hotels in the port all have little restaurants as well. The one at the **Hotel Behram** is the best, and also the most expensive, with meals for about 2,500TL ($3.50) to 4,000TL ($5.60). The very basic **Sahil Lokantası,** by the Jandarma post, is the cheapest place in the port. But don't expect village prices here: all food must be brought in from Ayvacık, and is therefore not cheap, but moderately priced.

THE RUINS OF ASSOS: As you approach the town you will pass (on your left) a nice **humpback bridge,** built by the Ottomans in the 1300s. Turn left at the fork and the road mounts the hill to the ancient **Acropolis.** The center of the modern town is right where the old one was, and the Acropolis now has a few little restaurants and souvenir shops, tea houses, and the inevitable bust of Atatürk.

At the very top of the hill is the spectacular view of the Gulf of Edremit, and also the **Murad Hüdavendigar Camii** (1359–1389), a simple, very early Ottoman-era mosque. The lintel over the door is carved with Greek crosses, showing that it was "borrowed" from an earlier Byzantine church, now in ruins.

Other than the mosque and the view, you can look at the site of the **Temple of Athena,** built in 503 B.C., ruined over the centuries, and about to be rebuilt.

SOUTH TO AYVALIK: Heading east and then south from Ayvacık brings you around the Gulf of Edremit and past the resort villages of **Akçay** and **Ören.**

Then 96 miles (155 km) from Ayvacık is the town with the similar name, Ayvalık.

4. Ayvalık

As you might imagine from a glance at the surrounding countryside, the cultivation of olives is important to this region. Actually, the Aegean coast was heavily populated by Greeks during the Ottoman Empire's time, and these communities controlled a big part of the olive commerce. After the exchange of populations, Turkish settlers took over the industry in Ayvalık. Today the olive oil from this region is known all over Turkey.

The town itself stretches for several kilometers along the waterfront, and there are smaller "suburbs" on nearby islands and peninsulas.

Besides its olive and olive oil produce, Ayvalık is also known as a fine, restful little resort town where city people come for a week or two in the summer, rent a room in a hotel or in one of the town's many old mansions (now pensions), and swim, spend hours over dinner, take a boat tour, or find a disco in the evening.

GETTING THERE: Unless you are careful to catch a bus that goes specifically to Ayvalık's Otogar, your bus will drop you at the northern turnoff for Ayvalık and you'll be three miles from the main square—you'll have to hitch a ride into town.

If you've been careful to get a bus that goes into Ayvalık, you will descend at the **Şehirlerarası Otobüs Garajı,** exactly a mile north of the square. You can catch any municipal bus ("Ayvalık Belediyesi") going south past the bus station, or you can hoof it. The walk downtown to the main square takes only 15 or 20 minutes.

ORIENTATION: The better part of the town is clustered around this square and up the slopes of the hill curving up from the water. The main street goes south along the coast past sections called **Orta Çamlık** and **Çamlık,** where many of the better hotels and pension choices are, and then past two or three discothèques and on to **Sarmısaklı Beach,** a few kilometers from the town. Ayvalık's plush motels are on this beach, as are some more modest hostelries and some restaurants. The **Tourism Information Office** (tel. 6631/2122) is less than a mile south of the main square opposite the yacht harbor.

HOTELS: Those used to staying in comfort have their choice of two attractive beachfront hotels on Sarmısaklı Beach, or another in a quiet, shady hideaway on another shore. The hotels right in Ayvalık are mostly very plain, but also clean and cheap.

Near Şeytan Sofrası

The **Murat Reis Oteli,** Sarmısaklı Mevkii, Ayvalık (tel. 6631/1680 or 2788), is located not on Sarmısaklı Beach, as its address might suggest, but at the base of the road to the Şeytan Sofrası, north of the beach. Secluded in a grove of pine trees, with its own beach, this attractive small resort hotel offers double rooms with bath for 20,350TL ($28.50) with breakfast, 27,000TL ($37.80) with breakfast and dinner, or 33,550TL ($46.95) for two with all meals included. Full board may be required during the busy summer season.

Right on the Beach

On Sarmısaklı Beach, the two nicest hotels are these:

The **Otel Ankara,** Sarmısaklı Plaj (tel. 6631/1195), has 57 rooms with bath priced at 12,000TL ($16.80) single, 15,900TL ($22.25) double, breakfast included, and that marvelous beachfront location. In summer they may rent rooms but only with all three meals included, in which case you will pay a total of 29,000TL ($40.60) double.

Virtually next door is the similarly attractive, 112-room **Büyük Berk Oteli,** Sarmısaklı Plaj (tel. 6631/2311), a modern building with a swimming pool, discothèque, playground, billiard and table-tennis room, and lots of water-sports equipment such as rowboats and sailboards. All rooms have balconies, bathrooms, and telephones, and cost 24,500TL ($34.30) double, breakfast and dinner included.

Downtown Hotels

Low-budget travelers will be delighted with the selection of plain but clean hostelries right near the main square. Though they are not on the beach, and do not usually have such luxuries as private bathrooms, they are certainly at the center of the action. Getting to the beach is cheap and easy by municipal bus.

The **Motel Kıyı,** Gümrük Meydanı 18 (tel. 6631/1438), is in "Customs House Square," a small plaza on the bit of land which juts into the water near the main square. The same plaza holds the Sahil Restaurant (see below). Not a motel at all, it's in an older building that has been given a nice facelift. Rooms, some of which have views of the water, cost 3,300TL ($4.60) single, 5,500TL ($7.70) double, 6,600TL ($9.25) triple, without private bath.

The very modest, old-fashioned **El Otel,** Safa Caddesi 3, at Talat Paşa Caddesi (tel. 6631/2217), is a block off Ayvalık's main street. It's clean if very plain, and a room with washbasin rents for 1,650TL ($2.30) single, 2,750TL ($3.85) double, 3,300TL ($4.60) triple.

Not far from the El Otel is the **Canlı Balık Oteli,** Gümrük Caddesi 20 (tel. 6631/2292), next door to the restaurant of the same name. Prices here for the simple but fairly quiet rooms are 3,000TL ($4.20) double for a room with running water, but no private bath.

The artfully hidden **İpek Oteli** (tel. 6631/1201) is 200 yards south of the main square, and half a block off the main street, but it's behind another building. When you find it, you'll discover a fairly modern structure bright with fluorescent lights, bare of much ornamentation, but clean. The double rooms, equipped with washbasins, cost 5,000TL ($7) double.

By the time you arrive in Ayvalık, the new **Önen Hotel,** on the main street just to the north of the main square, may be open. Guessing from the construction, it will be a cut above the other downtown places, though not as comfortable as the places on the beach.

RESTAURANTS: Those staying at one of the better hotels may have the meal question answered by a full-board requirement. If not, the first place to try is Ali Bey Island (see below). After that, there are several little places in the center of Ayvalık.

Seafood is the specialty, of course, and the best place in town to try it is the **Sahil Restaurant,** on Gümrük Meydanı (tel. 1418). In good weather you will want to grab one of the outdoor tables to dine under the stars. Order a fish in season, and a full dinner, beverage and tip included, might cost 3,000TL ($4.20).

In the narrow streets near the Gümrük Meydanı are numerous other small eateries serving up even cheaper fare in slightly less romantic surroundings. For instance, a meal at the **Ayvalık Restaurant** or the **Anadolu Pide ve Kebap Salonu** might cost only 1,400TL ($1.95).

WHAT TO SEE AND DO: Water sports and seafood dining are Ayvalık's forte, but before putting on your bathing suit or your napkin, take a stroll around this little town.

A Walk Around Ayvalık

The big olive-oil processing factories are right near the waterfront, but if you go back into the town you'll see some pretty streets of old classical-style architecture (another hint of the empire times). Walk on the street just out of the main square on which you find the Canlı Balık restaurant, and after a few blocks you pass the **Çınarlı Mosque,** an Orthodox church converted into a mosque. The iconostasis (the wall between the congregation and priests) is all in bright-blue, white, and gold; all of the pictures of saints have been removed in keeping with the Muslim ban on representation of the human form, and a Muslim pulpit has been made out of the original one. Remember to take your shoes off before entering.

Look for another minaret near the one on this mosque and you'll see another place of worship with the same history. Also, walking along the winding streets you pass carpenters' shops, bakeries, children tending goats, and shady little squares, always with a few tables and chairs for customers of a nearby tea house.

Harbor Tours

Right off the main square, boats load up each morning, afternoon, and evening for tours among the dozens of little islands and many peninsulas which make this coastline so interesting. An average tour costs 1,200TL ($1.70), or 5,000TL ($7) if a meal is included in the price.

Beaches

Besides the little beaches on Ali Bey Island (see below) and at Çamlık, Sarmısaklı Beach, reached from the town square by bus or dolmush, offers you almost 12 km (7½ miles) of sand and sun. Some of this is taken up by private establishments, some more has been claimed by little huts thrown up just for the summer. If you walk in the direction of Lesbos toward the tip of the peninsula, you'll find deserted stretches of beach. The really private areas are all the way around on the far side of the peninsula. If you're willing to walk you can have a whole beach to yourself.

Şeytan Sofrası

Overlooking the beach, in fact the whole area and all the way out to Lesbos, is the hilltop called **Şeytan Sofrası,** the Devil's Dinner Table. A side road off the main road near Sarmısaklı leads to the top, and it takes about a half hour to walk. In the late afternoon or evening take a cab from the main town square for the trip to the top, where there's a snackbar.

An Excursion to Ali Bey Island

Across the water from the main part of town, on what is technically a peninsula, though it's called an island, is a settlement called Ali Bey Island, or **Cunda.** You can get there by taxi, but the cheapest way (and more fun) is to take one of the motor launches that plies back and forth between the dock near the town square and the island. Boats leave on the hour from 7 in the morning until 11 in the evening (there's a full schedule posted by the dock) and charge 100TL (14¢) for the 20-minute ride, one way. If you walk to your right as you come off the wharf you pass a row of small outdoor fish restaurants right on the water. I took an early-evening boat to the island with two friends and we picked out one of these places—a difficult task, since they're almost identical—named, oddly enough, the **Canlı Balık** ("The Live Fish"). You might be able to tell it by the fish net and floats hung over the eating area. We had a table right on the water, and a friendly waiter brought us, in the course of the evening, four plates of fish, one plate of eggplant paste (patlıcan ezmesi) made with garlic and spices to eat on bread, one plate of *barbunye* (large flat beans in oil), two plates of *patates köfte* (light, soft cylinders of whipped potato rolled in crumbs and browned in a frying pan), two salads, one plate of sliced eggplant with yogurt, bread, and three full bottles of a local red wine (quite drinkable). The bill, for the three of us, came to 18,000TL ($25.20). During the summer months, be sure to try kalamar, fried squid. It's not cheap but it may be the best in all the Aegean. The food on Ali Bey Island is, in general, much better than that found in the town proper, and the setting was perfect. I can't recommend this sort of evening highly enough.

The town on Ali Bey Island used to be a large, busy community of 15,000 people, but the exchange of populations emptied it out. The people who stayed are mostly Greek-speaking Turkish families, about 2,000 people altogether. The town has a sleepy, slow quality and is obviously too big to be filled by its present number of citizens. It's an old settlement—the streets have a medieval, built-in central gutter—with some charming old houses and a large, now-unused Orthodox church. Across the water from the town is another island, with the ruins of a monastery on it, and in between the two islands, the boats between Greece and Turkey thread their way through a narrow channel marked by rows of buoys.

LEAVING AYVALIK: Most visitors who come through Ayvalık are on their way south to Bergama and İzmir. But Ayvalık also has direct ferry connections with the Greek island of Lesbos (Mytileni).

Boats to Lesbos

Every day from late May or early June through September, boats (both Greek and Turkish) carry passengers between Ayvalık and Mytileni. Leave from Ayvalık any weekday at 9 a.m. on the Turkish boat, or at 5 p.m. on the Greek boat. On Saturday departures are at 5:30 a.m., on Sunday at 6 p.m. At other times of year there may be one or two boats a week. In bad weather, and in the winter, there may be no boats at all.

Cost of the one-way trip on either the Greek or Turkish boat is $15; a round-trip ticket costs $25. Buy your ticket and surrender your passport the day before you plan to leave.

A number of small agencies near Ayvalık's main square sell tickets for these boats. Look in the streets near Gümrük Meydanı for **Ahmed Cemil Erener, Eresos-Tur,** or **Ayvalık Tur.**

Onward to Bergama

It's only 25 miles (40 km) between Ayvalık and Bergama, a journey of less than an hour. The easiest times to get a bus or dolmush are morning and early afternoon. You can buy bus tickets at bus company offices in the main square. **Sebat** has ten buses a day to İzmir (800TL, $1.10), and six or seven a day to Bergama (400TL, 56¢). **Dikici** has ten daily buses to Bursa (4½ hours; 2,000TL, $2.80), with continuing service to Ankara.

5. Bergama (Pergamum)

The Turkish city of Bergama is an agricultural center, as was the Byzantine town before it. There has been a town here since Trojan times, but Pergamum's importance reached its peak after Alexander the Great swept through. In the period from 241 to 133 B.C. Pergamum was the richest and most powerful principality in Anatolia, ruling a surprisingly large amount of territory, until the Romans came to dominate Asia Minor. Today Bergama welcomes thousands of tourists who come to visit the striking ruins of its grand Acropolis, its famous medical center (Asklepion), and its mysterious Red Basilica.

GETTING THERE: Though you will probably approach Bergama from Ayvalık, you might also come from İzmir. If so, you'll want to know that **Bergamalılar** runs buses every 30 minutes from 6 a.m. to 7:30 p.m. between İzmir's Otobüs Garajı and Bergama's Santral Garaj. The 60-mile (100-km), two-hour trip costs 500TL (70¢). In addition, **Aran** has four daily buses to and from Ayvalık for 400TL (56¢); the last bus for Ayvalık departs Bergama at 5 p.m.

First thing to do if you intend to visit this very historical city is to make sure the bus you're riding actually goes *into* the city. Many buses on the route from Çanakkale to İzmir just pass by on the highway, and if they drop you out there you'll be seven kilometers from town. So ask the bus conductor, *"Bergama Santral Garajına gidiyor musunuz?"* ("Do you go to Bergama's Central Garage?"). If you do get dropped at the crossroads, it's often possible to hitch your way into town.

ORIENTATION: Bergama's Central Bus Station (Santral Garaj) is on **Hükümet Caddesi,** the main street, which is the continuation of the road into town from the highway. East of the Archeological Museum, Hükümet Caddesi changes names and becomes **Uzun Çarşı Caddesi.**

The **Tourism Information Office** (tel. 5411/1862 or 1848) is over a mile west of the Archeological Museum, on the main road out to the highway, at the beginning of the Asklepion road. They have simple maps here, and speak some English.

HOTELS: The accommodations in Bergama aren't as good as what you'll find in Ayvalık or İzmir, but there are a number of hotels that will do if you find yourself stranded here too late in the day to reach either of these cities.

The 42-room **Tusan Bergama Motel** (tel. 5411/1173) is near the intersection of the coastal highway and the road into Bergama. Rooms are fairly cheap at this, the best place in town: with bath, they cost 7,200TL ($10.10) single, 9,600TL ($13.45) double.

By the way, not far from the Tusan is a construction site which promises, in time, to yield the **Hotel Berksoy,** which, when done, will doubtless steal the crown as "best place in town."

Other than these, there are a few very basic, plain, and cheap places such as the **Park Oteli,** Park Otel Sokak 6 (tel. 5411/1246), close to the bus station and the Archeological Museum—follow the signs. The rooms, though very simple, are often all full. The price is 1,760TL ($2.45) double, without private bath. The hotel boasts a shady patio and a quiet location.

Right on the main street in the center of town are two pensions catering to the backpacking set. Easiest to find is the **Pergamon Pansiyon,** Uzun Çarşı Caddesi (tel. 5411/2395), set up in an old stone house; they charge 5,000TL ($7) for a double room with breakfast, without bath. The **Akıncı Pansiyon,** a bit farther along (tel. 5411/1184), has similar accommodations at similar prices.

RESTAURANTS: Uzun Çarşı Caddesi is lined with shops and some little restaurants, among them the **Kardeşler Restaurant** (tel. 1050), just past the post office, which has a bounteous offering of ready-food dishes and at least one or two waiters who speak a smattering of English. Go back to the kitchen, choose your dishes, and the check will come to something like 1,700TL ($2.40).

You might also try the **Hacılar Restaurant,** just past the Kardeşler and even cheaper. For dessert or a snack, there's the **Hülya Pastanesi.**

For a fancier meal than at the little hazir yemek places on Uzun Çarşı Caddesi, the place to go is the **Bergama Restaurant,** between the bus garage and the Archeological Museum on the main street. Colorfully decorated tables with shiny cutlery and glassware are set out next to the sidewalk under an awning. There's a menu in English; a three-course meal selected from it will cost between 2,800TL ($3.90) and 3,200TL ($4.50).

SEEING THE SIGHTS: The ruins of Pergamum lie in three areas around the modern city of Bergama. Besides the ruins, you'll want to visit the Archeological Museum in the center of town.

Getting Around

Athletic types with lots of time may want to walk to all of the ruins, hitching an occasional ride with another tourist. But most people will choose to take a taxi to at least one of the two out-of-town sites.

For **taxi tours,** the customary rates and times are: up to the Acropolis, one hour's waiting time at the top, and return, 3,500TL ($4.90) total for the entire taxi. To the Asklepion and back into town, with a 30-minute wait at the ruins, the charge is 1,500TL ($2.10). The total tour for both sites costs 5,000TL ($7). Perhaps the cheapest way to do it is to take a cab to the top of the Acropolis and plan to walk down, stopping at the Red Basilica on the way back into town, and also to walk the several miles to the Asklepion.

The Archeological Museum

To start, take a look in the **Arkeoloji Müzesi,** on the main street (Hükümet Caddesi) in the center of town. It's a pretty little museum fronted by a terrace and garden dotted with the usual collection of larger pieces of sculpture. It's open every day from 9 a.m. to noon and from 1 to 7 p.m. in summer (to 5:30 p.m. in winter); admission costs 500TL (70¢), half price on Sunday and holidays.

Coming out of the museum, turn left and follow the main road through the town, heading for the Acropolis, which looms above the houses. When you pass the ruins of a huge red-brick basilica on your right and the road bends around to the right, turn left and wander through the residential streets toward the Acropolis. You'll end up on the paved road leading to the top. The **Red Basilica** was supposedly built as a temple to the Egyptian god of medicine in the 3rd century A.D., later converted into a Roman temple, finally to a basilica by the Byzantines. What's still habitable today serves as a mosque.

Acropolis

It's three miles (five kilometers) from the museum to the top of the Acropolis along a road which spirals up the hillside. At the top is a parking lot, souvenir shacks and a snack stand, and also a ticket booth. Entry to the site costs 400TL (55¢), half price on Sunday and holidays. The Acropolis is open to visits every day from 9 a.m. to noon and 1 to 7 p.m.; the auto road is open from 8:30 a.m. to 7:30 p.m.

To the west of the parking lot is the **Altar of Zeus.** The ruins of the altar are impressive because of their size and location on a cliff overlooking the town and the plain, but the altar itself, carved with beautiful reliefs, was taken to Berlin by the Germans who excavated Pergamum. There is now only a simple altar of stone blocks to give you an idea of the size of the original altar and the way it fit in with the scheme of the building.

If you walk down the hillside from the Altar of Zeus, you can explore what was known as the **Middle City,** with its **Altar and Temple of Demeter, Gymnasium** (school), **Lower Agora,** and **Roman bath.**

Around the hillside from the Altar of Zeus is the famous **theater,** surely one of the steepest and largest of its kind. The 80 rows of seats include traces of the royal box in the center near the stage. Someone will certainly be down on the stage demonstrating the acoustics to friends—imagine the experience of seeing a play or listening to a speaker in the evening, the whole plain below spread out for miles, and the town and river valley as a backdrop.

At the very top of the hill are several temples (those of **Trajan** and of **Athena**), the foundations of a royal palace, parts of the city walls, and the famous **Library of Pergamum,** which rivaled the great Egyptian library at Alexandria. There were said to have been 20,000 books in the collection, most of them written on parchment, which was invented here when the supply of paper from Egypt was cut off. When the library in Alexandria was damaged by fire, Mark Antony stole Pergamum's collection to restore that of Cleopatra. The path down to the parking lot takes you to a gate in the first wall, the original first line of defense for the city.

Before you start down the hill again, take a look across the river valley (the river is the ancient Selinos) to the other main site, the **Asklepion.** You can see the outlines of a stadium and part of a Roman theater, traces of wall and aqueduct, and the outline, farther to the left, of the Red Basilica.

Asklepion

The Asklepion is just over two miles (three kilometers) west of the museum. Bear right at the Tourism Information Office and go up the hill, and through an army base (no photographs allowed!) to reach it. The site is open at the same times, for the same prices, as is the Acropolis.

The insignia on the marble altar in the Asklepion is a familiar one: the snake-entwined staff of Aesculapius, the Greek god of medicine. The complex of buildings constructed in his honor and for his practice seems today like so much sham. A patient would visit the sacred spring, then run down the long sacred tunnel to the temple of Telesphorus, a god of healing, with the priests of Aesculapius yelling encouragement to him as he ran. The importance of the site doesn't come from these pretty buildings and mystic cures, but from groups of medical men who gathered here to study and to confer with one another, and from the library which they used and supported. The most important figure to emerge from this group was Galen, whose authority in the medical field was unquestioningly accepted between the time when he lived (the 2nd century A.D.) and the 16th century. Besides providing such men as Galen with a place to work and study, the worship of the gods and goddesses of medicine has supplied us with several words for medical things: Telesphorus had two daughters, named Hygeia and Panacea.

The long **Sacred Way** leading to the altar of Aesculapius started in the ancient town. The ruins of the entrance gate still exist at the town end.

Chapter X

İZMİR AND VICINITY

1. Orientation and Arrival
2. İzmir's Hotels
3. İzmir's Restaurants
4. İzmir's Sights
5. An Excursion to Sardis
6. An Excursion to Çeşme

THE TYPICAL TURKISH TOWN is made up of old and new, more or less in equal proportions. Minarets are everywhere, and there is at least one large mosque complex surrounded by Islamic theological seminaries, hospitals, and soup kitchens. But İzmir presents a totally different impression, for the old city was predominantly Greek at the turn of the century. At that time the city had three non-Turkish inhabitants for each Turkish one, and was one of those part-native, part-Levantine, part-European cities which were to be found all over the Middle East. With the collapse of the Ottoman Empire, armies from Greece occupied İzmir and pushed inland, trying to secure as much of the rich hinterland around the city as possible.

The War of Independence was on, and the new Turkish armies defeated the Greeks in a series of the most bitter battles of the war. The oncoming armies traveled so fast that the Greeks were literally driven into the sea in İzmir. The day this happened is now a national holiday in Turkey (Victory Day, August 30th). The war itself, a great fire that broke out after the final battle, and the exchange of populations at the end of the war have changed the face of İzmir completely. Some of the old houses remain on the waterfront and halfway up Kadifekale, the fortress-topped hill dominating the town, but İzmir today is principally a modern city of steel-and-glass buildings, palm-tree-lined boulevards, and prosperous Turkish businessmen.

1. Orientation and Arrival

İzmir is big, smaller only than Istanbul and Ankara among Turkish cities, so some tips on how to approach it would certainly be good to have.

ORIENTATION: İzmir is a clean and orderly city, with many wide boulevards and a waterfront drive. Though it is well ordered, the many streets which radiate from squares like spokes from a wheel hub make İzmir an exceptionally easy city to get lost in. It pays to get to know some landmarks.

First, the waterfront drive is officially named **Atatürk Caddesi,** and will be so named in official addresses; but everyone in İzmir calls this street the **Birinci Kordon** (First Cordon); and the one parallel to it and one block inland is the **İkinci Kordon** (Second Cordon), even though its official name is **Cumhuriyet Bulvarı.**

The two principal squares of the city are located on these two streets. **Cumhuriyet Meydanı** has an open plaza paved in marble and concrete, and an equestrian statue of Atatürk; the square is dominated by the gardens and great bulk of the Büyük Efes Oteli (the Grand Ephesus Hotel), İzmir's swankest place to stay. A half dozen blocks southwest of this square is **Konak Square,** the main stopping point for municipal buses. İzmir's symbol, an Ottoman clock tower, is in Konak, as is the dock for ferries which cross the bay to the suburb of Karşıyaka.

From Konak, the city's most colorful and interesting street wends its crooked way through the market areas, ultimately to terminate near Basmane train station. This is **Anafartalar Caddesi,** and a stroll along it is a requirement of a visit to İzmir. Finally, the city is dominated by **Kadifekale,** the "Velvet Fortress" (as it translates), dating from the time of Alexander the Great.

ARRIVING IN İZMİR: İzmir, like Istanbul, is a city to come to by sea, though in this case coming from the north by bus gives you a similar panorama. You approach the city heading southeast, sliding between the marshy flats on the left and the peninsula on the right that helps to form İzmir's magnificent harbor. The city, growing at an amazing rate, extends from a point along the peninsula all the way around the bay.

Once behind the peninsula, you head due east. The city stretches along on your right, backed by a chain of mountains rugged and high at the extreme right, lower around the rest of the city. The twin peaks in view are, according to legend, the home of Nemesis, the Greek goddess of law and order—and revenge. The only thing in the area approaching the twin peaks in height is the NATO radar station on a nearby hill.

To help you on your arrival in this fast-growing city, here follows some necessarily detailed information.

By Bus

All intercity bus service terminates at the city's **Otobüs Garajı,** on the eastern outskirts of the city. From the bus terminal, municipal buses run into the center of town—just walk out of the garage complex to the main road, where there's a municipal bus stop. The more expensive bus lines, such as Varan, are sometimes allowed to take their buses into the center of the city if it's early in the morning or late at night; Varan also has shuttle-bus service from its office across the street from the Büyük Efes Oteli to the bus terminal—ask about it when you buy your departure ticket from İzmir.

By Air

Çiğli Airport (tel. 51/29-1414) is north of the Bay of İzmir, about 30 minutes by bus from downtown. The airport bus (550TL, 75¢) will drop you right in the center of town at T.H.Y.'s office in the Büyük Efes Oteli complex. A new airport is under construction at Cumaovası, south of İzmir.

By Ship

İzmir's new commercial port, the **Yeni Liman,** is at Alsancak Point, and your ship will dock here. As you leave the port area, turn left and walk to Alsan-

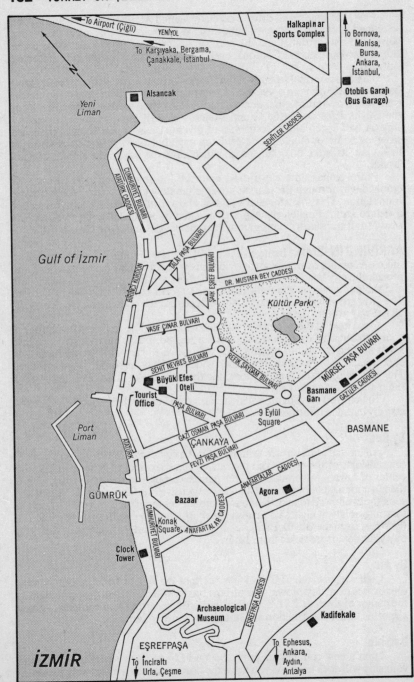

To Airport (Çiğli)
YENİYOL
To Karşıyaka, Bergama, Çanakkale, İstanbul

Halkapınar
Sports Complex

To Bornova, Manisa, Bursa, Ankara, İstanbul,

Otobüs Garajı
(Bus Garage)

Yeni Liman

N

Alsancak

ŞEHİTLER CADDESİ

CUMHURİYET BULVARI

ATATÜRK CADDESİ

Gulf of İzmir

BİRİNCİ KORDON

TALAT PAŞA BULVARI

ŞAİK EŞREF BULVARI

DR. MUSTAFA BEY CADDESİ

Kültür Parkı

VASIF ÇINAR BULVARI

ŞEHİT NEVRES BULVARI

REFİK SAYDAM BULVARI

MÜRSEL PAŞA BULVARI

GAZİLER CADDESİ

Büyük Efes Oteli

Tourist Office

Basmane Garı

PAŞA BULVARI

GAZİ OSMAN PAŞA BULVARI

9 Eylül Square

BASMANE

Port Liman

ÇANKAYA

FEVZİ PAŞA BULVARI

ANAFARTALAR CADDESİ

ATATÜRK

GÜMRÜK

Bazaar

Agora

CUMHURİYET BULVARI

Konak Square

ANAFARTALAR CADDESİ

Clock Tower

Archaeological Museum

EŞREFPAŞA CADDESİ

Kadifekale

EŞREFPAŞA

To İnciraltı Urla, Çeşme

To Ephesus, Ankara, Aydın, Antalya

İZMİR

cak Station. Nearby, buses and dolmushes pass heading for Cumhuriyet Meydanı (for the Büyük Efes Oteli) and Konak, the town's central square.

By Train
Intercity trains arrive at İzmir's **Basmane Garı,** right at the end of a main thoroughfare called Fevzi Paşa Bulvarı and very near 9 Eylül Meydanı (Dokuz Eylül Square). Most dolmushes and buses heading down Fevzi Paşa Bulvarı away from the station go to Konak; for buses and dolmushes going to Cumhuriyet Meydanı and the Büyük Efes Oteli, go to 9 Eylül Square and wait on Gazi Bulvarı.

USEFUL FACTS: When you get into İzmir, you might find some addresses handy.

American Express: The company's İzmir agent is **Egetur Travel and Tourism,** Talat Paşa Bulvarı 2B (tel. 51/21-7925), behind the NATO headquarters building. Go here to pick up your mail, or with credit-card or traveler's-check questions.

Car Rentals: Several agencies have desks at the airport. **Avis** has an office downtown at Şehit Nevres Bey Bulvarı 19/A, Alsancak (tel. 51/21-1226 or 21-6139), and another at Çiğli Airport (tel. 51/29-1410, ext. 282). **Budget** is at Gazi Osman Paşa Bulvarı 1/1E (tel. 51/25-8012 or 25-8013), next to the Büyük Efes Oteli. **Europcar/National** has its town office at Şehit Fethi Bey Caddesi 122/F (tel. 51/25-4698 or 12-1521); it has an airport office (tel. 51/29-1410, ext. 283) as well. For **Hertz,** go to Cumhuriyet Bulvarı 123/1B, Alsancak (tel. 51/21-7002 or 22-3880), or at the airport (tel. 51/29-1410, ext. 292). **InterRent** has its office at Cumhuriyet Bulvarı 151/B, Alsancak (tel. 51/21-4236).

Consulates: The **American Consulate** is on the Birinci Kordon at Atatürk Caddesi 92 (tel. 51/13-1369). The **British Consulate** is in Alsancak at Mahmut Esat Bozkurt Sokak 49 (tel. 51/21-1795).

Health Care: As there has been a large American military presence in İzmir for years, the city is well provided with doctors and dentists who speak English and who treat foreign patients. Contact the consulate, or ask at the **American Military Hospital,** behind the Büyük Efes Oteli on 1375 Sokak (tel. 51/21-7028).

Post Office: The main PTT is on the southwest side of Cumhuriyet Square, in front of the Büyük Efes Oteli.

TOURISM INFORMATION: İzmir's Tourism Information Office (tel. 51/14-2147) is in the same building as the Büyük Efes Oteli, next to the Turkish Airlines office.

2. İzmir's Hotels
İzmir is a large and wealthy city, and it is surprising that the hotels here are not better run and better kept; many of the city's hotels offer disappointing rooms and service at too high a price, and this goes for the very classy ones as well as the moderately priced ones and the modest ones. Standards here used to be a lot higher, and I hope they will be brought up to their old level again in the near future.

And a special warning is in effect for the time from about August 26 to September 15 each year, for that's when the annual İzmir International Fair is held and hotels throughout the city are booked solid. If you must be in İzmir during this time, be sure to make reservations well in advance, or else plan on staying in Kuşadası, an hour to the south.

With these caveats, here are the best bets in İzmir accommodations.

NEAR CUMHURİYET SQUARE: The **Kısmet Oteli,** 1377 Sokak no. 9 (tel. 51/14-4385), is very near the Büyük Efes (see below) and has lots of luxury features, but it's about half the price. Though there are none of the fine sea views one can get at the Efes, the Kısmet is in a quiet location which is worth a lot in itself—noisy hotels are the bane of İzmir. The 64 rooms with bath all come with breakfast and service included, and cost 14,300TL ($20) single, 20,700TL ($28) double. The Kısmet is air-conditioned, has covered garage facilities, an elevator, and a restaurant. To find the hotel, from Cumhuriyet Square (Meydanı) walk up Şehit Nevres Bulvarı—the Büyük Efes will be directly on your right side—and look for 1377 Sokak, on the left. Turn left down this street, and the hotel is at the end of it one block down, on the left-hand side.

The **Otel Anba,** at Cumhuriyet Bulvarı 124 (tel. 51/14-4380), one block out of Cumhuriyet Square toward Konak, on the left-hand side of the street, has some of the cheapest air-conditioned rooms in İzmir at 14,700TL ($20.60) single, 26,100TL ($36.55) double, breakfast included. All 54 rooms have bath or shower, and the garage below stores your car for a fee.

NEAR BASMANE STATION: As the railroad used to be the status mode of transport, station precincts are always full of the "better" hotels of a bygone era. In the case of İzmir, these are not at all fancy or especially modern, but many of the rooms have private facilities, and prices are not bad. However, beware of traffic noise from busy Fevzi Paşa Bulvarı. Here are Basmane's hotels, starting from the station door and heading down Fevzi Paşa Bulvarı.

The **Otel Billur,** Basmane Meydanı 783 (tel. 51/13-6250), faces Basmane Station across the madly busy intersection. The rooms here are priced at 12,155TL ($17) single, or 17,160TL ($24.05) double, with bath, breakfast included, and are comfortable enough, if you can find one that's quiet (that is, not overlooking Fevzi Paşa Bulvarı).

Not too far along the boulevard is the **Hotel Nil,** Fevzi Paşa Bulvarı 155 (tel. 51/13-5228 or 13-5620), on the right-hand side. Though this is an older hotel, the streetfront and the lobby have been nicely refurbished, an elevator has been installed, and the guest rooms have been spruced up, yet the prices are surprisingly low: 3,250TL ($4.55) single, 6,500TL ($9.10) double, with shower.

Farther along Fevzi Paşa Bulvarı, at the intersection with Gazi Osman Paşa Bulvarı, is the section called Çankaya. Overlooking the intersection is the **Babadan Oteli,** Gazi Osman Paşa Bulvarı 50 (tel. 51/13-9640), which is very used to foreign guests (particularly Americans and NATO staff). Many of the bath-equipped rooms have little refrigerators, which are a nice luxury during İzmir's sweltering high summer days. The penthouse room is particularly nice and particularly quiet. Double rooms have either one large bed or twin beds, and cost 14,000TL ($19.60) to 26,000TL ($36.40).

THE BIG SPLURGE: İzmir's prestige address is, of course, the **Büyük Efes Oteli,** on Cumhuriyet Meydanı (tel. 51/14-4300). The first real luxury hotel in İzmir, it still draws the wealthy and the expense-account traveler, and though its standards have sagged in recent years, it still has much to offer. All of the almost 300 rooms have bath or shower; many are—surprisingly—quite small, but with magnificent views. Other services include air conditioning throughout, small refrigerators in some rooms, a delightful swimming pool in its own park-like garden area, a restaurant, bar, lounge, hairdresser, newsstand, and all the other accouterments of a luxury hotel. It's not cheap. To give you the full impact, the following prices include the 10% tax and 15% service: single rooms are $52 to $70; double rooms, $65 to $79. Higher-priced rooms have the fine views of the bay which you get from the front of the building. Reductions in price of 15% are offered January through March and October through December; children are granted reductions year round. Even if you can't afford to stay at the Efes, you can afford a drink out by the pool (there's a terrace bar by a glassed-in portion of the pool, and you can watch the swimmers from "underwater,") or a lunch on the terrace overlooking the pool and gardens.

The bright, modern **Otel Karaca,** Necatibey Bulvarı 1379 Sokak 55 (tel. 51/14-4445 or 14-4426), is the virtual equivalent of the Büyük Efes Oteli in terms of creature comforts, but it lacks the Efes's swimming pool, gardens, and views of the bay. Prices at the Karaca are significantly lower, however, and air-conditioned rooms cost only 21,750TL ($30.45) to 26,220TL ($36.70) single, 31,800TL ($44.50) to 34,600TL ($48.45) double, breakfast included. The higher-priced rooms come equipped with TV sets and little refrigerators.

A close rival to the Büyük Efes, and also its close neighbor, is the 128-room **Etap İzmir Oteli,** Cumhuriyet Bulvarı 138 (tel. 51/14-4290), facing the main post office just off Cumhuriyet Square. Operated by the same French hotel chain which oversees the Etap Marmara and Etap Istanbul, this luxury-class hotel has rooms with all the comforts, including air conditioning, television, and refrigerators, for which it charges $52 single, $65 double, $81 triple in high summer, with reductions offered at other times of year.

THE STARVATION BUDGET: Now to the rock-bottom hotels for students and intrepid types who want something even cheaper than a youth hostel, but with similar accommodations. From the station, turn left and walk along Anafartalar Caddesi for a block and a half, then turn right onto 1296 Sokak. This little back street is lined with small hotels on both sides; most of them are converted town houses. Many of the hotels have long names incorporating the names of several Turkish towns and cities, perhaps to attract truck drivers who drive on these routes. A lot of these places are unsuitable for one reason or another, but many are spotlessly clean, newly refurbished, and cheerfully run places. In almost every one you will find a lobby filled with knickknacks, Arabic and Turkish religious plaques, mirrors, tassels, baubles, souvenirs, and sometimes an old man or two drinking tea. The rooms will have as many as six beds, but there are some singles as well. The bedding consists of a sheet safety-pinned to a quilt, village style. Prices per bed are between 700TL ($1) to 1,200TL ($1.70), depending on how many beds there are in the room. Showers are often available only cold, though some places have tanks in which you build a fire to heat your water. No specific recommendations—look before you buy.

3. İzmir's Restaurants

İzmir's most pleasurable dining is certainly along the waterfront, but you may also want to grab a bite near your hotel at Basmane Station. In addition, there are numerous very cheap eateries in the bazaar.

WATERFRONT RESTAURANTS: Many of the small sidewalk restaurants along the Birinci Kordon north of Cumhuriyet Square provide fine places to sit and people-watch, or to take in the marvelous sunset on the bay. This is perhaps the best area of İzmir to sit with a few plates of meze and a glass of beer or wine, and let the world go by.

The İzmir Palas Oteli has its street-level **Deniz Restaurant,** where seafood is a specialty (*deniz* means "sea"), and you should be able to enjoy the view and a dinner of fish in season here for about 4,000TL ($5.60) to 5,000TL ($7). Many more, similar, restaurants and cafés line the waterfront farther north.

South of Cumhuriyet Square there are also a few waterfront places, not quite as posh but perhaps better at preparing food and providing attentive service. The **Mangal Restaurant,** for example, serves good seafood at moderate prices of about 4,500TL ($6.30) to 5,500TL ($7.70). Most of the tables are inside, but if you come early in the evening you can probably grab one of the sidewalk ones.

NEAR BASMANE STATION: Walk down Fevzi Paşa Bulvarı from the station, turn right onto 1368 Sokak, and you'll come upon several small, fairly quiet, inexpensive, good—in fact delightful—and very Turkish restaurants. The **Zeybek Mangal Restaurant,** 1368 Sokak 6A (tel. 13-5231), for example, serves good döner kebab, but has various other kebaps as well, and often some fresh fish. A meal of three courses, with a main course of döner kebap, might come to 2,600TL ($3.65), but you can eat for less if you're not famished. Similarly, the **Güzel İzmir Restaurant,** very nearby at 1368 Sokak 8B (tel. 14-0501), has lots of ready-food dishes, and sidewalk tables. Prices are equally low.

IN THE BAZAAR: Buses from all parts of the city terminate or pass through Konak Square, the central station for city buses. From the famous clock tower, walk to the right of the little park and enter the bazaar on Anafartalar Caddesi. This main street winds through the bazaar for blocks, then crosses Gazi Osman Paşa Bulvarı to continue its wanderings all the way to Basmane Station. There are restaurants of every description all along this street and on the side streets around it. It's a great place to search out budget discoveries of your own. Here are some suggestions to start you off:

The **Ali Galip Pastanesi** is an İzmir institution, having stood here just a few steps along Anafartalar Caddesi from Konak Square for the better part of a century. This is İzmir's equivalent of Ali Muhiddin Hacı Bekir in Istanbul. Ali Galip bakes excellent baklava, cookies, and pastries all year round, and in winter, succulent halvah.

Budgeteers will like to know that there is a way to have a good, nourishing, filling lunch for a very low price, while getting a good look at craftsmen at work at the same time. Head for 872 Sokak, off the fish market (see below under "İzmir's Sights" for detailed directions), my favorite street in all the bazaar. One block past the canary-sellers' shops, on the left-hand side of the street, you'll find the **Afiyet Fırın** ("Health Bakery"), a tiny marbled place where the baker kneads, flours, pounds flat, and garnishes the football-shaped pide. The garnishes include ground lamb, eggs, cheese, tomato sauce, onions, and other good things. Once garnished, the pide is shoveled into the wood-fire oven and a few minutes later comes out golden brown, piping hot, and ready for the hungry customer. The price of this wizardry? A mere 650TL (90¢) (slightly more or less, depending on the garnish). There are other fırıns along the street near the Afiyet, some with tiny upstairs rooms for the footsore, but as the rooms are right above the ovens, it might not be as cool there as in the shady street.

4. İzmir's Sights

Because of the destruction during the many wars that have hit İzmir, especially the War of Independence, there's little left of the ancient city of Smyrna, or even of the Ottoman city. Some residential quarters on the side of Kadifekale escaped the fires of recent wars and are much as they were a century ago, but modernization is threatening even these.

GUIDED TOURS: Travel agencies offer tours of the city and the hinterlands, and if your time is limited it's not a bad idea to use İzmir as your base and take daily forays into the countryside by bus tour.

Every agency offers a half-day tour of İzmir itself, which typically includes seeing Konak, the Culture Park, the museums, the Agora, the bazaar, and a trip to the top of Kadifekale for the view. These tours run year round. Full-day trips to the major archeological sites of Ephesus, Pergamum, and Sardis are operated from April through October on certain days of the week. Longer tours of 3 to 14 days which go to just about all the major sights in Turkey are also available in summer; one agency at least offers an Aegean cruise to Turkish and Greek ports in the southern Aegean and the Mediterranean. As the quality of service on a tour can vary even within the same organization, I can't recommend any one company in particular. Ask around at your hotel to see if anyone else has taken a tour they liked, and then contact a travel agent for details.

AGORA: The Agora of the ancient city is still extant. From Cumhuriyet Square or from Fevzi Paşa Bulvarı near the Babadan Oteli, cross Fevzi Paşa and walk toward the citadel on Gazi Osman Paşa Bulvarı, which soon changes its name to Eşref Paşa Caddesi. When you get to 816 Sokak on the left, turn left and follow this street to the Agora. It's open every day between 9 a.m. and noon, and between 1:30 and 5 p.m. in the afternoon; entrance costs 200TL (28¢). The Agora was the Roman marketplace, and the present site is a large open space with columns and foundations still standing. Some underground vaults at the far end of the Agora, supported by massive stone ribs, must have been storage areas for the market. Nearby, a few statues found on the site gaze out over the empty market square, now protected by a plastic shelter that makes them look as though they're waiting for a bus. Actually, the Agora is a lot more impressive when seen from the top of the mountain, on the walls of the fortress, where it appears as a big empty patch of land among a jumble of tile roofs, a peculiar sort of anachronism.

KADİFEKALE: To get to the fortress, particularly for the view, take bus 25 from Konak Square to the last stop, or a Kadifekale ("K. Kale") dolmush. You'll be dropped off in a little square with a statue in the center. From here, walk up the hill past the modernistic "spaceship" mosque to the entrance to the fortress. The front walls of the fortress have been restored recently, mainly because they make a romantic sight when lit up at night. Inside there's now a water tower, a television transmitting station, several smaller buildings, ruins of some of the fortress's underground storage areas, part of its keep, and most probably, at least four teams of young boys playing soccer. If you walk along the massive six-foot-thick walls, you're sure to see a fragment from some old temple or column, since these walls have been built and rebuilt of rock swiped from other buildings. Walk up one of the numerous stairways for a view from the top of the walls over the entire city and the bay. It's easy to see the Agora from here, as well as the huge green patch of the Kültür Parkı, the site of İzmir's annual international fair.

THE KÜLTÜR PARKI: İzmir's annual fair is held in the Kültür Parkı. And while I'm on the subject—unless you're planning to attend the fair, don't arrive in İzmir around August 20, for then all of the city's hotels are full of the crowds coming to the grand opening. The fair has exhibits from scores of countries, most tending toward the commercial or industrial, but many of a "world's fair" type. The pavilions of the various nations which participate in the fair are permanent, though only open for one month out of the year. But the park's other facilities are open all year round, so you can visit them any time you're in İzmir.

THE BAZAAR: The only other thing of interest in İzmir is the bazaar. It's just a normal bazaar, uncovered, but in my opinion, one of the more charming ones to be found in Turkey. Enter it from Konak Square, walk to the right of the Konak on Anafartalar Caddesi. Crowds of vendors sell shoes, socks, underwear, shirts, belts, and everything imaginable out of carts or suitcases which they hurriedly close up and spirit away when they see the blue uniform of a municipal government official coming their way, since a city ruling forbids them to block the streets. When they're not running, they're calling out prices with voices that have no need of loudspeakers.

Follow Anafartalar past modern stores and banks ("Commercial Bank of Turkey, Bazaar Branch") and passages leading off the main street, lined with even more shops. The cook/owners of little restaurants along the street interrupt their work to lean out the doors of their places and coax you to try their latest specialty. Shops no bigger than a large telephone booth are lined from floor to ceiling with bottles of wine, beer, soft drinks, cigarettes, and incidental items. A music shop displays a large stringed instrument like a medieval lute, called an *ut*, brought from Arabia centuries ago. Beside it is a graceful Turkish *saz*.

At no. 173–175 (on the left) is the entrance to the fish market. Turn left off Anafartalar into the fish market to get to a small square with a *şadırvan*, or ablutions fountain, in the center. Turn right and head down 872 Sokak, to my mind one of the prettiest streets in the bazaar. At the very beginning of the street are the sellers of canaries and other songbirds with several examples of their "wares" hung out in front of their shops under the street's cover of vines. Turks are great lovers of songbirds. Many small, humble restaurants hang them in the dining room to entertain customers, a custom which is, unfortunately, dying out. Beside the canary shops are the vegetable stands, and farther along are shops displaying strands of big red onions; hat racks, rolling pins, and other woodwork; feed bags for horses (very colorful, strong, good as tote bags); huge wool shepherds' cloaks a half inch thick and stiff as wood; and various types of baskets; peaches as big as softballs; string and rope. Linking together all of these specialty stalls is a covering of grapevines or canvas tarps which protects the wares and cools the customers.

At the end of 872 Sokak turn left to get to a hidden şadırvan (an ablutions fountain used by Muslims before prayer) and a little coffeehouse with chairs and tables outside. Then if you duck back under the mosque on the right (for that's what the building is), turn left and walk through the clothing section, you will emerge within view of another şadırvan. The little street running past it is 913 Sokak, center of the clothing and blanket district.

To leave the bazaar, continue along 913 Sokak until you reach Fevzi Paşa Bulvarı; or head back toward the şadırvan and the countless streets of the bazaar. If you get lost, ask for Anafartalar Caddesi and you'll always be able to find your way out.

ARCHEOLOGICAL MUSEUM: South of Konak Square, near the beginning of the winding road (Varyant) which climbs the hillside toward Kadifekale and Ephesus, is İzmir's new Archeological Museum. You can walk there from Konak, or take a taxi. Hours are 9 a.m. to noon and 1 to 5:30 p.m.; admission costs 500TL (70¢).

NIGHTLIFE: As a port town, İzmir has lots of nightlife, much of it in slightly raunchy clubs called *pavyon*s. For a more refined atmosphere, head for the club in the Büyük Efes Oteli.

In the warm summer months, İzmirlis preserve the old tradition of *piyasa vakti* ("plaza time"), the hour or two just before sunset when everyone heads home from work, freshens up, changes clothes, and heads out for a stroll along the waterfront to take the air, to see and be seen. It's a delightful custom, and a long section of the Birinci Kordon, north of Cumhuriyet Square, is closed off to vehicular traffic each summer evening to accommodate strollers.

You can continue your evening by having supper in one of the little restaurants along the Kordon.

A favorite vantage point for watching the sunset is Kadifekale. Right in front of the entrance to the fortress are several small tea houses with terraces overlooking the vast panorama of the city, the bay, and the encircling mountains. To sit here as the light turns to gold and to watch the city lights twinkle on, and to hear the calls of a hundred muezzins sweep across the scene, is an unforgettable experience.

After sunset or after dinner, take a budget cruise across İzmir bay on one of the commuter ferries departing from Konak for Karşıyaka. For 300TL (42¢) you can cruise over and back, listening to the soothing sound of the sea as the ferry plows a furrow in the water, and admire the fairyland of lights which covers the slopes all the way from Konak to Kadifekale.

TRANSPORTATION FROM İZMİR: İzmir is important as a center for excursions to the more interesting parts of Turkey, so some details on the transportation situation might be helpful.

You can buy bus tickets right in 9 (Dokuz) Eylül Square, next to Basmane, and thus save yourself the trip out to the Otogar. Look for the bus company ticket offices at the beginning of Gazi Bulvarı, just off the square. For tickets on the premium-service Varan line, go to the Varan ticket office (tel. 51/25-5921), directly across the street from the main entrance to the Büyük Efes Oteli.

Heading South

Buses: If you're headed for Selçuk, Ephesus, and Kuşadası, don't bother buying a ticket in advance, and don't go all the way out to the bus station. Rather, go to the southern end of Konak Square, where there is a stop for **Elbirlik** (tel. 51/16-3127) buses going to these places. Buy your ticket right on the bus.

Trains: Three diesel *mototrens* pull out of İzmir's Basmane Station each day headed for Selçuk (Ephesus), Aydın, Nazilli (for Aphrodisias), and Denizli (for Pamukkale). Departures are at 8:10 a.m., and at 3:30 and 6 p.m.; a ticket to Selçuk costs 300TL (42¢), or 250TL (35¢) for a student. If you're only going as far as Selçuk, there's also a daily mototren which goes to Söke (not Denizli), departing Basmane at 6:45 p.m.; a ticket on this one costs 450TL (65¢) one way, or 400TL (55¢) for a student.

Heading North

Buses: For buses to Bergama, just go out to the Otobüs Garajı and catch the next bus out; they run every half hour throughout the day.

Flights: Turkish Airlines (tel. 51/14-1220) flies at least three times daily to Istanbul. Flight time is less than an hour.

Heading East

Buses: For Sardis, go out to the Otogar and catch a bus for Salihli, the large town just beyond Sardis. A ticket will cost about 200TL (28¢).

Trains: The fastest and most luxurious train on the route between İzmir and Ankara is the *Mavi Tren*, departing Basmane at 7:35 p.m. daily; a ticket to Ankara costs 3,300TL ($4.60), or 5,600TL ($7.85) round trip.

The *Ege Ekspresi* (*Aegean Express*) departs Basmane for Ankara at 7:35 a.m.; the *İzmir Ekspresi*, hauling sleeping cars and a restaurant car, leaves Basmane at 5:45 p.m. A first-class ticket on either express to Ankara costs 2,600TL ($3.65); second class costs 1,900TL ($2.65); a student pays 1,700TL ($2.40).

Flights: Turkish Airlines (tel. 51/14-1220) flies at least twice a day nonstop to Ankara (other flights are via Istanbul), and once a week (on Sunday) to Antalya.

Heading West

Buses: Buses and minibuses of the **Çeşme Turizm** line (tel. 51/14-1783) run to Çeşme every 15 minutes throughout the day in summer. You can catch the bus at the Otogar, or at the southern end of Konak Square. At Çeşme there are boats to the Greek island of Chios (see below).

Flights: Turkish Airlines (tel. 51/14-1220) has a nonstop flight to Athens on Tuesday in summer, and flights via Istanbul to Athens on every other day except Saturday.

5. An Excursion to Sardis

Living as we do in a materialistic age, it's difficult to conceive of what the world was like before the invention of money. There was indeed such a time, but it ended half a millennium B.C. in an ancient town an hour's drive east of İzmir. The town is Sardis, one-time capital of Lydia, ruled by King Croesus (560–546 B.C.) who, it is said, thought up the idea of hammering little discs of precious metal with his portrait, and using these discs (coins) as an intermediary means for the bartering of goods. Croesus must have liked his invention, for the phrase "rich as Croesus" rings in our language to this day.

Croesus, for all his wealth, didn't last that long (though his invention did). The Persians swept into Lydia and put an end to his reign, and also ruined his capital (no pun intended). By the 3rd century B.C. Alexander the Great had come through and conquered Lydia. After him an earthquake brought much of Sardis down, but it was too important a city to die, and when the Romans arrived they began to build it up again. Most of the ruined buildings you see at Sardis today date from Roman times.

If you go to Sardis in high summer, start out early so that you can tour the ruins before the sun becomes too hot. There's a good deal of walking to do here.

There are two small Turkish villages near ancient Sardis, surrounded by vineyards, olive trees, and fields of melons and tobacco. The one you want is **Sartmustafa**, right on the highway. The tea houses on the highway in Sartmustafa are where you wait to catch a bus back to İzmir once you've finished seeing the sights. The other village, **Sartmahmut**, is about half a mile north of the highway, at the train station.

GETTING THERE: Sardis is 56 miles (90 km) east of İzmir along the highway to Ankara. Travel agencies in İzmir run full-day tours to Sardis, including a stop in the nearby city of Manisa, for about $16 per person, lunch included. Contact any travel agent for details. You can do the trip yourself with a bit more trouble, but at a fraction of the price of a tour.

Buses to **Salihli**, the next big town east of the ruins, depart frequently from İzmir's Otobüs Garajı. The trip to Sardis takes about 1½ hours and costs 200TL (28¢). Tell the ticket seller and the bus driver that you want to get off at Sart.

TOURING THE RUINS: The ruins of Sardis are mostly at two different sites. The first site is a short stroll east of Sartmustafa along the highway; the other is two-thirds of a mile south of Sartmustafa along a village road.

Start with the site east of the village, which is the most extensive part of the ruins. It's open from early morning till dusk; a ticket costs 400TL (55¢), half price on Sunday and holidays. You must pay an equivalent fee at the other site also.

After buying your ticket, you enter the ruins along the **Marble Way,** lined with Byzantine-era shops. Note the water and sewer pipes buried in the stone walls. Signs on the shops identify their purposes, and even sometimes their owners.

At the eastern end of the Marble Way, turn left and enter the **synagogue,** which is large and beautifully decorated with mosaic paving and artfully cut colored-stone panels. Excavation and restoration (1965–1973) of the synagogue was supported by the Sardis American Excavation Fund, and a plaque within the structure lists names of donors to the fund.

South of the synagogue is the impressive façade of the great **gymnasium,** in this case a combination school and athletic facility. Behind the façade is an oval swimming pool.

At the other site, south of the village, is the **Temple of Artemis,** Sardis's most famous building. Take the road beside the tea house and walk for ten minutes to reach the temple. The great temple is now in ruins, and in fact it was never, in its long history, ever completely whole. It just never got finished. Now only two of its tall columns remain standing, but they give a fertile imagination the idea of what the magnificent structure must have looked like in its prime. Next to the temple is an altar which was here even before the temple was built. Alexander the Great, and later the Romans, used it for religious ceremonies.

At the temple's eastern end is a small brick Byzantine chapel. All this site needs is a little mosque to continue the tradition and it will have been sacred to man and divinity since earliest times.

6. An Excursion to Çeşme

Çeşme is a little town at the tip of the peninsula which shields the mouth of the İzmir bay from the Aegean storms. Its location makes it a natural jumping-off place for trips to the Greek island of Chios, and the long, white beaches of the Ilıca district make it İzmir's most popular sand-and-sea spot.

In the village of Çeşme proper is a fortress built by Sultan Mehmet the Conqueror's son, Beyazıt, for protection against the Knights of St. John from Rhodes, and from Mediterranean pirates. Picturesque old houses line the narrow, winding streets of the village around the town square and its inevitable tea houses.

GETTING THERE: Çeşme is 56 miles (90 km) west of Konak Square. Buses of the **Çeşme Turizm** company shuttle between İzmir (Otogar and Konak) and Çeşme, departing every 15 minutes or so from 6 a.m. to 6 p.m. throughout the day, for 600TL (85¢).

ORIENTATION: The center of life in Çeşme is the town's main square, called Cumhuriyet Meydanı or İskele Meydanı (Republic Square, or Dock Square), on the waterfront right by the fortress. The town's better hotels are all at the edges of the square. The **Tourism Information Office** is right down by the dock at İskele Meydanı 8 (tel. 5492/1653).

HOTELS: Accommodations can get scarce in Çeşme during the summer months, so if you plan to stay the night you'd do well to reserve in advance.

A Caravanserai Hotel

Prime place in town is the **Çeşme Kervansaray Oteli**, at the southern end of the main square (tel. 5492/6490, 51/14-1720 in İzmir), a caravan "motel" built in 1528 during the reign of Sultan Süleyman the Magnificent. It has been restored well beyond its former Süleymanic glory, and is now a beautiful hotel decorated in a blend of modern and traditional Turkish styles. Summer-season rates for room with bath and breakfast are 20,000TL ($28) for a single room, 27,000TL ($37.80) for a double, 37,000TL ($51.80) for a suite; off-season reductions of 20% are offered. The Kervansaray is one of the few good places to eat in town. A set-price lunch or dinner costs 4,000TL ($5.60).

Modern Tourist Hotels

Right on the main square is the modern 60-room **Ertan Oteli**, Cumhuriyet Meydanı 12 (tel. 5492/6795). Some of its rooms have fine views of the sea; all have private baths. The hotel has an elevator, a bar, and a terrace restaurant with a sea view. Room prices are a bit high, but nice rooms are scarce in Çeşme, and the Ertan is often completely filled by tour groups (as is the Kervansaray, in fact). The rates in summer are 18,500TL ($25.90) single, 20,300TL ($28.40) double.

The room situation might be eased somewhat with the opening of the new **Rıdvan Oteli**, presently under construction right next door to the Ertan.

The Big-Splurge Resort

Çeşme is the locale for a number of resort motels and hotels, and also *la crème de la crème* of Turkish holiday villages, the **Golden Dolphin (Altınyunus) Holiday Village** (tel. 5492/1250). All these resorts are located in the section of beach called Boyalık Köyü, and you'll need a car or taxi to get there. The Golden Dolphin is a mammoth establishment, very impressive in its size and whiteness when seen from the water, and it boasts every conceivable service: sauna, tennis, waterskiing, sailing, private beach, even its own gas station. You can get a double room with breakfast here for about 48,000TL ($67.20), or a double with all meals for a cool 75,000TL ($105). Reductions of 15% are offered January through March and October through December.

Family Pensions

Çeşme has lots of little family pensions, called *ev pansiyonu*. You will see little hand-painted signs throughout town directing you to one or another of these comfy if simple places. Prices for beds in rooms without private facilities range from 2,500TL ($3.50) to 4,000TL ($5.60), depending on what you get.

Among the quieter pensions are the ones up the hill above the fortress, such as the **Deniz Pansiyon** (tel. 5492/6122), and the **Çelik Pansiyon** (tel. 5492/6153). Handier to the square, but somewhat noisier, is the **Kervan Pansiyon** (tel. 5492/6061), just south of the main square and the docks.

RESTAURANTS: As one might anticipate, Çeşme has a good number of waterfront seafood restaurants. The long-running favorite here is the **Sahil Restaurant**, on the main square just a few steps from the Ertan Oteli. Outdoor tables, some facing the square, others the sea, are perfect for people- or sunset-watching, or generally lazing away the better (nonbeach) parts of the day. Full meals at the Sahil run 2,000TL ($2.80) to 2,500TL ($3.50), somewhat more if you order seafood, but these prices are typical of all the waterfront restaurants. The Sahil opens early for breakfast.

For slightly fancier surroundings, drop in at the Kervansaray for their set-price meal (see above).

For those on a very slim budget, Çeşme's main shopping street harbors many small, very cheap eateries. Perhaps the best of these, often filled with budget-minded foreign tourists, is the **Hasan Abi Lokantası,** about a block and a half inland from the main square.

WHAT TO DO: The prominent fortress, with its eventful history, has been tamed, and is now the **Çeşme Fortress and Museum,** open every day from 10 a.m. to noon and 1 to 5:30 p.m., for an admission charge of 400TL (55¢). Facing the fortress from the main square, with the sea behind you, the entrance is up the hill on the right-hand side.

Otherwise, there are the **beaches.** The peninsula which forms İzmir Bay has a number of them. Most popular are those at **Ilıca,** a ten-minute, 100TL (14¢) minibus ride away; and **Çiftlik,** also reachable by minibus from the bus stop near the wharf in the main square.

BOATS TO CHIOS (GREECE): The ticket agency for the little ferryboats to Chios is right in the main square, south of the fortress, near the Tourism Information Office. It's the **Ertürk Travel Agency,** Cumhuriyet Meydanı 11/A (tel. 5492/6768 or 6876). They'll sell you a one-way ticket between Çeşme and Chios for $18; a same-day round-trip ticket costs $20; a round-trip ticket valid for one year costs $30. Children 4 to 12 years old get a 50% reduction. Motorcycles, cars, even travel trailers and minibuses, can be carried on some of the ferries. The fare for a normal-sized car is between $40 and $60.

In high summer (mid-July through mid-September) there are daily boats (except Monday) departing in the morning at 9:30 or 10 a.m.; a few boats depart at 4 p.m. Extra boats may run if there is enough demand.

During the winter boats run on Thursday, weather and customers permitting; they run on Sunday and Thursday in early May; on Tuesday, Thursday, and Sunday from mid-May till mid-July and also from mid-September through October.

The Thursday summertime boat can be used for a day trip to Chios: leave Çeşme in the morning, spend the day on Chios, and return in the evening.

The Ertürk people can also usually give you accurate information about onward connections from Chios to Piraeus (daily except Saturday at 8 p.m.), to Athens by air, and to Samos, Lesbos, and Thessaloniki by boat.

Chapter XI

THE SOUTH AEGEAN

1. Ephesus and Selçuk
2. Kuşadası
3. Priene, Miletus, Didyma, and Altınkum Beach
4. Aphrodisias
5. Pamukkale and Denizli
6. Bodrum

THE REGION SOUTH OF İZMİR holds some of Turkey's most interesting ancient cities and a few of the most beautiful beaches. The countryside itself is distinctly Mediterranean, the hills and plains dotted with olive and cypress trees, or covered by tobacco fields, food crops, or wildflowers. Ancient temples and fortresses seem to grow by the side of the road along with the pine trees.

I must warn you that accommodations space can get tight in this very attractive and popular region in the high summer months of July and August. Try to arrive at your destination early in the day to look for a bed if you have no reservations, and then use one town as a base for visiting the surrounding ones.

1. Ephesus and Selçuk
Aside from Athens, the city of Ephesus is perhaps the most famous and interesting of the old Hellenic cities. In its heyday it was one of the greatest cities in Asia, with its busy commerce and famous cult of Artemis, also called Cybele and Diana, the continuation of a tradition almost as old as Anatolian civilization itself. Ephesus is said to be the last place of residence of the Virgin Mary; it was visited by St. Paul and St. John; it served as the capital of a Turkish emirate. Today the settlement on the site of the great city is the sleepy little town of Selçuk, surrounded by the ruins of its past.

GETTING THERE: Buses leave at least every half hour from the Central Garage in İzmir on the 1½-hour ride to Ephesus. The ticket hawkers in the garage will be glad to show you to the proper window. Minibus dolmushes also run through Selçuk on their way to Aydın. Catch them in Konak. A bus to Kuşadası, the little resort town on the coast, takes you through Selçuk and to a crossroads within a half mile of the principal ruins of Ephesus. Take this bus from the Central Garage if you want to start outside of the town of Selçuk and work your way back in.

Believe it or not, it's possible to take a train to Selçuk, and in my opinion it's the only way to go. See "Transportation from İzmir," in Chapter X, Section 4.

ORIENTATION: When you arrive in Selçuk you get off the bus in the center of town right at the dolmush and taxi stand on the main highway south from İzmir. Back toward İzmir one block is St. Jean Sokak, which leads to the Basilica of St. John and the İsa Bey Mosque. The Kuşadası road, curving off to the right from the main highway just before the dolmush stand, takes you past the town museum, only a few blocks from this intersection, then past the left-hand turn into the main ruins a mile or two from the town.

The **Tourism Information Office** (tel. 5451/1328) is in a group of shops across from the museum, open daily from 8:30 a.m. to 6:30 or 7 p.m. Besides providing maps and advice, they are willing and able to help you find a room in one of Selçuk's many inexpensive pensions.

GETTING AROUND: Do your traveling early in the day, and if you have to travel in the late afternoon or evening, make sure that there will be a bus or minibus to take you where you want to go. The frequency of service declines as the day winds down, and if you wait too long to head homeward, you may end up going by taxi.

That having been said, let me now inform you that **dolmush** service between Selçuk and Kuşadası via Ephesus is fast and furious from morning to late afternoon. **Minibuses** run at least every half hour in summer, charging 300TL (42¢) for the ride. There are also plenty of dolmushes to Söke; at Söke you change for Priene, Miletus, Didyma, and Altınkum (see below).

HOTELS: Because Selçuk is near İzmir and Kuşadası, most people visit it on a day trip and don't plan to stay overnight. Indeed, there are very few comfortable hotels in Selçuk, though there are many simple pensions.

The most comfortable hotel in Selçuk is the **Tusan Efes Moteli,** at the turnoff to Ephesus (tel. 5451/1060), a ten-minute walk from the entrance to the ruins. The 12 rooms in this small and unpretentious place come with private bath, and cost 9,800TL ($13.70) double.

There's also the simpler, 21-room **Hotel Aksoy,** Namık Kemal Caddesi 17 (tel. 5451/1040), between the highway and the train station. Set right in the middle of the town's tiny business district, the plain rooms here cost 3,850TL ($5.40) double with shower.

Facing the Aksoy, across the street, is the new **Ürkmez Oteli,** Namık Kemal Caddesi 18 (tel. 5451/1312), where the rooms are marginally more comfortable, and a good deal brighter, but otherwise much the same. All rooms have showers, and go for 5,000TL ($7) double.

As for those small **ev pansiyons,** Selçuk has several dozen of them. The best way to find one is simply to walk the streets looking, or drop by the Tourism Information Office and ask them to help. Out in front of the office is a big signboard with names, addresses, and telephone numbers of all the pensions. The average cost for a room without bath is 1,650TL ($2.30) single, 3,300TL ($4.60) double; some of the pension rooms come with private shower, and these cost 3,500TL ($4.90) single, 7,000TL ($9.80) double.

RESTAURANTS: Most of Selçuk's restaurants are small, simple, and cheap, though in a few places some touristic pretensions and higher prices have appeared. The place to look for an inexpensive meal is Cengiz Topal Caddesi, one of the two commercial streets which run between the highway and the train station. A full meal at the **Ephesus Pub**, for instance, might run to 2,000TL ($2.80). The **Girne Köftecisi** and the **Lezzet Lokantası** are two more, even cheaper, places on this street.

Personally, my favorite restaurant hereabouts is the **Villa Restaurant** (tel. 1299 or 1331), at the beginning of the highway to Ephesus and Kuşadası, more or less opposite the site of the famous Temple of Artemis. Trees and vines provide cooling shade, as do awnings. Service is a bit slow, but friendly; the grill is always hot, the drinks are always cool, and a tasty meal based on kebap and salad always seems to cost 1,800TL ($2.50) to 2,800TL ($3.90).

SIGHTS: The sights to see in town include the **museum,** where you might as well start. It's open every day from 9:30 a.m. to 6:30 p.m., and costs 500TL (70¢) to enter. The outstanding things in the museum, apart from the standard collection of frieze fragments, inscriptions, jars, and implements, are the two statues of Cybele (Artemis), each with several rows of breasts, a fitting symbol of fertility for the cult of which she was the center. There are some other statues of note, especially the exquisite little bronze of the *Boy on a Dolphin.* Don't write this museum off without a visit. You'll be glad you saw the statuary. There is one exception, however, and if you blush easily you should probably pass up this particular statue. It's a little replica of the god Bes. After a gander at Cybele and Bes, one has second thoughts about what life was like in ancient Greece.

For further sightseeing, start up St. Jean Sokak, and at the top of the hill you will come to the ruins of **St. John's Basilica,** said to have been built over the tomb of the saint (under the altar). It was built in Justinian's time, the 6th century, over the spot where a small chapel had been, also dedicated to St. John. An earthquake pretty well destroyed the church a little less than 1,000 years later, and what was left after the earthquake was ravaged by Tamerlane when his armies swept through the area.

Down the hill at the other end of St. Jean Sokak is the **İsa Bey Mosque.** The roof is gone, but the rest of the structure, dating from 1375, is in pretty good shape. The style and decoration of the building is a conglomeration of several types of architecture afoot at the time: Seljuk, Byzantine, Roman, classical. The ruins of the mosque are open all day every day, for free.

The fortress on top of the hill has been almost totally rebuilt, and has little inside it, so your next stop is the site of Ephesus's most impressive ruins, a few miles from the center of town.

The Ruins of Ephesus

Personally, I like to walk between Selçuk and the ruins in the evening, but during the day it's hot. Go to the dolmush and bus station on the highway to catch a bus or Kuşadası dolmush. Either will drop you a kilometer from the entrance, but as you walk through ruins to get there, you can consider it all part of your tour. Taxis are 550TL (75¢) one way. If you have more than five people, rent a minibus. For the Virgin Mary's House, which is several miles away on top of a mountain, a taxi is about the only way to get there. Taxi drivers want 2,200TL ($3.10) per carload for a round trip to the house, with waiting time included in the price. For 4,500TL ($6.30) you can get them to drive you to the main ruins, wait, and then take you to the Virgin's house.

You pass some ruins on the way to the entrance gate, enter the parking lot, pay 1,000TL ($1.40) for admission, and walk into the city. **Mount Pion** is on your left, with the city's big theater scooped out of its side. The original seats are gone, the marble having been used to build other things when the city was moved from this site to where it is now. Leading from the theater to what was once the waterfront is the marble-paved **Arcadian Way.** The silting-up of the harbor was one of the prime reasons for the decline of the city, and the waters of the Aegean are now almost a mile from the end of this street.

Walk down the marble pavement and you'll come to the **Port Baths** on the right, built by the Emperor Constantine II, which haven't been fully excavated yet, but are worth a look because of their sheer size. You might have noticed that there's an empty space under the Arcadian Way. Trenches that were part of the city's complex plumbing system are under all of the main streets. Turn right in front of the theater, and, walking down this street, you'll be able to see a good deal of this system. At the end of the street is the **Brothel,** to which a lot of the clay water pipes were headed, because the Brothel's many pools and fountains required a great deal of running water. Take a look inside, and don't miss the floor mosaics.

Incidentally, hidden in a maze of little walkways behind and to the right of the Brothel is an old hand pump which brings up the most glorious fresh cold spring water from a hidden well. Don't be afraid to stick your head under the spout—on one of Ephesus's many very hot days, there's nothing like it.

Across the street from the Brothel, what would you expect to find? The library, of course! This one is the famous **Library of Celsus** built in honor of Celsus by his son. The elder Celsus is buried in a vault under the floor at the rear of the library (you can peek in at the vault through little openings cut out of the stone). The library held a rich collection of manuscripts and scrolls, all protected by special insulation: there's a system of double walls with an air space in between.

Continuing along the street, following it up the hill, you pass the **Temple of Hadrian** on the left, one of Ephesus's most impressive temples. The head of Hydra over the door is to keep evil spirits out. Across the street, the honeycomb of tunnels, arches, and alleys is actually a **residential section** for the wealthy. The houses are tiny, but in the days of the close-knit community there were public places for reading, eating, bathing, and talking, thus no need to have space for these things at home. The **Odeon,** or small theater, near the Magnesia Gate at the end of the marble way, is a real jewel and in a good state of preservation. Forget the heat and walk all the way to the end to see it.

If you're a good scrambler and have suitable clothes, take off across the fields at the end of the Arcadian Way toward the Aegean in order to climb to **St. Paul's Prison,** not really a prison but a square guard tower in the old Hellenistic walls which surrounded the city. The walls run along the top of the mountain ridge to the south. From this tower there's a grand view of the city, the plain, Selçuk, and the Aegean. A second choice for a look at the whole area is from the top of Mount Pion, a bit closer and easier to climb.

Around on the other side of Mount Pion is the **Grotto of the Seven Sleepers.** The legend goes that seven young men took shelter here from religious persecutors. The Roman persecutors sealed these early Christians in the grotto, where they slept for 200 years, awakening when Christianity (after Constantine's conversion) had become the accepted state religion. Thinking that they had slept only a night or two, the seven crept back into the town, looking for refuge and their friends. They found easy refuge, but only the tombstones of their friends; they were accepted as heros by the believers in the town.

Unless you've made other arrangements, your best plan for getting to the **Virgin Mary's House** is to find a taxi in the parking lot near the ruins. Besides the fine view from the hilltop where the house is, you find the house itself, very much reconstructed by now. The foundations are said to date from the first century. Though the Church of the Dormition in Jerusalem claims also to be the place where the Virgin spent her last moments, several popes have indicated the

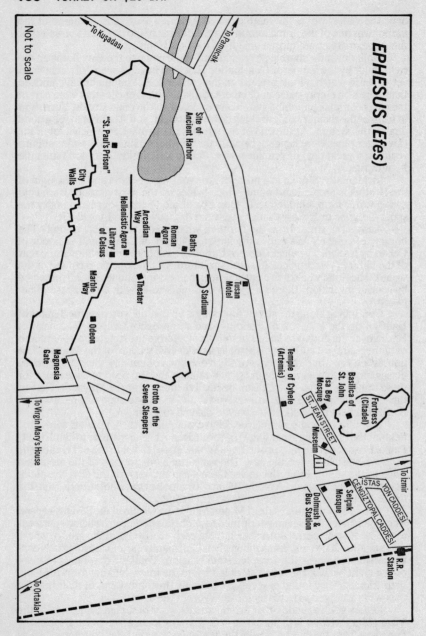

EPHESUS (Efes)

Not to scale

To Kuşadası

To Pamucak

Site of
Ancient Harbor

"St. Paul's Prison"

City
Walls

Hellenistic Agora

Arcadian
Way

Library
of Celsus

Roman
Agora

Baths

Tusan
Motel

Stadium

Marble
Way

Theater

Odeon

Magnesia
Gate

Grotto of the
Seven Sleepers

To Virgin Mary's House

Temple of Cybele
(Artemis)

Basilica of
St. John

Fortress
(Citadel)

Isa Bey
Mosque

ST. JEAN STREET

Museum

To İzmir

İSTAS YON CADDESİ

CENGİZTOPAL CADDESİ

Dolmuş &
Bus Station

Selçuk
Mosque

R.R.
Station

To Ortaklar

significance of this spot. Services are sometimes held in the chapel, which is open to private individuals all day.

2. Kuşadası

The bus trip takes you past Selçuk and Ephesus. The road winds through olive groves and tobacco fields. Riding along the road from Ephesus, suddenly you round a corner and the intense blue of the Aegean leaps up from the bottom of the cliffs which the road follows. This is your first taste of Kuşadası, and it's a valid one. After you've come down from the heights, the road takes you past the yacht marina, then into the little town itself. Today this town is a vacation resort and draws visitors solely for that purpose. The only two really historic buildings in the town are the Mehmet Pasha Caravanserai, rebuilt and turned into a luxury hotel for the Club Méditerranée, and the small fort on the "island" at the end of a causeway in the bay. This has also been rebuilt and is now a nightclub-discothèque; the rest of the island has been fixed up with gardens, walkways, restaurants and snack places, and a souvenir shop.

GETTING THERE: Buses are operated by **Elbirlik** from İzmir via Selçuk to Kuşadası at least ten times per day in each direction from 7 a.m. to 7 p.m., at a fare of 600TL (85¢) for the 1½- to 2-hour trip.

Going between Kuşadası and Selçuk, there are usually dolmushes departing on the hour and half hour, charging 300TL (42¢) one way.

For your onward journey, catch a dolmush in Kuşadası for Söke, and from Söke to Priene, Miletus, Didyma, and Altınkum, unless you plan to take a minibus tour right from Selçuk or Kuşadası (see below). From Söke there are also buses to Nazilli (for Aphrodisias) and Denizli (for Pamukkale).

ORIENTATION: The town is fairly long because it runs along the waterfront, the land which everyone wants a piece of. The only important street perpendicular to **Atatürk Bulvarı** (also called **Hükümet Caddesi**), the waterfront street is **Barbaros Caddesi,** right beside the caravanserai in the center of town. The dolmush stop is at the junction of this street and Barbaros Caddesi. The official bus and dolmush garage is about a half mile east along Kahramanlar Caddesi, which is the continuation of Barbaros Caddesi.

The beaches in and around the town vary in size from moderate to very small—in some places you swim from docks and wharves. The town is interesting for walks during the day, and at night several discothèques and nightclubs swing into action. But the talk of big hotels and clubs should not scare you, for Kuşadası is still basically a little coastal Aegean town, complete with fishermen and farmers.

The **Tourism Information Office** (tel. 6361/1103) is on the wharf where the cruise ships tie up, directly in front of, but two blocks away from, the Club Caravanserail.

HOTELS: Kuşadası has a full range of hotels from which to choose. Within the town center are luxury places, lots of moderately priced rooms, and also many very cheap beds in pensions. Take your pick. Another rich area of lodgings is the quarter to the north of the center, on the way to the yacht harbor.

Moderately Priced Downtown Hotels

An all-around good choice is the moderately priced, fairly large (42 rooms) **Hotel Akdeniz,** on Arslanlar Caddesi near Kahramanlar Caddesi (tel. 6361/1120). The hotel, though undistinguished, is bright and clean; some of the rooms (mostly those on the higher floors) have a view of the town and the bay.

Because every room in this oddly shaped hotel is different, you might want to see exactly what you're paying for before you buy, though you might not have much of a choice as the Akdeniz is a popular place for tour groups to put up for the night. When you look at a room, also listen to the noise level, as some face noisy streets. A double room without bath costs 6,600TL ($9.25), or 14,850TL ($20.80) with bath; breakfast is included in these rates.

Trudge up the steep slope on Arslanlar Caddesi, which goes to the right of the Hotel Akdeniz, to reach the **Aran Turistik Oteli,** Kaya Aldoğan Caddesi 4 (tel. 6361/1076 or 1325), with 22 rooms, each equipped with a solar-heated shower. Many rooms have excellent views, and all benefit from the quiet of the hotel's somewhat inconvenient location (inconvenient if you hate clambering up steep hillsides on broiling hot days). Still, the view and the quiet are well worth the effort. To stay here, you pay 6,900TL ($9.65) single, 11,350TL ($15.90) double, breakfast included.

Also up on this hillside above the town is the tidy **Hotel Stella,** P. K. 110, Kuşadası (tel. 6361/1632 or 3787), where you'll be impressed by the warm reception you get from the friendly management, and also by the panorama spread out below. The rooms are modern and nice, and the price is at the top of our budget, but worth it: 18,600TL ($26.05) double with shower, breakfast included.

Can't take the climb? Then stand facing the Hotel Akdeniz, and on your left will be a little market street called Eski Pazaryeri Sokak, on which stands the **Otel Güler Tur,** Eski Pazaryeri Sokak 26 (tel. 6361/2996), a recently remodeled hotel which is simple and friendly, with some oddly shaped rooms, most of them quite small, but clean and presentable. You might try bargaining with the desk clerk if the hotel seems less than crowded, but in normal times the price for a room here is 5,000TL ($7) single, 8,000TL ($11.20) double, with bath.

There are two hostelries in town named the **Hotel Pamuk Palas** (tel. 6361/ 3191). Both share the same telephone number, but one is a very basic place downtown on Barbaros Caddesi (see below); the other is a much more upscale establishment with a tiny swimming pool near the bus station. Though you're a few blocks from the waterfront, the hotel is among the newest in town; it charges 15,000TL ($21) for a double room with shower, breakfast included.

A block inland from the waterfront street, starting from Barbaros Caddesi opposite the caravanserai, is a quite narrow little street named Cephane Sokak which holds three good, convenient, quiet little hotels. The 19-room **Alkış Oteli,** Cephane Sokak 4/A (tel. 6361/1245), charges 8,800TL ($12.30) for a simple but clean and convenient double room with shower.

Just past the Alkiş is the **Minik Otel,** Cephane Sokak 8, Kuşadası 09402 (tel. 6361/2359 or 2043), a modern little hotel with 45 rooms, all with baths and telephones, renting for 12,000TL ($16.80) double, with breakfast. Other services here include a cafeteria, bar, and rooftop sunning area.

Right next to the Minik is the even fancier **Bahar Pansiyon,** Cephane Sokak 12 (tel. 6361/1191), which, despite the "pension" moniker, is actually a moderately fancy lodging in which all rooms are bath equipped, and the front-facing rooms also have balconies. For this extra dose of comfort, one pays the highest prices on Cephane Sokak: 8,000TL ($11.20) single, 14,000TL ($19.60) double, breakfast included, and well worth the price.

North of Downtown

Because of the lay of the land, Kuşadası has expanded northward, and the mile of shoreline to the north of Barbaros Caddesi is thus another fertile area for hotel hunts.

The **Posacı Turistik Pansiyon,** Leylak Sokak 5 (tel. 6361/1151), one block off the shore road, has 18 good rooms, some with views of the bay, most without private facilities, for $11.50 single, $17 double, breakfast included.

Right on the shore road is the older **Günhan Oteli,** Atatürk Bulvarı 52, Kuşadası 09400 (tel. 6361/1050), often busy with Turkish families or foreign couples who find the rooms comfy, the location not inconvenient, and the price right at 8,800TL ($12.30) double, 12,375TL ($17.35) triple, with bath, breakfast included.

Walk up İstiklal Caddesi, a street going inland from the shore road, and you'll come to yet more good, modern pensions, including the **Çi-dem Pansiyon,** İstiklal Caddesi 9 (tel. 6361/1895), a cheery place with a long-running reputation for friendliness, and single rooms for $9 with washbasin, or $13.50 with shower, and doubles for $11 with washbasin, $16 with shower. The **Yunus Pansiyon,** right next door, is quite similar in both accommodations and price.

Also right here is the **Hotel Akman,** İstiklal Caddesi 13, Kuşadası 09401 (tel. 6361/1501), open from March through November only, and when it's open, often filled with Europeans on a tour. Rooms here have either showers or tubs, and are priced on the outer ranges of our budget at $22 single, $31 double, breakfast included.

THE BIG SPLURGE: Your ultimate splurge might be in one of the ancient but beautifully refurbished rooms of the Mehmet Paşa Kervansaray, an Ottoman caravan way-station which has become the Club Méditerranée's **Club Cara-vanserail,** Atatürk Bulvarı at Barbaros Caddesi (tel. 6361/2457 or 2423). You enter through the building's massive armored front doors and come to a lush courtyard paved in marble and shaded by palm trees. At the center is a tinkling fountain, and all around, on two floors, are the attractive, tastefully furnished guest rooms, brightened up with pieces of Turkish folk art. Room prices, quoted in dollars, are high for Turkey, but eminently reasonable for what you get: a double costs $36.60 for room, breakfast, tax, and service, but you're usually required to buy "half pension" (breakfast and dinner), which brings the cost to $53.75 double, which is not actually that far out of our budget. To experience the fine old building and a bit of the posh life without going over the budget, come for lunch or dinner, or just sit in the courtyard and have a drink.

Utterly different are the accommodations at the **Hotel Efe** (P. K. 49), Güvercin Ada Caddesi 37 (tel. 6361/3660), facing the cruise-ship dock very near the little island. All of the guest rooms are on the front of the hotel, which is quite dramatic, with stepped terraces ascending the hill. Each room has a little balcony and an unequalled view of the sea and the town, as well as a private bathroom. The price to stay here is 25,300TL ($35.40) double, breakfast included—which, if you spend your dining dollars with care, is actually not a splurge at all.

Among Kuşadası's first upscale hotels was the **Tusan Oteli,** a mile or so north of town (tel. 6361/1094 or 2080), on its own stretch of sand beach. The Tusan is an older hotel, and fairly simple, but well situated for water sports and quietness. Room prices depend on the view and location, but range from 17,000TL ($23.80) to 19,000TL ($26.60).

The Starvation Budget

Kuşadası began its resort career as a town of little pensions, and luckily for budget travelers this tradition is alive and well. The pensions are scattered throughout town, with many located on the hillside overlooking Barbaros Caddesi. The typical pension room has a washbasin, but not a private shower or bath. Double rooms cost 4,400TL ($6.15) to 6,600TL ($9.25).

To find a rich concentration of pensions, go up Barbaros Caddesi, turn right toward the Akdeniz Hotel, and then walk to the right of the hotel, up the hill on Arslanlar Caddesi. Soon you will come to several little places, including the **Hotel Rose** (tel. 6361/1111), the **Pansiyon Su** (tel. 6361/1453), the **Şafak Pansiyon** (tel. 6361/1764), and others. Also look at the **Öven Pansiyon,** on Eski Pazaryeri Sokak (tel. 6361/3963) near the Hotel Akdeniz.

Budgeteers should also consider two hotels right on Barbaros Caddesi in the center of town. Watch out for noise when you pick a room here. That's the disadvantage. The advantages are low prices and a very central location. Try the **Otel Atlantik,** Barbaros Caddesi (tel. 6361/1039), which has rooms for 3,300TL ($4.60) single, 5,500TL ($7.70) double, without bath; and the aforementioned **Hotel Pamuk Palas,** Barbaros Caddesi (tel. 6361/1080), which offers doubles with shower for 7,150TL ($10).

RESTAURANTS: Kuşadası can be divided neatly into three parts when one thinks of food. Assuming that you are not having your meals at your hotel or pension, and that you don't wish to indulge yourself with the 10,000TL ($14) table d'hôte dinner at the Club Caravanserail, your options are to go down to the waterfront, where the town's better and higher-priced restaurants are stretched along the quai; to have a snack or light lunch in one of the dockside tea gardens; or to go up Barbaros Caddesi, around (or under) the police station and onto the street's continuation, called Kahramanlar Caddesi. On Kahramanlar Caddesi there are a half dozen cheap eateries—köftecis, kebapçıs, and hazır yemek restaurants—where the townfolk eat and the prices are minimal. Now for some details.

On the waterfront you'll find the **Toros Canlı Balık Restaurant** (tel. 1144), **Kazım Usta's Restaurant** (tel. 1226), and the **Diba Restaurant** (tel. 1063). Cheapest of these is the Diba, but basically all offer about the same food at the same prices. My current favorite is the Toros. If you just want to enjoy the waterfront ambience (which is very nice indeed), a plate of macaroni, a serving of stuffed peppers, and mineral water will provide you with a filling meal for about $2. But the specialty along the waterfront is fish, and the favorite is trança, an Aegean fish, served up as a shish kebap. Depending on season, it's about 2,500TL ($3.50) and well worth it. Expensive as they are for the budget traveler, these restaurants are nice, with pleasant Aegean customs: in some of the restuarants—indeed, all over Kuşadası—sweet basil plants are nurtured in big clay pots and put on tables for enjoyment. Run your fingertips across the top of the plant, then smell them (don't break off leaves to get the smell, there's no need to). Superstition has it that a sprig of sweet basil taken on a journey assures a safe trip.

The tea gardens near the waterfront offer such snacks as *çöp kebap,* small morsels of meat left over from the butcher's block, spitted on split bamboo, and roasted over charcoal; lokma, sweet honeyed fritters, and various kinds of börek. For about a half dollar you should be able to have a fine snack on these.

A moderately priced restaurant on Barbaros Caddesi is the **Çatı Restaurant,** with a shaded rooftop terrace offering a view of the busy street and good, standard Turkish fare. Plan on spending 3,500TL ($4.90) to 4,500TL ($6.30) for a full fish dinner with wine.

Also, for inexpensive but delicious kebaps, visit the **Öz Urfa Kebapçısı,** on Cephane Sokak facing the Hotel Alkış (tel. 3244), where a lunch or dinner of kebap, salad, and beverage costs about 2,200TL ($3.10).

Finally, the places on Kahramanlar Caddesi all offer about the same things for the same prices. The best place to go is, unfortunately, the one which is, at the moment, the busiest. It seems, on this street, one cook at one restaurant gets himself all fired up and cooks up a storm, building up the business in the process.

Then suddenly he'll relax, business will dwindle, and somebody else on the street will take over where he left off. My advice: follow the crowd. At any of the places, a meal of cacık (yogurt, grated cucumber, and garlic), salçalı köfte (ground meat rissoles in savory sauce), bread, and a beer will cost about 1,800TL ($2.50). Current favorites include the **Konya Restoran** and the **Nazilli Pideci,** near the mosque and the bus station, where you can chow down for 800TL ($1.10) to 1,500TL ($2.10).

For breakfast, there are pastahanes on Kahramanlar Caddesi where a pudding or pastry and a big glass of tea will cost about 600TL (85¢).

ENTERTAINMENT, DAY AND NIGHT: The town's beaches are all along the road on the ride into town. The best one, **Pamucak,** must be reached from Selçuk by taxi, so let's consider the ones closer to Kuşadası. The beach near the Kısmet Hotel is reached by horse-drawn "beach buggy." These quaint vehicles leave from near the caravanserai frequently during the daytime, and charge 200TL (28¢) for the ride to the beach. There's another beach, mostly pebble, at the other end of town, past the fort on the island. Swimming off the causeway is also possible.

The closest beach out of town is **Kadınlar beach,** a 200TL (28¢) dolmush ride; catch the dolmushes on Barbaros Caddesi, beside the caravanserai.

For those in the mood for some strolling and shopping, start on Barbaros Caddesi; the shops there display standard Turkish craft items, standard junk, and such oddities as suede neckties, suede patchwork handbags, Mexican-type straw hats, and curious evil-spirit chasers made from woven wheat stalks. In the middle of Barbaros Caddesi, near the dolmush stop, is a little fountain. The inscription cries out for a translation: "Çıplak İbrahim Özsürücü" means that the fountain was put up in memory of Naked Abraham the Pure Drover.

FERRIES TO GREECE: Kuşadası is a port for a good number of Greek island, Aegean, and Mediterranean cruise ships, and there is frequent service to the nearby Greek island of Samos. Any travel agency in town can book you on one of the ferries that operate every day during the summer. Boats leave at either 8 a.m. or 5 p.m., depending on which country's boat you take: Turkish in the morning, Greek in the afternoon. The trip takes 2½ hours and costs $25 one way. Get to the office the day before you wish to sail if you can, so you'll have a firm reservation. A hint: The morning trips are often less choppy than the evening trips. If you're at all prone to seasickness, try to get a morning boat.

The **Akdeniz Tourism and Travel Agency,** with an office right down near the dock and another near the little bridge on Atatürk Bulvarı, is the agent for Epirotiki Lines and for other international cruise ships. If you're interested in a longer trip than to Samos, contact them. If it's just to Piraeus that you want to go, get the ferry to Samos and pick up one of the two daily boats which leave from Samos.

LEAVING KUŞADASI: Dolmushes to Söke, the jumping-off point for the south Aegean coast, leave about every half hour from the garage at the end of Kahramanlar Caddesi. The fare to Söke is 300TL (42¢).

3. Priene, Miletus, Didyma, and Altınkum Beach

Though today this is farming and resort country, in ancient times the southern coast was dotted with rich trading cities. Wealthy and cosmopolitan societies supported and encouraged progress in the arts and sciences, and so philosophy and mathematics flourished. Priene is said to be the first city planned and built with a neat grid of streets, while Miletus was the home of the great Thales, granddaddy of great mathematicians. Didyma was the site of an enormous—

and enormously wealthy—temple, complete with oracle. This was the south Aegean during the Golden Age.

There is much to see among these sites. The three ancient cities south of Kuşadası, plus one of the better south Aegean beaches, can all be seen in a day or two, minimizing the tight hotel problem by allowing you to use Selçuk or Kuşadası as a base.

TRANSPORTATION: You can take a **minibus tour** which includes time to explore these three archeological sites, and also a swim at Altınkum Beach. Travel agencies organize them, but you may get a better deal by just going to the bus station and asking around. Sometimes the minibus drivers organize their own tours lasting from 10 a.m. to 7:30 p.m., including lunch, for 6,000TL ($8.40) per person. A tour is the best way to see these cities if your time is short, or if you mind doing a little hitchhiking.

To get around to these sites on your own, start by heading for the bus station in Söke. It has separate bus and dolmush sections, and acts as the regional transportation center. From the bus side of the station, municipal buses (Söke Belediyesi) leave for İzmir every hour on the half hour from early morning until late afternoon; a one-way ticket costs 700TL ($1). Also, buses go east to Denizli and Pamukkale, and south to Bodrum, Muğla, and Marmaris.

Start your explorations by catching a dolmush to Priene (8½ miles, 14 km) for 200TL (28¢); it may be marked "Güllübahçe," which is the name of the modern village nearby. From Priene, catch a passing dolmush to **Milet** (Miletus) or **Balat,** the neighboring village, 13 miles farther south (500TL, 70¢, from Söke). From Miletus, continue your tour by taking another minibus to **Didim** (Didyma), 35 miles (56 km) and 500TL (70¢) from Söke. **Altınkum Beach,** the farthest point on this excursion, is 38 miles (61 km) from Söke (500TL, 70¢). If you want to do all of this in one day from Selçuk or Kuşadası, start early in the morning. The dolmushes begin running just after dawn. If you don't care about swimming at Altınkum, begin by taking a dolmush to Didyma, the farthest site, and work your way back.

PRIENE: The dolmush will turn off the highway and drop you in a shady parking area next to the **Şelale Restaurant,** a charming place built on terraces beside a pool and a waterfall. The water falls from a fragment of the city's old system of aqueducts and cisterns. There's a signboard with all of the restaurant's prices on it, and it shows that you can have a snack or a light meal for 1,800TL ($2.50) to 2,600TL ($3.65). The restaurant has a public telephone and rest rooms.

From the restaurant, climb the slope to the **archeological zone,** which is open from 9 a.m. to 6 p.m. daily, at a cost of 400TL (55¢) for admission, half price on Sunday. Go through the gate and walk up the long flights of steps to get to the **Council Chamber.** This was the meeting place for the city government, located in a charming setting faintly reminiscent of Delphi because of the mountains behind and the plain below. The chamber is in pretty good shape, and from its top step there's a good view of the plain and the Meander River (Menderes in Turkish), which gave its name to the phenomenon of a winding, curving course —it's not hard to see why. The Meander filled in the entire plain with silt over the centuries, causing Priene to lose its port, and to end up as Ephesus did when the same thing happened there. The valley is very fertile because of the rich river deposits, and if you walk to the edge of the bluff in front of the Council Chamber, you'll look down on rich olive groves, manicured orchards, lines of cypress trees, and a small creek, now the only trace of Priene's harbor. While you're walking around these ruins, watch out for snakes. I stepped over a big one.

Walking farther on past the Council Chamber will bring you to a road downhill which once led to the port and which now leads to the ruins of the **Temple of Cybele,** the ancient Anatolian goddess. The road looked too good to be true—until I found out that it had been restored recently.

On the top of the hill is the **Temple of Athena,** Priene's most impressive temple, the drums of its huge columns standing in place or littered around the temple grounds. Behind the temple and a bit farther up the slope of the next hill are the ruins of a **Byzantine church,** almost too close to a pagan temple for comfort, I would think. The church adds an odd touch to the old city—something from a very different culture dropped into the middle of ancient Greece.

The town's **theater** is just behind the church, and is in a good state of repair. There are armchair-style seats for the town dignitaries with an inscription on each one, probably their names and titles or ranks. The heart-shaped leaf motif used for decoration throughout the theater is one that I have not seen anywhere else in Turkey.

There's something charming about the ruins of Priene. Although the city has undergone extensive excavations, the work was done so long ago (1895) that time has been able to rub out the traces of the work, giving the city the feeling that it has been deserted for centuries, and that it is now much like it was originally. It seems as though time was the only thing at work here, not modern science. I find it sad that the city is deserted. The people who built this city, like their peers in the other cities along this coast, knew how to pick a good site for a settlement.

MILETUS: This city flourished for more than a millennium, but about A.D. 700 its harbor was suffering from silt, commerce died out as at Ephesus, and the citizens of Miletus sought the good life elsewhere. Today Miletus is famous because of Thales, who is gone for good, and because of its **theater,** which is here to stay. It's impressive, it's huge, it stands alone, and it's in good condition. Honeycombed with walkways and passages, the theater is said to have held 25,000 spectators. Most of the seats are still in place.

Besides the theater, Miletus has numerous other buildings, most in a state of advanced disrepair. A ticket to see the theater and all the rest of the site costs 400TL (55¢), half price on Sunday; the site is open from 9 a.m. to about 6 p.m. every day. Services at Miletus include a snack and drinks stand, and a Seljuk Turkish caravanserai remodeled and restored as a souvenir bazaar.

Other buildings at Miletus include a **stadium,** several **agoras** (marketplaces), the **Baths of Faustina,** and the city council meeting place, or **bouleterion.** But the most significant structure other than the theater is the **İlyas Bey Camii,** built in 1404, at a time before the Ottoman architectural style had come to dominate the small Turkish principalities hereabouts. There are many Seljuk features of the style, and others that might be called pre-Ottoman. Though partly in ruins, it's a very sympathetic building which you will enjoy visiting. The mosque is open all the time. The easiest way to reach it is by walking across the fields, starting from the museum.

Speaking of the **museum,** it's about half a mile south of the theater, and it holds the usual collection of objects found at the site.

To reach Didyma, nine miles south of Miletus, catch a dolmush or hitch a ride by the theater, or walk the mile out to the highway and hitch there. Take anything that comes along; it may be going only to Akköy, the next town south, but from Akköy it's usually easier to catch something else southbound.

DİDYMA: The **Temple of Apollo** is all there is at Didyma, but it's the most interesting ruin in the area. Entrance is 350TL (50¢); hours are 8:30 a.m. to 6:30 p.m.

daily. The temple is colossal, on the scale of the Parthenon, the front part being a veritable forest of huge column drums with bases decorated in differing designs. Walk among these piles of stone, up a few giant steps, and then descend to the interior of the temple, now a large open courtyard. Indicated by a sign is the spot from which the oracle spoke, to be interpreted by the temple priests. You can climb to the top of the temple by means of stairs in the walls to get an idea of the temple's grandeur. Supposedly the temple was never really finished, though it was under construction for 300 years—right up to the birth of Christ. The workmanship is impressive; there's still a good deal of it evident after almost 2,000 years. The carved-marble decoration and the statuary, once incorporated in the temple and now strewn around the temple's "front yard," shows that the workmen who built this place were not interested solely in size, but in beauty and harmony as well. One of the carvings here is the famous colossal head that's reproduced on travel posters with a bikini-clad girl sunning herself in front of it.

After you've done the temple, consider having a cool drink or a meal across the road under the trees (shade!) where there are two restaurants and a tea house. These little eateries are not as cheap as they should be because of their location right next to a tourist attraction, but a meal of menemen (eggs cooked on top of sliced tomatoes, heavily spiced), a salad, pilav, and a drink comes to about 2,000TL ($2.80).

ALTINKUM BEACH: The Turkish name means "golden sand," and that's what you'll find here, three miles (five kilometers) south of Didyma. The beach has its own collection of small pensions and hotels, some beach restaurants, and a lot of that deliciously cool Aegean sea water, which feels particularly refreshing after a day's tramping through ruins. For the return trip to Selçuk or Kuşadası, begin by catching a dolmush to Söke, and change there for your final destination.

4. Aphrodisias

One of Turkey's most exciting archeological sites is the city of Aphrodisias, only recently discovered and still in the process of excavation. Those interested in old things should consider visiting it, for some of the things uncovered are almost as good as new. If you plan to go to Denizli and Pamukkale, this is only a short detour off your route.

GETTING THERE: There are direct buses from İzmir to Nazilli, your point of departure for the trip to Aphrodisias. From Söke, take a dolmush to Ortaklar to pick up this bus. It's about three hours from İzmir to Nazilli by bus, only about one hour from Ortaklar.

Once you get to Nazilli, get a dolmush to Geyre, the village right next to Aphrodisias. If none of these is running, your best bet is a dolmush to Karacasu. The driver of this one will probably spot you and come out to usher you to his minibus. To Karacasu it's a 45-minute ride (250TL, 35¢). If, by chance, you should catch a dolmush directly to Geyre, the trip will cost somewhat more for the extra 12 km (7½ miles) between Karacasu and Geyre. From Karacasu, dolmushes run out to Aphrodisias (and Geyre) during the morning and early afternoon; if you want a private vehicle, rent a taxi or a minibus (5,000TL, $7, round trip). I didn't want to wait for the dolmush, so I hitched a ride with an oil tanker.

THE RUINS: The ruins and the nice little museum here are open from 9 a.m. to 6:30 p.m., for 400TL (55¢), half price on Sunday and holidays. One ticket admits you to both the ruins and the museum. You'll have to check your camera at the door of the museum, and the guard may blow his whistle if you try to photograph excavations in progress here; but otherwise, shoot away.

The city took its name from the great **Temple to Aphrodite,** which existed here from about 700 B.C. until taken by the Byzantines and converted to a church around A.D. 350. It got rich on pilgrimages to the temple in pagan times, and continued to prosper under the Byzantines, but Aphrodisias was despoiled and torched by Tamerlane in 1402, and never recovered.

Aphrodisias is in a valley right on the stream which probably did the most to cover the city up. One of the first things you'll notice on the way in is the **stadium,** in such good condition that with a bit of cleaning up it could be used again. All of the original building seems to be there: the seats, the tunnels leading into the arena, the track rimmed with stones. It has not been touched since the city was prosperous—not restored, tampered with, or changed—so it must look exactly as it did when in use. The **odeon,** farther on toward the hill, is in even better condition, because, unlike the stadium, the odeon was not exposed to the weather. The mud of the stream, still causing trouble by flooding the stage, was the agent which covered the odeon with mud and preserved it so that the marble seats and decorations look as bright and sharp as when they were cut. The nearby Temple of Aphrodite has some fine workmanship in its marble pavements and birds' nests on top of its columns. A smaller temple next to it has in it a strange, bowl-shaped stone, about ten feet in diameter. Could this have been some sort of altar?

Near the temple and the odeon are the large **Baths of Hadrian,** dating from the 2nd century A.D.

Among the most striking buildings at Aphrodisias is the **theater,** built into the side of the small hill, with marble used lavishly in its construction. It's a grand sight, uncovered and restored with the aid of the National Geographic Society.

When you're done tramping through the ruins, you can buy a cool drink from the little stand near the museum.

ONWARD TO PAMUKKALE: To get back to the highway, get a direct dolmush from Geyre to Nazilli, or take one to Karacasu and transfer. There's no need to go all the way back to Nazilli if you're going on to Denizli and Pamukkale. Get out of the dolmush when it meets the main highway and wait for a bus at the tea house across the road. Frequent buses come from İzmir and pass this point on their way to Denizli. The ride takes less than two hours.

5. Pamukkale and Denizli

Pamukkale, besides being the site of ancient Hierapolis, a Roman health spa, is also modern Turkey's most famous spa. Hot springs burst from the earth right near the old Hellenistic theater and run through channels carved in stone down through several motels and their private swimming pools, then tumble over a cliff, leaving bright deposits of calcium before rushing down into the valley below. The deposits have built up into enormous white falls and stalactites, and the appearance of these **travertines** has given the place its Turkish name, which means "Cotton Fortress."

On the way to Pamukkale is the agricultural city of Denizli, which has the bus and train stations which serve Pamukkale, and also some hotels to take the overflow of visitors to the spa. Though Denizli is a tidy, friendly place, you won't need to do much there except catch a bus or train, or find a hotel room if Pamukkale is booked up.

GETTING THERE: You can take a bus or a train from İzmir or Selçuk to get to Denizli. From there you must take a bus, dolmush, or taxi for the last 12 miles (7½ km) to Pamukkale.

Direct buses depart İzmir on the four-hour run to Denizli, charging 1,500TL ($2.10) for a one-way ticket. There are also direct buses from Kuşadası's bus station; the trip from there takes 3½ hours and costs 1,500TL ($2.10). If you miss these, take a dolmush to Selçuk, Söke, or Ortaklar and catch a bus there.

As for **trains,** two express *mototren*s depart İzmir's Basmane Station daily on the 6½-hour run to Denizli via Selçuk. The train, though it takes somewhat longer than the bus, is also a bit cheaper. A first-class one-way ticket from İzmir to Denizli costs 900TL ($1.25); from Selçuk to Denizli, the price is a mere 650TL (90¢).

From Denizli to Pamukkale

Municipal buses marked "Denizli Belediyesi" shuttle between the city and the spa every 30 to 45 minutes throughout the day, though service stops around dusk. On weekends, when there is heavier traffic, trips are more frequent. A one-way ticket costs 150TL (23¢).

Dolmushes also run this route, charging slightly more for the slightly faster ride.

A taxi will charge you about 3,800TL ($5.85) for the one-way trip from the Denizli bus station to Pamukkale.

ORIENTATION: Denizli's bus and train stations, and several of its better hotels, are all within a few blocks of one another, not far from the highway through town and the turnoff to Pamukkale. As for Pamukkale itself, it's about 12 miles (19 km) north of Denizli. Services at Pamukkale include a first-aid station, PTT, police station, and tourism office.

Tourism Information

The Tourism Information Office (tel. 621/13-393) in Denizli is in the train station on the main highway, just a block from the bus station. There is also a small Tourism Information Office at Pamukkale, in the row of shops to the left of the open area just at the top of the slope.

HOTELS: The prime place to stay during your sojourn here is at the top of the slope, above the travertines, right next to the ruins of old Hierapolis. This is where you will find the modern, comfortable motels. When the motels fill up, as they often do on summer weekends, you may have to seek equivalent accommodations in Denizli, not far from the bus and train stations. If you're willing to take a cut in comfort in exchange for a cut in price, or if you're traveling on a severely restricted budget, look for a room at the bottom of the slope in **Pamukkale Köyü,** the village of Pamukkale, where there are dozens of little pensions.

Motels at Pamukkale

The **Tusan Motel** (tel. 6218/1010) is part of the chain with motels throughout Turkey. It has 50 rooms, its own hot-spring swimming pool, an excellent, convenient location near all the ruins and the action, yet it's set slightly apart from the hubbub (you'll see what I mean). Prices run 18,400TL ($25.75) single, 23,000TL ($32.20) double, for rooms with private bath.

The **Motel Koru** (tel. 6218/1020) is the largest lodging place at Pamukkale with 130 rooms, many occupied by tour-group members. To handle the crowds, it also has a very large swimming pool. The restaurant is good, the gardens lovely, the situation fine. The Koru has a reputation as Pamukkale's prime place to stay. Prices for the privilege are 20,000TL ($29.40) single, 23,400TL ($32.75) double, with bath of course.

The 80-room **Beltes Motel** (tel. 6218/1014) has a name that's a shortened form of *Belediye Tesisleri* ("Municipal Installations"), meaning that it's owned and run by the city government. Whatever its management, the draw here is the motel's excellent location overlooking the valley—most rooms have panoramic views—and its unique swimming pool. One long pool stretches across the cliff side of the motel, and each guest room has its own portion of the pool right outside the door. You can swim and admire the view at the same time! Because of these advantages, and because the demand for rooms is so high, the Beltes normally only rents its rooms with breakfast and dinner included, at 32,000TL ($44.80) to 35,000TL ($49) double; the more expensive rooms have the private pools.

The **Pamukkale Motel** (tel. 6218/1024) is the oldest establishment on the hill, but it has been renovated recently, and is so popular that a block of new rooms is under construction. The attraction is a depression in the courtyard of the motel with drums of old fluted columns, inscription stones, statuary, and other artifacts left from the Greek and Roman periods. Filled with the natural hot-spring water, it becomes the swimming pool! The water is surprising: so clear that it appears to be ice cold, it is in fact the temperature of bath water. To stay at the Pamukkale Motel, you pay 12,000TL ($17.65) single, 15,000TL ($22.05) double, with bath.

The **Mis-Tur Moteli** (tel. 6218/1013) is at the northern end of the row of motels ranged along the cliff top. Less convenient to the center of the site, it's still within a 10- or 15-minute walk. Some of its rooms are little domed structures with very odd and somewhat disturbing acoustics; check one out before you buy. Single rooms with bath are priced at 12,500TL ($18.40), doubles at 18,000TL ($26.45), breakfast included. The Mis-Tur has a small camping area as well.

Village Pensions

Down at the base of the hill, below the gleaming travertines, is the village of Pamukkale. The village has grown up with the purpose of providing shelter to less well-heeled visitors to Pamukkale, especially foreign backpackers. The rooms in the village pensions are always quite simple and plain. Some have private showers, many do not, and a lot of the time you will find yourself doing without hot water. You can make up for the chilly water in the shower, however, by taking a dip in the hot water of the swimming pool, as most of these pensions, modest though they be, have some sort of pool. It may be makeshift, or oddly shaped, or no bigger than a hot tub, but it's still a soothing, relaxing place to spend some time. Some pensions serve all three meals; others provide only breakfast.

If you plan to stay at the base of the cliff, plan to do some walking. Several of the better pensions are a half mile from the village center, and the village itself is almost a mile from the installations at the top of the cliff.

The **Hotel Nebioğlu** (tel. 6218/1031), despite its name, is a pension much like the rest, though it's right next to the highway. Rooms with shower cost 6,600TL ($9.25) double, without private bath.

For a quiet pension well away from the highway, follow the signs to the **Anatolia Pension** (tel. 6218/1052 or 1085), half a mile from the highway. A bucolic location, English-speaking management, and a homey atmosphere are the advantages. The few rooms are newish, though plain. The water in the private showers is rarely hot, but there is a little pool. They charge 6,000TL ($8.40) single, 8,000TL ($11.20) double, for a room with shower. All meals are served.

The **Pension Mustafa** (tel. 6218/1240 or 1096) is among the better bargains in the village, as you can get room and meals here for the price of a room anywhere else. The rooms themselves are not beautiful, but clean, freshly painted, and tidy enough, without running water. The owner is an energetic village woman with the bearing of a genial sergeant, who charges 5,000TL ($7) double for a room, or 8,000TL ($11.20) with breakfast and dinner included. The pension has a small swimming pool.

If you don't find what you're looking for at these places, just wander around the village for 15 or 20 minutes and you'll turn up an agreeable room.

Hotels in Denizli

To some people, swimming in the warm waters at Pamukkale is not particularly important. Others will arrive at Pamukkale only to find all the rooms in the better motels occupied. The alternative to staying at Pamukkale is to find a hotel near the bus and train stations in Denizli. Hotels in Denizli tend to charge less for equal comforts than do the motels at Pamukkale. In the city, however, you don't have those marvelous views, swimming pools, and ancient ruins. But the frequent bus service makes staying in town only a minor inconvenience.

The first place to look is on İstasyon Caddesi, the street which begins directly opposite the Denizli Gar (train station). Closest hotel to the station is the modern and comfortable **Halley Oteli**, Cumhuriyet Caddesi at İstasyon Caddesi, Denizli 20100 (tel. 621/19-544 or 21-843), one very long block up the hill from the train station, on the right. For 12,200TL ($17) single, 16,500TL ($23.10) double, you get an attractive and comfortable room with bath in one of the city's better hotels.

Another choice is much farther into the city, a mile or two from the station. The principal plaza of the city is called Delikli Çınar Meydanı, and just off it is the **Kuyumcu Oteli**, Delikli Çınar Meydanı, Denizli 20100 (tel. 621/13-749 or 13-750), with modern rooms priced at 12,000TL ($16.80) single, 16,000TL ($22.40) double, with bath of course.

For much cheaper lodgings, look at the **Otel Sedir**, Cumhuriyet Caddesi, Denizli 20100 (tel. 621/16-998), just beyond the aforementioned Halley Oteli. The Sedir is one of the city's older hotels, but is quite respectable and favored by Turkish families. It has an elevator and a restaurant for breakfast, and rooms with or without private shower for 3,300TL ($4.65) to 4,500TL ($6.30) single, 5,000TL ($7) to 6,500TL ($9.10) double, the higher prices being for the rooms with shower.

RESTAURANTS: With the exception of the municipal facilities' terrace café and a small *pideci* (Turkish pizza place), there are no independent restaurants at Pamukkale atop the cliff. For sustenance, you go to one of the motel dining rooms. At the **Motel Koru,** for instance, a dinner of soup or appetizer, a main course, and something to drink might cost you 3,000TL ($4.20). All the other motels have decent dining rooms, many with even lower prices.

Down at the base of the cliff in Pamukkale village is an anomaly, a Turkish folk version of an American **Pizza Hut** restaurant, built by a Turkish pizza maker who had worked at the trade in Australia for many years. The building is a caricature, but the pizza is of much higher quality than the "real thing," so go and enjoy! Whole pizzas with various toppings are offered at prices ranging from 800TL ($1.10) to 1,800TL ($2.50).

SWIMMING: Stay in a motel or pension and you can use their pool. Otherwise, you can often pay a day-use fee at a motel just to take a swim. The most interesting place to do this is in the pool at the **Pamukkale Motel,** with its submerged columns. A ticket to use the pool for a day costs only 400TL (55¢).

Another public swimming place is the **Municipal Tourism Facilities (Bele-**

diye Turistik Tesisleri), with several large pools, some smaller family-size ones, and other services such as bathing-suit rental and a terrace café for tea, coffee, soft drinks, and snacks. Here's what you'll need to know to use the municipal facilities: *umumi havuzlar* means "public pools," and the charge here is 350TL (50¢) for two hours' swimming; an *özel aile havuzu* is a private family pool, which costs 1,050TL ($1.45) per hour to rent.

By the way, signs warn visitors that it's forbidden to walk, wade, or swim in the pools of the travertines, but almost everyone seems to ignore the signs. At some point the authorities will have to get strict about this rule in order to preserve the natural beauty of this fascinating geologic formation, but right now the rule seems not to be enforced.

THE RUINS OF HIERAPOLIS: Hierapolis was founded early in the 2nd century B.C. by the King of Pergamum. The king built a city here for the same purpose that modern Turks built motels here: so people could come and enjoy the healthful waters. Unfortunately, many visitors came with illnesses, hoping for a cure. Though many must have gone away sound and happy, many more stayed permanently to fill the city's several ominously large cemeteries, or *necropoli*.

To entertain visitors, and just because every Roman city had to have one, Hierapolis had a large **Roman theater,** which still stands. It has been very nicely restored and is scheduled to be used for summer shows and recitals.

Between the entry road and the theater is the impressive bulk of a ruined **Byzantine church,** and the **Temple of Apollo.** The temple had an oracle attended by eunuch priests, and did a brisk business issuing enigmatic "predictions" to hapless visitors.

THE MUSEUM: The stone structure close to the Pamukkale Motel which housed Hierapolis's mineral-water baths is now the **Pamukkale Museum,** open from 9 a.m. to noon and 1:30 to 5 p.m., for 400TL (55¢), half price on Sunday and holidays.

A VISIT TO LAODICEA: Once a prosperous, populous commercial city at the intersection of two major trading routes, Laodicea is today an archeological site west of the Denizli–Pamukkale highway. Turkey is littered with the ruins of old cities, but Laodicea's claim to fame is that it was home to one of the Seven Churches of Asia, which were among the first large and influential Christian communities outside the Holy Land. Anyone following in the footsteps of St. Paul and visiting all of the Seven Churches will want to make the pilgrimage to see what's left of Laodicea.

The "churches" referred to in the phrase does not mean buildings, of course, but Christian congregations. You won't see any church buildings at Laodicea (Laodikya in Turkish), and as a matter of fact you will see little else. There are ruins of a **stadium,** but most of the cut stones have been taken over the centuries to be used in building projects elsewhere. Two **theaters** are also visible, in a ruined condition.

Visitors with their own cars, or willing to rent a taxi for the trip, can see Laodicea easily by turning left (west) off the Denizli–Pamukkale highway 2½ miles (four kilometers) from the big traffic circle near the Denizli bus station. A yellow sign with black letters marks the turnoff. The site is open during daylight hours, for free.

6. Bodrum
The southwestern corner of Turkey is a ragged edge of Anatolia with low mountains, lush fields, and peninsulas jutting out into the seas, both the Aegean

and the Mediterranean. Along these peninsulas are little towns, festooned with palm trees, which have played host to at least several civilizations apiece. Ruined classical temples stand partly hidden in pine forests and fairytale castles dominate picture-perfect fishing villages. If you have an image in your mind after reading the above words, you can now put a name to it: Bodrum.

Once called Halicarnassus, Bodrum was the capital city of the ancient Kingdom of Caria, ruled over at its most famous period by King Mausolus, whom we remember because of his fabulous tomb, the Mausoleum, one of the Seven Wonders of the Ancient World. Today Bodrum is a beach and watersports resort, a yachting center with a fine marina, and the jumping-off spot for ferries to the Greek island of Kos.

GETTING THERE: The 168-mile (270-km) trip from İzmir to Bodrum takes about four hours by bus, which is the only public transportation available. From Selçuk or Kuşadası, the 93-mile (150-km) trip takes between 2 and 2½ hours. The trip is along a good, fairly fast road through beautiful scenery.

ALONG THE WAY: The route to Bodrum takes you south past the roads to Priene and Didyma, then past the pine-tree-lined shores of **Lake Bafa.** The ruins on the other side of the lake are of the old city of **Heraclea** (the Greek Latmos), famous in the myth of Hermaphrodites, the son of Hermes and Aphrodite. The handsome Hermaphrodites was supposedly fused with his lover into one body which had the characteristics of both male and female. There are fishermen willing to row you across the lake to the ruins for a price; check with them in the restaurant on the shores of the lake. Several small islands in the lake held Byzantine monasteries, now in ruins. As you leave the lake, look for a small ruined fortress on the left side of the road.

There are often camels on this road, usually hard at work carrying loads of grain or tobacco. They don't seem to fit in with the lushness of the countryside, with its rich fields and pine-covered hills. Some camels in Bodrum and Marmaris are fitted out for riding, but these are only for the tourist trade. The Turks wouldn't think of riding camels when there are horses around, but they know camels are first rate as beasts of burden.

After you pass through the village of **Selimiye,** keep an eye out on the left side of the road for the **Temple of Euromos,** one of the best-preserved in Anatolia. It was built by the citizens of Euromos, a town in the ancient Kingdom of Caria.

Not far after Euromos is another trace of the region's history, not from the time when it was Caria, but from its history as a Seljuk Turkish emirate. Parallel to the modern highway bridge over a stream is an old bridge built by the Seljuks.

The bus usually makes a short stop in **Milas,** an old town noted for its rugmaking, before heading on to Bodrum.

On the right side of the road shortly after Milas is the **tomb of a Muslim saint,** under a tree. The branches of the tree are a spooky sight—hung with ripped shreds of cloth. It's the customs for Muslims to tie a shred of their clothing on or near the tomb of a saint whom they've asked to intercede for them, as a reminder that they have a request pending.

After the hardship of the curves, the road heads down to the shore and the double bay, where the town spreads out before you, divided in the center by the romantic **Crusaders' castle** perched on a rocky peninsula between the two bays.

ORIENTATION: The bus leaves you at its office near the main crossroads in the town. The street you drove down while coming into town (and the one the post office is on) is called **Cevat Şakir Caddesi.** It changes names at the crossroads and continues on into the town, straight to the door of the castle, as **Kale Caddesi.** Facing Kale Caddesi, the road along the water on your right is **Neyzen Tevfik Caddesi;** on your left is the street the bus company office is on, the first of a number of streets in the market numbered in order: 1, 2, etc. Follow these numbered streets through the market to get to **Kilise Square,** where **Cumhuriyet Caddesi,** the one running along the shore of the other bay, begins. The **Adliye Camii,** the mosque right at the crossroads here in the center of town, is a good starting point for all your activities in Bodrum.

The **Tourism Information Office,** Oniki Eylül Meydanı (tel. 6141/1091), sometimes called İskele Meydanı, is right at the foot of the Crusaders' castle by the docks. Hours of operation are Monday through Friday from 8 a.m. to 8 p.m., on Saturday from 9 a.m. to noon and 3:30 to 7:30 p.m.; closed Sunday. These are the summer hours; winter hours are somewhat shorter.

HOTELS: Besides the town proper, there are several outlying areas with hotels, so you have quite a choice of locations when you stay here. You may not, however, have much of a choice of rooms if you arrive late in the day during high summer. Bodrum has a room shortage in the summer months, and reservations are advised.

Those looking for a cheap bed in a pension may find that when they descend from the bus, numerous pension proprietors have gathered to meet them and to lead them to just the sort of place they need, at a very reasonable price.

Starting from the Adliye Camii, let's explore the lodging possibilities on both the eastern bay, to the left of the Adliye Camii, and the western bay, to the right, before taking a look at hotels farther out.

On the Eastern Bay

Bodrum's greatest concentration of little pensions and hotels is along Cumhuriyet Caddesi. Starting from the Adliye Camii, walk through the market to get to this waterfront street and its hostelries.

The **Otel Baraz,** Cumhuriyet Caddesi 58 (tel. 6141/2570), is modernish, comfortable but not lavish, with rooms right on the water. The 24 double rooms with shower here rent for 12,500TL ($17.50).

Somewhat farther along Cumhuriyet Caddesi you'll see the **Artemis Pansiyon,** Cumhuriyet Caddesi (tel. 6141/2530), where the street runs right along the beach. Many of the 22 rooms at the Artemis have some colorful traditional folk pieces as decoration, and rent for 9,600TL ($13.45) double with shower, breakfast included.

At the farther limits of Cumhuriyet Caddesi is a district named Kumbahçe, where you will find the **Fesleğen Pansiyon,** Papatya Sokak 18/1 (tel. 6141/2910), by following the signs. The 13 double rooms here are quieter than most, and reasonably priced at 9,500TL ($13.30), with private shower.

On the Western Bay

Turn right at the Adliye Camii and Neyzen Tevfik Caddesi leads you past many yachts and excursion boats tied up at the quai, to the **Herodot Pansiyon,** Neyzen Tevfik Caddesi (tel. 6141/1093), very popular with the budget-minded portion of the yachting crowd. This cheerful place facing the marina and the castle has only 15 rooms, and it's not unusual for all of them to be full. But if you can get one, it will cost you 7,200TL ($10.10) double, without private bath.

Seçkin Konaklar, Neyzen Tevfik Caddesi 164/1 (tel. 6141/1351), is not really a hotel. The name translates as "select lodgings," which in this case means a dozen little apartments which can sleep four to six people, and also four large rooms with three or four beds in each. This is the perfect place for congenial groups or families to stay. The cost works out to something like 3,500TL ($4.90) to 4,000TL ($5.60) per person for a room with private facilities.

On Gümbet Beach

West of Bodrum proper is Gümbet Beach, a short dolmush or taxi ride, or a 15-minute walk, from the center of town. Because it has close access to good swimming, the hillside behind Gümbet has sprouted its own crop of hotels and pensions. If beach life appeals to you more than town life, this is the place for you.

You won't have much trouble spotting the **Esentepe Motel,** Gümbet Mevkii (tel. 6141/2045), a new, modern place perched right atop the hill which dominates the beach. The bath-equipped rooms here, though of moderate comfort, are actually budget in terms of price: 9,000TL ($12.60) for a double is the norm.

Right next door to the Esentepe is the very similar **Kıvanç Motel** (tel. 6141/2043), where you will pay the same price for a very similar room.

Down at the edge of the water is the **Ayaz Motel,** Gümbet Mevkii (tel. 6141/1174), which has its own swimming and boating dock, a camping area, and simple but adequate double rooms with private shower for 9,800TL ($13.70) per person, breakfast and dinner included.

The Big Splurge

The **TMT Motel,** Akçabük Mevkii (tel. 6141/1423 or 1440), about a mile east of the center of town in the district called Akçabük, is generally regarded as Bodrum's poshest place to stay. A large, modern two-story motel structure with 171 rooms set amid nice gardens, the TMT has its own swimming pools, beach, patio restaurant, and tennis courts, and is more like a mini-resort than just a lodging place. The motel usually rents rooms on a "half-pension" plan, so you get a bath-equipped room with a view of the bay, plus breakfast and dinner, for 25,500TL ($35.70) double.

The "in" place to stay for fashionable types is the **Halikarnas Motel,** Kumbahçe Mahallesi (tel. 6141/1073), at the far end of the eastern bay, a ten-minute walk from the Adliye Camii. The motel rents rooms, of course, but nightlife and good times are as important as slumber here. Lots of the people in the motel's disco-club have paid the 20,000TL ($28) to 30,000TL ($42) for one of the motel's 28 double rooms.

The Starvation Budget

As you strolled along Cumhuriyet Caddesi, east of the Adliye Camii, you passed lots of little pensions. The price to stay at any one of these little places is about 5,400TL ($7.55) double. Try any of these: the **Martı Pansiyon,** Cumhuriyet Caddesi 84 (tel. 6141/2605); the **Mercan** (tel. 6141/1111); or the **Uslu Pansiyon** (tel. 6141/1486).

If all of these are full, try exploring the little streets that head inland from Cumhuriyet Caddesi. These hold lots more pensions, and many of them are even cheaper because they're not located on the main street. One such place is the tiny **Kemer Pansiyon,** Uslu Çıkmazı 30 (tel. 6141/1473), with 17 beds in its severely plain, small, but clean rooms. Two people pay 3,600TL ($5.05) in a room without running water.

RESTAURANTS IN BODRUM: Some of the pensions have cooking facilities you can use, others have their own little restaurants. For more romantic ambience and fancier cooking, head for the waterfront. You'll find the **Körfez** and other restaurants on the water in the center of town near the Adliye Camii. They are not the town's cheapest, but they are the most pleasant. Fish, as everywhere these days, is expensive, and will run 2,000TL ($2.80) to 3,000TL ($4.20) a plate, depending on the fish and the season. There are kebaps for much less, about 900TL ($1.25), with the mixed grill (karisik kebap) costing slightly more. A kebap, salad, and beverage, with the tip, should cost about 2,100TL ($2.95).

Cheaper? There are several little eateries on Cumhuriyet Caddesi, some with their own little seaside tables (remember: the plainer, the cheaper), but for the lowest prices, the town's köftecis are near the Adliye Camii.

Light lunches and breakfast can be had in the same area at one of the town's pastahanes. My preference is the **Ender Pastahanesi,** in the market at no. 9 (there's also an entrance near the bus garage). Bread, butter, honey, and a large tea costs 800TL ($1.10); a more substantial breakfast with cheese and an egg costs just a bit more.

Another favorite is the **Mauzolos Restaurant,** where the two of us enjoyed a bounteous repast consisting of two appetizers, a large and perfectly grilled fish of the day, a big mixed salad, a bottle of white wine, and Turkish coffee, all for 13,000TL ($18.20) total, tip included.

Tea Houses

Sad to say, the nice old tea house right down by the docks has almost been destroyed by the ramshackle souvenir shop set up in the middle of it. It used to be one of the best places in town to sit and people-watch. Creeping commercialism cannot daunt the townfolk, however, for most evenings you'll see the chief of police, the Customs officer, and assorted boatmen drag their chairs out onto the waterfront and put their whole soul into the enjoyment of a glass of tea or a cup of coffee. This spirit of tranquil joy is called *keyf* in Turkish. It's a practice badly needed by modern society. The taste, smell, and color of the tea, the evening air, good company, relaxation are all the objects of serious concentration. Pascal may be right that "Man will not be happy until he learns to sit quietly in a room" and the Turks have a good start by learning how to do it outdoors.

A less-congested tea house is the one on Neyzen Tevfik Caddesi near the little white mosque. Soft drinks and beer are served also, and the panorama, if not the street traffic, is better than at the dockside place.

But in the evening, don't miss the activity down around the docks. This is the social center of the town, drawing long-haired hippies as well as the smart set living in the yachts moored nearby. In the evening the tables are spread out into the square nearby, the crowd livens up, and one of the local sailors will get out a village flute and put one of his mates to dancing. The town's strolling violinist is sure to stop by and give a change of pace to the proceedings as he makes his rounds of the restaurants and tea houses in the evening.

THE CASTLE AND THE TOWN: Bodrum is a strange town. Almost everyone who visits it falls in love with it. This could be because of its location, its history, or its amusing blend of cultures. It's not a typical Turkish town. One of my Turkish friends said that if the people didn't speak Turkish, he'd think it was a "foreign" town. Bodrum has preserved a great deal from the turn of the century, when the town was predominantly Greek, and some of it—the buildings, the customs, even the language—has blended with the Turkish way of life which has taken it over, and has produced a unique result.

When you start out to see the town, begin early in the day. Even as early as the late hours of the morning, the sun is burning hot.

Castle of St. Peter

The first place to go when you're out to see the sights is the castle. It's open every day from 8:30 a.m. to noon and 3 to 7 p.m. Entrance costs 400TL (55¢).

Wander around the lower levels of the castle for views of the town and the sea. Scattered throughout the interior of the castle, set into the walls, are plaques with Latin inscriptions honoring the medieval knights who built and manned the castle. In the keep there's an old church which served as a mosque for a while under the Turks, and is now a museum. The grounds of the keep are studded with amphoras, the big clay urns retrieved from the bottom of the sea around Bodrum. Other finds put on display in the yard include inscribed stones and some rusty anchors. Walk up the hill between the cactuses to the other museum buildings.

One museum holds the finds of a National Geographic excavation in this area, which include gigantic metal "coins" a foot square, used by the Byzantines in international commerce, fittings for Byzantine galleys, and a wonderful scale for weighing cargo, the counterweight of which is a bronze bust of a woman. The expedition, thanks to modern diving techniques, uncovered the hulk of a Byzantine cargo ship that had sunk intact.

Now to the top of the castle for an overall look. The castle is really something out of a storybook, making most castles, no matter what their historical importance, look like pale copies. Though it was indeed used in the defense of the town (even as late as World War I), the romantic Knights of St. John, the ones who built and garrisoned the castle, had more in mind than just defense. The medieval period was romantic in many respects, and the idea of crusading troops fighting Oriental hordes at the far end of the Mediterranean was one of the most romantic. The marble tablets on which are emblazoned the coats-of-arms of notable knights are meant to add to the effect, but they look so new that it's hard to believe the dates such as 1496 and 1513 that they bear.

A Walk Around Town

After exploring the castle, take a walk around the town to turn up native sights; a pomegranate tree right next to the town's oldest mosque, near the castle entrance; sponge sellers with their wares on Kale Caddesi; pottery covered with shells and amphoras covered with barnacles being sold in the souvenir shops; from a mosque, the raucous call of the muezzin amplified by a loudspeaker.

Starting in early September, Bodrum holds an **Arts Festival** for a week each year. Tickets entitle the bearer to the concerts, folk dancing, photography, and painting exhibitions put on in the castle and environs.

The Mausoleum

Though the famous Mausoleum was destroyed by earthquake and pillage centuries ago, recent excavations have revealed its foundations and various bits of decoration. You can visit the site of King Mausolus's tomb, one of the Seven Wonders of the Ancient World, inland from the western bay. Follow the signs from Neyzen Tevfik Caddesii, and walk two blocks inland.

Mausolus's grand monument was a great temple surrounded by columns, roofed with a stepped pyramid, and topped with a chariot drawn by four horses. Artists' renderings show that it was indeed a wondrous sight. Mausolus's widow had the tomb built on the late king's orders. Construction took five years and was completed in 350 B.C. Today, in the case of the Mausoleum, one picture is worth a thousand fragments of rubble.

BEACH EXCURSIONS: Though there is a pebble beach along the eastern section of Cumhuriyet Caddesi, the water in the eastern and western bays is not particularly clean. You can insinuate yourself onto the little beach at the TMT Motel, but a better plan is to walk, or take a ten-minute dolmush ride, to **Gümbet,** west of town. These are the nearest beaches.

Excursion boats will offer to take you on a day-long tour to various swimming and picnic spots for 2,000TL ($2.80) to 3,500TL ($4.90) per person.

Another possibility is a dolmush ride to the town of **Turgut Reis,** 11 miles (18 km) southwest of Bodrum. Turgut Reis, formerly known as Karatoprak, has a fine beach, several hotels, pensions, and restaurants, and a resort complex.

North of Turgut Reis is the beach hamlet of **Gümüşlük,** set on a picture-perfect bay with some sand beach and the partially submerged and very ruined remains of ancient **Mindos.** Dolmushes run out to Gümüşlük from Bodrum, and small pensions and restaurants provide food and shelter. Go here, but don't tell anyone else about it!

The mass of land just off the coast of Bodrum offers a chance for another outing. This is **Kara Ada,** the "Black Island," and there's a daily boat which leaves from the wharf at the castle end of Kale Caddesi at 9 a.m. and returns at 5 p.m. A round-trip ticket is 1,200TL ($1.70). The beaches on the island are not quite as good as the ones on the mainland, but there's a warm mineral spring you can bathe in, alternating this with a dip in the bracing sea water.

You can get a fisherman or a motorboat owner to take you to the island and back for about 4,500TL ($6.30), and he'll even wait around for you while you swim and explore the island. You'll have to strike a bargain with one of them; you can usually find one around the wharf or in the tea house. If you can find a few people who missed the daily boat, you can share the cost among you—the price is for the whole boat, not per passenger.

BOAT CONNECTIONS FROM BODRUM: Boats to the Greek island of **Cos** (İstanköy in Turkish) leave the wharf at 9 a.m. on Monday and Friday for the 75-minute trip; $21 one way. The boat arrives back in Bodrum at 7:30 p.m. the same day. Any local travel agency can take care of the arrangements for you. You'd better arrange for your ticket the night before in order to make sure there's time for Customs formalities.

Are you heading east along Turkey's Mediterranean coast? If so, you might consider taking a boat out of Bodrum rather than a dolmush or bus. During the summer months, **Karya Tour Yachting and Travel Agency,** Karantina Caddesi 13, Bodrum (tel. 6141/1759 or 1914), operates ferryboats between Bodrum and the little fishing village of **Datça,** on the narrow peninsula which begins near Marmaris. The boat departs at 8:30 a.m. from Bodrum, and returns at 5 p.m. from Datça on most days. On weekends the schedule changes: on Friday a second boat leaves Bodrum at 5:30 in the afternoon; on Saturday the one daily boat departs Bodrum at 6 p.m., and departs Datça at 8 a.m.; on Sunday boats depart Datça at 7:30 a.m. and 5 p.m. The price for a one-way passenger ticket is 5,000TL ($7), or 7,000TL ($9.80) for a round-trip ticket.

Chapter XII

MEDITERRANEAN TURKEY: THE TURQUOISE COAST

1. Marmaris
2. Datça
3. Fethiye and Ölüdeniz
4. Kalkan and Kaş
5. Antalya and Vicinity
6. Side
7. Alanya
8. The Eastern Coast

TURKEY'S MEDITERRANEAN COAST has flourished, to my knowledge, twice in history: the first time was when the Hellenistic cities along its shores were built; the second is today. In recent years there's been a real boom here, and European tourists by the planeload have been coming to bask in the sun, climb around the ruins, and take advantage of the miles of beaches.

The choicest portion of what the travel magazines have called the Turquoise Coast is on the shores of the Gulf of Antalya, 84 miles covered with ancient cities and white beaches, protected by the headlands on either side. Transportation center and largest town in this area is Antalya, the capital of the region, built on the site of the Roman city of Attaleia.

But Antalya is not the whole coast. The western coast between Marmaris and Antalya was in classical times the mountain-bound kingdoms of Lydia and of Lycia, remote areas which borrowed elements of classical culture and mixed them with local inspiration to produce a unique, if limited, civilization. And to the east of Antalya and Alanya lie areas just now being put on the tourist map. Though the eastern coast offers less interest per mile to the first-time visitor than does the western, you'll find many things to amuse and delight you, all the way to Antakya (Antioch).

TRANSPORTATION: A few general comments on getting around will help you to discover the Mediterranean coast with ease.

There are three **airports** on the south coast, at Dalaman, Antalya, and Adana. Adana, at the eastern end of the coast, has the most flights as it's an important agricultural, commercial, and industrial city. Antalya receives almost as many flights, including some direct charters from Europe. Dalaman, near Fethiye, is mostly for charter flights, though Turkish Airlines serves the western coast (Marmaris, Fethiye, Kaş) through Dalaman with flights from Istanbul and Ankara in the summer months.

As for **bus** service, it's not as frequent or as convenient as you might expect. There is some service between Marmaris and Antalya, and a few more buses daily between Antalya and Adana, but in general you must check the bus transportation situation carefully before making plans.

Between towns, particularly on the western reaches of the coast, you will probably find it most convenient to take a **minibus.** Check the day before you travel so as not to be disappointed. There may only be a few minibuses per day.

1. Marmaris

Not long ago Marmaris was a sleepy little fisherman's village which received, every now and then, a handful of travelers passing through town to and from the ferryboat to Rhodes. Then a number of things happened: a new road was carved through the mountains, the tourist crush hit the Greek islands like a tidal wave, and Turkish tourists bought cars and hit the road in search of the perfect vacation spot. Marmaris, they decided, was *it.*

Marmaris is now undoubtedly a resort town, not a fishing village. Strung out along the curve of a beautiful bay, backed by pine-mantled green mountains, its quais thick with yachts flying the flags of a dozen nations, Marmaris has arrived as a full-fledged "destination," at least as far as the Mediterranean's cognoscenti are concerned. But I hasten to add that this does not mean it is Miami Beach, barricaded from the sea by high-rise hotel and condo towers, glutted with cars careening off expressways, inhabited by credit-card-toting big spenders. Marmaris still has a sort of simple charm, and you'll enjoy it.

GETTING THERE: Dalaman, with its airport, is about 60 miles from Marmaris. City buses (Marmaris Belediyesi) meet flights at **Dalaman Airport** and shuttle passengers to Marmaris for a mere 1,000TL ($1.40) each. A **taxi** from the airport to Marmaris costs 17,000TL ($23.80). During the summer months, bus traffic to Marmaris from northern cities is intense, even frantic. Direct **buses** from İzmir arrive 30 times a day. The six-hour trip costs 2,000TL ($2.80). Coming from Bodrum, there are nine buses a day via Muğla. A ticket on the three-hour trip costs 1,500TL ($2.10). To and from Fethiye, to the east, there are 22 daily buses; the trip, which takes from two to three hours, costs 1,500TL ($2.10).

ORIENTATION: At its heart Marmaris is a small village, and the heart of town is İskele Meydanı, the plaza next to the ferryboat dock. Near the dock, surrounded by sleek yachts, are the Customs house, tourism office, currency-exchange booths, several small and inexpensive hotels, and the market.

The street running along the shore is officially named **Atatürk Caddesi,** but to most locals it's the **Kordon.** A convenient landmark is the equestrian statue of Atatürk.

Atatürk Caddesi runs partway around the bay, but an interior road goes even farther, well around to Uzunyalı, the district where there are holiday villages and the Hotel Lidya.

The **Tourism Information Office**, İskele Meydanı 39 (tel. 6121/1035) is right by the ferryboat dock. Hours are 8:30 a.m. to 6:30 p.m., though you may find it open later on summer evenings.

HOTELS: Marmaris, like Bodrum, suffers from summer overstuffing, so it's good to have reservations, or at least to arrive as early in the day as possible so you have a good chance of finding a room.

Marmaris has several hotel areas. The older section of town, near the ferryboat dock and the market, has several small, plain hotels and one or two nicer ones. The Kordon, stretching for a mile or so around the bay, has dozens of hotels, mostly new. And well around the bay are several vacation villages and more luxurious hotels.

The **Hotel Kaptan** (tel. 6121/1251), more or less behind the Tourism Information Office, in the row of buildings facing the moored yachts, is the best hotel right in the center of town. It's a small, older building that has been well restored for a yachting clientele. Comfortable, though not fancy, rooms without bath rent for 12,000TL ($16.80), breakfast included.

From the center, walk out along the Kordon to explore other lodging possibilities. Within half a mile of the market are quite a number of other choices.

The **Hotel Acar,** Atatürk Caddesi, near the equestrian statue (tel. 6121/1117), is modern, located close to everything, and very attractively priced at 7,000TL ($9.80) to 8,000TL ($11.20) for double rooms with showers, the higher prices being for those on the front side, which have little balconies facing the bay.

The **Otel Karaca,** Atatürk Caddesi 48 (tel. 6121/1663 or 1992), is new and pleasant, with small but congenial, brightly decorated rooms with private baths. Breakfast is included in the rates here: singles cost 11,000TL ($15.40); doubles, 15,400TL ($21.55); triples are 19,300TL ($27) to 26,400TL ($36.95).

Very near the Karaca on Atatürk Caddesi is the **Karadeniz Hotel** (tel. 6121/1064 or 2837), a similar establishment with equally modern rooms, some with views of the bay, for 16,000TL ($22.40) double with shower and breakfast.

More expensive, but similar in most other regards, is the **Otel Yavuz, P. K.** 125, Marmaris (tel. 6121/2937), right with the other hotels on the Kordon. What makes the Yavuz stand out is its tiny rooftop swimming pool. You've got to decide whether the pool is worth paying extra for. A double with bath and breakfast here costs 20,000TL ($28).

Two older traditional hotels on the Kordon are waffle-fronted buildings facing the bay, about a mile from the market and the ferryboat dock. Though the hotel design gives front rooms nice little balconies from which to enjoy the view, it also exposes these same rooms to noise from the busy avenue, which can continue until quite a late hour. Check your room carefully for noise, or take a cheaper room on the back.

The **Otel Marmaris,** Atatürk Caddesi 30 (tel. 6121/1308), is one of these old favorites, its 63 double rooms with bath going for 18,000TL ($25.20), less for a quieter room facing the rear.

Right next to the Marmaris is the 40-room **Otel Atlantik,** Atatürk Caddesi 34 (tel. 6121/1218 or 1236), which is popular with Turkish families. Double rooms with shower are rented for 17,000TL ($23.80) and singles for 8,500TL ($11.90), breakfast included.

The Big Splurge

The **Otel 47** (that's not "forty-seven" but *kırk yedi*), Atatürk Caddesi 10, Marmaris 48700 (tel. 6121/1700 or 2730), has many luxury touches in its decor and furnishings, and is among the newest hotels in town. Definitely aimed at an upscale audience, the price of a room is still quite reasonable, considering that this is the most comfortable hotel right downtown: doubles are 23,400TL ($32.76), singles are 15,000TL ($21), and breakfast is included.

The other classy hotels are off to the west of town, set on their own stretches of beach, surrounded by gardens.

The **Hotel Lidya**, Uzunyali Mevkii (tel. 6121/2940), was Marmaris's first luxury hotel, built several decades ago and well maintained over the years. Though certainly not of world-class luxury, it is very comfortable and has the advantage of an experienced and attentive staff. There are fully 220 rooms, suites, and small apartments in a number of buildings set amid the Lidya's gardens. Prices during the summer season range from 18,000TL ($25.20) to 23,000TL ($32.20) double for rooms, twice as much for an apartment.

Those looking for an all-expenses-paid sojourn in a self-contained vacation complex should look into staying at one of the two holiday villages beyond the Hotel Lidya. The **Turban Marmaris Tatil Köyü**, Uzunyalı Mevkii (tel. 6121/1843), rents its 250 rooms with breakfast and dinner included, and charges slightly more than does the Hotel Lidya. The **Martı Tatil Köyü**, Uzunyalı Mevkii (tel. 6121/1930), is even more luxurious, with 213 rooms priced at 30,000TL ($42) double. Besides rooms, you get a full range of sports and entertainment facilities at these "villages."

The Starvation Budget

The small downtown hotels, clustered near the ferryboat dock, are mostly the same in terms of facilities and prices. The **Otel Sema** (tel. 6121/1595), the **İmbat Oteli** (tel. 6121/1413), the **Karaaslan Oteli** (tel. 6121/1867), and the **Kalyon Oteli** (tel. 6121/1085) all seem to charge 5,500TL ($7.70) for a double room without private bath, or 7,500TL ($10.50) for a double with shower. All are in or near İskele Meydanı (Dock Square), right by the dock and the Tourism Information Office.

Can you beat this price? Certainly. Go to the Tourism Information Office and ask them to help you find a room in one of the town's many **ev pansiyons.** Prices per room in private homes vary from 3,500TL ($4.90) to 6,000TL ($8.40). You probably won't have a private bathroom in an ev pansiyon, and you've got to watch out for trampoline-like beds, but otherwise these rooms for rent constitute the best lodging bargain in Marmaris.

RESTAURANTS: As with many resorts, firm restaurant recommendations are difficult to make here as the staff and management of most places change from season to season. It's more important to know about Marmaris's dining areas than about particular restaurants, for the area in which you dine pretty much dictates what you'll pay.

The most pleasant and romantic dining area is along the quai facing the larger moored yachts, behind the Tourism Information Office. The wide esplanade here is a succession of sidewalk restaurants, one after another. Prices are similar, though by no means identical, at these establishments. If I had to choose, I'd sit down at the **Birtat Restaurant** (tel. 1076), which has been here for decades and which has maintained a good reputation. But to choose wisely, look at the menus and the clientele in several of these waterfront places before you sit down. Seafood is the highlight of dinner here, and you can expect to pay 6,500TL ($9.10) per person for the works: appetizers, fish, salads, dessert, wine, and tip.

For much cheaper, standard Turkish fare, with not as much seafood offered, head into the little warren of market streets inland from İskele Meydanı and locate the **Ayyıldız Lokantası** (tel. 2158), which is a typical storefront eatery with a few tables set out in the market streets. Recently I paid 1,100TL ($1.15) for a delicious meal of döner kebap, bulgur pilav, salad, and beer. There are a half dozen other such inexpensive, not bad places in the market. Most of the patrons will be Turkish.

WHAT TO DO IN MARMARİS: You've probably guessed already that there's not a lot to do in Marmaris if you're looking for excitement. This is a place to relax.

There's a national park to the left of the town as you look out to sea, and you might want to settle down for the afternoon there with a book. For exercise, try climbing around on what's left of the little fortress right downtown.

Other than these things, there's **swimming,** of course, from beaches spread along the coast from the end of Kordon Caddesi to the Hotel Lidya, or you can rent a boat and swim from that.

Save your walk around town for the evening, when these other activities are not practical, and the town is just quieting down for the night. The town has a folk-dance troupe, but it usually performs on order from a tour agency for the tours from Greece, or in one of the big hotels. For a free peek, keep an eye out for where they're dancing in the afternoon.

In a market area behind the town square, it's so busy during the afternoon one almost fails to notice that the indoor shopping arcade is actually an ancient "Menzilhane" or Pony Express way-station left from the Ottoman Empire's crack messenger service. The plaque, in medieval Turkish in the Arabic script, says it was built by Sultan Süleyman the Magnificent in 1545.

If you intend to buy anything in Marmaris, wait until after the boats from Greece leave, for the prices charged the day trippers are about 50% more than normal. One of the local products is beautiful golden honey (*bal,* in Turkish).

A street with services—restaurants, barbershops, etc.—used by the townspeople and not just tourists is **Çeşme Meydan Sokak.** To find it, walk from the wharf through the market streets to the mosques and little fountain (çeşme). Then turn left and you're on Çesme Meydan Sokak.

You can't miss the town's many **excursion boats,** moored along Kordon Caddesi. As you walk by them, their mates will importune you in several languages to buy a ticket for tomorrow's cruise in the bay and among the islands. Departures are often at 9 a.m., and the cruise may last until 5 p.m. Things to find out before you buy: Where does the cruise go? Is lunch included? What is lunch, a dried-up sandwich or a freshly caught fish? When does the boat return? The price for a ticket on one of these cruises is generally around 1,000TL ($1.40), somewhat more if lunch is included.

There are also longer excursions by boat from Marmaris, including some to **Cnidos,** out at the tip of the Datça Peninsula. The Tourism Information Office or any travel agency can fill you in on the details.

FERRYBOATS TO RHODES: Almost any travel agent in town—there are many along the Kordon—can book you on a boat to Rhodes. The standard procedure is to buy your ticket and drop off your passport the evening before your morning departure. Boats make the run daily except Sunday in high summer, and even sometimes on Sunday if traffic warrants. Tickets cost $15 one way, $27 round trip, with a special excursion ticket (round trip in one day) priced at $20.

2. Datça

Extending west of Marmaris well out into the sea is the slender, mountainous Datça Peninsula, well known to ancient mariners sailing between the Levant and Piraeus or Rome, and now being discovered by intrepid foreign visitors. Besides a few national forest parks and campsites, the heavily forested, sparsely populated peninsula offers two attractions for the visitor: the idyllic little fishing village of Datça, and the ruins of the ancient city and port of Cnidos.

GETTING THERE: Datça is 46 miles west of Marmaris along a winding, sometimes mountainous road. The scenery is gorgeous, but the trip cannot be done at top speed. Various companies run over a dozen **buses** per day between Marmaris and Datça, charging 800TL ($1.10) for the two-hour ride.

Besides the buses, **excursion boats** often go to Datça on day trips. You can often arrange for them to drop you there, and perhaps even to pick you up for the return trip several days later.

For summertime **ferries** between Datça and Bodrum, see the section on Bodrum in Chapter XI, above.

ORIENTATION: Not much orientation is needed as Datça is small and strung out along its one main street, with the bus station located at the marketplace, in the center of town. Hotels, restaurants, and beaches are all within a few minutes' walking distance.

The municipality of Datça sponsors a **Tourism Information Office** (tel. 6145/1163) in the town office building right next to the bus station. Even if the office isn't open, you'll want to look at the bus and hotel information posted in the windows.

HOTELS: The **Dorya Motel** (tel. 6145/1036), at the very end of the street, and also at the end of the little peninsula which juts out from the town, is Datça's only really fancy hotel. Though the price for a double room with bath is a bit beyond our budget at 22,500TL ($31.50) for room and breakfast, 30,000TL ($42) for room, breakfast, and dinner, you might well think the extra dollar or two worth it. The motel's situation, set in its own beautiful gardens and surrounded by the sea, is extremely fine. For the evenings there's a "disco" with live entertainment(!).

Right next to the Dorya is a far more modest, much cheaper place, the **Esenada Oteli** (tel. 6145/1014), with plain, even bare rooms without running water of any kind priced at only 3,000TL ($4.20) double, 3,750TL ($5.25) triple.

As you get off the bus, you'll notice the little **Deniz Motel** (tel. 6145/1038), with the familiar plain, stark, waterless rooms going for 3,000TL ($4.20) double.

Apart from these, Datça has small pensions throughout town costing about 1,000TL ($1.40) per bed. I'd recommend that you choose your pension by location, to enjoy the blissful quietude that Datça has to offer. Try the **Bora** (tel. 6145/1327), the **Karaoğlu** (tel. 6145/1079), the **Huzur** (tel. 6145/1052), or the **Sadık** (tel. 6145/1196).

RESTAURANTS: As with the hotels, you'll have the restaurant situation under control shortly after arriving in Datça. The best place in town is the Dorya, of course, but the main street, up on the hill just before the peninsula, has several serviceable, pleasant restaurants, all charging about 1,200TL ($1.70) to 2,100TL ($2.95) for a full lunch or dinner. The **Taraca Restaurant** has a nice shaded dining area with a marvelous view of the little cove, the peninsula, and the sea, as does the more prominent **Liman Lokantası**.

BEACHES AND SIGHTS: The beaches are in the little cove where the yachts moor, and also back along the road to Marmaris. As yet they're uncrowded, unpolluted, and simply wonderful.

Other than swimming, sunning, reading, talking, and lazing the day away, there's nothing to do in Datça. For excitement, make the 22-mile trek out to the end of the peninsula to visit **Cnidos**, the ancient port city which once exhibited Praxiteles' most famous statue, his *Aphrodite*. The road to Cnidos is rough and often unpaved, and public transportation is scarce. If you go by land, you'll probably have to rent a taxi for the entire excursion, an expense of some 13,000TL ($18.20).

An alternative way to see Cnidos is on a day-long boat excursion, and this is much the preferable of the two, as you glide through the water, enjoying the scenery and getting some sun, rather than bashing over the mountains inhaling dust. Not only that, it's usually cheaper, as a day trip by boat costs only 3,000TL ($4.20) per person.

Once you arrive at Cnidos, you will find yet another perfect, idyllic harbor, a few very basic restaurants where local matrons cook up rough-and-ready grub, and a plain little pension with only a few rooms and only rare vacancies. All around are the ruins of the great commercial city which flourished here since about 400 B.C. Praxiteles' great statue is gone, and virtually every other building has been tumbled to ruins by the earthquakes of centuries. Even though there isn't a lot to see, the site is marvelous.

EASTWARD FROM MARMARİS: To continue your explorations of the Turquoise Coast, hop a bus eastward from Marmaris to Fethiye. The road passes through fragrant pine forests and lush farming valleys, skirting the ruins of a dozen ancient cities. If you have the time, make a detour at **Dalyan** to see the rock-cut Lycian tombs carved in a sheer cliff face above the Dalyan River, and to visit the ruined and largely undisturbed city of **Caunus.** Dalyan has a number of small pensions and restaurants, and boatmen who will take you on the excursion downriver to Caunus.

3. Fethiye and Ölüdeniz

FETHİYE: Called Telmessos in ancient times, Fethiye has seen a lot of history but has very little to show for it. It's a pretty enough place, set on a wide bay with an attractive waterfront esplanade, but the 1958 earthquake turned to ruins many of the last vestiges of Fethiye's long history. Today you can visit the town's museum, hike up to a striking rock-cut tomb, and marvel at the odd Lycian sarcophagi which are scattered through downtown. But you will soon find yourself in a dolmush bumping over the mountains to Ölüdeniz, the absolutely perfect ribbon of white sand beach which stretches from a shady pine-forest park to a hidden lagoon. Today, Ölüdeniz is why people come to Fethiye.

Getting There

Buses depart frequently from Marmaris to Fethiye. There are also six buses per day from İzmir and a few from other cities. The **Fetur** company operates minibuses from Dalaman Airport to Fethiye, serving each flight, for 1,000TL ($1.40) per person. A taxi from the airport to Fethiye charges 13,500TL ($18.90). Besides direct buses from Fethiye to and from Antalya, there are minibuses run by **Sunny Boy Tourism** to take you to intermediate stops such as Kalkan and Kaş. These aren't all that frequent, however, so check the schedules.

Orientation

Fethiye is a spread-out place, ranged along the main street, which is of course **Atatürk Caddesi,** skirting the eastern portion of the bay. Heading into town from the bus station, it's about half a mile to the museum and the commercial district, and about a mile to the yacht marina, the Hotel Likya, and the area of pensions. The town is backed by mountains, so it's long and narrow rather than deep.

The **Tourism Information Office** (tel. 6151/1051) is on İskele Meydanı next to the Hotel Dedeoğlu. They have maps, lists of accommodations, and lots of information on the area.

Hotels

Before rushing off to find a hotel at Ölüdeniz, you should know that there is only one comfortable, modern hotel there, and that the other little beachfront places are fairly primitive and not particularly cheap. You would do well to spend your nights in Fethiye and your days in Ölüdeniz.

The poshest hotel in Fethiye is the **Hotel Likya**, Yat Limanı (tel. 6151/1169 or 1690), facing the yacht marina at the very end of Atatürk Caddesi. The Likya has only 16 rooms, but they look out to the bay across the hotel's gardens, and all are equipped with private bathrooms. The hotel has a swimming pool and a nice restaurant. Rates are 19,000TL ($26.60) double, breakfast included. You should understand that the Likya is not a particularly fancy place, though it's very pleasant. The major difference between this hotel and others in town is the Likya's situation, amid its gardens and lawns, and its pool.

My favorite hotel in town is the older **Otel Dedeoğlu**, İskele Meydanı (tel. 6151/4010), next to the Tourism Information Office and not far from the yacht marina. The Dedeoğlu benefits greatly from its friendly, helpful, and experienced staff, who really make one feel welcome. Located right on the quai, the Dedeoğlu's 41 rooms have views of the water, private baths, and prices of 8,800TL ($12.30) single, 13,200TL ($18.50) double, breakfast included. This may be your best choice. Go to the next-door hotel only if the Dedeoğlu is full.

Much lower in price is the **Kordon Oteli**, Atatürk Caddesi 8 (tel. 6151/1834), not far from the Tourism Information Office, but more in the commercial center of town. The Kordon's older rooms have seen heavy use, but the location is excellent, and the price very refreshing: doubles with shower go for 7,700TL ($10.80), breakfast included.

Around the curve in the road from the Kordon is the **Otel Ulvi**, on Atatürk Caddesi (tel. 6151/1650), somewhat newer than the Kordon, with suitable though not fancy rooms, for 6,600TL ($9.25) double, with shower.

Looking to really save some serious money? The **Hotel Kaya**, Cumhuriyet Caddesi 6 (tel. 6151/1161 or 2469), is in the market, a block inland from Atatürk Caddesi; look for the jasmine vine climbing up the front of the hotel. Simple, very tidy small rooms here have private showers, and prices that won't make you take a bath: 6,000TL ($8.40) double, 4,000TL ($5.60) single, for rooms with private shower.

The Tourism Information Office can help you find a room in an **ev pansiyon,** or you can easily find one yourself. The several streets on the hillside above the yacht marina and the Hotel Likya hold rows of homes which rent out rooms for about 1,500TL ($2.10) to 2,000TL ($2.80) per bed. Rooms have no running water, and you must often provide your own soap and towels, but for those on a tight budget these pensions represent an unbeatable bargain.

Restaurants

You have your choice of several locales for meals in Fethiye, all of them pleasant. The dining rooms of the better hotels often have views of the water, experienced service, and good kitchens. But most people opt for the outdoor restaurants along the esplanade in summer when the weather is warm. A cheaper alternative is to wander through the market streets, where restaurants set out tables and chairs in the streets, and a carnival atmosphere prevails.

The yachting crowd has two favorites in Fethiye. Closest to the yacht marina is the aptly named **Yacht Restaurant,** near the Hotel Likya. With no street noise to bother you, and the sound of the waves lapping at your boat, you can enjoy a fish dinner at one of the patio tables for about 3,500TL ($4.90), drinks included.

The other favorite is not at all fancy, but quite friendly. Frosty glasses of beer crowd the tabletops, and smiles and good-natured banter set the mood at **Pizza 74** (tel. 1869), right next door to the Kordon Oteli. You can get a pizza here, which is in fact a Turkish *pide,* for 200TL (28¢) to 300TL (42¢), but they also have a full menu of grills, appetizers, and salads, so the "pizza" in the name is a bit misleading. In any case it's cheap, friendly, and very popular. At sunset you may not be able to find a seat outside.

Once the sun has set and the view no longer matters, head for Çarşı Caddesi, the main street in the market district, where half a dozen little places will offer to fill you up on shish kebap, döner, köfte, grilled lamb chops, and even the occasional fish, for only about 2,000TL ($2.80); many times the tab will amount to even less.

Seeing the Sights

As you wander around town, notice the odd **Lycian sarcophagi,** high-domed stone rectangles placed on elevated bases. Most of them have been here, in place, since 450 B.C. which, when you think of it, is pretty amazing. If perchance you don't run into one, go visit the one near the post office on Atatürk Caddesi.

Fethiye is backed by rugged cliffs, and high up the side of one are the ruins of a **Crusaders' castle,** built, it is said, by the Knights of St. John of Rhodes, who constructed their fort on foundations left by the Byzantines, and no doubt the Byzantines had built on earlier foundations. Some estimates say there has been a fortress here since 400 B.C.

Fethiye's only real expedition is the climb through the town and up a long flight of steps to the **Tomb of Amyntas,** carved from the living rock in 350 B.C., in the Doric architectural style. The tomb was broached long ago by grave robbers, so there's nothing to see inside, but the climb is worth it for a close inspection of the monumental façade, and for a look at the other, smaller tombs to the left.

The local **museum** holds, as you might imagine, many artifacts of extreme antiquity, but at this writing it's closed for renovations. Chances are good that it will be open again by the time you want to visit.

Any travel agent, and most hotel desk clerks, can sign you up for one of the daily **excursion boats** which cruises among the 12 islands in the Bay of Fethiye. The day-long tour costs between 2,000TL ($2.80) and 2,500TL ($3.50), and gives you a look at the terrain, a chance to swim, and some information on local history and lore.

Other tours, by boat or minibus, go to archeological sites in the region: **Caunus, Letoon, Kalkan, Kaş, Patara,** and **Xanthos.** Among the most fascinating excursions is the one to **Karmylassos,** which includes the chance to swim, and to explore an unexcavated Byzantine town, complete with temples, necropolis, and mosaic pavements, on uninhabited Gemile Island.

ÖLÜDENİZ: Though the name means "Dead Sea," this morbid moniker comes not from mineral-saturated waters, or fetid stench, but merely from the fact that the lagoon remains placid and tranquil when storms rage and Mediterranean waves buffet the neighboring coast and beach. It's peaceful, not gloomy.

Or at least it used to be peaceful. Since a paved road has been driven over the mountains from Fethiye, less than ten miles away, word has gone out that the beach at Ölüdeniz is simply breathtaking in its beauty. That has brought vacationers and disturbed the earlier perfect tranquility. But Ölüdeniz is far from "ruined," and you'll love it.

Getting There

Getting to Ölüdeniz from Fethiye is easy. Just go to the post office on Atatürk Caddesi. Behind it are dolmushes bound for the beach. Hop in, pay 250TL (35¢), and you'll be there in no time.

Orientation

The dolmush climbs into the hills through pine forests, then comes over a pass, and the panorama of Ölüdeniz is revealed. The great swath of beach is obviously too big to be easily crowded. The lagoon, to the right, is hidden at first.

Once you actually arrive at the beach, note these facts: the police (*jandarma*) station, post office, Ölüdeniz Piknik Yeri (picnic and beach park), and Motel Meri are to your right. Most of the hostelries, camping areas, restaurants, and Kıdrak Orman Parkı camping area and beach are to your left. Kıdrak is about two miles from the post office, along a road gouged from the side of the mountain.

Accommodations

The **Motel Meri**, Ölüdeniz Mevkii, Fethiye (tel. 6151/1430 or 1431, 1025 in Fethiye), is the only real hotel as such and, having a lock on the market, it charges what the traffic will bear. The motel's situation is nice, with blocks of rooms built on terraces ascending the hillside and overlooking the lagoon. Gardens of beach cactus and succulents add color and freshness, something that many of the rooms lack. If you're not a hiker you won't want to get a room on the highest terrace, as it's quite a climb from the entrance. But even with these disadvantages, the views are spectacular and the situation good. Because demand is great, the Meri makes you take breakfast and dinner when you rent one of its 75 rooms, and you pay 36,000TL ($50.40) double. The motel has its own beach and seaside restaurant. Note that the Meri is about half a mile from the main beach of Ölüdeniz.

The other lodging places here are very simple, even primitive, and often booked solid in advance during the summer months. Still, if you arrive off-season, you might want to look at the **Belcekız Motel** (tel. 6151/1430 or 1439), which is hardly what you'd call fancy, or even excessively comfortable, and yet the price for a double room is 20,000TL ($28) to 23,000TL ($32.20) with shower. Breakfast and dinner are included, however.

Another possibility is the **Çetin Motel** (tel. 6151/1430 or 1433), which is even more basic, but indisputably cheaper at 7,000TL ($9.80) for a double room without shower, 10,000TL ($14) with shower, breakfast included.

If you've brought your camping equipment, you'll be happy at Ölüdeniz, for **camping areas** abound. The prime camping spot is at Kıdrak, a park operated by the national forestry service. Prices are low, all is proper, and sites are shaded by whispering pines.

Restaurants

When I was last at Ölüdeniz, the **Han Restaurant,** at the camping area of the same name, was the most popular place based on quality of food and aptness of price. But you must be prepared to pay resort prices anywhere here, as all the food must be brought in from Fethiye, and restaurants must pay their bills with what they earn during the summer season. Also, you're a captive market unless you've packed a lunch. A restaurant meal which costs 2,500TL ($3.50) in Fethiye may cost almost twice that at Ölüdeniz.

Beaches

There's only one fact you need to know. The pay beaches at **Kıdrak** and in the **Piknik Yeri** are accessible for a fee of 200TL (28¢), a small enough price to pay for the right to use the changing rooms and toilets, and to enjoy these choice pieces of beachfront real estate. Other fees at Kıdrak, which has camping facilities, are like this: 300TL (42¢) to sleep on the beach; 1,000TL ($1.40) to pitch a tent. Kıdrak has a spring-water pump and toilets, and is usually fairly crowded.

4. Kalkan and Kaş

Everyone dreams of discovering that fast-vanishing touristic marvel, the perfect little unspoiled fishing village. Mediterranean Turkey's two entries into the international-fishing-village sweepstakes are the tiny hamlet of Kalkan, and the much larger, but still quite small, town of Kaş. Both of them, in different ways, approach the ideal.

The reason these places are unspoiled is simple. Until the new highway was cut between Fethiye and Antalya, access to Kalkan and Kaş was by boat or by Jeep. The old "road" around the Lycian peninsula was no more than a donkey track. As for the trip by boat, that was left to wealthy yachters, intrepid archeologists, and coasters bringing in supplies.

Now all of that has changed, of course, and the towns themselves are changing rapidly as more hotels rise and more restaurants open. But Kalkan and Kaş are far from "developed," though they have all the comforts.

GETTING THERE: Kalkan is 50 miles (81 km) east of Fethiye, and 17 miles (27 km) west of Kaş; it's 120 miles (192 km) from Kaş to Antalya. **Buses** between Fethiye and Antalya (there are at least four a day) stop in both towns. In addition, the **Sonny Boy Tourism minibuses** shuttle along the coast between Kaş and Fethiye.

KALKAN: Built on a treeless hillside falling down from the highway to the sea, Kalkan is really a tiny town. It does have many of the services you might need, however, such as a post office, bank, police station, pensions, and restaurants.

Hotels

The only real hotel in town is the **Kalkan Han** (tel. Kalkan 151), an old village house that has been restored with the aid of a government grant. The 16 tastefully decorated guest rooms have private baths, and Turkish handcrafts here and there in keeping with the age of the building. The price for a double is 17,000TL ($23.80). By the way, the hotel has a Telex machine.

If you don't stay at the aforementioned place, take a look at the modern **Patara Pansiyon** (tel. Kalkan 76), a hostelry also made from a renovated village house. It now has lots of white plaster and light-wood accents, and simple but bright and appealing rooms with shower, breakfast included, priced at 10,000TL ($14).

Kalkan's many pensions aren't fancy, but they make up for that in friendliness. The **Ay Pansiyon** (tel. Kalkan 58) is among the first ones you should look at, a family-run place offering double rooms with showers for 6,000TL ($8.40). Others, in which the rooms don't have private showers, are the cheaper **Akın Pansiyon** (tel. Kalkan 25) and the **Dalkıran** (no phone), which charge 4,500TL ($6.30) for a double.

Restaurants

Let's face it, one of the beauties of Kalkan is its simplicity, and the simple life doesn't normally provide fancy food. All of Kalkan's restaurants are pretty basic, and the food is plain and not so cheap because of transport. But the little restaurants down by the harbor do their best. You can sit down at the **Yakamoz,** or **Pala'nın Yeri,** the **Kalamaki,** the **Lipsos,** the **Kalkan,** the **Doy-Doy,** or the **Köşe Lokantası** and have fried fish, salad, and beer for 2,800TL ($3.90).

For cheaper meals, go up the hill to the tiny market district and sit down in the **Köşk Restaurant** (tel. 46), which may have the best cooking in town.

Water Sports

Get ready for this: the one thing I neglected to mention while singing the praises of this town is that Kalkan really has *no* beaches. It's surrounded by rock, but there is a small beach at **Kapıtaş,** and near it the **Mavi Mağara** ("Blue Cavern"). Excursion boats from Kalkan will take you there to swim and to explore on day trips.

KAŞ: If you haven't seen it before, you've imagined it: the little town, a cluster of old houses around the main square which fronts on the tiny harbor, and shady tea houses where fishermen and tourists mingle and while away the afternoon. On the outskirts, an ancient theater in good condition. That's Kaş, and all it lacks are big, wide beaches. The neighboring shores do have a few small patches of sand that you'll enjoy, but taking boat excursions and swimming from the boat or at remote beaches is more enjoyable still.

Orientation

Hop off the bus, start down the hill on Elmalı Caddesi, and you'll pass several of the better hotels. At the bottom of the hill as you face the little mosque, the **main square** is to your left. Go here for restaurants, pensions, and the Tourism Information Office. To your right is **Hastane Caddesi** (Hospital Avenue), which leads to more pensions, the little hospital, the ancient theater, and a short distance out of town, a little beach and a camping area.

The **Tourism Information Office** (tel. 3226/1238) is on the main square. It has some staff who speak English, and who hand out mimeographed sheets with information on hotels, pensions, and things to see and do.

Hotels

Right down the hillside from the bus station a few yards is the **Hotel Mimosa,** Elmalı Caddesi (tel. 3226/1272 or 1368), the most comfortable and, if you like, luxurious place in town. It's also the newest, having opened for business in August 1986. As in many such modern small-town hotels, the guest rooms are quite small, but each has a bit of sea view, a tiny balcony, and a modern tile shower. The hotel has a restaurant. Prices are 16,500TL ($23.10) double for each of the first three nights, 15,000TL ($21) per night thereafter.

Next hotel as you descend the hill is the **Oriental Hotel,** Elmalı Caddesi 10 (tel. 3226/1445), with somewhat older rooms costing 15,000TL ($21) for a double with bath and breakfast.

As far as comforts are concerned, the next place in line is the **Ali Baba**

Oteli, Hastane Caddesi (tel. 3226/1126), right at the start of the street near the little mosque. The hotel looks a bit more impressive than its guest rooms do, but they are still suitable, and quite well priced, at 6,500TL ($9.10) single, 8,000TL ($11.20) double, with shower, in season.

Among the larger pensions, I like the **Kısmet** and the **Mini,** which tend to charge 5,000TL ($7) to 8,000TL ($11.20) during the high summer season for a room with bath. Rooms may be extremely tiny and the plumbing primitive, but they're both congenial.

The **Yalı Pansiyon,** Hastane Caddesi 11 (tel. 3226/1132 or 1070), is in a quiet location (not that Kaş has many problems with noise), and gets lots of cooling sea breezes, but charges only 6,500TL ($9.10) for a double room.

Kaş has even cheaper **pensions,** those that charge a mere 2,000TL ($2.80) per bed. Look for them throughout the town, especially on the little streets behind the Hotel Mimosa, or ask at the Tourism Information Office.

Restaurants

Head down to the main square and you'll quickly get a look at all of Kaş's restaurants. Prices are fixed by the town council, so it doesn't matter much, at this stage of Kaş's development, where you eat in terms of price.

The **Mercan Restaurant,** right on the water, is a favorite for romantic dinners. The **Eriş,** on the main square near the Tourism Information Office, has about the only pretensions to decor in town, with its rustic tables and candlelight. Even so, prices are about the same. But the most popular, crowded, and, I must confess, noisiest place of all is the **Derya,** which fills an alley between the main square and the marketplace, inland. Under awnings and vines, a tiny cookshop spills out into the alley, its steam tables and refrigerator cases blocking the passage. Waiters scurry from kitchen to table, hollering orders and clattering dishes. It's chaotic but enjoyable, a bit of Kaş real life. A basic meal of shish kebap, salad, and a beer costs less than 2,000TL ($2.80) here at the Derya.

By the time you read this, you may have already patronized the **Noel Baba Pastanesi** ("Santa Claus Pastry Shop") on the main square, as many of the tables set out along the water are served from this little place. Wander into the shop, however, and you can see that they have more than tea and soft drinks: eclairs, tarts, and cookies are all served up. With a cup of Turkish coffee, a sweet treat might come to 300TL (42¢).

What to See and Do

Before taking off for an excursion by boat to any of several fascinating locales along the coasts, take a walk around Kaş. This town was the Antiphellus of ancient times. Up the slope by the road to the left of the Tourism Information Office is the **Monument Tomb,** one of those strange, very old Lycian sarcophagi. These imposing tombs were once scattered all over Kaş, but the smoothly finished rectangles were broken up to be used as pre-fab building stone.

The **theater,** a few hundred yards west of the main square along Hastane Caddesi, miraculously escaped being used for building stone, perhaps because the neatly worked blocks were not the proper size or shape. Anyway, the theater stands, virtually ready for performances, and you'll like it.

The **rock tombs** cut into the cliff face behind the town are illuminated at night, making for an eerie sight. You can hike up to the tombs for a closer look during the day, but you'd better start early because it's hot work.

Excursions by Boat

The Greek island of **Kastellorizon** is visible directly facing Kaş across the water, and this is among the more popular boat trips. However, be advised that you can only go on a day trip. The Greek authorities have not designated Kastellorizon as a port of entry, so there are no Customs or immigration facilities. Thus you cannot legally "enter" Greece here, though the local police will allow you to visit for the day.

Another trip takes you westward, to places you may already have visited: Kalkan, the Mavi Mağara (Blue Cave), and Kapıtaş. Instead of backtracking to these places, spend your time at **Patara,** a ruined classical city just inland from the most gorgeous and underpopulated stretch of beach on the entire south coast. The wide, brilliant swath of sand goes on for miles—literally.

Perhaps the most memorable excursion from Kaş is the one eastward to **Kekova** and **Üçağız.** Here, at a place where several rivers meet the sea, are the ruins of several ancient cities, some of them submerged. The scenery, the swimming, and the artifacts are outstanding. The cost for a day-long trip to Üçağız is 3,000TL ($4.20) per person, or 30,000TL ($42) to 50,000TL ($70) to charter the whole boat. By the way, there are a few extremely spartan pensions and restaurants at Kekova, but life in this untouched Turkish village is only for the intrepid.

EASTWARD TO ANTALYA: Four buses a day depart Kaş for Antalya via Demre. The trip takes five long hours and costs 1,300TL ($1.80). At first the bus climbs into the mountains behind Kaş, providing some very nice panoramas of the town and the sea. Then it's inland through mountainous country until the road descends on a terrifyingly narrow switchback which snakes its way down the face of a cliff to the fertile plain of Demre, 23 miles east of Kaş, where stood the Roman city of Myra.

DEMRE: This you won't believe, but I swear it's true. You are about to visit the home of Santa Claus.

In the 4th century A.D., when this was the Roman town of Myra, a local priest named Nicholas became famous for his generosity and compassion. In particular, he made a practice of secretly providing marriageable but poverty-stricken girls with money for their dowries. In one case he tossed a bag of money through a window at night. Another time the window was closed, so he dropped it down the chimney. Or so the story goes.

Whether the birth of the legend is accurate or not (and why not?), it is known for a fact that the Nicholas who preached and did good works here became St. Nicholas later (he was officially canonized), and became a revered symbol of generosity and compassion throughout the world.

If you simply must get off the bus, or if the legend has captured your interest, take a look at the **Church of St. Nicholas,** a Roman structure dating from the A.D. 400s, and recently restored. It's not a grand building, but remember that it dates from the early centuries of Christianity. When this church was built, Christianity had barely been the official, recognized religion of Rome for a century. Admission costs 250TL (35¢), half price on Sunday. By the way, the church is now a museum, not a house of God. No services are held here, although it's the site of a symposium on the history of St. Nicholas every December.

Another site to visit in Demre, if you have the time, is the ruins of **Roman Myra,** with its honeycomb of tombs cut into the rock face, and its theater. Take a taxi for the short ride inland from the main square near the church, or walk the mile or so to the site. It's open for free, all day.

Should you want to spend the night, the nicest place in town is the simple but homey **Kıyak Otel** (tel. 2092), which charges 2,200TL ($3.10) for a double room with private shower and one large bed, or 2,750TL ($3.85) for a double with two beds. Those prices are not misprints! The Kıyak is a ten-minute walk south of the main square, in the direction of the sea.

5. Antalya and Vicinity

Antalya, which was once the Roman town of Attaleia, has a breathtaking setting next to the sea, backed by jagged mountains shaded a hazy blue by the mists that surround them in the morning, changing to lush green in the late afternoon. In the town itself you'll find palm-tree-lined streets, a big park, and a charming old harbor area once used for Roman commerce but now reserved for fishing smacks and yachts. The area around the port is called Old Antalya (Eski Antalya), a neighborhood of picturesque Ottoman houses and narrow winding streets. The Ottoman ambience of Old Antalya is being preserved as the district is slowly restored for posterity.

Though Antalya is among Turkey's hottest tourist towns, its beaches are not the draw. They are covered in pebbles, lined with shacks, or are well out of town. Rather, Antalya is a good place to use as a base for visits to the archeological sites nearby, such as Termessos, Aspendos, and Perge. For beach time, head east along the coast to Side and Alanya.

GETTING THERE: Turkish Airlines has daily nonstop flights in summer between Antalya and Ankara and Istanbul, and one nonstop flight per week to and from İzmir.

As for **buses,** about 12 per day run between Antalya and Alanya along the coast via Side. Being a popular vacation destination, there are also direct buses between Antalya and Adana (12 hours; 4,000TL, $5.60), Ankara (2,200TL, $3.10), Denizli (5½ hours; 2,000TL, $2.80), Fethiye (6 hours; 2,300TL, $3.20), Kaş (5 hours; 1,300TL, $1.80), Konya (7 hours), Marmaris (8 hours), and Ürgüp and Nevşehir in Cappadocia (11 hours; 4,000TL, $5.60).

ORIENTATION: The center of Antalya is the plaza near Antalya's landmark, the **Yivli Minare** ("Grooved Minaret"). From here the main avenue of **Cumhuriyet Caddesi** heads west, changing names to **Akdeniz Bulvarı** and **Konyaaltı Caddesi** as it goes. This street passes the **Antalya Museum** on the outskirts before descending from the cliffs to **Konyaaltı Beach.**

Running north from the main plaza is **Kazım Özalp Caddesi,** also often called by its old name of **Şarampol Caddesi.** Antalya's **Otogar** (bus station) is several blocks up this street, as are some hotels.

Heading east from the main plaza is **Cumhuriyet Caddesi,** which soon changes names to become **Ali Çetinkaya Caddesi,** which goes through the market area. Only a block or so out of the main plaza on Cumhuriyet, **Atatürk Caddesi** goes off to the right, heading south past **Hadrian's Gate** to the luxury **Talya Oteli** and to **Kara Ali Park.**

The **airport** is several miles east of town. Minibuses to points of interest near Antalya (Perge, Aspendos, Side) depart not from the Otogar on Kazım Özalp Caddesi, but from a lot called the **Doğu Garajı** ("Eastern Garage"), a mile or so east of the main plaza. The easiest way to get there is by dolmush minibus (D. Garajı) from the Otogar for 60TL (8¢).

Tourism Information

The Tourism Information Office (tel. 311/11-747 or 15-271) is at Cumhuriyet Caddesi 73, several blocks west of the main square and the Yivli Minare.

HOTELS: Because of its booming popularity as a vacation destination for Europeans and Turks, Antalya's hotels charge the highest prices outside of the major commercial cities such as Istanbul, İzmir, Ankara, and Adana. You pay more and get less in terms of style and comfort here, but even so, the prices aren't bad, all things considered.

The first hotel to consider is the time-tested **Yayla Palas Oteli,** Ali Çetinkaya Caddesi 14 (tel. 311/11-913), only a block and a half from the main plaza. It has been here a while, but it has also been well kept up, and its longevity provides the benefit of experienced, friendly staff. Double rooms with private bath cost 19,800TL ($27.70); singles are 15,000TL ($21).

From the Yivli Minare, walk west along Cumhuriyet Caddesi, passing the dramatic monument to Atatürk on your left, and the next building on the left is the **Büyük Otel,** Cumhuriyet Caddesi 57 (tel. 311/11-499). The name means "Grand Hotel," and though it's obviously modest by today's standards, it was indeed Antalya's first "luxury" hotel. As such, it assumed the best location in town, overlooking Old Antalya and the harbor from the very edge of the cliff. The rooms are comfortable, though not luxurious, and have private baths. A double is priced at 15,000TL ($21), breakfast included.

If you arrive late at night at Antalya's Otogar, descend from your bus, scan the surrounding skyline, and you'll easily spot the tall **Hotel Bilgehan,** Kazım Özalp Caddesi (tel. 311/15-184 or 25-324), rising right near the bus station. Though undistinguished and reminiscent of the 1950s or 1960s, it's well maintained, comfortable, and rated as one of the city's better hotels. It has the priceless advantage, when you're exhausted, of being *right there.* You'll pay about 18,000TL ($25.20) for a double room with bath and breakfast.

Between the Otogar and the main plaza on Kazım Özalp Caddesi is the **Kervan Oteli,** Kazım Özalp Caddesi 138 (tel. 311/12-044), not quite so comfortable as the aforementioned place, but quite suitable, and priced at 16,500TL ($23.10) for a double with bath and breakfast.

A pleasant alternative to staying in one of Antalya's older-but-pricey hotels is to stay at a little pension in Old Antalya. Few of these places have rooms with private bath, but if this is no problem, head for the **Hadriyanüs Pansiyon,** Kılınçarslan Mahallesi, Zeytin Çıkmazı (tel. 311/12-313), an Old Antalya house with an enclosed garden. The friendly proprietors will give you a pleasant welcome and show you the refurbished guest rooms which rent for 7,500TL ($10.50) for a double room without running water. You'll like it here, as it's quiet, convenient, and decently priced.

The Big Splurge

The most luxurious hotel in town is the **Talya Oteli,** Fevzi Çakmak Caddesi (tel. 311/15-600), a modern, world-class 150-room place overlooking the Mediterranean, offering all the services you'd expect at a top-class place, and charging top-class prices of 77,000TL ($107.80) to 100,000TL ($140) double. The Talya is completely air-conditioned, and has a swimming pool, tennis court, restaurant, bar and nightclub, hairdresser, and exercise room.

A different sort of luxury awaits you at the **Turban Adalya Oteli,** in the old harbor area (tel. 311/18-066), a waterfront warehouse from Ottoman times which has been beautifully restored and converted into a small, service-oriented hotel of only 28 air-conditioned rooms, all with bath, telephone, and piped-in music. The location is more convenient than is the Talya's, though only a few rooms have views of the sea. At the Turban, a double room costs 51,500TL ($72.10) in the high summer season, breakfast included.

The Starvation Budget

The best place to look for a budget-priced room is along the narrow streets and alleys of Old Antalya where, in recent years, little pensions have sprung up.

Most of these little hostelries offer rooms without private bath, even without running water, but at prices to delight the slimmest of budgets.

For example, the **Tunay Aile Pansiyonu,** Selçuk Mahallesi, Mermerli Sokak 7 (tel. 311/24-677), has rooms as described, but the bonus of a rooftop terrace and the quiet Old Antalya location. A double room costs only 3,000TL ($4.20).

There are half a dozen other, similar pensions in Old Antalya. Wander into the quarter, follow the little signs, and you might end up at the **Harika Pansiyon,** Selçuk Mahallesi, Mermerli Sokak 11 (tel. 311/24-677), right next to the aforementioned Tunay Aile Pansiyonu. The Harika charges 5,000TL ($7) for a waterless double room. There are lots more.

For a clean and modern place just off the main plaza, search out the **Ülker Pansiyon,** Posta Sokak 6 (tel. 311/29-636), right across Cumhuriyet Caddesi from the statue of Atatürk and the Büyük Otel. The price per person in stark, waterless, but clean, bright rooms is 2,000TL ($2.80).

RESTAURANTS: Antalya has a good number of restaurants, most of which are sufficient, few of which are exceptional. As in many other towns, the district you eat in is as important as the restaurant you choose.

Antalya's most charming place to dine is down in the old harbor. Several restaurants here have outdoor dining areas for those balmy summer evenings, and feature seafood. One such place, with a name suggesting seafood specialties, is the **Ahtapot Restaurant** ("Octopus"). Despite its attractive location and its selection of marine delicacies, prices here are quite moderate. For a full meal of soup or appetizer, fried squid (kalamar) or fish, a salad or side dish, dessert and coffee, and a beverage, you can expect to pay 3,200TL ($4.50) to 5,000TL ($7).

In the center of town near the main plaza are several traditional restaurants worth a try. The **Parlak Restaurant** stands across Cumhuriyet Caddesi from the statue of Atatürk, and serves up the standard menu of Turkish fare in an attractive dining room with a view of the bay for prices ranging from 2,500TL ($3.50) to 4,500TL ($6.30) for a full meal.

For a slightly lower tab, and a dinner without the view, try the **Şehir Restaurant,** right behind the Parlak.

The place to go for the cheapest meals in town is the corner of Cumhuriyet/Ali Çetinkaya and Atatürk Caddesis. Walking to this intersection from the main plaza, look to your right just before you get to the intersection and you'll see a small market street named **Eski Sebzeciler İçi Sokak,** a Turkish mouthful that can satisfy your appetite, as this little street has become one long low-budget dining room. A half dozen little restaurants along both sides of the street dish up the traditional soups, stews, salads, and kebaps at bargain prices, and you can sit down to a full repast and pay only about 1,800TL ($2.50).

WHAT TO SEE AND DO: First you'll want to explore Antalya itself, then go out to the beach for a swim, and later venture farther afield into the mountains or along the coast to visit other ancient cities.

A Walking Tour

The place to start is at the symbol of Antalya, the **Grooved Minaret.** It was built around 1200 by the Seljuk Turkish sultan who ruled all of central Anatolia at the time, Alaeddin Keykubat I. The sultan had converted a church here to a mosque, and the mosque needed a minaret. As you will see when you visit Konya, the Seljuks were very stylish and creative architects and builders.

Walk east along Cumhuriyet Caddesi to Atatürk Caddesi. On the left-hand side of the street is the **bazaar,** which you should take some time to explore later at your leisure.

At Atatürk Caddesi, turn right. Several blocks along, on the right-hand side, is **Hadrian's Gate** (Hadriyanüs Kapısı), a monumental city gate to Old Antalya constructed in honor of the Roman Emperor Hadrian in A.D. 130.

Continue along Atatürk Caddesi all the way to **Kara Ali Park.** Spend some time enjoying the shade, the flowers, and the marvelous views of the Mediterranean, and then make your way to the northern end of the park, which overlooks the harbor and Old Antalya. The ancient stone tower here is called the **Hıdırlık Kulesi.** Archeologists disagree over its purpose. Some say it was a defensive point in the city walls. Others think it was a lighthouse to guide ships to Attaleia's harbor. Yet another says it's built in the form of a Roman senator's tomb, and must be a monument to some local worthy. In any case it dates from Roman times, and was probably built about the same time as Hadrian's Gate.

From the Hıdırlık Kulesi, descend into Old Antalya and you'll soon come to the **Broken Minaret** (Kesik Minare), which is just what its name says. As with the Grooved Minaret, this one was built next to a church, the 5th-century Church of the Panaghia. The church was converted to a mosque in the 1200s under the Seljuks and the minaret was erected at that time.

Enjoy yourself getting lost in the twisted streets of **Old Antalya.** From Roman times right through the end of the Ottoman Empire, for almost 2,000 years this *was* Antalya. The rest of this burgeoning city dates from the most recent half century.

The **old harbor area** has recently gotten a complete facelift, and is now a delightful place with pleasant restaurants and cafés, shops, and the very nice Turban Adalya Oteli. You might enjoy taking a break here, or instead climb to the top of the cliff behind the Büyük Otel (there are several stairways) and sit in one of the tea houses right at the edge of the cliff to sip something refreshing, and to take in the view. It's especially nice here at sunset.

Antalya Museum

Catch a bus or dolmush in the main plaza heading west along Cumhuriyet Caddesi to the **Antalya Müzesi,** about a mile and a half from the plaza. Even if you generally ignore museums, and have no interest in the ones in small Turkish towns, you should make the trip here because of the richness and variety of the collection. The museum is open from 9 a.m. to noon and 1:30 to 6 p.m.; closed Monday. Admission costs 500TL (70¢), half price on Sunday.

The collections are well displayed, and include everything from prehistoric fossils and Stone and Bronze Age artifacts to Ottoman costumes and kitchen implements. Among my favorite rooms is the **Gods Gallery,** with statues of 15 classical gods, from Aphrodite to Zeus. Other rooms hold exhibits of jewelry, vases, glass items and statuettes, and a small collection of Christian art, including icons, and a few of the bones of St. Nicholas from Myra (Demre). If you are at all interested in the history and culture of this region, don't miss this museum.

Beaches

The best of Antalya's beaches is the **Lara Plaj,** east of the city, reachable by minibus from the Doğu Garajı. Lara has its own collection of hotels, motels, and pensions, inhabited mostly by vacationers who come for a week or two. The beach itself is sand, but actually not as attractive as those at Side or other spots farther east along the coast.

The alternative is **Konyaaltı Plaj,** a sweeping arc of pebble beach to the west of town, between the city and its modern commercial port and industrial area. Konyaaltı is several miles long, but many of those miles are filled with fairly tacky beach installations, shacks, camps, and such. You might head out here one day for a dip, but save your serious beach time for Side and Alanya, farther east.

Archeological Sites

Having been prosperous and beautiful for a long time, the region around Antalya is rich in impressive classical ruins. If your time is short, you'd do well to take a tour to see these places, particularly Termessos, which is difficult to get to by bus and dolmush. If you have more time than money, however, you can in fact see all but Termessos on your own. There's some hiking involved, though.

All of Antalya's travel agents are able and willing to book you on a tour, and the cost is quite reasonable. A half-day tour to Termessos, with a stop at the Düden Waterfall picnic spot, costs only about 5,000TL ($7); a full-day tour to Perge, Aspendos, and Side costs 9,000TL ($12.60). Some people have complained that the tour bus doesn't stay at Termessos long enough to see everything, so you might ask how long you'll have at any one site. Also, find out if the bus stops at any shops. The practice of taking captive groups of tourists to shops which pay a kickback to the tour agency is often a waste of your time and money. If you pay for a tour of archeological sites, that's what you should get.

If you can get together four or five people, you can bargain with a taxi driver for a tour of several sites. That way you get to stay as long as you like at any one site.

The two most accessible sites are Perge and Aspendos.

Perge: No one is sure how old Perge is. We do know that Greek colonists came and staked a claim sometime after the Trojan War, but they may well have driven out earlier settlers. In any case, Perge flourished at the time of Alexander the Great, several centuries B.C., and continued to prosper through the Roman era and into the Byzantine. But before the coming of the Ottomans it was a dead city, as it still is.

Doing a tour on your own, catch a minibus eastward from the Doğu Garajı to the town of **Aksu,** eight miles (13 km) east of Antalya, and from there hike inland another mile and a half to the ruins. Perge is open from about 8 a.m. to 7 p.m., for 400TL (55¢).

First thing you'll notice here is the **Great Theater,** which is in quite good condition, but can't compare at all to the almost-complete theater at nearby Aspendos. Walking from the theater to the main part of the city, you pass a large **stadium** in an excellent state of repair, though it's now half-buried by the dust of centuries.

Into the city proper, walk along the main street toward the towering **gate** with two cylindrical bastions, which dates from Hellenistic and Roman times. The **colonnaded street** is reminiscent of Ephesus, and is almost as fine. The **acropolis,** on the hill behind (north of) the city, has little of interest in it, so you can save yourself a hot hike.

Aspendos: Two attractions draw visitors to the site of Aspendos, 29 miles (47 km) east of Antalya. The first is a Seljuk-era **humpback bridge** over the river on the way to the site. The other is the magnificent **theater,** said to be the best-preserved Roman theater anywhere.

If you're not on a tour, get a minibus from the Doğu Garajı to the Aspendos turnoff, then hike inland 2½ miles (4 km) to the theater. Hours for the site are 8 a.m. to 7 p.m. daily; admission costs 400TL (55¢), half price on Sunday.

What a theater! Turkey has hundreds of old Roman cities and each has at least one theater, but all are at least partially in ruins, and at none—except Aspendos—can one really get a full idea of what a classical theater was supposed to be. The acoustics in the ruined theaters are excellent, but in the one at Aspendos they are superb. The richness of the decoration, the harmony of the curves and porticoes, are all truly wonderful. It is perhaps appropriate that the theater of Aspendos was built during the reign of Emperor Marcus Aurelius (A.D. 161–180), that most enlightened of Roman rulers.

You must remember, though, that there was in fact a city here. Fragments of buildings—a stadium, an agora, a Byzantine basilica—stand in the neatly tilled fields in the river flood plain, and several arches from an aqueduct add effect, but little else is left of old Aspendos.

Termessos: Some 21 miles (33½ km) north of Antalya, in a high mountain valley, is the Pisidian city of Termessos. The city was built and inhabited in Roman times by a recluse people who didn't want much to do with the rest of the world. They achieved their desire, for their city was a virtual fortress, and not even Alexander the Great thought it worth his time to conquer them.

Today Termessos is situated in its own national park, off the highway north to Burdur. Entry to the park costs 250TL (35¢) for a car, 100TL (14¢) for each person, and this includes entry to the ruins and also to a little museum with photographs and artifacts from the ruins, plus displays touching on the botany and zoology of the park. Near the museum are camping and picnic spots.

You ascend the mountains to arrive at a parking place which was once the city's **agora,** or marketplace. The setting of Termessos, as you will see immediately, is truly magnificent.

Get your hiking shoes on, because a visit to the rest of the city involves climbing up to the high end of the valley, noting along the way the **Temple of Hadrian,** the **city gate,** the well-preserved **theater,** the **gymnasium,** a **Corinthian temple,** and the upper **city walls.** Finally, after about a mile of climbing, you will arrive at the spooky **necropolis,** or cemetery, a chaos of huge stone sarcophagi— overturned, broken, violated. Earthquakes and grave robbers have done the damage, but the scene looks for all the world like a preview of the Judgment Day.

HEADING EAST: Leaving Antalya is easy. Go to the Doğu Garajı and catch a minibus if you're only going as far as Side. Otherwise, head for the Otogar on Kazım Özalp Caddesi and find a bus for Alanya.

6. Side

The early Greeks who settled in Side (pronounced *See*-day) knew how to pick a location: they checked the winds, tides, currents, the productivity of the sea and the soil, and the site's aesthetic value. It's no coincidence that they settled in Side, and that the Romans and Byzantines followed them, and made a thriving community of the old city. I don't know how much people of that time went in for swimming, but if it was popular then, this must have been a big factor in selecting the site of the city. On either side of the promontory on which the city rests, white beaches stretch for miles. You can find places with fairly good surf (for this region) and places that are relatively calm; you can swim from the ruins of a Roman temple dedicated to Cleopatra (who is said to have dropped anchor here while on a trip to see Anthony) or from a wild region of sand and tufts of grass that looks as though it's been untouched by civilization.

The land around Side is fertile, planted with orange and banana groves mingled with pomegranate trees—supposedly the name "Side" means "pomegranate." One of the specialties of the region is the kind of bitter orange used for making marmalade. In among the ruins of the old city lies a small village of Turkish people who were moved from Crete during the exchange of populations. Until their coming, the last people to inhabit the region had been the Byzantines. These settlers cultivated the fields which lie around the village until tourists started wandering into the town a few years ago. Then they started to run pensions.

ORIENTATION: Side is about 47 miles (75 km) east of Antalya, a bus ride of about an hour and a half. The large town on the highway is **Manavgat;** the village of Side is about two miles south of the highway, on the shore.

The road from the highway goes past a number of pensions, and then, on the left, the **Tourism Information Office** (tel. 3213/1265). On the right is a turn for the motel district along the western beach. After that intersection, the road into the village pierces the ancient city's walls, passes the museum (on the right) and the grand theater (on the left), before ending at the parking lot behind the theater. Most vehicles must stop at this point. Buses have their ticket offices facing the parking lot.

The road continues through the village as its main street. Shops, restaurants, and pensions are on both sides, and on side streets. The **post office** is on a side street to the right (west). The main street ends at the shore.

ACCOMMODATIONS: The village of Side is positively jammed with little pensions, from the very simple to the moderately comfortable. Few have more than a dozen or so rooms, and most have fewer than a half dozen. Anytime a room is vacant, the little sign goes up on the side of the house: *"Boş oda var"* ("Vacant Room Available"). Prices for rooms range from about 4,000TL ($5.60) or 5,000TL ($7) for a double room without any plumbing, or with only a washbasin, to twice that amount for a nice room with private shower and pretensions to decor. It's difficult to guide you, as there are so many pensions, with so many different, unique rooms, and in high summer the rooming situation is guaranteed to be very tight. You'll probably end up staying in what's available, not in what you prefer.

All that being said, take a look at the **Köseoğlu Otel** (tel. 3213/0303), on the eastern side of the village, which, even though it calls itself a hotel, is actually just a fancier pension with bare modern rooms priced at 10,000TL ($14) double, with private bath and breakfast. At the cheaper end of the scale, ask in the little square on the western side of the village for the **Hermes Pansiyon.** There's no sign, but someone will direct you to the house, and the lady who runs it will show you a room looking out onto a little garden. One or two rooms have showers, but most share communal facilities. A kitchen in the garden with refrigerator and gas stove is available for your use for a small daily charge. Depending on the room and the season, you'll pay between 4,500TL ($6.30) and 6,500TL ($9.10) for a room here.

Facing south across the western beach are numerous motels, and at the far end of the built-up area, some larger hotel and low-rise condominium complexes. My first choice here would be the **Motel Side** (tel. 3213/1022). It's one of the closest places to the village, which means you can walk into the village and shop or people-watch pretty easily. It has a nice restaurant with a terrace for sitting, sipping, and gazing out to sea. Prices for the double rooms with bath are 22,000TL ($30.80), breakfast and dinner included.

The nearby **Subaşı Motel** (tel. 3213/1215 or 1047) is even closer to the village, yet still on the beach, with comfortable double rooms with bath going for

12,000TL ($16.80), breakfast included. Some of the rooms have views of the sea.

Among the more luxurious layouts, though not actually deluxe, is the **Motel Turtel** (tel. 3211/2225), which has regular motel-style rooms and also little bungalows for rent. With breakfast, a room at this very comfortable place costs 16,000TL ($22.40).

RESTAURANTS: During the high season restaurant meals in Side tend to be fairly expensive by Turkish standards, as this is an extremely popular place for the city folks from Istanbul and Ankara to "resort" to. Even so, by home standards everything is very reasonably priced.

To enjoy Side's seaside location, head for the **Afrodit Restaurant,** overlooking the water right at the seaside end of the main street. Vines and flowers shade the dining terrace, and soft incandescent lights set a romantic mood at night. Fish is the specialty here, and a seafood dinner might cost in the range of 6,000TL ($8.40).

The **İlgi Restaurant,** in the middle of the village right on the main street, is one story above street level, with a shaded but open dining area from which you can watch the flow of traffic below. Though they serve seafood, the specialty is kebaps, which they prepare in several original ways. The atmosphere here is more summer-beach-fun than moonlight-and-romance. The lighting is fluorescent, the waiters are overworked, but the food is quite good and the prices are reasonable: a three-course kebap repast comes in at about 3,800TL ($5.30) or less.

For some of the town's better food, at the best prices in town, search out the restaurant called **Enişte'nin Yeri** ("Uncle's Place"), near the beach end of the main street, on the right-hand (west) side. A few tables are set out on the porch in front of the bare glassed-in dining room, but the choice place to dine is at a table on the patio on the south side, lit by garish fluorescent tubes, but surrounded by greenery, with lots of space to breathe. Enişte's is one of those places where you choose a table, mark it with a hat or newspaper, then head for the kitchen to see what's cooking. Select several dishes or order a kebap or a grilled fish, decide on a beverage, then head back to your table. Service may be inexpert, but it's always friendly, the food's good, and the price for a three- or four-course repast may come to only 2,600TL ($3.65) to 3,500TL ($4.90).

The **Nergiz Tea Garden,** at the very end of the main street on the beach, gets a crowd of locals and out-of-towners sipping rakı or beer and batting the breeze every evening. But in the morning it also serves a good, inexpensive breakfast on a stainless-steel cafeteria tray for only 500TL (70¢). Having got your tray, it's great to sit here, sip tea, slowly break the fast, and watch the early part of the day unfurl.

BEACHES: If you are in Side, you are most likely there for the beaches, which need little explanation. The beach to the east is about a kilometer long, with no buildings on it and not that many people, just pure sand. There is one danger: a section of the old town wall which has fallen into the water about a third of the way along the beach. At low tide it's readily visible; at high tide, make sure you keep track of where it is.

OLD SIDE: The ruins are all around you. The most spectacular, the **theater,** is beautiful in its weathered state, but is being carefully restored. From the top row of seats there's a fine view of the village, the other ruins, and the sea. Entrance to the theater and the other ruins is supposedly 400TL (55¢), but there was no ticket seller in sight the whole time I was there. The modern **museum,** housed in a reconstruction of the old Roman baths, holds an assortment of things found in the area of the ruins. It's open from 8:30 a.m. to noon and 1:30 to 5:30 p.m. every day except Monday; entrance is 300TL (42¢). The **gymnasium,** near the theater, is the building next best preserved after the theater, and has interesting ceiling and column decorations. The **Temple of Apollo** and the **Temple of Athena,** its massive columns lying like benches for sea-watchers, are out on the tip of the peninsula, an especially good place to watch sunsets.

LEAVING SIDE: Dolmushes to Manavgat leave all through the day from the parking lot in Side, and drop you off at the tea house in Manavgat not far from the bus stop, on the route to Alanya. At least ten buses a day pass this point, as do some minibus-dolmushes. The fare to Alanya is 500TL (70¢); the 37-mile (60-km) trip takes a bit less than an hour.

7. Alanya

Alanya is an impressive sight. As in Side a peninsula juts into the water, wide beaches spread out from either side of it, and ancient ruins abound. But here the peninsula is a promontory, and the ruins, dominating the town and the bay, are those of a great Seljuk Turkish fortress.

Though Alanya has some commercial life outside of tourism, it is first and foremost a vacationers' town. But the vacationers are mostly Turkish. Alanya has yet to be discovered by hordes of foreigners.

GETTING THERE: Bus is the only way, unless you've got a car or a yacht. Most of the **bus** traffic, even from such places as Ankara and Istanbul, comes via Antalya. There are ten buses daily to and from Antalya (800TL, $1.10), and several which come into town from cities on the eastern coast. For details on travel to and from Silifke, Mersin, Adana, and Antakya, see the end of this section.

ORIENTATION: Alanya's **Otogar** (bus terminal) is two miles west of the middle of town, just north of the highway. Municipal buses travel from the Otogar through the town about every 30 minutes. The fare is 100TL (14¢). Or you can take a taxi into town for about 650TL (90¢).

With one exception the more expensive hotels and motels are all scattered along the eastern beach, some distance from downtown. Buses and dolmushes shuttle along the eastern beach, and travel between the town and the motels is not really inconvenient.

In town, huddled at the base of the promontory, are many of the cheaper hotels and restaurants. The **Tourism Information Office** (tel. 3231/1246), the museum, and the bus stop for buses going to the top of the hill are all at the northwestern foot of the promontory.

HOTELS: The hotel situation here is a bit of feast or famine: the better beach-front places exceed our budget and most of the downtown places are very basic.

Perhaps the best of the downtown places well within our budget is the **Hotel Kent,** İskele Caddesi 12 (tel. 3231/2754), which is well located on the street that leads to the famous Red Tower and the harbor along the eastern side of the promontory. The Kent is neat and newish with pretentions to style, clean rooms with bath and view of the town and the harbor, and a price of 7,000TL ($9.80) double.

Another good choice is the **Hotel Günaydın,** Kültür Caddesi 30 (tel. 3231/1943), which, because of its inland location a block or two from the waterfront, has no views. But it does have a quiet location, bare but tidy rooms with private showers, and low, low prices—4,000TL ($5.60) single, 6,000TL ($8.40) double.

The Starvation Budget

A longstanding favorite of the budget set is the **Yayla Palas Oteli,** İskele Caddesi 48 (tel. 3231/1017 or 3544), a converted house with a number of rooms, all different, all without private bath or even washbasin, priced at 4,000TL ($5.60) double. The location is good, right near town, and some of the rooms even have that expensive view of the harbor.

Two more low-budget choices in this area are the **Baba Hotel,** İskele Caddesi 8 (tel. 3231/1032), a simple, offbeat sort of place where doubles without bath cost 4,000TL ($5.60), 5,000TL ($7) with bath. Right next door is the **Alanya Palas Oteli,** İskele Caddesi 6 (tel. 3231/1016), which charges even less: a mere 2,250TL ($3.15) single, 3,000TL ($4.20) double, or 4,000TL ($5.60) for a double with shower.

The Big Splurge

The anomaly downtown—a fairly expensive, air-conditioned hotel—is the very comfortable, 45-room **Kaptan Otel,** İskele Caddesi 62 (tel. 3231/2000 or 1094), not far from the Red Tower. If you don't mind taking a dolmush to the beach, you can be right at the center of the town's activity for 22,500TL ($31.50) single, 29,700TL ($41.60) double, with bath.

It is generally agreed that Alanya's most comfortable rooms are at the longstanding beachfront favorite, the **Club Alantur** (tel. 3231/1224 or 1924), four miles east of the center. This 99-room resort motel has what is, for Alanya, a lavish spread of gardens, swimming pools, beach, restaurant, and other services. Air-conditioned double rooms go for 50,000TL ($70) in season.

RESTAURANTS: The street along the waterfront downtown is named **Gazi Paşa Caddesi.** The seaward side of the street is lined with little restaurants. You enter through a storefront and pass a tiny kitchen, then enter an enclosed dining room which has the requisite refrigerator cabinets and perhaps a steam table. Past the dining room is a terrace shaded by trellises and arbors of grapes, honeysuckle, and jasmine. Beyond the terrace is the waterfront and the sea. These little restaurants are Alanya's most pleasant places to dine, and none of them is very expensive.

As you walk along Gazi Paşa Caddesi, you will pass the **Şirin Lokantası,** the **Yönet** and **Havuzbaşı** restaurants, and also the **Mahperi.** All serve seafood, kebaps, and ready food, and at none will your check amount to much more than 3,200TL ($4.50) for lunch or dinner.

For a light meal or snack at truly bargain prices, wander through the little streets perpendicular to Gazi Paşa Caddesi, in the bazaar. Tea houses, pidecis (Turkish pizza joints) and kebapçıs will fill your needs and satisfy your appetite for little more than 1,600TL ($2.25).

BEACHES: If your hotel-motel doesn't have a beach, find your own section of beach anywhere along the shoreline. There are two public beaches with shower and changing facilities in Alanya, the first farther down Gazi Paşa Caddesi and, the second on the other side of the hill.

WHAT TO SEE: The **fortress** on top of the hill is good for as much time as you wish to spend, for the walls enclose a very big area with mosques, old and new houses, ruins, and heights from which there are splendid panoramas of the Mediterranean. At the highest point are some remains of a palace built by Alaeddin Keykubat, the great Seljuk Turkish emperor responsible for most of the fortifications on the hill. There are three systems of walls, in all about eight miles of them! Endless paths lead by ruined houses and churches from the Byzantine era, among cactuses and cicadas, through little throngs of curious, smiling girls offering you handmade silk scarfs for sale, down to the **Red Tower,** a mass of red stone and brick which helped to guard the harbor and the shipyards from pirate raids. The shipyards of the Seljuk emperor, the old **Tersane,** are a little farther out the promontory.

During the summer months the sun is hot even at 9 a.m., so I'd recommend getting up fairly early for your hike around the ruins. Then go to the Tourism Information Office at the northwestern foot of the promontory, and catch a city bus (100TL, 14¢) for the two-mile ride to the top. The buses run every half hour or so all day.

When you're done touring the top of the hill, return to the Tourism Information Office for a look at the nearby **Alanya Müzesi.** The museum has some Greek and Roman stuff, but much more from the times of the Seljuks and the Ottomans, including a good little ethnology exhibit of Ottoman costumes and woven home furnishings. The museum is open daily from 9 a.m. to noon and 1:30 to 6:30 p.m.; admission costs 200TL (28¢), half price on Sunday.

From the museum, walk out the western side of the promontory to **Damlatas Mağarası,** or Cave of Dripping Stones. You pay a small amount and enter, waiting for a half minute while the ticket taker gives you a spiel in Turkish about the age of the cave, the waters dripping through it, the rock formations and what and whom they resemble (much playing with light switches; flashing lights illuminate different parts of the cave), and about the medical properties of the air in the cave, which is supposed to relieve asthma if breathed for a while. The cave doesn't offer a lot to see, but the admission fee is not a lot to pay. Suit yourself.

MOTORBOAT TOURS: The entire coast of southern Turkey is riddled with caves. Most of the really big ones are off the main roads, accessible to those with private cars. You can get a taste of the better ones by taking a boat tour offered by the boatmen of Alanya. From Gazi Paşa Caddesi, walk down to the wharf near the Red Tower. A standard tour in a seven-passenger motorboat with pilot costs 600TL (85¢). The tour takes about a half hour and goes around the promontory, stopping at several caves: the **Pirates' Cave,** where early buccaneers were said to have kept a harem of their most comely captives; the **Lovers' Grotto,** a phosphorescent cave; and **Cleopatra's Beach**—this town, too, abounds with Cleopatra legends.

LEAVING ALANYA: The south coast from Alanya to Adana is similar to the area you've just covered, but with a higher concentration of castles and fortresses. None of the towns along the eastern coast is as interesting as Antalya, Side, or Alanya, however. If your time is short, you may want to end your Mediterranean explorations here and head north up to the central Anatolian plateau for a look at Ankara, Cappadocia, and Konya.

Heading east from Alanya, you should know that there are seven daily buses to Adana (2,500TL, $3.50) via Silifke and Mersin (2,300TL, $3.20).

Heading north, most buses backtrack to Antalya and ascend the plateau via Burdur or Isparta, as the road via Akseki is tortured by short curves and switchbacks for scores of miles. From Alanya proper there are five buses per day to Ankara (2,800TL, $3.90) via Konya (10 hours; 2,000TL, $2.80) or Nevşehir (12 hours; 4,000TL, $5.60), and also two to İzmir (11½ hours), and two to Istanbul (3,800TL, $5.30). One bus heads west for Marmaris via Kaş (6 hours; 2,000TL, $2.80, to Kaş). If you can't get a seat on any of these direct buses, get to Antalya and look for one there.

HEADING EAST: The road from Alanya eastward to Silifke, the next major town, twists along the mountainous shore, providing beautiful scenery, and slow going that gives you perhaps more than enough time to enjoy it. The distance is 167 miles (270 km). At **Anamur** is a massive castle erected in 1240, several small pensions, and lots of beachfront camping areas. Finally the highway descends from the mountains to arrive on level ground in the town of Silifke.

8. The Eastern Coast

Turkey's eastern Mediterranean shore has seen an awful lot of history. Alexander the Great swept through here over 2,000 years ago, and after his death the generals of his army struggled to gain control of his domains. The eastern coast fell to Seleucus I Nicator in the 290s B.C., and he founded an empire along this shore. The Seleucid rulers exerted a great deal of influence in the region until the coming of Rome.

Other empires and kingdoms came and went, but for such a tumultuous history, the eastern shore has surprisingly little to show for it. **Silifke** (its name is the Turkish form of Seleucia) has one great ruined temple, but is mostly a transportation point, not a tourist destination. From Silifke, buses climb into the mountains for Konya and Ankara. Ferryboats depart from Silifke's port suburb of Taşucu for northern Cyprus. And buses trundle along the coast through Silifke, linking Antalya with Mersin and Adana.

Mersin is a modern city less than half a century old. It was built as a port for the important industrial and commercial region of the Çukurova, the Cilician Plain. **Adana,** though it has a few ancient buildings downtown, is basically a new and modern commercial, industrial, and agricultural center populated by businessmen, workers, and farmers, not tourists. The ancient Roman city of Antioch, now called **Antakya,** has somewhat more to hold your interest, as its older section is pronouncedly Arabic or Syrian in flavor, and the Antakya Museum holds Turkey's most important and striking collection of Roman mosaics.

SİLİFKE: High above this dusty coastal town a fortress broods on its hilltop perch. Between the bus station on the highway and the town center half a mile inland are the ruins of a grand Roman building, the **Temple of Jupiter.** Silifke is also useful as a place to change buses, or to stay the night if you're exhausted. The people at the town's **Tourism Information Office,** Atatürk Caddesi 1/2 (tel. 7591/1151), on the northern side of the Göksu River right at the traffic circle, are helpful and friendly, and have lots of information on Silifke and its hinterland.

Hotels

None of Silifke's hotels is at all fancy, but you must take what there is. The **Hotel Akdeniz,** Mut Caddesi 66 (tel. 7591/1285), is clean and tidy but very basic, and charges only 2,500TL ($3.50) for a bathless double, 3,500TL ($4.90) for a double with private shower. It's in the commercial district at the opposite end of İnönü Caddesi from the bus station.

Very close to the Akdeniz is the **Hotel Eren** (tel. 7591/1289), which is a bit the worse for wear, but with more pretentions to comfort. The rates are 3,300TL ($4.60) single, 5,500TL ($7.70) double, both with shower.

Ferryboats to Cyprus

Passenger ferries depart from **Taşucu,** a suburb of Silifke, for Kyrenia (Girne) in Turkish Cyprus. Taşucu has its own little Tourism Information Office (tel. 7593/1234) right at the ferry dock. The Deniz Otobüsü ("Sea Bus," or hydrofoil) departs Taşucu on Monday, Wednesday, and Friday at 10 a.m. on the two-hour trip to Kyrenia. A one-way ticket costs $23, twice that amount for a round trip. Besides the hydrofoil there are regular steamers which carry cars as well as passengers, operated by the **Ertürk Company** (tel. 7593/1033 or 1325) on Tuesday, Thursday, and Saturday at 10 a.m. The trip on the car-ferry takes six hours. A one-way ticket costs $18; to go and return costs $29.

Onward from Silifke

Heading north, the bus to Konya takes 4½ hours and costs 2,000TL ($2.80); to Ankara, the bus trip takes eight hours and costs 3,000TL ($4.20).

The bus route eastward from Silifke to Mersin (53 miles, 85 km), Tarsus and Adana (95 miles, 153 km) has lots of traffic, so you should have no trouble finding a seat. The **Silifke Koop** company runs buses about every 15 minutes throughout the day. Times and prices from Silifke are like this: just over an hour to Mersin, two hours to Adana (1,000TL, $1.40).

The most exciting event on the coastal ride is your first sight of the **Kız Kalesi** ("Maiden's Castle"), a wondrous castle floating above the azure Mediterranean waters about a mile offshore. Another castle faces it from the shoreline. Both were supposedly built in Roman or Byzantine times.

If you have your own car, head inland opposite the village of **Narlıkuyu** for a look at the great limestone caverns named **Cennet ve Cehennem** ("Heaven and Hell").

MERSİN: Unless you need a bed, or are going to take your car on the big Turkish Maritime Lines ferryboat to Cyprus, you have little reason to stop in Mersin. If you do stop, however, head for the **Tourism Information Office,** İnönü Bulvarı Liman Giriş Sahası (tel. 741/11-265 or 12-710), down near the docks.

Hotels

For a nice, interesting hotel room in a quiet district not far from downtown, search out the **Otel Ege,** off İstiklal Caddesi at 33 Sokak no. 24 (tel. 741/21-419). The best policy might be to take a taxi here, as the hotel is tricky to find. Many Turkish craft items have been used in the decor, and a room with bath costs a moderate 11,000TL ($15.40) single, 14,000TL ($19.60) double.

The **Hosta Otel,** Fasih Kayabali Caddesi 4, Yeni Hal Civarı (tel. 741/14-760), is one of the city's older hotels, well kept up and fairly conveniently located across the street from the fresh produce markets, just a few blocks from downtown. A single room with shower is priced at 5,000TL ($7); a double goes for 7,000TL ($9.80).

To get the air conditioning that's so blissful in Mersin's sticky summer heat, you've got to stay at the best place in town, the 116-room **Mersin Oteli,** Gümrük Meydanı 112 (tel. 741/12-200). Located right at the very heart of the downtown district, the hotel hosts visiting sheiks and potentates in its very comfortable bath- and refrigerator-equipped rooms. It charges prince and proletarian alike 25,000TL ($35) single, 36,000TL ($50.40) double. If you stay here, have at least one meal in the hotel's rooftop restaurant.

Need to crash, cheap, right near Mersin's bus station? The place to find is the **Otel Murat,** Zeytinli Bahçe Caddesi 208 (tel. 741/24-681), a block and a half north (to the left) as you walk from the bus station. Though not at all fancy, it's the best there is close to the bus station, and they'll rent you a double room without private bath for 3,000TL ($4.20).

Car-Ferries to Cyprus

Turkish Maritime Lines operates the M/F *Yeşilada* car-ferry from Mersin to Famagusta (Magosa) all year, departing Mersin on Monday, Wednesday, and

Friday at 10 p.m. on the ten-hour cruise. Fares range from $26 for a Pullman "sleeper-seat" to $50 per person for a luxury cabin; middle-range cabins rent for $30 per person. The cost to take a car is $21.

Onward to Adana

The **T. O. K. bus company** operates a shuttle service between Mersin and Adana, with buses departing Mersin's bus station every 15 or 20 minutes throughout the day.

Just 17 miles east of Mersin along a fast highway lies the industrial town of **Tarsus,** where St. Paul was born almost 2,000 years ago. Virtually nothing is left of ancient Tarsus, certainly nothing to help you to feel that you are traveling "in the footsteps of St. Paul." The best you can do is look at the landscape and ponder how it might have been almost two millennia ago; but the industrial scenery doesn't help you out much.

ADANA: The Cilician Plain, or Çukurova, north of Adana, is a marvelously fertile agricultural region. Of all its crops, cotton is king, and the wealth from cotton cultivation has made Adana rich during the last few decades.

With the income from cotton, local entrepreneurs have begun industries and commercial concerns that contributed even more to Adana's explosive growth. Today it's Turkey's fourth-largest city, and still growing fast.

The speed of Adana's expansion hasn't left much time for planning or architectural niceties, so it's not a particularly attractive city. But it is a transportation hub, and it does have one or two places which you will want to visit.

Getting There

As one of Turkey's most important cities, located right near the pass through the Taurus Mountains known as the Cilician Gates, Adana is the crossroads of the southeast.

Turkish Airlines, Stadyum Caddesi 1 (tel. 711/37-247 or 43-143), runs two nonstop flights a day between Adana and Istanbul (1¼ hours), and also between Adana and Ankara (one hour). There is airport bus service from Adana's Şakirpaşa Airport into the center of town. The fare is 350TL (50¢).

Adana's Otogar has direct **buses** to and from most major cities, including Adıyaman and Kahta, near Nemrut Dağı (seven buses per day; six hours; 2,200TL, $3.10), Antalya (eight hours; 3,000TL, $4.20), Alanya (seven hours; 2,500TL, $3.50), Diyarbakır (nine hours; 3,000TL, $4.20), Konya (6½ hours; 2,500TL, $3.50), and Şanlıurfa (six hours; 2,000TL, $2.80).

Adana is also a major rail junction, with six **trains** a day westward along the coast to Mersin (300TL, 42¢), and express trains northward to Kayseri, Ankara, and Istanbul. A first-class train ticket to Adana costs 2,100TL ($2.95) from Ankara, 3,500TL ($4.90) from Istanbul, or 1,100TL ($1.55) from Kayseri, in Cappadocia.

Orientation

The **airport** is two miles west of downtown, just off the main highway. The highway itself roars right through the center of town and passes the **Otogar** before crossing the **Seyhan River,** which borders the eastern edge of the downtown area. Adana's **train station** is at the northern end of the broad boulevard named Ziya Paşa Bulvarı, a mile or so north of downtown. To get into town, take a bus from the airport, a taxi from the train station. From the Otogar, take a taxi or a bus, or walk for 20 minutes if your bags aren't too heavy.

When you get downtown, you will discover that the main street is **İnönü Caddesi.** It's not particularly wide or impressive, but it has most of the city's recommendable hotels, several restaurants, and its prettiest museum. The **Tourism Information Office,** Atatürk Caddesi 13 (tel. 711/11-323), is just half a block north of İnönü Caddesi along Atatürk Caddesi.

Hotels

Depending on when you visit, Adana might be the town in which you go all out and splurge on a hotel that's air-conditioned. The summer climate here is one of heat and sticky humidity which does not abate even by midnight. The air stays gooey all day and night. But first, here's a look at the moderately priced lodging possibilities.

Adana's two old standards are both on İnönü Caddesi, downtown. The **Otel Duygu,** İnönü Caddesi 14/1 (tel. 711/16-741), is a moderately comfortable older place with restaurant and bar, elevator, and double rooms equipped with fans (very necessary) and private showers, priced at 7,500TL ($10.50) single, 11,000TL ($15.40) double.

Not far from the aforementioned, and still on İnönü Caddesi, is the **Otel İpek Palas,** İnönü Caddesi 103 (tel. 711/18-743), which has similar-quality rooms at prices that are only a bit higher.

The Big Splurge: Among Adana's newest upscale hotels is the snazzy **Zaimoğlu Oteli,** Özler Caddesi 72 (tel. 711/13-366), just around the corner from the western end of İnönü Caddesi, more or less behind the Adana Sürmeli Oteli (see below). Service is attentive, the lobby gleams with lots of polished stone, and the rooms are moderate in size, with nice tiled bathrooms, little drink refrigerators, and air conditioning. Rates are 16,500TL ($23.10) single, 22,000TL ($30.80) double, 30,250TL ($42.35) for a suite, 41,250TL ($57.75) for an apartment.

The Sürmeli hotel firm owns and operates Adana's two top hotels, the **Adana Sürmeli Oteli,** İnönü Caddesi 142 (tel. 711/22-701), and the **Büyük Sürmeli Oteli,** right behind it on Özler Caddesi (tel. 711/21-944). Both of these hotels are fully air-conditioned, and both have elevators, restaurants, bars, nightclubs, and helpful staff. To stay at the Adana Sürmeli costs 50,000TL ($70) double; the price at the Büyük Sürmeli is just slightly less.

The Starvation Budget: For a very inexpensive room right on İnönü Caddesi, search out the little **Mehtap Oteli,** 123 Sokak no. 6 (tel. 711/21-954), just off İnönü Caddesi opposite the big Adana Sürmeli Oteli. Though this plain little place is right in the center of town, it's fairly quiet and undisputably cheap: double rooms without bath go for only 1,000TL ($1.40) single, 1,800TL ($2.50) double.

Restaurants

If I were a hungry traveler in Adana looking for lunch or dinner (as I have been), I would immediately head for the **Yeni Onbaşılar Restorant,** on Atatürk Caddesi (tel. 14-178), between the main highway and İnönü Caddesi, opposite the Tourism Information Office. The restaurant is up one flight, and has a rooftop terrace dining area up a second flight. This is the place to go, for it's cooler and pleasant on one of Adana's sticky hot nights. The restaurant specializes in grilled kebaps, chief among which is the spicy but not fiery-hot Adana kebap, rissoles made of ground lamb and charcoal-grilled on flat skewers. It's served with the traditional accompaniments of paper-thin village bread, thicker flat pide bread fresh from the restaurant's own bakery, sliced red onions, and chopped parsley. With a salad and a cold bottle of beer or a soft drink, such an authentic Adana meal costs less than 2,000TL ($2.50), all included.

Museums

While you're here, be sure to see the **Adana Ethnography Museum,** or Adana Etnoğrafya Müzesi (tel. 22-417), on a little side street just to the left of the Adana Sürmeli Oteli. Though the exhibits of Turkish carpets, swords, manuscript books, and tombstones are interesting, the building is even more so. It was built by the Crusaders as a church, and is in that attractive, plain but harmonious Burgundian style of early medieval France. The church was used until the present century, when it became a museum. The museum is open from 9 a.m. to noon and 1:30 to 5:30 p.m., closed Monday; admission costs 200TL (28¢), half price on Sunday.

The **Adana Regional Museum,** or Adana Bölge Müzesi (tel. 43-856), is more the standard archeological museum found in most Turkish towns. The modern glass-and-concrete museum building holds lots of statuary and a few mosaics, as well as the other standard produce of local archeological digs. It's very near the Otogar, right on the riverbank. You can visit any day but Monday from 8:30 a.m. to 12:30 p.m. and 1:30 to 5:30 p.m., for 400TL (55¢).

Adana's other noteworthy sight is the Roman stone bridge across the river, called the **Taşköprü.** It's still in use, and, begrimed by the traffic, is not all that impressive, though it might be if it were a well-preserved footbridge in a nice park. Looking at it, you must remember that building a stone bridge 300 yards long was quite a feat in Roman times.

EASTWARD INTO HATAY:

After the War of Independence, the Turkish republic was founded and its borders established. The government under Atatürk immediately declared that it had no interest in reclaiming or reconquering any of the formerly Ottoman lands. But as World War II approached (and Atatürk saw it coming), it became clear that to protect its southeastern border Turkey needed to hold the port of Alexandretta (İskenderun), the city of Antakya, and its hinterland, then under a French protectorate. A plebiscite was held and the population, though predominantly Arabic by race and speech, voted to become Turks. Turkey preserved a precarious neutrality during the war and Hatay never had to play its strategic role, but it is still happily part of the Turkish republic.

Hatay is different, still very much an Arabic town in its old section, and intrepid travelers wishing to see the museum's fabulous Roman mosaics, and willing to brave the city's oppressive summer heat, will get to know a unique city, and also take in some impressive castles on the way.

Just south of the highway, 22 miles (35 km) east of Adana is the **Yılan Kalesi,** or "Snake Castle," dramatically sited atop a hill in the midst of a pancake-flat plain. The castle dates from the 1200s and, though not restored, is worth a visit if you have your own car. Then, 23 miles (37 km) farther east the highway divides at a "Y" right around the **Toprakkale,** or "Soil [or Earth] Castle," which is as large and as impressive, though not nearly so well preserved, as the Yılan Kalesi. Take the right fork for Antakya.

Along the way, the road skirts the port city of **İskenderun,** founded by Alexander the Great and later called Alexandretta in his honor. From İskenderun the road climbs into the mountains which, Atatürk knew, could help block the progress of invading troops and protect the port. Descending the other side of the range, you see a vast, hot, but fertile plain cultivated in a patchwork of tawny fields. Sitting in the midst of the plain is Antakya, the ancient city of Antioch.

ANTAKYA:

Having been here since its founding in 300 B.C. by Seleucus Nicator, Antakya has lived through a lot of history. The city on the eastern bank of the Asi River looks old, and combines Ottoman, Arabic, French Protectorate, and modern styles among its buildings. On the western bank is the new, modern, tidy Turkish republican city.

Getting There

Lots of buses depart Adana's Otogar on the 2½-hour journey around the bay and over the mountains to Antakya. A one-way ticket is priced at 1,100TL ($1.55).

Orientation

The **post office** and **museum** are in the modern part of town, not far from the major bridge over the river. The **bus station** is in the old town on the east bank. Most hotels and restaurants are also in the old city, though a new and fairly luxurious hotel has opened in the modern part of town, only steps from the museum.

There is no national Tourism Information Office here, but the provincial **Tourism Office** (tel. 891/12-636) does a fine job of providing visitors with maps, information, and assistance. It's located on a traffic circle over a mile north of the traffic circle on which you'll see the museum and the post office, in the modern part of the city.

Hotels

Antakya's climate in summer is hot, hot, hot. You might want to pay for an air-conditioned room. If so, you'll find it at the brand-new **Antakya Oteli,** near the museum in the modern part of town. Construction on the hotel was still under way when I last visited so I can't give you any details, but when it opens, this will be the best place in town.

Otherwise there are the older hotels in the old part of town, such as the 28-room **Atahan Oteli,** Hürriyet Caddesi 28 (tel. 891-11/036 or 11-407), the first choice before the newer Antakya Oteli came on the scene. At the Atahan a room with bath and fan costs 8,000TL ($11.20) single, 12,000TL ($16.80) double. You'll find one of the best restaurants in town here.

The next choice would be the **Divan Hoteli,** İstiklal Caddesi 62 (tel. 891/11-518 or 11-735), fairly near the bus station in the northern reaches of the old city. The Divan is well used, but its 23 rooms with shower rent for only 6,000TL ($8.40) single, 7,500TL ($10.50) double, 9,300TL ($13) triple.

If your hotel has a restaurant, your best plan would be to dine there, as the rest of the town's eateries tend to be extremely cheap and basic.

What to See

The **Antakya Museum** is what you've come to see. It's open from 8:30 a.m. to noon and 1:30 to 5:30 p.m., except on Monday. Admission costs 500TL (70¢). Inside are the absolutely wonderful mosaics, including an outstanding one of Oceanus and Thetis, another of Orpheus, yet another of Iphigenia in Aulis, one of Dionysius in his usual inebriated state, and countless spirits, cherubs, chimerae, gods, and goddesses. The modern museum displays them well.

After visiting the museum, bargain with a taxi driver for the trip out to the **Church of St. Peter** (Senpiyer Kilisesi, or just Senpiyer). The price should be about 1,500TL ($2.10) for the round trip. This little cave in the rock was the worshipping place for an early Christian congregation. The Crusaders, very concerned over holy places, built the façade and consecrated it as a church. If you happen to visit on the first Sunday of the month, you can attend mass at 3 p.m.

After seeing the museum and Senpiyer, wander through old Antakya's market streets to feel the peculiarly Syrian-Arabic spirit of the place. Most Antakyans speak Turkish as a second language, learned in school, and Arabic as a first language, learned at home. The scents in the bazaar are also more Levantine, with lots of mint and coriander.

To escape the city's heat, hop in a dolmush minibus bound for **Harbiye,** called Daphne in ancient times. It was to Daphne, five miles from Antakya, that the citizens of Antioch would go to get a breath of fresh, cool air. There was an oracle here, and pilgrims would come to get answers to their questions about the future. They paid the priests handsomely for what was probably questionable advice, and the money often went into building sumptuous villas. Many of these had mosaic floors, and many of those wonderful mosaics are now in the Antakya Museum.

There's a good beach at **Mağaracık,** not far from the town of Samandağ, about 18 miles south of Antakya.

Onward from Antakya

You may want to backtrack to Adana in order to continue your Turkish adventure northward to Ankara or Cappadocia. For those interested in taking an eastern tour, buses leave Antakya's bus station for Gaziantep (four hours; 1,000TL, $1.40), a modern city with a few good hotels for the night, and **Şanlıurfa** (seven hours; 2,500TL, $3.50), the ancient city of Edessa, with many things to see and do.

Chapter XIII

ANKARA

1. Getting There and Getting Around
2. Ankara's Hotels
3. Ankara's Restaurants
4. Ankara's Sights
5. The Hittite Cities

UNTIL THE WAR FOR INDEPENDENCE in the early '20s, Ankara was a sleepy Anatolian town noted for its curious goats and cats, whose hair was exceedingly long and fine. Mohair is still a thriving trade here, but the city's specialty now is government. After the war, Atatürk had a complete plan made for his new capital city, and laid out wide boulevards, large parks, an artificial lake, and complexes of government buildings. Today Ankara is a city of about 3½ million people, and growing fast.

Ankara is a city of government clerks, embassies, legations, and businesses. There's little to draw you to the city unless you have some official business. But if you're passing through, you can spend a day or two pleasantly enough.

1. Getting There and Getting Around
All roads in Turkey lead to Ankara, and there's not a town of a decent size which does not have at least several buses a day to the capital. Ankara is also the transfer point for virtually all domestic flights, so there's never a problem getting there.

BY PLANE: Though most international flights land in Istanbul, Ankara has lots of domestic service, with flights arriving from Adana, Antalya, Dalaman, Diyarbakır, Erzurum, Istanbul (six or more flights daily; 30,000TL, $42), İzmir, Malatya, Samsun, Trabzon, and Van. Most of these flights take place every day, or at least five times per week, and cost between 30,000TL ($42) and 32,000TL ($44.80).

Ankara's **Esenboğa Airport** is 19 miles (30 km) north of the city. The USAŞ company operates **airport buses** which meet each flight. Don't dally around the airport after you land, though. The bus into town will leave shortly after landing, and there may not be another one for several hours. The alternative, a **taxi**, can cost as much as 5,000TL ($7), whereas the bus costs a mere 550TL (75¢). Another hint: USAŞ buses supposedly depart from the Air Terminal in Ankara bound for Esenboğa Airport 1½ hours before domestic flight times, 2¼ hours before international flight times, but in fact they may fill up and leave *early*, so get on the bus well before these times! Minimum check-in time for any flight is 45 minutes.

The **Turkish Airlines Air Terminal** (tel. 41/12-62-00 for reservations, 12-49-10 for information), next to the train station, is open every day from 7 a.m. to 8 p.m.; on Sunday the ticket counters are only open from 8:30 a.m. to 5:15 p.m.

BY TRAIN: Let me recommend my favorite way of getting from Istanbul to Ankara (or vice-versa). The **Ankara Ekspresi,** an all-sleeping-car train, has first- and second-class berths and a dining car (for breakfast only). It departs at 9:40 p.m. from both cities, and arrives the next morning at 8:30 a.m. It's the pride and joy of the Turkish State Railways. A similar train, the **Anadolu Ekspresi,** is a night train with first- and second-class coaches, sleeping cars, and a dining car, which leaves at 9 p.m. from both Istanbul and Ankara, and arrives the next morning about 8 a.m. Considering that you'd have to pay for a hotel room otherwise, the full fare for a first-class sleeping compartment isn't bad at all: including train ticket, sleeping-car charge, and sleeping car porter's 10% service charge and 5% tip, the total would come to about 16,100TL ($22.55) per person in a two-person compartment.

If a sleeping car is just too expensive, consider taking the comfortable and speedy **Blue Train** *(Mavi Tren),* an all-reserved super-first-class train with club cars and a dining car. Two Blue Trains depart each city daily, around lunchtime and late in the evening, making the run in about 7½ hours.

The regular first-class train is the **Bosphorus Express** *(Boğaziçi Ekspresi),* with club cars and a dining car, leaving at breakfast time (8 a.m.) and arriving at dinnertime, making the trip in about nine hours.

From İzmir there's a fast **Blue Train** at night (seats only, no sleeping cars); a slightly less-fast first-class express during the day called the **Aegean Express** *(Ege Ekspresi),* and a slow but comfortable sleeper train which leaves in late afternoon and arrives early the next morning, the **İzmir Express.**

BY BUS: Not only is it easy to get to Ankara by bus, as virtually every city and town has direct buses, it's also cheap. Fares vary from around 2,000TL ($2.80) for the nine-hour trip from Istanbul to 5,000TL ($7) for the 14-hour trip from Trabzon. I know of no fare higher than 7,000TL ($9.80) or 8,000TL ($11.20), which means that you can get to Ankara from virtually anywhere in Turkey for less than $12, and probably more like $3 or $4.

When it comes time to leave, just wander down to Ankara's Otogar and buy a ticket on the next bus out. Plan ahead if you can, and get your tickets in advance if it's convenient. But to major destinations, seats should be in good supply anytime.

ARRIVAL: All of Ankara's travel termini are grouped conveniently near the Ministry of Transportation. The Otogar is a block northwest of the Gar (train station), and the THY Air Terminal is right beside the train station. All of these termini are only a mile from Ulus, two miles from Kızılay.

GETTING AROUND: Though Ankara is a big city, and spread out, transportation is fast and cheap. The national government makes sure the capital city runs efficiently. Several years ago the city government decided to lighten the traffic load on Ankara's streets by doing away with dolmushes, so you won't find any of these downtown. However, it's easy to get around on Ankara's inexpensive and extensive bus system.

By Bus

The fare for a ride on a municipal bus is 100TL (14¢); buy your tickets *before* you get on the bus, at one of the little kiosks located at major bus stops.

Also, you should know that some buses are privately owned. For these, you can purchase a ticket right on the bus, for slightly less than the cost of a city bus ride.

Some of the most useful routes are these: bus 8 ("Çankaya") runs the entire length of Atatürk Bulvarı, from Ulus all the way up to the Presidential Palace at Çankaya; buses 16 ("Bahçelievler") and 64 ("Emek") will take you from the train station, air terminal, or Otogar up the hill to Ulus, and bus 44 ("Terminal") will take you from those places to Kızılay. To get from Ulus or Kızılay to the Anıt Kabir, Atatürk's mausoleum, catch bus 63 ("Anıttepe").

By Taxi

As in other large cities, all Ankara taxis have meters, and they run them. The meter starts at 260TL (35¢) and a normal ride from, say, the bus, train, or air terminals to Ulus or Kızılay would come to 700TL ($1) to 1,000TL ($1.40).

ORIENTING YOURSELF: The city is divided into two general regions: the **old city** spreading down from the **Citadel,** with **Ulus Square** as its center; and **Yenişehir,** literally "new city," with its center about a mile from Ulus in **Hürriyet Square.** Hürriyet Square is the official name for the square right next to the large Gima department store and Ankara's tallest building, but nobody uses the official name. If you want to get there, ask for **Kızılay.** Connecting Ulus and Kızılay is **Atatürk Bulvarı,** the city's main thoroughfare and reference point for all your wanderings in the city.

The local **Tourism Information Office** is in the headquarters of the **Ministry of Tourism,** Gazi Mustafa Kemal Bulvarı no. 33 (beginning in Kızılay), in the section called **Demirtepe.** You can walk there in about ten minutes from Kızılay. Head west out of the square, and make sure that you're on the left (southern) side of the street, because soon there will be a barrier down the middle of the street, and you won't be able to cross; you'll have to walk about half a mile out of your way just to get across the street! The lettering over the door of the Ministry reads "Kültür ve Turizm Bakanlığı" (tel. 41/29-29-30, ext. 95). The actual Tourism Information Office is around to the right side, on Özveren Sokak. There are also small Tourism Information desks at the airport, and at the Otogar.

Ulus

Ulus Square is a vivid demonstration of lesser economics. Every conceivable product and service is offered here; nothing that will provide an honest (or sometimes otherwise) living is left out. On the sidewalk, with a big new department store as a backdrop, a man washes his hands while speaking into a microphone, plugging the brand of soap he is demonstrating. The shoeshine boys are everywhere and have boxes every inch as elaborate as those in Istanbul, some even including such gadgets as electric bells (to attract the attention of would-be customers), portable radios (for music to work by), and tiny lamps directed at the work area (for working at night). Elsewhere, an old man in a gay knit cap is manning an ancient doctor's scale, by means of which he'll determine your weight in kilograms for a charge of 100TL (14¢). Men dressed in white circulate through the crowd pushing carts filled with flaky, pastry-like börek. A battered old station wagon has been parked on the sidewalk, its tailgate let down to display an assortment of men's shirts which the driver-proprietor is offering for sale at bargain rates. In the midst of the loudspeaker spiels by countless hawkers, one old man sits quietly and contentedly on a stool with a box of metal shoe cleats and a ganglion of laces before him. You don't even have to remove your shoes in order to have him tap a cleat on with his little hammer. Behind all this bustle and diversity, a window of the department store is filled with row upon row of jars filled with golden honey which light up when the sun catches them.

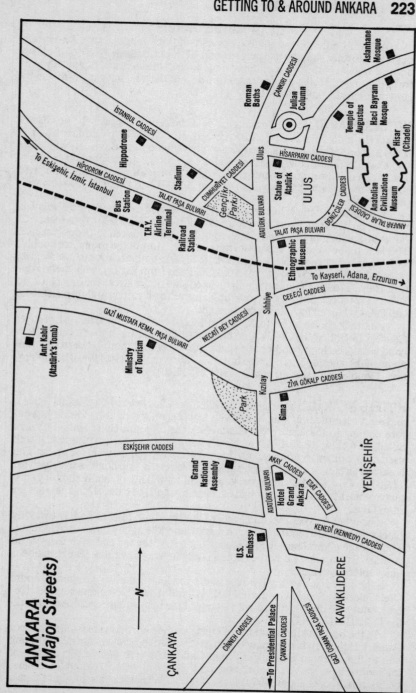

**ANKARA
(Major Streets)**

N

ÇANKAYA

YENİŞEHİR

KAVAKLIDERE

ULUS

İSTANBUL CADDESİ

Hippodrome

HİPODROM CADDESİ

To Eskişehir, İzmir, İstanbul

TALAT PAŞA BULVARI

Stadium

Bus Station

T.H.Y. Airline Terminal

Railroad Station

CUMHURİYET CADDESİ

Gençlik Parkı

AtATÜRK BULVARI

Ulus

HİSARPARKI CADDESİ

Statue of Atatürk

DENİZCİLER CADDESİ

ANFARTALAR CADDESİ

Roman Baths

ÇANKIRI CADDESİ

Julian Column

Temple of Augustus

Hacı Bayram Mosque

Aslanhane Mosque

Hisar (Citadel)

Anatolian Civilizations Museum

TALAT PAŞA BULVARI

Ethnographic Museum

To Kayseri, Adana, Erzurum →

Şıhhiye

CEEECİ CADDESİ

GAZİ MUSTAFA KEMAL PAŞA BULVARI

NECATİ BEY CADDESİ

Ant Kabir (Atatürk's Tomb)

Ministry of Tourism

Kızılay

Park

ZİYA GÖKALP CADDESİ

Gima

ESKİŞEHİR CADDESİ

Grand National Assembly

AKAY CADDESİ

ATATÜRK BULVARI

Hotel Grand Ankara

ESAT CADDESİ

KENEDİ (KENNEDY) CADDESİ

U.S. Embassy

CİNNEH CADDESİ

To Presidential Palace

ÇANKAYA CADDESİ

GAZİ OSMAN PAŞA CADDESİ

2. Ankara's Hotels

Ankara's hotels come in all types and all price ranges, but the weight is definitely toward the more expensive end of the price scale. No doubt this is because the life of the city is oriented more toward business and diplomacy than toward tourism. Hotels are scattered throughout the city, but we'll list them by general area, starting with—

HOTELS NEAR KIZILAY: Perhaps the best choice in the area is the new **Hotel Sultan,** Bayındır Sokak 35 (tel. 41/31-59-80), off Ziya Gökalp Caddesi. The hotel's location several blocks from Kızılay, but on a quiet side street, will allow you to sleep. The public spaces as well as the rooms are bright and modern. There's an elevator, and an enclosed parking garage for guests' cars. The price stretches the top limit of our budget a bit, at 20,800TL ($29.10) for a double with private bath.

On the same street, but several blocks away and even nearer to Kızılay, is the 41-room **Otel Gül Palas,** Bayındır Sokak 15 (tel. 41/33-31-20), on a section of Bayındır Sokak that has been closed to traffic and dedicated to pedestrian use. This is an older building, kept quite presentable. Most of the rooms are doubles with private bath, and cost 13,500TL ($18.90); bathless rooms are singles, priced at 10,700TL ($15). To get to the Gül Palas from Kızılay, walk down Atatürk Bulvarı toward Ulus on the right-hand side of the street for one block, to Sakarya Caddesi. Turn right, walk up Sakarya to Bayındır, and turn left. The Gül Palas is half a block down on the right.

Another choice close to Kızılay is the 64-room **Ersan Oteli,** Meşrutiyet Caddesi 13 (tel. 41/18-98-75), one block east off Atatürk Bulvarı, on the left-hand side. The lobby and public spaces are nicer and more modern than are many of the guest rooms, but the hotel's location makes it worthy of consideration. Doubles with shower cost 18,150TL ($25.40).

HOTELS NEAR ULUS: Walk up the hill from Ulus toward the Citadel (Kale), and after several fairly long blocks you will see, on the right-hand side just before coming to the foot of the citadel hill, the 53-room **Hotel Hitit,** Firuzağa Sokak 12 (tel. 43/10-86-17). The Hitit's fairly large rooms are pleasant, if well used, and look out onto the small side street away from the noise of traffic. The hotel has an elevator, an English-speaking desk clerk, and doubles with bath for 11,000TL ($15.40). Staying here, you're within walking (actually climbing) distance of the Museum of Anatolian Civilizations and the Citadel, and also not far from Ulus.

For other inexpensive hotels near Ulus, go south toward Kızılay two long blocks and turn left into a big open area where lots of city buses are gathered. This is İtfaiye Meydanı, or Firehouse Square. At the far end of it, away from Atatürk Bulvarı, are numerous hotels charging very low rates. The situation is quiet and convenient.

The first place you will notice is the modern if undistinguished 50-room **Otel Güleryüz,** Sanayi Caddesi 37 (tel. 41/10-49-10), which offers comfortable, bath-equipped double rooms with a view of the busy square and Gençlik Parkı for 12,100TL ($16.95).

In the opposite direction out of Ulus, heading north on the continuation of Atatürk Bulvarı, which is named Çankırı Caddesi, a block and a half will bring you to the 35-room **Otel Taç,** Çankırı Caddesi 35 (tel. 41/24-31-95). Most of its rooms have private baths and cost 8,500TL ($11.90) double; others, without bath, cost about 1,000TL ($1.40) less. Whatever you do, don't take a room on the front (street) side, as the traffic noise will be sure to keep you awake.

For emergencies only, you should know that there is a hotel right in the Otogar building. The **Terminal Oteli**, Hipodrom Caddesi 3 (tel. 41/10-49-49), is not that old, but looks much older, due to the hard use it has received. But if for some reason you simply can't get in a cab and find another place, you can stay here for 7,700TL ($10.80) in a double room without bath, 9,900TL ($13.85) with.

THE BIG SPLURGE: Were I to decide to stay in comfort in Ankara, I'd head immediately for the **Ankara Dedeman Oteli,** Büklüm Sokak 1 (tel. 41/13-96-90), a block up the hill on Akay Sokak from Atatürk Bulvarı, in the section of town called Bakanlıklar. The Dedeman is a well-established first-class hotel with 252 air-conditioned rooms. The gleaming marble in the lobby lends class to the place, but the services lend even more: a private parking garage, music piped into the rooms, a swimming pool, and a very fine view from the rooftop restaurant. In this lap of luxury, singles cost 36,000TL ($50.40), doubles cost 46,000TL ($64.40).

Quite convenient and comfortable, though not particularly smacking of luxury, is the tidy **Etap Mola Oteli,** Atatürk Bulvarı 80 (tel. 41/33-90-65), the local representative of the French hotel chain which also runs the Etap Marmara and Etap Istanbul in Istanbul, and another Etap hotel in İzmir. Rooms here are air-conditioned, not huge but big enough, with a decor of soft, soothing tones and sparkling-clean tile baths. The price to stay here is 32,000TL ($44.80) single, 40,000TL ($56) double.

For the time being, Ankara's poshest hotel is the **Büyük Ankara Oteli,** Atatürk Bulvarı 183 (tel. 41/34-49-20), more or less across the street from the Grand National Assembly, Turkey's parliament. The Grand Ankara Hotel is an asymmetrical high-rise tower with 208 air-conditioned guest rooms, a swimming pool, a tennis court, various restaurants and bars, and a status address. For all this, the price is fairly reasonable: 42,000TL ($58.80) single, 71,000TL ($99.40) double.

Soon the Grand Ankara will have some competition for the carriage trade, as Hilton International is building a large luxury hotel in this city.

THE STARVATION BUDGET: The place to look for a truly cheap room is İtfaiye Meydanı, mentioned above. Besides the several hotels already described, there are lots of much cheaper places on Sanayi Caddesi, Kosova Caddesi, Tavus Sokak, and near the large post office building on Atatürk Bulvarı.

For instance, the modern **Otel Akman,** Tavus Sokak 6 (tel. 41/24-41-40), is popular with European tourists because its rooms are bright and clean; it has an elevator, a parking lot, and a television lounge; and rates are a low 7,700TL ($10.80) for a double with bath.

Very nearby is the older but still quite serviceable **Otel Devran,** Tavus Sokak 8 (tel. 41/11-04-85). This was no doubt in the city's better class of hotels a half century ago, and so it was built with marble staircases, brass ornamentation and accents, and little chandeliers. Though it has obviously hosted lots of guests since it was new, it remains a suitable and presentable place to stay, with neat double rooms going for 5,600TL ($7.85) with shower, 6,600TL ($9.25) with bathtub.

Near the post office is the **Hotel Zümrüt Palas,** Posta Caddesi 16 (tel. 41/24-51-65), another older but well-kept place, this one a favorite with Turkish families visiting the capital. A double with only a washbasin costs 5,000TL ($7); for a double with private shower, the charge is 6,500TL ($9.10).

3. Ankara's Restaurants

Government employees in Turkey get paid low salaries but must maintain a fairly high standard of living because of the status of their positions. When they have lunch or dinner in restaurants, they expect the food and service to be good, and the prices low. Because of this situation, and because Turkey in general has low dining-room prices, some of the best restaurants at reasonable prices to be found in the country are in Ankara.

RESTAURANTS NEAR KIZILAY: As we've seen, several of Ankara's better medium-priced hotels are on Bayındır Sokak, the street parallel to Atatürk Bulvarı but several blocks east of it. The same goes for medium-priced restaurants.

First place to consider is the **Körfez Lokantası,** Bayındır Sokak 24 (tel. 31-14-59), half a block north of Ziya Gökalp Caddesi. The several plain indoor dining rooms are virtually deserted in the warm summer weather, as all the patrons obviously prefer to sit at the outdoor terrace tables, some of which are shaded, others open-air. The restaurant's name means "Gulf Restaurant," so seafood is well represented when it's in season. At any time, though, the kebaps are excellent. A meal based on a kebap plate might cost 2,200TL ($3.10); one based on fish, 4,000TL ($5.60). The Körfez is simple, unpretentious, inexpensive, and very good.

One of Ankara's most famous and longstanding restaurants (it's been here for over two decades) is the **Piknik,** Tuna Sokak 1 (tel. 33-06-63). Walk toward Ulus out of Kızılay, and the Piknik is two blocks down on the right, near Atatürk Bulvarı 73. The restaurant has a few tables squeezed into a tiny strip of outdoor dining area and a menu which can boast numerous items not normally found in Turkish cuisine, such as chicken salad and smoked tongue. As long as you don't order something too exotic (watch out for such things as caviar!), you can have a very filling meal, with wine or beer, for only about 2,100TL ($2.95).

If you come out the front door of the Piknik, you'll be walking along Selanik Caddesi, a pedestrian street which has a few little eateries to note. The **Cihan Kebap Lokantası,** Selanik Caddesi 3 (tel. 33-16-65), is just the sort of place Ankara's restaurateurs do best. Small but tidy, with pretentions to decor and even snazz, an inside dining room and a shaded terrace, the Cihan serves a limited menu of soups, salads, kebaps, desserts, and soft drinks. Service is friendly and fairly good, and the prices are just unbelievable: a bowl of soup, a plate of kebap, and a soft drink need cost only 1,600TL ($2.25).

For a much more lavish spread, follow Bayındır Sokak to its northern end, where it meets Süleyman Sırrı Sokak near Sıhhiye Meydanı. There you'll find a building set into a slope, overlooking an open plaza on the far side of which is Atatürk Bulvarı. This building was once the Turkish Airlines Air Terminal, but is now the **Beyaz Saray Restaurant.** The name means "White Palace," which is the Turkish translation of "White House" (as in Washington, D.C.), and while the presidential chef might not cook up all the Turkish delicacies you'll find here, the president might well wish he did. Though there are lots of dining rooms to choose from, the choice spot is on the front terrace overlooking the plaza. As you pass the food preparation areas, choose from among the dozens of salads, purées, appetizers, fish, kebaps, and other treats, and let a waiter know what you want, asking prices as you go. This will save you struggling with a basically useless menu later. Though the service here is sometimes abominably slow, it's never unfriendly, and the food can be delicious. Prices are high for

Ankara, but not really bad. A four-course tuck-in would cost about 4,000TL ($5.60) to 5,000TL ($7), with wine or beer.

RESTAURANTS NEAR ULUS: There are several nice and quite inexpensive restaurants in or near Ulus, handy if you're staying here or sightseeing nearby. The safest bet is to walk north out of the square along Çankırı Caddesi, on the right-hand side of the street.

The first place to check out is the attractive **Çiçek Lokantası,** Çankırı Caddesi 12/A (tel. 11-59-97), where you can dine from a standard menu of Turkish specialties well prepared, and served with care, for less than 1,800TL ($2.50). They've installed a little fountain in the center of the dining room to lend the soothing tinkle of falling water to your meal.

A few steps farther along Çankırı Caddesi is the **Ender Lokantası,** Çankırı Caddesi 10/A (tel. 11-85-43), where you'll find white tablecloths, attentive waiters, good food, and similarly low prices.

Right next to the equestrian statue in the square is a big office building complex. If you walk in front of it along Atatürk Bulvarı, at no. 3 there's an entrance to a courtyard in the middle of the building. At the other end of the courtyard is a pastry shop with the best selection of exotic Turkish desserts that I've ever encountered. It's the **Akman Boza Ve Pasta Salonu,** Atatürk Bulvarı 3, open for breakfast, an afternoon snack, or an evening coffee, with tables and chairs set out in the courtyard among potted shrubs and trees, around a pool with a fountain. Tea is 250TL (35¢), coffee, 450TL (65¢). Try *boza,* a strange Turkish drink made from fermented millet juice, very thick, with a slight tang and a very delicate taste something like apple (winter only). Their continental breakfast special costs 750TL ($1.05), if you don't want to do-it-yourself by picking a pastry or a roll to eat with tea, or perhaps have an omelette.

The rage in Ankara these days is **Hacı Bey,** an eatery which serves only Bursa-style döner kebap. Busy whenever it's open with the hungry and happy, it serves everyone from cabinet ministers to clerks with the same delicious kebap topped with browned butter and tomato sauce. Ankara being a diplomatic center, many of the international set even make the trek to Devren Sokak 1/B to chow down. Plates of kebap cost 950TL ($1.35) for the normal size (and quite sufficient), or 1,250TL ($1.75) for a large (and an awful lot of food). No alcoholic beverages are served, but the buttermilk-like ayran is a favorite with the kebap, or you can choose üzüm suyu, a very refreshing unfermented grape juice. The total bill for the small kebap plate, beverage, and coffee will be about 1,600TL ($2.25). To get to Hacı Bey's, tell the bus driver anywhere along Atatürk Bulvarı to let you off at the Opera. Across the boulevard from the opera house is a street climbing a grade. That's Devren Sokak, and Hacı Bey's is a short walk up, on the left.

4. Ankara's Sights

The Turkish word *gezmek* means "to walk about, inspect, especially for pleasure." Though Ankara is not primarily a sightseeing city, there are a few places which you should not miss while you're there, and several others which you might want to take in on your "gez."

THE ARCHEOLOGICAL MUSEUM: Above all you should go to the **Museum of Anatolian Civilizations,** known informally as the Hittite Museum, though it includes non-Hittite materials as well. The museum is housed in a restored han, or caravanserai, and a restored covered bazaar, near the Citadel. What is not very old in the buildings is very modern, but well blended with the ancient style. To get to the museum, take a taxi from Ulus for 800TL, ($1.10) or walk up Hisarparkı Caddesi to Anafartalar Caddesi. Turn right and walk up Anafartalar, and continue straight on up the hill even though the main road bears right. Keep glancing to your left; when you can see the Citadel, you've come to the small road which leads to the museum.

The museum is open every day but Monday; entrance costs 500TL (70¢), half price on weekends. Without paying a very hefty fee, you are allowed to photograph only the displays in the central court of the museum. No flash or tripod allowed, and no movie cameras. A pamphlet guide to the museum, in English, costs 650TL (90¢), and is well done and very helpful.

The Turkish abbreviation for B.C. is M.Ö. You'll find an original cave painting and similar Stone Age relics to start, but the museum's real wealth comes just after these, in the Hittite section. Here you can see the famous deer statues with graceful, stylized antlers, the Hittite bulls, ironwork designs, and earthenware pitchers and vessels showing ingenuity and a high standard of art. Most items like these in museums interest me because of the way people lived millennia ago, and once I've seen a few examples I usually lose interest. But the Hittite objects are different. They seem to give off a feeling of joy in creation; the stylizations are graceful and well proportioned, capturing the spirit of the objects or animal involved. To me, the famous Hittite stag, here in the hexagonal glass case, is a much greater accomplishment than the massive figures carved from stone to be seen elsewhere in the museum, though those probably demanded more time and energy. And the water pots and bowls—things to be used every day—are made to be practical, but at the same time are works of art showing a great deal of ingenuity and pleasure in creation. Some gold jewelry found at the Hittite excavations is here too, as are runic tablets, artifacts from civilizations other than the Hittite, and wall maps showing where the discoveries were made.

In the central part of the old han are the works in stone: long friezes depicting victories, weddings, celebrations by Hittite warriors and kings, statues big enough to stand guard at royal portals, sphinxes, hieroglyphics. Many of the things on display are accompanied by photographs which show how they looked in their original sites, thereby lessening the damage done by removing the old objects to a museum. At the end of your tour through the museum you pass through a small classical section, with some fine Greek and Roman gold jewelry, coins, and other small finds from a country rich in such old things.

Next along is a small refreshment stand. It's so nice the way the museum staff keeps songbirds and an aquarium full of tropical fish in this last section "just for pretty." It's also very Turkish, and the time is not long past when many establishments of every description (restaurants especially) kept songbirds. Sitting down at the end of your tour through the museum is the time to admire the fine building you're in.

THE ANIT KABİR: The other sight you shouldn't miss in Ankara is the Anıt Kabir, **Atatürk's Tomb.** You've probably noticed it, the giant stone rectangle on a hill in the midst of the city, built in a modern but simple and appealing style. To get to it, take a bus from Kızılay along Gazi Mustafa Kemal Bulvarı. Just mention the Anıt Kabir to the driver and he'll let you off at Anıt Caddesi. Turn left and walk up this street, which leads right up to the grounds of the mausoleum. It's about a 15-minute walk to the top through a manicured park, past the military guards, and down a "triumphant way" lined with stone lions.

The tomb itself is quite impressive, surrounded by tall, simple columns cut from a local stone that seems to capture both the beauty and the wildness of Anatolia. Inside, past the high-stepping guards out front, is a room paved in marble, roofed with gold mosaic in old Turkish patterns, leading to the sarcophagus in front of a large window with a view of the city. I couldn't help remembering, at this point, what a friend once said about this place—that it was the symbol of a recent heroic age (along with such monuments as Lenin's Tomb in Moscow), all the more long gone for its having been so recent. Can you imagine a contemporary politician or statesman who would aspire to such a resting place, or who might deserve it?

The other buildings, surrounding the courtyard in front of the tomb, house such things as the official cars Atatürk used (mostly Lincolns), the gun carriage used in his funeral procession, and so forth. The small museum, open from 9 a.m. to 6 p.m. every day, holds some of Atatürk's personal effects and memorabilia, part of his library, presents from monarchs and other heads of state, and photographs. One of the best things to see from the tomb is the city, for like the Citadel, the hilltop location here gives you a panoramic view.

During the summer, **Sound and Light** shows are sponsored at the Anıt Kabir. Shows are given in German, French, English, and Turkish on different nights. Consult the *Turkish Daily News* for the dates of the various languages.

ÇANKAYA KÖŞKÜ: While I'm on the subject of Atatürk, you should know that his Ankara home can be visited and toured. When Ankara became Turkey's capital, its first president had a small "koisk" *(köşk)* or lodge built among the Çankaya hills in what was then the city's outskirts. The little house is now within the grounds of the **Presidential Palace** (called the **Cumhurbaşkanlığı Köşk);** the palace grounds are open to the public each Sunday afternoon so citizens can enjoy the formal flower gardens and visit Atatürk's retreat. The house is very solidly built in a style borrowed from alpine countries, and is furnished very much in the style of the '30s. The Çankaya Köşkü gives one many insights into the early history of the republic. To get to the kiosk—remember that it's open for free from 1:30 to 5:30 p.m. on Sunday afternoons only—take bus 8 ("Çankaya") along Atatürk Bulvarı running south (away from Ulus toward the center of town). Get out and ask to be pointed in the direction of the Çankaya Köşkü. Admission to the palace grounds is free (but you must have your passport), and the view from up here is very good.

ROMAN ANKARA: A Roman city occupied the site of modern-day Ankara, and several vestiges of this old city still exist. All of these are near Ulus, and a walking tour of them, throwing in the non-Roman Citadel along with the bazaar and the city's two most famous mosques, will take you only a few hours, a morning at most.

Start off down Çankırı Caddesi, in the hotel district. At no. 43 is the entrance to the **Roman baths,** open from 8:30 a.m. to 12:30 p.m. and 1:30 to 5:30 p.m. for 200TL (28¢); closed Monday. You can still see the oval-shaped pool with a seat running all the way around, used for soaking, and several rooms used for steam, identifiable by the piles of round red bricks which held up the floors and allowed heat to circulate below, fed by furnaces in the corners. Some of the plumbing is still extant, though the aqueduct which used to bring water for steam from the distant mountains is long since gone. A colonnaded way, a palaestra or sports ground, a few inscriptions, and other fragments complete the site.

Walk back up Çankırı Caddesi toward Ulus, turning left onto Armutlu Sokak about a block before the square. At the end of this street, turn into the square on the right, which has a small park and fountain, and the **Column of Justinian,** an odd monumental column said to have been built as a commemorative for the emperor's visit to the city. On top there's a stork's nest said to be almost as old as the column.

From the column, walk up the hill, turn right, then turn left onto Bayram Caddesi, a street lined with religious bookshops, stores selling green cloths inscribed in gold with Arabic inscriptions from the Koran, and a number of stands with large piles of Muslim rosaries. At the end of the street are two more things to see: the ruins of the **Temple of Augustus and Rome,** and the **Hacı Bayram Mosque,** one of Ankara's oldest. Not a great deal remains of the temple: some high walls, decorations, windows with bars carved in stone. The mosque has been restored many times since it was first built in the early 1400s, but still offers a striking contrast to the Byzantine-influenced mosques of Istanbul. The Hacı Bayram seems more modern, with rectangular rooms and wood paneling. The tomb of Hacı Bayram himself, builder of the mosque and founder of an order of dervishes, is right near the entrance to the mosque grounds. It's open every day except Monday: on Tuesday from 3 to 5 p.m., on other days from 8 to 11 a.m. and 3 to 5 p.m. Remember to take your shoes off before entering. A sign posted out in front states that "no candle-lighting is allowed." (The practice of candle-lighting was reportedly borrowed by Muslims from Catholic and Orthodox churches, to signify the same thing as tying a bit of one's clothing to the window bar on a saint's tomb: it's a reminder to the saint that you've asked for help some way—but it's a no-no here.)

If you'd like to wander around old Ankara on your own, the Hacı Bayram Mosque is a good starting point. Behind the mosque and the temple is a little alley called Gaziantep Sokak, which winds through the old city, past wooden houses with bright-blue doors, windows festooned with green and red peppers drying in the sun, children with bright dark eyes smiling at you from behind partly opened doors. Keep bearing right as you descend and you'll end up on Kevgirli Sokak, down in the valley. Follow this street toward the Citadel, turn left onto Hisarparkı Caddesi, and walk up the hill to the Citadel.

THE CITADEL: The **Citadel,** or **Kale,** has two defensive walls, the outer one near the bottom of the hill, and the fortress wall itself. In between there is now a park. Inside the fortress proper is a continuation of the old town: houses, shops, mosques, and cobbled streets. Look as though you're lost and a child will point the way to the very top of the hill, from which you can view the whole city. Not far from this tower of the fortress is a gate through the wall which brings you to the **market,** just above the Archeological Museum. Here are wide canvas tarps covering piles of melons, sacks of beans and rice, sheepskins drying in the sun, and warehouses which trade in tiftik—gora goat hair. Follow this street to the right to pass the Museum of Anatolian Civilizations and to reach Ulus. To the left is more of the market, some of its most interesting parts, and the **Aslanhane Mosque,** the oldest mosque in Ankara, built in the late 1200s.

Next to the Aslanhane mosque is Talat Paşa Bulvarı. Walking down the hill on this street will bring you to the **Ethnographic Museum,** on the left, open from 8:30 a.m. to 12:30 p.m. and 1:30 to 5:30 p.m. (closed Monday); entrance is 400TL (55¢). The museum has a collection of folk costumes, Turkish carpets, Anatolian handwork and sewing, and assorted relics—a good sampling for a taste of Anatolian peasant life.

Right next door is the **Painting and Sculpture Museum,** open at the same times, for the same price.

GENÇLİK PARKI: Near Ulus on Atatürk Bulvarı is an entrance to **Gençlik Parkı,** Ankara's "Youth Park," a combination amusement park, world's fair, and city park. It offers shady walks, refreshment stands, full-fledged restaurants, tea gardens, rock-and-roll bands with singers (even during the daytime), outdoor movies, a ferris wheel and other rides, and an artificial lake where boats can be rented. Entrance to the park is 50TL (7¢).

ANKARA'S NIGHTLIFE: In the mood for dancing? Ankara is well endowed with spots for you to look over for the evening. Most of the big hotels, including the **Grand Ankara**, the **Balın**, the **Dedeman**, and others, have rooftop clubs with live bands, singers, dance floors, cover charges of several dollars or so, and drinks for a dollar apiece.

For a cheap, Turkish-style evening out, take a look at the **Luna Park Aile Gazinosu.** The gazino is in Gençlik Parkı, in a subdivision called the Luna Park. Entrance to the Luna Park grounds is several hundred liras (on top of the admission to Gençlik Parkı). You can bring your own soft drinks and a picnic dinner, or buy such things inside. Inside is a tarpaulin-covered seating area with a stage at one end where Turkey's popular music greats perform nightly, amplified to ear-splitting level. The best stars come on late, as usual, but you must get to the gazino early to get a good seat. Turks like long evenings out, so 7:30 p.m. is not too early to get your seat; the big stars start about 11 p.m. But before you decide to pay your money, you'd better know what you're getting into—walk by the gazino and listen for a minute first.

If a nightclub, rooftop place is your idea of a splurge, try the roof restaurant of the **Hotel Dedeman** (described above). The view from this roof is breathtaking. Ankara is well suited for such views because of its location in a basin surrounded by mountains, with the outskirts of the city sprawling over miles and miles of mountainsides, twinkling their lights back to the center. The prices at the Dedeman are in the meal-for-$10 range; the menu is a mixture of Turkish and continental dishes. Until 10 p.m. the roof is a restaurant; at 10 it becomes a nightclub, with a band, a singer, and a small dance floor. The restaurant remains open past 10 p.m., and you can sit outside on the terrace, more or less separated from the club atmosphere—but when the band begins to play, a minimum charge comes into force. If you have this first drink with dinner, the whole thing doesn't inflate your bill too much, and subsequent drinks are less expensive. To get to the Dedeman, walk or take a dolmush up two long blocks of Atatürk Bulvarı from Kızılay, away from Ulus, and turn left onto Akay Sokak. The Dedeman is plainly visible, about two blocks up the street.

5. The Hittite Cities

From 1600 to 1200 B.C. Central Anatolia and Syria were the domain of a mysterious people known as the Hittites. A people with some relation to Indo-European races and civilizations, they are thought to have migrated here from the East. Between about 1400 and 1200 B.C. Hittite kings ruled Cappadocia and most of central Anatolia during the empire's Golden Age, and their armies threatened Babylonia and Egypt. They had a hieroglyphic alphabet for their Indo-European language, a code of laws developed independently of Babylon, and the knowledge to smelt iron—one of the first peoples to know how to do so.

Even though the Hittites are mentioned several times in the Bible, knowledge of their culture and civilization was largely lost until the present century, when excavations and research revealed the accomplishments of this surprisingly sophisticated people. Their artworks, which you have already seen in Ankara's Museum of Anatolian Civilizations, are superb. To see where many of those treasures were discovered, make an excursion to Boğazkale.

TOURS: Numerous companies run tours to Boğazkale from Ankara, and taking a tour isn't a bad idea. The ancient city sprawls across a vast hillside, and seeing it all entails a lot of walking. Also, transportation to and from the site is not really the best, and accommodations nearby are severely limited, so a day tour is recommendable. Any travel agency can set you up. Two that are running tours at this writing are **Konvoy Tur,** Atatürk Bulvarı 233/8, Kavaklıdere, Ankara (tel. 41/26-16-31), which has a full-day Boğazkale tour for $35; and **Duru Turizm,** Atatürk Bulvarı 83, Kızılay, Ankara (tel. 41/34-48-44), which operates a tour priced at $50. Lunch is included in these rates.

GETTING THERE ON YOUR OWN: Hop on a bus from Ankara's Otogar to Yozgat. At the bus station in Yozgat, hawkers will approach you to sell you a minibus tour of **Boğazkale,** which you should sign up for.

An alternative is to catch a bus from Ankara to **Sungurlu,** from which you catch a minibus to **Boğazkale.** At Boğazkale you must hire a taxi to take you around; taxis may be scarce. If you rent a taxi from Sungurlu for the whole trip —to Boğazkale, around the ruins, and back to Sungurlu—the cost might be 8000TL ($11.20) for the entire car. The distance from Sungurlu to Boğazkale is about 17 miles (27 km).

A HOTEL: If you don't take a tour, and thus expect to spend the night near the ruins, your first task upon arrival in Boğazkale should be to nail down a room at the village's one hotel, the 25-room **Aşikoğlu Turistik Moteli** (tel. Boğazkale 4). A double room without private bath is high priced for what you get, but it's what there is, and costs 5,000TL ($7). The hotel is open only from mid-March until mid-November. It has a restaurant.

THE MUSEUM: The little museum near the hotel in Boğazkale is open from 8 a.m. to noon and 1:30 to 5:30 p.m. The one ticket you buy for 500TL (70¢) admits you to both the museum and the ruins. All of the best pieces discovered on the site have been carted away to endow Ankara's Museum of Anatolian Civilizations, but much of the remainder is here.

THE RUINS: What's left of ancient Hattuşaş is, as I've mentioned, spread out over a large area on a hillside. The ruins are memorable because of their situation and their antiquity, but not because of the buildings you see. Most are just rough, low stone foundations, many of them reconstructed. Look particularly for the **Great Temple of the Storm God;** the **Fortress,** where the great kings of the Hittite Empire had their palaces; and the **Sphinx Gate,** now guarded by replicas of the original lions. The gate leads to a tunnel topped by a **corbelled arch,** not really a true arch (the principal of which would only be discovered later, and by other peoples), but just two large stones leaned one against the other to close off a narrow passage from the sky.

Of particular interest are the relief pictures and inscriptions at **Yazılıkaya** ("Rock-with-Writing"), two miles from the main part of Hattuşaş. Near the end of their golden age, Hittite artists chiselled images of some of their 1,000 gods and goddesses in rockfaces here. The place is thought to have been a temple or other religious sanctuary, though much of its use is still a mystery.

Chapter XIV

CAPPADOCIA

1. Nevşehir
2. Ürgüp
3. Göreme, Çavuşin, and Zelve
4. Kayseri
5. The Underground Cities
6. Konya

CAPPADOCIA IS THE VERY CENTER of Anatolia, a region of wildly different kinds of topography, inhabited since the earliest times. Civilization upon civilization has come to this area to take refuge from the military invasions and campaigns which are so much a part of Anatolia's history. Hittites, Arabs, early Christians, Seljuk Turks, Armenians, and Ottoman Turks have all lived in this part of Anatolia and have added something to the impression you get when you visit it.

The most famous sights in Cappadocia are Mount Erciyes, the 13,000-foot peak which dominates the town of Kayseri, and the rock churches and caves in the area around the Göreme Valley. To see these things and the other sights that Cappadocia has to offer, begin your trip in Ankara.

TRANSPORTATION: If you want to travel by train or plane, and if you want to spend a day in Kayseri, come to Ürgüp by way of Kayseri. But if you want to take a bus directly from Ankara to Ürgüp, there are at least eight buses a day from Ankara's Otogar (bus station). Just walk to the ticket counters and a hawker will direct you to the proper counter for Ürgüp or Nevşehir. The ride takes four hours and costs 2,000TL ($2.80). Unless you see Ürgüp very quickly by taxi-tour, you'll have to plan to stay overnight.

1. Nevşehir

Nevşehir is the provincial capital, and has a number of hotels you might consider. Other than for a night's lodging, you'll probably look upon Nevşehir as a transportation point. There is none of that striking Cappadocian scenery here, just a farming town.

ORIENTATION: The layout here is pretty simple. The bus station is a large open lot with several bus company ticket offices facing it. The town's main street, Atatürk Bulvarı, comes right by the bus station and descends a slope to the center of town. Walk down the slope to find hotels, restaurants, banks, and dolmushes to nearby towns (leaving from Nevşehir's main crossroads). There is a little booth for tourism information right at the bus station, and a larger **Tourism Information Office** at Lale Caddesi 22 (tel. 4851/1137), downtown.

HOTELS: At the top of the scale is the 80-room **Hotel Orsan Kapadokya**, Kayseri Caddesi (tel. 4851/1035 or 2115), which rents comfortable, modernish double rooms with private bath for 15,000TL ($21). The big bonus at the Orsan is a swimming pool.

The **Hotel Göreme**, Hükümet Caddesi 16 (tel. 4851/1706), is right in downtown Nevşehir, and you can't miss it. This 11-floor "skyscraper" is built to resemble the cave dwellings of Cappadocia. This is not really possible, as you'll see when you look at the building; but they tried. Inside this elevated cave are 75 comfortable guest rooms with private baths renting for 12,000TL ($16.80).

Not far from the Hotel Orsan Kapadokya is the smaller (24-room) **Hotel Viva**, Kayseri Caddesi 111 (tel. 4851/1326 or 1760), not fancy, plain but presentable, with a popular dining room and tidy double rooms with showers going for 6,000TL ($8.40).

RESTAURANTS: Try the **Aspava Lokantası**, Atatürk Bulvarı 29 (tel. 1057), right downtown, a bright and popular place with low farm-town prices and a standard selection of Turkish dishes. Among the specialties are kebaps, and pide topped with everything from ground meat to eggs or cheese. Soup, kebap, and dessert will cost about 1,700TL ($2.40).

2. Ürgüp

Ürgüp is the hub of tourism in Cappadocia. In summer its streets are thronged by visitors from a dozen countries, talking in many languages, haggling with shopkeepers for carpets, antique brass and copper utensils, clothing, and trinkets, and enjoying the balmy evening air at some outdoor café or restaurant. In winter, Ürgüp reverts to what it has done forever: farming. Vineyards dot the volcanic landscape, fields of grain fill the river valleys, and fruit orchards crowd tiny backyard garden plots. Local wineries produce simple but in some cases appealing vintages.

Its status as hub for tourism came to Ürgüp because it's the closest real town to the Göreme Valley, and thus it's also your most convenient base of operations.

GETTING THERE: Ürgüp is linked with other towns by dolmush routes which begin and end in Ürgüp's bus station. There are hourly minibuses to and from Nevşehir (200TL, 28¢), and almost as many to Kayseri (700TL, $1). Minibuses to Avanos are far less frequent. Traveling to and from Göreme Village (formerly called Avcılar) involves being dropped off by the Motel Paris and walking over a mile, or going all the way to Nevşehir and taking another dolmush back out to the village.

ORIENTATION: This is not a large town, and you should have no trouble orienting yourself here. The bus or minibus from Nevşehir comes in past the turnoff for Göreme (and in the opposite direction, for Ortahisar), past the Motel Paris, then past the big new **Turban Ürgüp Motel**, on the left. Descending the hill on a winding road, you enter Ürgüp. The modern little bus station is right next to the market square, and just below the town's main square, which has several recommendable restaurants and most of the souvenir shops. From the main square,

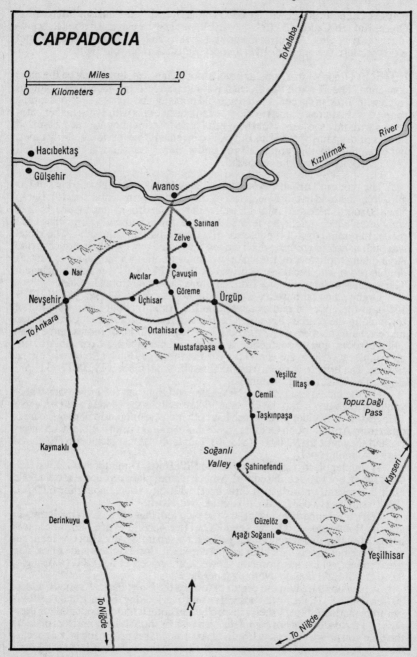

Kayseri Caddesi runs down the slope gradually, past the **Tourism Information Office,** Kayseri Caddesi 37 (tel. 4868/1059), and past a cluster of hotels, including the Büyük Otel. As you come down Kayseri Caddesi, when the Büyük Otel is on your left, the quarter called Sivritaş Mahallesi is on your right.

HOTELS: Ürgüp's most popular hotel is not its fanciest, but it may be the most congenial. The 54-room **Büyük Otel,** Kayseri Caddesi (tel. 4868/1060), is decorated with Turkish carpets, crafts, and old implements. It has a spacious dining room, a wide staircase, and two floors of smallish rooms with even smaller bathrooms with tiny showers. But thoughtful little touches abound, such as sealed bottles of drinking water. The Büyük is convenient to everything, fairly quiet, but often filled by tour groups. If you find a room vacant, it will cost 12,600TL ($17.65), double, breakfast included.

Ürgüp's showpieces are the two large motels on its outskirts.

The modern **Turban Ürgüp Motel** (tel. 4868/1490), on the outskirts of Ürgüp along the road to Göreme, is run by the quasi-governmental Tourism Bank. The 160 rooms here are "mini-suites," with bath, bedroom, and alcove, built in complexes which might be termed "village town houses." Furnishings are meant to remind one of the interior of a traditional Turkish home. The motel was built to accept groups, which it does, and you'll meet group members in the large dining room and by the small swimming pool. It's a nice place to stay. A double room with breakfast is priced at 19,300TL ($27), breakfast included. The motel is walking distance from Ürgüp, a short ride from Göreme.

Ürgüp's newest hostelry is the **Hotel Boydaş,** P. K. 11 (tel. 4868/1259 or 1659), at the opposite end of town from the Turban, about half a mile out of town along the road to Kayseri. The Boydaş also was designed for the group market, being a series of low-rise buildings holding 127 guest rooms, three bars, a dining room, and a discothèque. More rooms, perhaps more congenial to single couples traveling, are across the road in the **Tepe Hotel,** also owned by the Boydaş. The price for a room with breakfast in either place is 13,200TL ($18.50) single, 17,400TL ($24.35) double.

On the main road between Nevşehir and Ürgüp, at the crossroads where you turn to go down into the Göreme Valley itself, is the **Motel Paris** (tel. 4868/1435, ext. 99), an older place which has both motel rooms and camping facilities open from April through October. Its 24 motel rooms are all doubles with shower, and they rent for 9,800TL ($13.70) double, breakfast included. The motel has a swimming pool.

A simpler place, right in town, is the **Hitit Hotel,** Dumlupınar Caddesi (tel. 4868/1481), not to be confused with a much plainer place on another street. The Hitit is a recently refurbished little hotel with nice rooms going for 6,000TL ($8.40) single, 11,000TL ($15.40) double, with bath.

If it's atmosphere you want, try the twin lodgings of the **Göreme Pansiyon** and the **Hotel Şato,** next to the Büyük Otel (tel. 4868/1146 or 1149). These two halves of a large two-family village house have separate names but one management. The interior public spaces are plastered with local carpets and kilims. The guest rooms, which have private showers, are priced at 5,000TL ($7) single, 8,000TL ($11.20) double. Nothing fancy here.

A new hotel right in the center of town is the **Hotel Park,** Avanos Caddesi 20 (tel. 4868/1883), facing the post office and overlooking the park and the Tourism Information Office. When I inspected the hotel it had just opened for business and the decor was not complete, so it may be more homey and less plain by the time you arrive. The view from a front room makes up for any lack of decor, though. A room with shower costs 5,000TL ($7) single, 8,000TL ($11.20) double.

The Big Splurge

For the true comfy life, you must go to the neighboring town of Üçhisar, and sign up for room and meals at the Club Med's **Kaya Oteli** (tel. 4851/1488, ext. 7). Built partway into a volcanic hillside, the Kaya (which means "rock") claims title as Cappadocia's most dramatic hotel. Rooms are rented only with breakfast and dinner, for 17,000TL ($23.80) per person.

The Starvation Budget

Ürgüp's collection of pensions is in the quarter called **Sivritaş Mahallesi.** In the small grid of streets here are half a dozen little pensions with small, homey rooms for fairly low prices. Some of these places have pretensions to hotel status, however, so ask around at a few before bedding down.

Elgin Sokak has four such places to consider. The **Hotel Divan,** Elgin Sokak 4 (tel. 4868/1705), gives you a choice of prices and conveniences. It rents rooms for 2,500TL ($3.50) to 3,000TL ($4.20) single, 3,750TL ($5.25) to 4,500TL ($6.30) double, 4,500TL ($6.30) to 6,000TL ($8.40) triple; the higher prices are for rooms with bath. Nearby, the **Hisar Oteli,** Elgin Sokak (tel. 4868/1261), has similarly spartan but acceptable rooms with bath priced slightly cheaper, at 4,500TL ($6.30). Cheapest of all is the **Otel Villa,** Elgin Sokak (tel. 4868/1906), by no means fancy, but quite alright if your budget is constrained. Doubles without bath cost 3,750TL ($5.25), or 4,500TL ($6.30) with bath.

RESTAURANTS: I should perhaps warn you that, off-season, Ürgüp's restaurants don't do a lot of business and the quality of the food can suffer. But during the warm months most of the town's restaurants are full, the food is great, and the prices aren't bad, even in this touristic mecca.

You will spot the **Cappadocia Restaurant,** on the main square above the bus station (tel. 1029), very soon after you arrive in Ürgüp. What can I say? Big, bright interior dining room, small outdoor place with a few tables, friendly waiters, and lots of good food at moderate prices. At dinner I spent 2,200TL ($3.10) for three courses.

The **Uğrak Restaurant** is just opposite the vehicular entrance to the bus station. The sidewalk tables are the draw here, as are the prices, which are even lower than the already low ones just mentioned above.

For meals that are a cut above in quality and ambience, yet hardly what one might call expensive, try dining at one of the better hotels or motels. The place to try first is the **Büyük Otel,** which has a set-price, table d'hôte (fixed-menu) meal for only 3,000TL ($4.20). Add the cost of wine or beer, plus the tip, and you may be out of pocket $6 or $7 per person.

For the lowest prices in town, stroll along **Dumlupınar Caddesi,** on the opposite side of the bus station and marketplace from the main square. The few little kebapçıs and pide places here can fill you up for amazingly small amounts of money, and still the food will be good. Full meals can range from 850TL ($1.20) to 1,900TL ($2.65).

3. Göreme, Çavuşin, and Zelve

On the trip into town you probably got a glimpse of what this area is like. Nothing else can really compare to it—a wide, flat plateau with valleys gouged out of its middle, and the valleys filled with tall, ghost-like pinnacles of rock, some with square holes cut into them. According to some sources, the Hittites were the first people to live in this area and leave a mark, several thousand years ago. They found that the rock of the plateau and of the pinnacles was soft volcanic rock, easily worked with primitive tools, and that they could make safe, secure homes for themselves relatively easily. You could call them "cavemen," I suppose, though their civilization was far too advanced for this term to apply.

Early Christians who fled Roman, and later Arabic, persecution came to this area and found refuge in the rock caves. They hollowed out houses, stables, work and storage rooms, churches—entire communities—from the soft rock. Passages leading into these refuges were built so that massive stone wheel-doors could be rolled across the narrow places, preventing attackers from reaching the interior. There are hundreds of caves in the valley of Cappadocia; no one has ever visited them all. The strangest and most appealing of these cave communities are to be found in and around the Göreme Valley, but even in Ürgüp itself there are caves.

TOURS: As the sites in this area are somewhat spread out, you may want to sign up for a tour if your time is limited. Several companies compete, selling full-day tours of the region for 2,500TL ($3.50) to 3,000TL ($4.20) per person. Watch out, though: part of the tour time will be spent in a souvenir shop, where you will be dropped, like it or not, and from which the tour operators get a kickback on everything you buy.

The alternative is to organize your own tour by gathering a group of like-minded people and bargaining with a taxi or minibus driver for a full day of his services. Such a tour would cost 20,000TL ($28) to 25,000TL ($35) for the entire car or minibus.

THE GÖREME VALLEY: The road winds down through sandy vineyards to a parking lot with a post office, guard post, and souvenir stand. The rock pillars surround this spot and are especially thick on the left of the road. Pay the 600TL (85¢) entrance fee and head off into the valley.

The principal churches are all marked by signs displaying their intriguing names: the Dark Church, the Slipper Church, the Buckle Church. If you have a flashlight, it's a good idea to have it along, since the lighting in the churches is only what leaks in from outside. Inside the churches, the walls and ceilings are covered with early Christian paintings of saints and angels and biblical scenes. Almost all of the paintings of humans have literally been "defaced," this having been done before the valley was protected. The soft volcanic rock, spewed forth from Erciyes centuries ago, has been worked into columns and vaults, domes and niches. More than one of the churches has a burial vault hollowed out underneath the sanctuary.

Churches are not the only places to be found in the valley. A whole community once inhabited it. It's not hard to guess the function of any place you might scramble into. Everything needed for a bakery, or a stable, or a workshop is all evident, only it's all carved right from the rock.

The **Tokalı Kilise** (Buckle Church) is outside the enclosure. Follow the road down the hill from the parking lot: the church is on the right. It's the biggest of the churches in this area. The name was stuck on the church by the Turkish conquerors for some reason now obscure. There's a burial vault which you can explore beneath the ground level of the church. Among the graffiti on the walls and ceiling is one in modern Greek—I wonder what that says.

The village of **Avcılar** is a kilometer (half a mile) farther down the road. Don't miss a quick look at it if you're interested in Turkish village life: Old men sit in the shade outside a tea house; veiled women glide back and forth from their houses to the town fountain; the only women without veils are some pretty, young schoolteachers, probably on their first assignment from Ankara, who walk together, looking a bit self-conscious. The rock tower in the center of the town has perhaps the only ruin of its kind: two ruined columns, carved from the rock, with the bottoms missing, not the tops. Everywhere in the soft rock are cut rows of little cubbyholes like apartment house mail boxes. These are for raising pigeons—the original pigeonholes. Start on the right of the town fountain and walk up the path into the town. There's an open-air mosque, houses in the rock with precarious toe-hole ladders by which to enter, and near the top, a flour mill cut completely from the rock. Vineyards fill the ridge above the town, from which you can take a look at the whole countryside for miles, all the way to Mount Erciyes, the cause of it all.

ÇAVUŞIN AND ZELVE: To visit another valley, from Avcılar get a dolmuş to Avanos, but get off at the turnoff to **Çavuşin,** a similar valley with a high concentration of rock churches, these with better paintings. Soon after the turnoff to Çavuşin the road passes a sideroad to **Zelve,** still another valley, this one with fewer churches but more houses and workshops. You can visit these valleys directly from Ürgüp, but only by taxi. If you're willing to take a chance, get a taxi only one way. When the time comes to return, wait at the refreshment stand (there's one in every valley, it seems) and catch a taxi as it returns after dropping newcomers off.

AVANOS: Avanos, reached by dolmuş from Avcılar or Ürgüp, is an old town formerly inhabited mostly by Greeks, now completely Turkish, which specializes in alabaster. Lamps, ashtrays, chess sets, vases, bowls, trays, even whole liqueur services are carved from the bright, translucent stone and sold here for a fraction of the price asked anywhere else in the world.

A SELJUK CARAVANSERAI: The **Sarı Han** is an old Seljuk Turkish caravanserai, located about three miles from Avanos in the lonely rolling hills around the town. A taxi will take you there from Ürgüp for 1,400TL ($1.95), but if you're a hiker, an hour's walk will bring you to this old way-station for caravans, now surrounded by bare hills and a sheep or two. The han is, of course, in ruins, but most of the decoration is still in place. The outer walls have been pillaged recently in order to get stone for the new bridge across the river in Avanos.

These caravanserais were major outposts on trade routes and, befitting their importance, included stables, sleeping quarters, a mosque, a treasury, storerooms, and baths. The Seljuks constructed them all over their empire in order to facilitate trade, and from the looks of the Sarı Han, defense.

SİNESON: From Ürgüp you might like to take another side trip. Early in the morning and at several other times during the day, a dolmuş leaves from Ürgüplü Caddesi on the short trip to Sineson, also called **Mustafapaşa.** This goodsize town was formerly Greek, resettled by Turks after the exchange of population. The town has rock churches, a monastery, and houses as well, but all of them fairly contemporary—all of these were used and kept in good condition until 50 years ago; consequently, they're very well preserved. A tour of all the churches has to be done with the town guide since he has the keys, and it requires an hour or so because the churches are spread out. The dolmuş will drop you off in the main square of Sineson. Walk across the square to the mill. There will probably be an old man lashing bags of freshly ground flour to his burro. Behind him is the town mill; the miller is also the tourist guide. If business at the mill is slack he'll take you around. You might give him a tip at the end.

4. Kayseri

Kayseri is a big town, but it still gives the impression of a frontier post. There's not a lot to see here, but the transportation between Ankara and Kayseri is good, so you might want to take the longer (but more comfortable) route to Göreme by way of Kayseri.

GETTING THERE: Trains on the express run to Kayseri leave at 6:40 and 10:40 a.m. on the seven-hour trip. The first-class fare from Ankara to Kayseri is 1,300-TL ($1.80) on these trains.

Turkish Airlines has only a Sunday flight from Ankara to Kayseri, but no flights vice versa.

The Erciyes bus company, Kayseri's biggest, runs buses every hour between Ankara and Kayseri, charging 1,800TL ($2.50) for the trip and leaving from Ankara's new bus garage, the Otogar. The trip by bus takes about 4½ hours.

ORIENTATION: Upon arriving in Kayseri, the place to go to get your bearings is **Cumhuriyet Square** in the center of town. This is a short walk from the airline office, a short cab ride (600TL, 85¢) from the bus station on the west side of town, and a half-mile ride from the railroad station by city bus (60TL, 8¢), carriage, or taxi (600TL, 85¢).

Cumhuriyet Square is dominated by Kayseri's old fortress walls, and is surrounded by Seljuk and Ottoman religious schools and mosques. The four streets which meet in the square are **Talas Caddesi** and **Sivas Caddesi,** both main routes leading out of town; **İstanbul Caddesi,** going to Düvenönü Square before heading for Ürgüp and Göreme; and **İstasyon Caddesi,** coming from the long, stretched-out railroad station. **Atatürk Bulvarı** runs parallel to İstasyon Caddesi between the station and Düvenönü Square.

Walk out of Cumhuriyet Square to the left of the fortress to get to the **Tourism Information Office,** Kağnı Pazarı Honat Camii Yaui 61 (tel. 351/11-190). From here, keep walking around the walls to get to **27 Mayıs Caddesi** (pronounced *"yeer*-mee yeh-*dee* may-*uhs"*), your baseline for hotels.

HOTELS: The best in town is the **Hattat Oteli,** İstanbul Caddesi 1 (tel. 351/19-331), right in the middle of everything on Cumhuriyet Square. All 67 rooms here come with bath, and the prices reflect the place's status: doubles are 16,000TL ($22.40); singles, 11,000TL ($15.40).

The town's old faithful is the **Turan Oteli,** Turan Caddesi 8 (tel. 351/11-968), off 27 Mayıs Caddesi a few blocks southwest of the Citadel, or fortress. Five of the 70 rooms here come without bath, and you can get them for 5,000TL ($7) single, 8,000TL ($11.20) double; rooms with bath are 8,800TL ($12.30) single, 15,000TL ($21) double. The Turan has an elevator, someone who speaks English, and a rooftop restaurant with a splendid view of Erciyes—if you stand up to eat! They've built a plastic divider high around the wall, blocking the view, apparently because the neighbors complained of hotel guests peering down at them.

RESTAURANTS: For restaurants, 27 Mayıs Caddesi is again your best bet.

The **İskender Kebap Salonu,** across the street from the Divan Hotel at 27 Mayıs Caddesi no. 5 (second floor), has big windows overlooking the activity on the busy street below. It's a pleasant place, busy at lunch, and a big plate of döner kebap with melted butter and tomato sauce, with a soft drink, is only 1,600TL ($2.25). Recommended.

The **Divan Pastanesi,** on 27 Mayıs Caddesi at Mevlevi Caddesi, is a good place for a light breakfast at prices lower than those charged by hotels. Hot milk and sugar is always available, as are puddings, cookies, and various pastries. Try a serving of su böreği, a noodle-type dish made with white cheese.

THE SIGHTS: Kayseri is a strange town, with the early-morning activity including young girls in black dresses with white collars and knee socks going to school, but dominated by the sight of shrouded village women with bright baggy trousers called shalvar. The basic tone of the place is conservative; even in summer some women dress completely in black.

Another strange sight is the snow on the sides of Mount Erciyes, viewed while baking in the summer heat downtown—if that's any relief.

Kayseri is the sort of place where you can find out what it's like to be a celebrity, for everyone will notice your presence, smile at you, ask where you're from, or want to know if you need some help.

The Citadel

Start your sightseeing at the old **Citadel,** where there's now a **market.** Near the entrance look for the perfume seller, with a case of small bottles of every sort of scent imaginable, including oil pressed from rose petals. Pencils from Russia and Rumania are sold along with sacks of potatoes, dates, figs, and raisins. The market's most colorful section is the fruitsellers', a vine-covered area in the very middle of the market. On the street along the walls, walk into the shop at no. 62, go all the way through, and you'll find yourself at a stairway leading up to the top of the walls, where you can see the market and the town in company with the town's watchman, a tall and utterly dignified stork. Back down in the market, pass an ironmonger's shop to see the ugly, frightening collars made of iron, fastened around the necks of Anatolia's muscular sheepdogs to protect them from neck bites by wolves. In a nearby window are hundreds of orange and yellow bottles, slightly different shades of each color, filtering the sun through the liquid inside: it's cologne, made from lemon juice and used as a refresher all over the Middle East, especially in Turkey.

The Covered Market

An even older market is just down the street. Ask anyone for the **bedesten,** and you'll be shown the town's original covered market. Wend your way to the very center and you come to the meat market, in which the preparation as well as the selling of the meat is done. This is recommended only for those with strong stomachs. Past this are several old hans, two-story buildings built around a courtyard. Members of a certain guild come in from the country with their wares, sheepskins, leather, or whatever, store their goods and tether their animals in the stalls below, and sleep in the rooms above.

If you come across something to buy, remember that the Kayseri people have a reputation throughout all of Turkey for craftiness and hard bargaining. One story goes that a boy borrowed a donkey from his father, painted it, and sold it back to him for 100% profit.

Huant Hatun Mosque and Ethnographic Museum

Most of Kayseri's well-preserved historic buildings are near the Citadel, which was the center of the ancient city. The **Mosque of Huant Hatun** (Huant Hatun Camii) dates from the year 1228, when it was constructed for a lady named Huant Hatun, wife of the Seljuk Sultan Alaettin Keykubat. Huant Hatun is buried here.

Next to the mosque of Huant Hatun is another building in her mosque complex, a former religious seminary dating from 1237 which now houses the **Ethnographic Museum** (Etnoğrafya Müzesi), open from 8 a.m. to noon and 1 to 5:30 p.m.; admission costs 200TL (28¢). The marvelous old edifice conforms to the Seljuk canon for religious schools, plain and simple but very harmonious, with splashes of decoration here and there. The museum holds exhibits of weapons, articles and utensils from daily life, costumes, and home furnishings.

Other Buildings

Other buildings near Cumhuriyet Square include the **Sahibiye Seminary** (Sahibiye Medresesi), on the north side of the square. This religious school dates from 1267, and has an especially beautiful Seljuk doorway.

The **Kurşunlu Cami,** or Ahmet Paşa Camii, just west of the Sahibiye, dates from 1585, is Ottoman in style, and has a distinctive lead-clad dome.

Two other religious schools, the **Giyasiye** and **Şifaiye** medreses, are located in a maze of narrow back streets north of Atatürk Parkı and the Kurşunlu Cami. Ask for the "Çifte Medrese" ("Twin Seminaries"). The schools are right next to one another, and were built in 1206.

The **Ulu Cami** ("Great Mosque"), near Düvenönü Square, was under construction for almost a century, having been started by a Danishmendid Turkish emir of Kayseri, and completed by the conquering Seljuks. Construction lasted from 1135 till 1205. This accounts for a lack of harmony in the style.

The "Revolving Tomb"

The Seljuks built many tombs in an odd cylindrical or octagonal style. Kayseri's most famous of these is the **Döner Kümbet,** literally the "Revolving Tomb," built in 1276. Though it never really "revolved," it almost looks as though it might. To take a look at it, walk from the Citadel out Talas Caddesi about half a mile toward the Archeological Museum, and look for the tomb on the right-hand side of the street. The neighboring **Sırçalı Kümbet** is slightly later in construction, and was even fancier, having been covered in colored faïence.

Archeological Museum

Out past the Döner Kümbet, and to the left off Talas Caddesi, is the Archeological Museum, where you can examine finds from the early Hittite city of Kanesh (Kültepe), which lies close to Kayseri. Other displays include items from Kayseri's Hellenistic and Roman past. The museum is open from 8 a.m. to noon and 1 to 5:30 p.m.; closed Monday. The admission fee is 400TL (55¢).

An Excursion to the Sultan Han

If you have yet to explore a Seljuk caravanserai, take the opportunity to visit the Sultan Han, a beautifully restored "desert motel" on the outskirts of Kayseri. There may be a dolmush running out here from the Otogar, but if you want to make the trip quickly and comfortably, without having to worry about how you will return to the city, rent a taxi. The entire round trip might cost 3,500TL ($4.90) and take less than two hours. Settle on a price for the trip out, the half-hour wait, and the return trip, before you get in the car.

The Sultan Han is on the Sivas highway, 28 miles (45 km) northeast of downtown. Along the way, about 12 miles (19 km) out of town, there is a sign for the turnoff to **Kültepe** (Kanesh). You might want to stop and get the mood of this 4,000-year-old Hittite city, but don't expect much in the way of impressive ruins.

Admission to the Sultan Han supposedly costs 100TL (14¢), and visiting hours are 9 a.m. to 1 p.m. and 2 to 5 p.m. But what usually happens is that you'll arrive to find the gate locked, and soon after your arrival someone will appear with the key and a book of admission tickets. If the gate is locked, ask anyone nearby for the *anahtar* (key).

The Sultan Han was built in 1236 and was the last stopping place on the caravan route before the city of Kayseri. Caravans would enter the great front gate, pass through the open courtyard with its fine little *mescit* (prayer room), built on legs to raise it above the hubbub, and then bed down in the great covered hall (at least in bad weather).

Caravanserais had all the necessary services, including fodder for the beasts of burden, a treasury for storing precious items, a Turkish bath, repairmen, and servants.

For a good view of the entire building and the village, climb up to the roof by the stairway located to the right of the main gate as you enter.

5. The Underground Cities

I found the rock-pinnacled valleys of Cappadocia to be about as strange a sight as I'd hoped to see—until I saw the underground cities. The rock churches are only half of the whole picture in Cappadocia.

GETTING THERE: Take a dolmush from Ürgüp to Nevşehir and walk to the Belediye (Municipal) building to pick up a dolmush for Kaymaklı and Derinkuyu. These villages are about 15 miles south of Nevşehir. If you're short on time, you need only go as far as the first village with an underground city, called Kaymaklı. Actually, I prefer the city at Kaymaklı to the one at Derinkuyu, for it has more passages and is more complex.

KAYMAKLI: At Kaymaklı, a guide employed to watch over the city will turn on the lights for you, take your ticket (400TL, 55¢), and guide you down. At Derinkuyu, tours are organized by the Tourism Information Office next to the entrance. To find the entrance to the cities in either village, ask for the *yeraltı şehir,* although I'm sure the villagers will anticipate your question. Hours are 9 a.m. to noon and 1:30 to 6:30 p.m.

When I heard there were "underground cities" here, I pictured homes for a few families hollowed out of the rock. No such thing. Here there were full cities in every sense of the word, reaching down seven stories into the earth, cities which were inhabited by an estimated 60,000 people! So far the cities have only been cleaned out of the dirt of centuries and wired for electricity down to the third level. The first two levels are thought to have been begun by the Hittites, though most of the work was done by Byzantine Christians who retreated here to escape the fury of Arabic Muslim raids in the 7th century. Take a sweater and a flashlight, if you have them, and start down.

The guide at Kaymaklı will point out and explain (in sign language, with a few words of English) the communal kitchen (necessary because of the smoke-ventilation problem), stables, the massive round wheel-doors to close off the passage against enemies, a wine press complete with storage urn below, an old storage vat, a salt-pulverizing block, living quarters, and workshops. Finally the guide takes out a crumpled piece of newspaper he's brought with him, lights it, and drops it into one of the city's wells. Down, down, down it drops, the flame roaring as it passes through the still air in the well. A few hundred feet down it lands—finally. Some of the city wells, now partially filled in, are 400 feet deep. Near the well you'll be able to peer up one of the city's many ventilator shafts which ascend to hidden vents on the surface.

If there ever was a real labyrinth, it must have been this. Even with a guide it's possible to get lost; if you don't pay constant attention, you'll be in the position of having to follow the electric wires out of the cave rather than the mythical silver thread. Voice contact does little good. You're always within shouting distance of your party, but they may be a good distance away, or even on another floor. And so you wander around in what reminded me of nothing so much as the inside of a gigantic sponge, from room to room, through tunnel after tunnel.

The temperature underground seems quite low at first, and I wondered how people could bear it for years at a time. But the temperature is bearable, with the proper food and clothing, and is no colder in winter than it is in summer. Since the temperature is cool enough to keep food fresh, citizens of this strange place, troglodites, could store up enough for years on end if harvests allowed. If they ran out of food, they could borrow from the "neighbors" in the next city, for it's been found that there are several underground cities in Cappadocia, all connected by incredibly long tunnels.

DERİNKUYU: The city at Derinkuyu is the one most favored by the Ministry of Tourism, and recently many new excavations have been made, so that one can now go eight levels beneath the surface of the earth. The city is a bit better laid out and more regular than the one at Kaymaklı, and the "stories" are more easily distinguishable. There's a fine rock church (but with little painted decoration) about halfway down. Entry to the site is at the same times, and price, as at Kaymaklı.

6. Konya

So far Turkey has unveiled to you only a few suggestions of the artistic achievements of the Seljuk Turks. If these fragments have intrigued you at all, consider a trip to Konya, the central Anatolian city which was the capital of the Seljuk Empire. It was here that the order of "whirling dervishes," called Mevlevi, was founded by the great poet and mystic Celaleddin Rumi, called Mevlana. Konya was the home of this dervish sect for centuries until the sect was disbanded under the republic. The dervishes still whirl, however, once a year in December at a memorial service for Mevlana.

The city is still about the most religious in Turkey. Many women are veiled, Islamic law is observed by most of the townspeople, and the tomb of Mevlana has become a place of pilgrimage. The city is filled with old mosques, religious schools, and dervish convents, some of which have been turned into museums.

GETTING THERE: From Ankara, you could make the trip to Konya and back in a day if you got a very early bus (6 a.m. or so), ran around to see the sights, and took an evening bus back, but the bus trip, one way, takes four hours, so you'll probably want to stay overnight. There are frequent—if not hourly—buses from the Ankara Otogar costing 1,500TL ($2.10) one way.

ORIENTATION: To get your bearings in Konya, the first street you must get to know is **Alaettin Caddesi.** It stretches from the foot of the hill on which the old city stood, now the **Alaettin Park,** down through the center of town to the tekke, or dervish monastery, of Mevlana. Around the base of this hill and on its top are most of the important Seljuk buildings, except for the tekke. Halfway down the boulevard, in **Hükümet Square,** are most of Konya's hotel choices, as are a good number of the restaurants.

The bus pulls into Konya's new bus terminal, within view of the Alaettin hill, but slightly outside the center of town. Walk through the bus station to the other side in order to find taxis, buses, and dolmush minibuses. Catch a bus or minibus going to the Çarşı or **Konak,** and at the end of the short ride you'll be dropped in Hükümet Square.

Konya's **Tourism Information Office** is at Mevlana Caddesi 21 (tel. 331/11-074), across the square from the Mevlana Museum.

HOTELS: Two of Konya's best places to stay are right next to the bus station. As you will probably be spending only one night in Konya, consider staying here.

However, be advised that these places may be booked. Call in advance if you plan to arrive late in the afternoon in the height of the summer season.

Near the Bus Station

The 90-room **Özkaymak Park Oteli,** Otogar Karşısı (tel. 331/33-770), faces the bus station and provides a comfortable, though not luxurious, refuge for weary travelers. Each room has a private bathroom with shower and twin beds. Two elevators, a restaurant, and private parking are added services. The reception desk staff can be frosty, but don't let it bother you. Rooms are priced at 13,000TL ($18.20) single and 20,000TL ($28) double.

The other choice right by the bus station is considerably cheaper. It's the 33-room **Hotel Sema 2,** Otogar Yanı (tel. 331/32-557 or 30-138), fairly well used but still presentable (for the price) and utilitarian. Prices are the best part: 6,000TL ($8.40) for a double without bath, or 10,000TL ($14) for a double with bath; a bathless single costs 4,000TL ($5.60).

Downtown Hotels

Downtown Konya has mostly older hotels, fairly simple places but comfortable enough for a night, with everything you need for a short stay.

Find the Tourism Information Office, facing the Mevlana Museum across a large open square, and you will also have found the **Konya Oteli,** Turizm Ofisi Arkası (tel. 331/19-212 or 16-677), which is right behind it. The Konya Oteli is one of those older but serviceable places. Officially the price for a room with bath here is 9,000TL ($12.60) single, 14,000TL ($19.60) double, but if business is slack you can rent one for less.

The 40-room **Başak Palas,** Hükümet Alanı 3 (tel. 331/11-338), just off Alaettin Caddesi near the government buildings, is another older hotel, even simpler, where you walk up a flight of steps to reach the front desk, then continue to your room by elevator. Again it's simple and basic, but so is the price: bathless singles cost 4,500TL ($6.30); doubles with bath cost 10,000TL ($14).

The Starvation Budget

Konya is full of highly religious types, and this clerical atmosphere acts on its cheaper hostelries. You'll find no scenes of revelry here, nor will the proprietors welcome any from you, but you'll find many very inexpensive, very clean and tidy, very cheap places to stay, all over town. Some are in converted houses, others are in tiny hotels. Chances of finding a room with private bath, or an English-speaking owner, are slim; chances of finding a comfy bed with spotless sheets for only a few dollars are great.

Among the higher priced of Konya's budget offerings (believe it or not) is the **Saray Oteli,** Mevlana Caddesi 15 (tel. 331/19-990), near the Tourism Information Office. A single with private shower here costs 3,300TL ($4.60); a double, 5,500TL ($7.70). Watch out for street noise when you choose a room.

RESTAURANTS: Konya's restaurants, like its hotels, are serviceable though not at all fancy.

The restaurant which is most convenient to the center of town and the Mevlana Museum is the newish **Şifa Lokantası,** Mevlana Caddesi 30 (tel. 20-519), with a plain, modern dining room and quite decent food. A full lunch or dinner here, from the standard Turkish menu, will run you 1,500TL ($2.10) to 2,000TL ($2.80).

Even cheaper is the **Çatal Lokantası,** Turizm Ofisi Arkası (tel. 14-439), right next to the Konya Oteli behind the Tourism Information Office. Kebaps are the specialty, no alcohol is served, and a meal in the plain dining room costs only about 1,400TL ($1.95).

You can, of course, dine in your hotel. The **Özkaymak Park Oteli** has fairly good food in a slightly richer atmosphere, but at prices considerably higher than the aforementioned places.

THE SIGHTS: For your first look around town, climb to the top of the old city hill in the **Alaettin Park.** The Seljuk building taking up a good portion of the hilltop is the **Alaettin Camii,** famous as one of the finest surviving Seljuk mosques. Unfortunately, it is closed for renovation at this writing.

İnce Minare Museum

On the other side of the hill, directly opposite the end of Alaettin Caddesi, is a partially destroyed minaret and a grand, ornate doorway. This is the İnce Minare Museum, once a mosque, now one of Konya's most famous attractions. The decoration of the doorway takes some time to digest. Those wide bands of Arabic calligraphy running up the sides of the doorway and intertwining above can be found in the Seljuk works. This one was built in 1251 as a mosque and was used for worship until recently, when it became the town's museum for Seljuk wood and stone-carved works. The artifacts inside are of more than casual interest: there are bits of design from Seljuk buildings that have fallen to ruins, drawings of what the great Seljuk palace of the sultans looked like, some tombstones, and several examples of the wonderful eagle and double eagle motifs found often in Seljuk art. This, too, is closed temporarily for renovation.

Büyük Karatay Museum

Coming out of the museum, turn left and walk around the base of the hill. At the intersection of the Ankara road, the remains of a **Seljuk palace** are on the right—one large corner edge protected by a modernistic concrete shelter. On the left is the **Büyük Karatay Medrese,** a Seljuk religious school which is now, like the İnce Minare, a museum. It was built in the same year as the İnce Minare, but has a doorway different in both style and construction, this one made of marble. This museum is open from 8:30 a.m. to noon and 1:30 to 5:30 p.m. It costs 200TL (28¢) to enter, half price on weekends.

The Karatay Medrese was built by the Seljuk Turkish statesman Celaleddin Karatay, founder of a good number of other important Seljuk buildings. Karatay, who died in 1254 after serving three sultans, is buried in the medrese. You can see his tomb in the small room to the left and rear of the main hall.

The first thing you notice inside is the roof, decorated with the tiles the Turks made so beautifully. The graceful Arabic lettering forming a nonstop commentary around the roof draws its material from the Koran and the name of the first caliphs. All the different styles of pottery and tiles which the early Turks did are represented here. The medrese itself is as much a delight as the tilework: notice the pool in the center of the floor, and the drain designed to make the water draining off give out the pleasant sound which aids concentration and meditation. Be sure to see the display, in one of the side rooms, of the tiles brought from the ruins of another Seljuk palace, on the shores of Beyşehir Lake —they used to decorate the sultan's living quarters. Many of them have the same interesting edge designs as in the İnce Minare.

Other Seljuk Buildings

Ask around to find a street named Ressam Sami Sokak, on the south side of the Alaettin hill, and follow this narrow, winding street south to several other good examples of the Seljuk architects' art.

The **Sırçalı Medrese,** built in 1242, is now a museum for funerary monuments, better known as gravestones. Around its grand main door were designs in blue tilework which were said to resemble crystals, and the seminary took its common name (*sırça* is "crystal") from this. (The museum is closed for renovations at this writing, but you can still see a lot by peeking through the doorway.)

Next along Ressam Sami Sokak is the **Sahip Ata complex,** a group of buildings around a mosque dating from around 1283, and founded by Sahip Ata, the same man who built the İnce Minare Medrese. The Sahip Ata Medrese here is now set up as Konya's **Archeological Museum,** with statuary in the garden courtyard and exhibits in the building. Museum hours are 8:30 a.m. to noon and 1:30 to 5:30 p.m.; admission costs 400TL (55¢).

As you face the Sahip Ata complex, turn to the right, walk a block or two, and you'll reach the **Ethnographic Museum,** open at the same hours as the Archeological Museum, for 400TL (55¢).

Mevlana Museum

Now walk to the far end of Alaettin Caddesi to see the tekke of the whirling dervishes, Konya's most famous attraction. Officially, this is the Mevlana Museum, but most people in town remember it as the place where the dervishes once whirled, the same building in which the founder of the order is buried. It's open from 9 a.m. to noon and 1:30 to 5:30 p.m. every day during the summer; closed Monday at other times. Entrance is 150TL (21¢).

> *Whoever you may be, come*
> *Even though you may be*
> *An infidel, a pagan, or a fire-worshipper, come*
> *Our convent is not one of despair*
> *Even though you have broken*
> *Your vows of repentance a hundred times, come.*

This verse from Mevlana, posted on the wall of the museum, best describes the spirit of the order. Dervish orders, like monastic orders in Christianity, were not specifically set up in the holy book, but developed after the writing of such early documents. Mevlana was interested in communion with God, and expressed his theories on this subject in his poetic and philosophic works. His chosen method of communion was through music and the dance, in a context of Islam. The worship ceremony of his order is a mystical, dignified rite beginning with the dervishes, arms folded over their chests, passing before the sheik, or leader of the order, who whispers something—a passage from Mevlana's writings, perhaps—in each one's ear before the dervish begins to whirl. Slowly at first, then faster and faster, the arms unfolding, one hand palm up to receive the blessings from heaven, the other palm down to communicate them to earth, the dervishes go into a trance, their eyes half-closed, skirts billowing gracefully around them. As the individual dervishes turn, so does the entire group of dervishes. When one full revolution of the room has been made, the dancers sink to the floor and are covered with long robes to keep them warm. The whole ceremony is performed three complete times, after which prayers are offered for the dervish and the spectators, and the service ends. All through the ceremony you hear the voice of the special choir, and the orchestra, used only for this service. Besides the drums and chants of the choir, the most interesting thing about the music is the sound of the long, open pipe called a ney. It's a type of flute, but is extremely simple—just a long, straight hollow tube—but very difficult to play. The sound is low, mournful, breathy, and mysterious, a perfect vehicle for expressing the spirit of the ceremony.

You may hear ney music when you walk around the Mevlana Museum. The museum has several recordings of it, and the staff often plays them during the hours when the museum is open. With this mystic background, people kneel and say prayers before the tomb of Mevlana, covered by a magnificent 90-pound cloth made with thread of gold. The tombs of other leaders of the order, and of Mevlana's oldest son, are nearby. Other rooms display good collections of rugs, illuminated Korans, examples of Arabic calligraphy, and religious items.

Perhaps the two most interesting exhibits are the "April Rainwaters" basin and the silk prayer rug. The basin is a large object of bronze worked with gold and silver, very beautifully done. The first rains of April were looked upon as particularly healthful and holy, and used for all sorts of treatments. The prayer carpet is an exquisitely lovely work of art highly prized when it was made, and virtually priceless today. It is not large, but because of the fineness of its working has been estimated to contain about 3,000,000 individual knots (144 per square centimeter—and one of the prime gauges for quality in a rug is the high number of knots per square centimeter). The April basin is to the left shortly after you enter the main room of the building; the prayer carpet is in the first room to the left.

The dervishes used to whirl in this building. Though the yearly service now takes place in the Spor Salonu (Sports Hall), if you see the dervishes in action you realize they are not just performing a dance, but are worshipping just as their predecessors did. Likewise, the ancient tekke is now a museum, but it is still held sacred by Muslims around the world.

Unfortunately, the dervish ceremony only takes place in December, usually in the second week of that month. If you happen to be in Turkey at that time, you'll be able to get tickets to the performance easily, in Konya or from the Tourism Information Office in Ankara. Hotel rooms, however, are at a premium; most of them are reserved well before the week begins. If possible, write early in November to the Konya Tourism Information Office on Mevlana Caddesi to ask about rooms.

Other Things to See

There are other mosques and old buildings to see in town, but you might find a walk around the town just as interesting. Near the Mevlana Museum is a big open-air **bazaar,** dotted with mosques. I peeked into one during a reading of the Koran, and found a young schoolboy, in the uniform of his school complete with military-like cape, reciting from the Koran to groups of old men seated cross-legged on the floor. He was probably a student at a religious school as well, perhaps training to be a muezzin, the one who chants the call to prayer from the minaret five times a day, or perhaps even a hafiz, a man who has memorized the entire Koran.

The market can be a bustling place if you see it on the right day, when all of the people from the surrounding villages have brought their produce into town to sell. But on other days the entire town seems to be pervaded with an undefinable somber mood, lonely as the city is on the wide, flat ground of the Antolian plateau, kept company only by the spooky twin mountain peaks just outside the city. The twin peaks remind me of the tall conical hats of the dervishes, said to represent their tombstones.

If you have the time, the walk around town can turn up surprising things: a small Catholic church—in this bastion of Islam—and the bright, modern **Ordu Evi,** or Army House, a collection of work and entertainment facilities for Turkish army units stationed in Konya.

EASTERN TURKEY

A TOUR OF THE WILD, BEAUTIFUL EAST was a bold adventure only a decade or so ago, but with the building of good, new highways and hotels, the East is open to all.

Despite the "opening of the East," there are still many elements of adventure to an eastern tour, so you must plan ahead. In this chapter I'll explain what's involved on a tour through the wild and beautiful eastern portion of the country, and then lead you city by city on a circuit that includes the highlights of the Black Sea coast, the eastern plateau, and the Southeast.

1. An Eastern Tour

Planning your eastern tour involves four elements: when to go, what route to take, how to travel, and where to stay. Here's what you'll need to know on all four points.

WHEN TO GO: Unlike most parts of Turkey, the East has a visiting season limited by extremes of temperature. The problem is that different climatic zones in the East suffer extremes at different times of year.

Winters on the high eastern plateau (Erzurum, Ararat, Van, Nemrut Dağı), fenced in by lofty mountain ranges, are alpine in their intensity and severity. Heavy snow, blizzards, and temperatures well below freezing are normal. Spring and fall can be uncomfortably cold and windy as well, so the only time to tour the plateau comfortably is in high summer.

But the southeastern region (Diyarbakır, Mardin, Şanlıurfa, Gaziantep) is only pleasant in the spring and fall. In midsummer, temperatures regularly soar as high as 120°F!

As for the Black Sea, the climate there tends to be equable, fairly pleasant year round. However, it's rainy much of the year; the driest time is in midsummer.

Thus in planning your eastern tour you're faced with a choice: visit the

Black Sea and the plateau in high summer, when it's comfortable, and suffer from the heat when you get to the Southeast, or visit in the spring when the plateau is still wintry but the Southeast is pleasant.

PLANNING YOUR ROUTE: Your itinerary will depend on the sights you want to see, and when you go. Points of interest in the East seem to have arranged themselves in something of a circle, so it makes sense to travel thus. Start with a ride from Samsun to Trabzon along the Black Sea coast, then head up into the mountains to Erzurum. Make a side trip to Kars and Ani, then head for Doğubeyazıt for a look at Mount Ararat and the Ishak Pasha Palace. From Doğubeyazıt, catch a bus to Van. Take a side trip to Akdamar for a look at the wonderful Church of the Holy Cross, then continue your travels to Diyarbakır, city of massive medieval walls. Make a day-trip by minibus to ancient Mardin, near the Syrian border, then head for Şanlıurfa, the ancient city of Edessa. After Urfa (as it's often called), the next stop is Nemrut Dağı, the mountain with the fantastic colossal statues on top. From Nemrut Dağı you can head southwest to Antakya, Adana, and the Mediterranean coast, or due west to Cappadocia and Ankara.

You can, of course, follow this itinerary in reverse. If time is short, abandon the idea of doing the whole circuit by road and fly to one or two points from Ankara.

The entire circle can be done in a rental car in about two weeks, but you'll feel much more comfortable spending three weeks. By bus, plan on three weeks to see everything.

A warning: Don't fall into the trap of glancing at a map and thinking you can pour on the steam and do it all in a week or ten days. Eastern Turkey is vast, and the roads, though good, can be twisty and slow in the mountains. Don't expect to whiz at high speed along expressways out here.

TRANSPORTATION: In planning your eastern tour, you must consider all means of transport: rental car, bus, plane, train, and ship.

By Car

Perhaps the most convenient and independent way to see the East is in a rental car. Pick up the car in Ankara or Samsun, drive at a leisurely pace along the verdant Black Sea shore, then climb through the mountains up to the plateau. A rental car offers comfort and a free schedule, but it's perhaps the most expensive way to go. Total rental costs, including fees, insurance, and fuel, can easily reach the lofty realms of $500 or more for a two-week tour. You don't save any money by renting in Samsun and dropping the car in Adana, as there are hefty return fees.

By Bus

Seeing eastern Turkey by bus is fairly convenient and very, very cheap. With a little more time, and a willingness to put up with a bit of discomfort in order to have the full experience, you can tour the East in two or three weeks. To speed up your itinerary, and reduce the discomfort, mix your bus travel with the occasional flight or cruise: take the Istanbul–Trabzon boat, or fly from Istanbul or Ankara to Erzurum to begin your journey. At the end of your itinerary, fly from Malatya (near Nemrut Dağı) or Adana back to the western part of the country.

By Ship

Weekly ferryboats cruise from Istanbul eastward along the Black Sea coast to Trabzon, carrying cars as well as passengers. It's a pleasant and fairly fast way of traveling the length of the country. See the Black Sea section, below, for details.

By Plane

Turkish Airlines runs numerous flights from Istanbul and Ankara eastward. Unfortunately, there are virtually no flights from point to point in the East. To fly from Erzurum to Van, you must go via Ankara.

Here's an idea of flight frequency. The numbers in parentheses indicate how many flights are operated per week from Istanbul via Ankara: Diyarbakır (7), Erzurum (7), Malatya (5), Trabzon (7), and Van (5).

By Train

As with air travel, train routes tend to be from east to west rather than from north to south, which means that you can take a train from Ankara to get to Erzurum or Van, but not to go between Erzurum and Van. Trains in eastern Turkey tend to be slow, late, and fairly uncomfortable. Buses are always faster, more frequent, and more comfortable. Though a trip by bus can cost two or three times the train fare, I'm still talking about very small amounts of money here. For instance, if a train ticket costs $1, the comparable bus fare might be $2.25.

In general it's a good idea to forget about train travel when touring the East.

ACCOMMODATIONS: The best hotels in eastern Turkish cities often resemble moderately priced hotels in the western parts of the country. For $15 or $20 you can rent a double room with private shower and breakfast in a building with an elevator, restaurant, and lounge. But there are fewer of these hotels in eastern cities, and they can fill up with business travelers or tour groups. You might arrive in Şanlıurfa, or Erzurum, or Doğubeyazıt, to find the two or three best places in town full up. The rule, then, is to plan ahead and arrive in town by mid-afternoon (not late at night) if possible. Or have your hotel call ahead to the next city to locate a room. You can, if you like, write or call for reservations weeks or months in advance, but this is quite a hassle and isn't really necessary.

2. The Black Sea Coast

Turkey's Black Sea coast is a region apart, a lush, green, often rainy littoral backed by mountains. Though the history of the region is deep, its towns and cities have little to show for it. Samsun, for instance, presents a completely modern, commercial appearance. Trabzon, called Trebizond in ancient times, has much more to offer, including a fine Byzantine church, numerous other Byzantine buildings, and on the outskirts, a spellbinding monastery clinging to a sheer rock wall.

This is rich agricultural country. Turkey's best milk and butter come from the fat, sleek cattle which graze on the coast's lush greenery. Hazelnuts (filberts) are a mainstay of the economy, and are exported to yield millions of dollars in foreign exchange. Cherries have been cultivated here since olden times, and one city, Giresun, even has "cherry" *(kiraz)* at the root of its name. Also, and perhaps most important, the eastern end of the coast is covered in tea plantations. Virtually every glass of *çay* you drink in Turkey was born of the leaves grown on steep hillsides in the humid air east of Trabzon.

GETTING THERE: The Black Sea coast between Istanbul and Samsun is somewhat difficult of access. There is no fast, beautiful coastal highway except the traditional one of the sea. Thus a land-based tour of the coast best begins in

Samsun, which has frequent bus service from Ankara and other points. From Samsun, the ride eastward 224 miles (360 km) to Trabzon is easy and beautiful.

Getting to Samsun is easy, no matter how you choose to travel. Turkish Airlines runs three flights per week from Istanbul, and also three from Ankara. If you plan to go by bus, catch one at Ankara's Otogar for the 260-mile (420-km) trip, which will take six or seven hours.

Cruising the Coast

Among the most enjoyable ways of getting from Istanbul to Samsun or Trabzon is aboard the weekly Turkish Maritime Lines car-ferry. The ship leaves Istanbul each Monday evening, arrives in Samsun on Tuesday evening, and departs a few hours later to arrive in Trabzon Wednesday morning. Departure from Trabzon for the return trip is late Wednesday evening. You dock in Samsun on Thursday morning, stopping for only about 90 minutes before casting off for the final leg of the journey to Istanbul, arriving Friday at noontime. There's not much point in making a round trip, but you might well take the opportunity for this "mini-cruise" one way.

The price for a reclining aircraft-type Pullman seat, from Istanbul to Samsun, is 7,200TL ($10.10); from Istanbul to Trabzon, it's 8,500TL ($11.90). Prices for cabins range from 10,000TL ($14) to 25,700TL ($36) per person from Istanbul to Samsun, or from 10,700TL ($15) to 34,300TL ($48) per person from Istanbul to Trabzon, depending on the number of berths, whether you want a private shower, and placement of the cabin (some locations are choicer than others). You buy your meals (not included in these prices) in the ship's dining room, or in port, as you like.

The ferry takes cars, of course, at a cost of 22,150TL ($31) from Istanbul to Samsun, or 29,300TL ($41) from Istanbul to Trabzon.

SAMSUN: This is the largest city on the Black Sea coast, a major commercial port and industrial center. Though there has been a city here for several millennia, the city you will visit is completely modern. The life of the old city ended in the 1400s, when Genoese forces attacked and burned it to the ground. It was not rebuilt until modern times.

Orientation

Coming by bus, you will land at Samsun's **Otogar,** less than a mile east of downtown. City buses heading westward along the coast road will bring you into town.

Samsun's main commercial thoroughfare, with hotels, banks, restaurants, and the post office, is named **Kazım Paşa Caddesi,** also sometimes called **Bankalar Caddesi.** It's one block inland from the coast road.

The **Turkish Airlines office** in Samsun is at Kazım Paşa Caddesi 11/A (tel. 361/18-260 or 13-455). The airport bus (200TL, 28¢) provides transportation to and from flights.

Hotels

As there is little to see in the way of sights here, your prime purpose for visiting Samsun may well be to find a decent bed for the night. That's not a difficult task, as the city's commercial life demands that there be many good, moderately priced hotel rooms available.

The best in town is the 117-room **Turban Büyük Samsun Oteli,** Sahil Caddesi, Samsun 55002 (tel. 361/10-750), between the coast road and the sea, right downtown. The entire hotel is air-conditioned, and offers a swimming pool as a way to further beat the heat. The very comfortable rooms go for 14,250TL ($19.95) to 16,000TL ($22.40) single, or 19,000TL ($26.60) to 21,500TL ($30.10) double, with bath, breakfast included.

On the aforementioned commercial thoroughfare is the smaller, more modest, but still modern and comfy **Hotel Burç**, Kazım Paşa Caddesi 36 (tel. 361/15-479), with 38 bath-equipped rooms priced at 10,000TL ($14) double.

For a look at an alternative, find the larger (65-room) **Vidinli Oteli**, Kazım Paşa Caddesi 4 (tel. 361/16-050), where all the rooms have private showers and cost 9,000TL ($12.60) to 10,000TL ($14) double.

Should you want merely to bed down between bus trips, the 44-room **Terminal Oteli**, Samsun Otogar (tel. 361/15-519), is right in the Otogar itself. As with most bus terminal hotels, it tends to be well used but it will do for a night, and the price of a room with bath certainly won't break you: 7,000TL ($9.80) double.

EASTWARD TO TRABZON: The journey eastward to Trabzon can be done in a day, by either bus or car. Here are some of the spots you'll pass along the way:

Ünye

This small port town is in the midst of the rich hazelnut-growing region of the coast. Most local people make their living raising, harvesting, and preparing the flavorful nuts, and in fact the entire economy is based on hazelnut culture. For instance, local people buy huge sacks of hazelnut shells and use them as home heating fuel instead of wood, coal, oil, or gas. The Turkish word for hazelnut is *fındık,* by the way. You'll see them on sale, taken from the shell and ready to eat, in shops and bus stations, for the unbeatable price of about $1 or $2 per pound.

Another local crop is tobacco. The leaf raised here tends to give a strong, full flavor.

Ordu

About 44 miles (70 km) east of Ünye lies Ordu. The name means "army," but the town is known for crops of hazelnuts and tobacco, and as a fishing port. There are some nice old houses here.

Giresun

Though mostly modern in appearance, Giresun is a very old town, founded some 3,000 years ago. Fishing has always been important, but the Romans added cherry orchards to the economy, and they still flourish and provide all of Turkey with their fresh fruit *(kiraz).* The Turkish word for cherry, as well as the town's modern name, are both derived from the town's Roman name, Cerasus.

Should you want to break your trip, this is the place to do it. Stay at the **Giresun Oteli**, Atatürk Bulvarı (tel. 0511/2469 or 3017), a small but modern and presentable hotel on the shore road, one block from the Belediye Sarayı (City Hall). They'll charge you 4,800TL ($6.70) single, 6,600TL ($9.25) double, for a room with bath. In your spare moments take a look at the ruins of the medieval castle here.

When you're back on the road heading eastward, you'll have 93 miles (150 km) to cover in order to reach Trabzon.

TRABZON: The fabled port of Trebizond, once a far outpost of trade made lively by intrigues among magnates, consuls, ship captains, spies, and pretenders to royalty, is now a fairly quiet Turkish port city involved in the transshipment of goods from Black Sea ships to Iran. Much of the city is perched on a promontory above the harbor. Its streets, paved in stone blocks, and its numerous old buildings, make Trabzon an enjoyable walking town, even though the sky here is often overcast.

Orientation

Coming by ship, you'll arrive in Trabzon's harbor, at the foot of the promontory. By plane or bus, you end up several miles east of the port, on the shore. Take a taxi or dolmush to reach **Taksim Square,** the heart of the city, up on the promontory. This is where you'll find most of the city's hotels and restaurants, and also the **Tourism Information Office,** Taksim Caddesi 31 (tel. 031/12-722). The **Turkish Airlines office** is at Kemerkaya Mahallesi, Meydan Parkı Karşışı (tel. 031/13-446 or 11-680), not far out of Taksim, to the west. The airport bus costs 200TL (28¢).

Hotels

Trabzon has no very fancy hotels, only a few of those comfortable-but-simple places.

Perhaps the most comfortable hotel in town is the 45-room **Hotel Özgür,** Taksim Caddesi, Trabzon 61100 (tel. 031/11-319 or 12-778), overlooking the main square (a few of the rooms have minuscule balconies). The hotel has a restaurant and a breakfast room, and quite presentable guest rooms with bath which go for 8,500TL ($11.90) single, 11,500TL ($16.10) double, 14,000TL ($19.60) triple. Over half the rooms here have twin beds; ten have single beds, five are triples, and five are junior suites.

Another place to look is the 72-room **Hotel Usta,** Telgrafhane Sokak 3, Trabzon 61100 (tel. 031/12-843 or 12-195), facing the main square, Taksim. When the guest rooms here are not filled by members of a visiting tour group, you can have one, with bath, for 7,000TL ($9.80) single, 11,000TL ($15.40) double, with bath.

Even cheaper is the 42-room **Otel Horon,** Sıra Mağazalar 125, Trabzon 61100 (tel. 031/11-199 or 12-289), also on Taksim Square. Rooms here come with either washbasin, or bathroom with shower, and one, two, or three beds. Prices reflect the conveniences: you pay 4,300TL ($6) to 5,700TL ($8) single, 6,400TL ($8.95) to 8,500TL ($11.90) double, the lower price being for a room with washbasin, the higher with shower or bath. A triple-bedded room with shower costs 10,000TL ($14).

At the eastern end of Taksim, up the hill behind the İskender Paşa mosque, is the little **Benli Palas Oteli,** İskender Paşa Mahallesi, Cami Çıkmazı Sokak 5, Trabzon 61100 (tel. 031/11-022 or 11-750). Plain and somewhat old-fashioned, with 42 severely bare rooms, the Benli offers such unexpected luxuries as views of the sea (from some rooms) and private showers (most rooms have only washbasins, however). Prices are 1,500TL ($2.10) to 1,750TL ($2.45) single, 3,000TL ($4.20) to 3,500TL ($4.90) double, 4,500TL ($6.30) to 5,250TL ($7.35) triple; the higher prices are for the rooms with showers.

Restaurants

Trabzon is not busting out with restaurants, and you will probably find yourself having lunch and dinner at one of the principal hotels. But a stroll around Taksim will reveal a few alternative places, such as the **Meydan Kebap ve Yemek Lokantası,** opposite the statue of Atatürk in the square, and the **Kuyu**

Restaurant, which is one of the few places to serve alcoholic beverages. The **Gaziantep Kebapçısı & Baklavacısı** is the place to go for an inexpensive plate of kebap followed by a portion of Turkey's favorite dessert.

Trabzon's Sights

For most of Trabzon's sights you must catch a bus or dolmush, or take a taxi. But first let's start with a walk around town.

A Walking Tour: Start from Taksim Square and head west along **Uzun Yolu,** the "Long Road" which meanders from Taksim through the oldest parts of the city to the Citadel. Along the way you will pass, on your right, the **Basilica of St. Anne** (Küçük Ayvasıl Kilisesi), which dates from the 800s.

Cross over a gorge, turn left onto Kale Sokak, and make your way to the **Citadel** (Kale), where you'll find the 10th-century **Church of Panaghia Chryso- kephalos,** converted later to become the Ortahisar Camii.

Aya Sofya Church: Two miles west of Taksim Square, standing above the coastal highway on a hill, is the 13th-century **Church of the Holy Wisdom (Aya Sofya Kilisesi),** now a museum. Compared to most other Byzantine churches existing in Turkey, this one is very late, and a careful observer will notice ele- ments of Seljuk architectural style and decoration here and there. Trabzon was an outpost of the Byzantine Empire. It held out against Turkish conquest longer than most other Byzantine cities, and it retained its Roman-Greek ambience long into Ottoman times. The church is a vivid symbol of this survival. Note the fine wall paintings, mosaic floors, and the church's fine bell tower.

Atatürk's Villa: On the outskirts of Trabzon is a white gingerbread villa which was given to modern Turkey's founder and first president as a vacation getaway spot. In fact it was more of a ceremonial residence, not used much by the great leader, but nonetheless beautiful for all that. As a turn-of-the-century Black Sea Victorian period piece, it can't be beat.

The best way to get to the villa, called the Atatürk Köşkü in Turkish, is by taxi, but there are also occasional city buses from Taksim.

A Side Trip to Sumela Monastery

No one should come to Trabzon and leave without visiting the famous Monastery of Sumela, which clings improbably and dramatically to a mist- shrouded rock cliff in the wild mountains south of the city.

Start your excursion with a visit to the Tourism Information Office on Tak- sim Square. Ask about buses and dolmushes. In high summer on weekends there are often enough prospective visitors to warrant a bus run. If so, buses depart after breakfast and charge 500TL (70¢) for the round trip to Sumela. If business is slack the Tourism Information Office will help you to find a taxi to operate as a dolmush. Fill all the seats in the car and the charge will be about 2,500TL ($3.50) per person for round-trip transportation, plus a two-hour wait at the site.

Note that the monastery is open only from 8:30 a.m. to noon and then from 2 to 5 p.m. These times may be a bit flexible, but don't chance it. Since you must hike for the better part of an hour after you travel the 33 miles (54 km) to the site, you must arrive at the site before 10 a.m., or before 3 p.m., if you are to have a worthwhile visit. The optimum schedule might be this: depart Trabzon at 9 a.m., reach the site by 10 a.m., and hike to the monastery, arriving before 11 a.m. After an hour's exploration (perhaps only a half hour), hike back down and enjoy a picnic lunch before heading back to town. Or leave Trabzon after lunch (1 p.m.) to arrive at the site by 2 p.m. Hike to the monastery, arriving at the top before 3 p.m. Whatever you do, don't arrive at Sumela just after 11 a.m. and rush up the steep slope just in time to see the caretaker walk away for his two-hour lunch break!

The trip to Sumela begins by leaving Trabzon along the highway to Erzurum. At Maçka, 19 miles (31 km) from Trabzon, turn left onto the road for Sumela, or Meryem Ana (meaning the Monastery of the Virgin Mary). After climbing up the slopes for another 14 miles (23 km) you'll come to the "base station," deep in cool pine forests by a rushing mountain brook.

From the base station, which has a snack stand and a picnic area, you must hike up the steep slope through the forest to the monastery itself. Allow a half hour for the hike if you're in good shape, 45 minutes if you're out of shape, and an hour if you're not much of a hiker. At the end of the hike you'll be more than 800 feet above the base station.

Arriving at the monastery, huffing and puffing, you'll be greeted by a caretaker seated at a small table, selling admission tickets for 500TL (70¢).

After paying the admission fee, you are in Sumela, an eerie aerie begun during Roman times in the 6th century, about the time that Justinian was building the great church of Sancta Sophia in Constantinople. Monks lived at Sumela through the end of the later Roman and Byzantine periods, through Ottoman times, and up to the founding of the Turkish republic in 1923. At that time, with the Ottoman Empire crumbling, there was a movement to revive a Greek Orthodox Kingdom of Pontus, with Trabzon as its capital and Russia as its protector. But the movement failed, the Turkish republic gained control, and many supporters of the kingdom scheme, including the monks of Sumela, left for good.

The monastery is a warren of little cells, chapels, workrooms, and common spaces, with decoration dating from various periods of its long history. There are some good mosaics and gilded paintings, but much had been damaged by neglect and carelessness before it was protected by the government and preserved from further deterioration. If you are subject to acrophobia (fear of heights), watch your step here, as there are many steep drops and frightening vistas.

3. Erzurum, Kars, and Ani

Capital of the eastern plateau, control center for defense of Turkey's eastern frontier, transportation point from north to south and east to west, and cultural fount for the wild territories surrounding it, Erzurum is actually two cities in one.

The first Erzurum is an old city of winding, narrow streets dominated by the high walls of a citadel which is centuries old. The Byzantines founded Erzurum, which they called Theodosiopolis, on the site of an even earlier city, and people have been living here in numbers, on this lonely plateau, ever since.

The second Erzurum is the modern city which has grown up around the old, a tidy, orderly, sprawling assemblage of wide tree-lined boulevards, university buildings, and military barracks.

Guarding the eastern approaches to Anatolia, the land bridge between Europe and Asia, Erzurum has always been an important military post and garrison town. The Seljuks used it as such, and built a good number of fine public buildings which survive, and which are one of the main reasons for visiting this city.

GETTING THERE: As Erzurum has such strategic importance, access is easy, frequent, and convenient, no matter what your means of travel.

By Bus

You can get a direct bus to Erzurum from almost any part of the country, but be prepared for a fairly lengthy ride. Erzurum is, as they say, equally inaccessible from all parts of the country.

To give you an idea of what you're in for, here are some sample travel times and fares: from Ankara, 14 or 15 hours, 5,500TL ($7.70); from Diyarbakır, 11 hours, 4,000TL ($5.60); from Doğubeyazıt, 4½ hours, 2,000TL ($2.80); from Istanbul, 20 or 21 hours, 8,000TL ($11.20); from Kars, 3½ hours, 1,500TL ($2.10); from Trabzon, eight hours, 3,700TL ($5.20); from Van, seven or eight hours, 3,500TL ($4.90).

By Car

Assuming that you are following the itinerary of this chapter and coming from Trabzon, head out of town on Hwy. E-390 toward Gümüşhane, Bayburt, Aşkale, and Erzurum. The road is twisty and mountainous for much of the way, and fairly slow going. The distance to Erzurum is just over 200 miles (325 km).

By Air

Turkish Airlines, 100. Yıl Caddesi, SSK Rant Tesisleri 24 (tel. 011/18-530 or 11-904) in Erzurum, runs daily flights from Istanbul via Ankara to Erzurum. The fare for the one-hour flight from Ankara is 30,000TL ($42).

By Train

Two express trains connect Ankara with Erzurum. Neither one would be called a delight to ride, but if you're an inveterate train buff with lots of time, climb aboard either the **Eastern Express** *(Doğu Ekspresi),* departing Ankara at 10:40 a.m. daily, or the **Soldier's Express** *(Mehmetçik Ekspresi),* departing at 5:15 p.m. Don't expect either of these trains to depart or arrive on time. They are often hours late coming in from Istanbul. The journey, as scheduled, takes over 24 hours, but may in fact be longer. A first-class ticket from Ankara to Erzurum costs 3,300TL ($4.60).

The most comfortable way to travel is in a sleeping compartment, which I recommend that you do, even though it will raise the price of your ticket up to the realms of air fare. Only the *Eastern Express* hauls sleeping cars. Both trains haul first- and second-class coaches and dining cars.

ORIENTATION: During most of your visit you can walk from place to place or take the occasional taxi ride. Upon arrival, however, you should know what your options are.

Arrival

Erzurum's central bus station, or **Otogar,** is several miles out of town on the road to the airport. Municipal bus no. 2 stops in front of the station, and will carry you right to the center of town for 50TL (7¢).

When you plan to leave Erzurum by bus, note that many bus companies maintain little ticket offices downtown, not far from the train station and the bazaar, at the southern end of İstasyon Caddesi, facing Gürcü Kapı Square.

The **airport** is six miles from downtown. The airport bus departs after each flight, charges 400TL (55¢) for the ride, and stops at both the Otogar and the Otel Oral (see below) on the ride into town. If you miss the bus you'll have to pay about 2,000TL ($2.80) for a taxi ride to the center, less if you're only going as far as the Otel Oral.

If you're flying from Erzurum you can catch the airport bus from Turkish Airlines' air terminal near the western end of Kazım Karabekir Caddesi. It leaves for the airport 105 minutes before flight time. If you take a taxi, be at the airport at least 30 minutes before flight time.

The **train station,** or Erzurum Garı, is at the northern end of İstasyon Caddesi, north of the bazaar about 400 yards. You can walk from the station to several hotels, but not to the Otel Oral. City buses trundle by the station every half hour or so, and will take you to the main commercial district. A taxi from the station to almost any point in town costs about 700TL ($1).

Getting Around

You can walk to almost everything downtown, except the popular Otel Oral, which is on the outskirts of town about half a mile from the bus station. Erzurum's main downtown boulevard is **Cumhuriyet Caddesi,** but the western end of the boulevard has a different name, **Cemal Gürsel Caddesi.** Where the name-change occurs there is a large traffic circle with a big statue of Atatürk, a pool, and a fountain. This circle is called **Havuzbaşı** ("At the Pool"), and is a convenient point of reference to get your bearings downtown.

Tourism Information

The **Tourism Information Office,** Cemal Gürsel Caddesi (tel. 011/15-697 or 19-127), is on the south side of the main street one block west of Havuzbaşı.

HOTELS: Most of Erzurum's hotel rooms are rock-bottom class. Some hotels have no bathing facilities in the entire hotel, let alone private baths in the rooms. However, there are a number of much more comfortable places. Prices for even the best hotel in town are surprisingly low.

Generally acknowledged to be the best place in town is the 90-room **Otel Oral,** Terminal Caddesi 3 (tel. 011/19-740), only about a half mile from the bus station, on the road into town from the airport. The Oral has many advantages: comfortable rooms with private showers, a friendly and helpful staff, and a decent dining room which attracts most of the foreign travelers visiting the city. But there are several disadvantages you should know about. The hotel is inconveniently located on the outskirts, which means you may end up taking taxis in and out of town. This isn't a great expense, just slightly inconvenient. Also, the hotel's location on the main street out of town means that there's a good deal of noise from trucks. In the warm months, when you may want to have the windows open, ask for a room on the rear side of the hotel, away from the noise. Prices for the tidy rooms, all of which have showers and telephones, are 8,535TL ($12.55) single, 10,665TL ($15.70) double.

Most tourists stay at the Oral. Erzurum's other hotels, downtown, are much more basic, but will do quite well if you are watching your budget carefully and don't mind a bit less snazz in exchange for a convenient downtown location.

Best of the rest is the 36-room **Hotel Sefer,** İstasyon Caddesi at Aşağı Mumcu Square (tel. 011/13-615 or 16-714). Though hardly fancy, it's sufficiently comfortable, especially at a price of 4,400TL ($6.15) single, 6,600TL ($9.25) double, for rooms with bath, located only blocks from the train station or Cumhuriyet Caddesi, right at the edge of the bazaar.

You might also want to look at two modest places just off Cumhuriyet Caddesi in the center of town. The 51-room **Kral Hotel,** Erzincankapı 18 (tel. 011/16-973 or 11-930), is right across Cumhuriyet Caddesi from the Yakutiye Medresesi (see below). The hotel has obviously seen long, hard years of service, but to compensate for the worn furniture, the staff tries to be particularly friendly. Rooms here have showers, and prices of 4,400TL ($6.15) single, 5,500TL ($7.70) double, 6,600TL ($9.25) triple.

The smaller, 32-room **Akçay Otel,** Cumhuriyet Caddesi 1 (tel. 011/17-330), has similarly "experienced" rooms, at identical prices. To find this place, look for a tiny side street (Kamil Ağa Sokak) running south off Cumhuriyet Caddesi opposite the Yakutiye Medresesi and the Lala Mustafa Paşa Camii.

The Starvation Budget

Should you want to find lodging for prices even lower than those surprisingly low prices noted above, make your way to **Kazım Karabekir Caddesi,** which runs from the Turkish Airlines air terminal to Aşağı Mumcu Square, near the bazaar. The street is more or less parallel to, and near, İstasyon Caddesi. Being near the train station, Kazım Karabekir Caddesi is lined with simple, inexpensive hotels. Four of these are among the more presentable ones.

The **Hitit Otel,** Kazım Karabekir Caddesi 26 (tel. 011/11-204), is at the southern end of the street, near the bazaar. The price for one of its 32 older, simple rooms is 2,700TL ($3.80) for a single with bath, 3,000TL ($4.20) for a double without bath, 3,400TL ($4.75) for a double with bath. It's one of the better places on the street.

Next door to the Hitit is the 35-room **Örnek Otel,** Kazım Karabekir Caddesi 24 (tel. 011/11-203), which offers similar accommodations at virtually identical prices.

The 55-room **Otel Şan,** Kazım Karabekir Caddesi 8 (tel. 011/15-789), is perhaps the snazziest of these low-budget places. It has the feeling of a real hotel, even though the price for one of its 55 rooms is incredibly modest: 3,000TL ($4.20) for a single with bath, 3,400TL ($4.75) for a similar double.

The 60-room **Otel Polat,** Kazım Karabekir Caddesi 4 (tel. 011/11-623), the last place to consider along this street, is fairly sympathetic, with a family atmosphere, an elevator, and rooms with bath for 4,400TL ($6.15) single, 5,500TL ($7.70) double, 6,600TL ($9.25) triple.

RESTAURANTS: Once you have walked up and down Cumhuriyet Caddesi in the heart of town a few times, you will have located all of Erzurum's presentable restaurants except for the dining room of the Otel Oral. The food at these downtown eateries is extremely tasty, the decor is usually pleasant, and the prices are unbeatable.

The **Salon Çağın,** Cumhuriyet Caddesi (tel. 011/19-320), not far from the traffic circle near the Yakutiye Medresesi, on the south side of Cumhuriyet, is clean and bright. The steam tables are laden with goodies at both lunch and dinner, and a three-course meal of soup, main course (a stew or kebap), and dessert need cost only 1,200TL ($1.70).

The **Güzelyurt Restorant,** Cumhuriyet Caddesi (tel. 011/11-514), is about the same in terms of pleasantness, convenience, and quality, with similar prices —all of which are set by the municipal government, by the way. Main meat courses are priced at 600TL (85¢) or 700TL ($1), so a full meal for $2 or under is a simple accomplishment.

A WALKING TOUR: You can easily walk to all of Erzurum's sights, which consist mostly of beautiful old Seljuk religious buildings. After you've visited these, wander through the old part of town and its lively bazaar.

Start your tour at the eastern end of Cumhuriyet Caddesi with Erzurum's most famous landmark.

Seminary of Twin Minarets

The Çifte Minareli Medrese dates from 1253, the height of Seljuk Turkish power and influence in Anatolia, when it was built under the auspices of Sultan

Alaettin Keykubat II. Walk beneath the twin minarets and visit the seminary any day, during daylight hours, for free.

The harmonious main courtyard has four great niches, or *eyvan*s. On both sides of the courtyard are students' cells, both at ground level and one flight up (stairways are in the corners of the court). Behind the southern eyvan is a unique feature, not found in other seminaries. It's the **Tomb of Huant Hatun** (Hatuniye Türbesi), the daughter of Sultan Alaettin Keykubat II, a 12-sided room with a crypt beneath it.

Great Mosque

Right next door to the Çifte Minareli Medrese, to the west, is the Great Mosque (Ulu Cami), built in 1179 by a pre-Seljuk ruler of Erzurum, a Saltuklu Turkish emir. The outside of the mosque is severely plain, with just high walls of limestone blocks. Inside is a simple forest of columns, with the only outstanding architectural features being a stalactite-decorated dome, another wooden dome, and two bull's-eye windows above the mihrab.

Seljuk Tombs

Perhaps you remember seeing Kayseri's famous Döner Kümbet tomb. If so, you'll see a lot of similarities in Erzurum's "Three Tombs" (Üç Kümbetler). Walk south between the Twin Minaret Seminary and the Great Mosque. When you come to a "T" intersection, turn left, then right (there are some signs), and walk a short block up the hill to the tombs, which date from the 1100s.

The Citadel

North of the Twin Minaret Seminary, across Cumhuriyet Caddesi and a block up the hill, Erzurum's ancient Citadel (Kale) overlooks much of the town. The Romans (Byzantines) under Theodosius started it when they founded Theodosiopolis in about A.D. 400, and later occupants strengthened and expanded it. As you enter, you'll pass a **Clock Tower** (Saat Kulesi), topped by a Turkish flag, which was a minaret in the time of the Saltuklu Turks (they who built the Great Mosque). There's little to see inside the citadel walls except a scattering of old cannons with Russian and Ottoman Turkish inscriptions.

Along Cumhuriyet Caddesi

As you walk back to the center of town along Cumhuriyet Caddesi to continue your tour, you pass several small Ottoman mosques, including the **Caferiye Camii,** which dates from 1645.

Shortly after passing the mosque you come to a major intersection. Erzurum's provincial government headquarters and city hall are here, and you may well see the governor's sleek black car with red license plate parked out front. Cross the street, still on Cumhuriyet, and the building on your right is the **Lala Mustafa Paşa Camii,** put up in 1563 by a grand vizier during the Golden Age of the Ottoman Empire.

Yakutiye Seminary

West of the Lala Mustafa Paşa Camii is the **Yakutiye Medresesi,** which is one of Erzurum's most interesting old buildings because it was built by the invading Mongols in 1310, after they swept into Anatolia from the East. The Mongols, a nomadic people, did not normally have much use for stone buildings, but a local Mongol warlord set himself up here as emir and copied many elements of the Seljuk style. He built himself a tomb behind the school, but somehow never ended up occupying it.

Unfortunately, the interior of the seminary has yet to be restored, so it is not now open to visitors.

Erzurum Museum

Continue westward along Cumhuriyet Caddesi, and at Havuzbaşı, turn left and walk up the tree-lined boulevard to reach the **Erzurum Müzesi** (tel. 11406). The museum is just before the next intersection, on the left (east) side of the street, and the walk here from the Yakutiye will take 10 or 15 minutes. You can visit anytime from 8 a.m. to noon and 1:30 to 5:30 p.m.; admission costs 400TL (55¢), half price on Saturday and Sunday, closed Monday.

Though Erzurum has had a long history, and though many relics of its ancient past are preserved in this simple, modern museum, the most fascinating displays are the ethnographic ones. Look for the exhibits of carpets and kilims, old costumes, tools, and home furnishings. Don't neglect the upstairs exhibition rooms, which hold displays primarily of old weapons and coins.

Strolling Through the Bazaar

Walk back to the main intersection with the provincial government headquarters, then head north from the Lala Mustafa Paşa Camii into the narrow streets of the bazaar. It's impossible to direct you here, but you needn't get hopelessly lost. If in doubt, as for İstasyon Caddesi, at the northern end of the bazaar, or the Lala Mustafa Paşa Camii. As people point the way to these places, you'll easily find your way out of the labyrinth.

Within this bazaar you see more than the normal amount of traditional craftwork: tinsmiths are busy fashioning little grills and samovars from bright metal, ironmongers retrieve unwanted scrap, and in an ancient caravanserai, artisans carve a light black mineral substance called *oltutaş* into Muslim rosaries *(tespih)*. There is a small fruit-and-vegetable market in the bazaar too.

AN EXCURSION TO KARS AND ANİ: Unfortunately, it is difficult to make a day excursion to Kars and Ani from Erzurum due to the distance involved and the necessity of obtaining official permission before visiting the ruins at Ani. This is unfortunate because the lodging situation in Kars could hardly be worse. At the end of the road and rail line, on a dead-end route to the Soviet border, Kars is little more than a military outpost and farming town. It gets few visitors, touristic or commercial, and so it's difficult for hotels to maintain high standards of comfort.

But the trip is definitely worth considering, as Kars is a very untypical Turkish town, and the ruins of ancient Ani, capital of a short-lived Armenian kingdom in the 1200s, are simply fascinating. If you have your own car you can in fact do the trip in one long day. By bus it's possible, but you should perhaps be prepared to stay overnight in Kars.

Getting There

It's 124 miles (200 km) from Erzurum to Kars, and the trip by bus takes about 3½ or 4 hours. Fare is 1,000TL ($1.40) to 1,500TL ($2.10), depending on the company you ride.

Orientation

When you alight from your bus you will notice the 36-room **Yılmaz Oteli** (tel. 0211/1074 or 2387) right next to the bus station. As of this writing, the Yılmaz is the one suitable place to stay and dine in Kars. Check out the room situation as soon as you arrive. The price for a double room with bath is 6,300TL ($8.80).

Upon leaving the Yılmaz and wandering around town a bit, you will see that Kars is laid out on a street grid, and that it has lots of Russian-style buildings. This region was in fact captured and held by the Russians for a period of 50 years, but control reverted to the Turks in 1920. The **fortress** (Kars Kalesi) dominating the town was greatly rebuilt as recently as 1855, and is still used in defense of this highly vulnerable town. It is off-limits to visitors.

Kars does not have a Tourism Information Office of its own. For help with any question or problem, contact the museum (see below).

What to See and Do

Kars has a large number of government personnel, including clerks, policemen, soldiers, and inspectors. All are posted here from other parts of Turkey, and all of them have about the same opinion of what to do in Kars: get out of town. The climate here is usually chilly and cold, the accommodations poor, the food worse. But before you get out of town, heading for Ani, you should do several things.

The first place to visit is the town's nice, modern **Kars Museum** (Kars Müzesi), open from 8 a.m. to noon and 1:30 to 5:30 p.m.; closed Monday. The museum is the information point for the town and for Ani, besides having good exhibits of local finds, from Old Bronze Age artifacts to recently woven carpets and kilims. Read the section on Ani, below, before visiting the museum, so you will know what to do.

Church of the Apostles: Called the **Drum-Dome Mosque** (Kümbet Camii) in Turkish, this striking and obviously un-Turkish structure by the river beneath the citadel was built in 938 by a Bagratid ruler, King Abas. Officially a museum, the church awaits restoration and is not presently open to the public. Armenian churches always seem to have marvelous decoration on the exterior, however, and the church's namesakes, the apostles, are clearly visible on the drum-shaped cupola.

Kars's **Stone Bridge** (Taşköprü) dates from the 1400s and is still in use. You'll spot it spanning the river not far from the Church of the Apostles.

A VISIT TO ANİ: Right on the Russo-Turkish frontier, 27 miles (44 km) east of Kars, the ruined city of Ani is perched above a rocky gorge cut by a stream. On the eastern side of the gorge, sinister watchtowers are manned by Soviet border guards who scan the horizon for violations of their border, and shoot to kill at anyone or anything moving within the 700-yard-wide "sanitary zones" on either side of the border. Beneath their watchful gaze, the crumbling, 1,000-year-old churches of Ani preserve the last memories of an almost-forgotten kingdom.

Sound dramatic? It is. I find Ani spellbinding, but also a bit dangerous. The ruins lie within the sanitary zone, and were they not here, providing a legitimate excuse for approaching the border, anyone standing this near the gorge which marks the border would be shot dead by the Soviet guards, *even though they were standing on Turkish soil.* Ask anyone in Kars, or at the guardpost in Ani, and they can tell you about a recent incident in which Turkish soldiers, while carrying out their duties, inadvertently entered the zone on their own side and were shot.

Rules Governing Visits

The Turks want no trouble with the Soviets along this border, but neither do they want to prevent tourists from visiting the marvelous ruins, so they have worked out a system for visitors. First you obtain official permission from the security people in Kars (this is usually routine, but can take an hour or two), then you tour the ruins in the company of a Turkish soldier whose presence signals to the Soviets that you're on a touristic visit. The soldier also makes sure that you obey the rules governing a visit to Ani, which include these: do not stare or point your finger toward the Soviet side; do not carry or use binoculars or cameras; do not linger long in any one spot, or take notes, or picnic in the ruins; and stay together in a group with your soldier-guide. Please *take this warning seriously.*

You obtain permission for a visit to Ani by applying at the museum in Kars. Take your passport with you, and give the museum officials the information they require. The museum people may try to arrange transportation for you, but this may turn out to be expensive as they may cut a deal with a taxi driver who's a friend of theirs, and take a commission. You should check with a few drivers about a round-trip excursion to Ani, before going over to the museum, so you'll know the going rate.

From the museum, you must go to the Directorate of Security (Emniyet Müdürlüğü), where police officials in green uniforms will approve your application. Having received their approval, you face the task of actually getting to Ani.

Transportation

Unless you have your own car, the way to get to Ani is by striking a deal with a taxi driver in Kars for the round trip. Plan a visit of about a half hour at the ruins, which is about all you'll need and about all the guard will allow. In all, then, you should not need the taxi's services for more than two hours at the most. The rate for such a tour, as of this writing, is about 7,000TL ($9.80), total.

Sometimes there are buses or minibuses from Kars to Aniköyü, the village near the ruins. If they're running, they will depart from the bus station at 6 a.m. and 1 p.m.; the last bus returning from Ani runs at 4 p.m. Though this is cheap, it's also inconvenient and chancy. A taxi is a much better bet.

As you travel across the rolling steppe tawny with crops of wheat, you'll be surprised by the massive walls of the ancient city, rising from the featureless land and running for a half mile.

When you reach Ani, report immediately to the **Jandarma** (Gendarmerie) station, where a soldier-guide will be assigned to take you around the ruins.

Touring the Ruins

Earliest records show that the Urartians, one of Anatolia's oldest peoples, had a city here, at the edge of the gorge along which runs the Arpaçay stream. But Ani lies at a crossroads of armies, today as in the past, and it did not long remain in anyone's hands. The Armenian Bagratid kings, who made it their capital and who reigned here in splendor for less than a century, from A.D. 953 to 1045, lost the city and the kingdom to the Byzantines, who soon lost it to the Seljuk Turks of Persia, who were forced to yield it to the King of Georgia, who gave it up under duress to Kurdish emirs, who in 1239 fled the advancing Mongols. These nomadic warriors had no use for cities, and Ani's beautiful churches were left to fall in ruins after the Mongol conquest.

You pass through the great city wall at the **Alp Arslan Kapısı,** a double gate. The view of the city from within the gate, with a few ruined buildings rising above a grassy field, makes it difficult to imagine what it must have looked like when it was a cosmopolitan city of some 100,000 people.

The tour consists of short visits to eight churches. Of these, the **cathedral** is the most impressive building. Seat of the Armenian Catholics after 993, it was built between 989 and 1010. Other structures include the **Church of the Holy Savior,** built in 1036, and the **Church of St. Gregory,** dating from 1215.

4. Mount Ararat and Doğubeyazıt

At the very easternmost limit of the Turkish republic, near where the frontiers of Turkey, the Soviet Union, and the Islamic Republic of Iran meet, majestic Mount Ararat (17,000 feet) rises into the clouds. According to legend, this is where Noah's Ark came to rest when the waters of the Great Flood finally receded.

At the foot of Ararat is a broad, dusty plain on which lies the frontier town of Doğubeyazıt. Today it's a stopping place for long-distance truck drivers on the road to Iran, but it was once the seat of an independent Kurdish principality, the monarch of which built a grand fortress-palace complex on a hilltop just out of town.

In this far corner of Turkey, the charm of Istanbul, the bustle of İzmir and Ankara, the cosmopolitan feeling of the Aegean and Mediterranean resorts seem far away indeed. Here the scope is vast, the landscape forbidding but absolutely magnificent, the life wild and primitive.

GETTING THERE: Doğubeyazıt lies 176 miles (284 km) east of Erzurum, and only 22 miles (35 km) from the Iranian frontier. You can come out here on a long day trip from Erzurum for a look at Ararat and a visit to the Ishak Pasha Palace, or you can stay the night here, though good hotels are very limited in number. If you're coming primarily to see (or to photograph) Ararat, note that the snowy summit is clear of clouds only at daybreak, for an hour or less.

Several daily buses run from Erzurum to Doğubeyazıt and vice versa; the trip takes about four hours.

Coming from Kars, transportation is a bit more difficult as there are no direct buses. Take a bus or minibus from Kars to Iğdır and change there for Doğubeyazıt.

HOTELS: Doğubeyazıt is mostly mud-brick buildings, so it's a surprise to find a good hotel here, let alone two. The reason they're here is the truckers, of course. International drivers are paid well, and they can afford to stay in comfortable places. Rooms can be scarce, though, so call ahead, or get into town and pin down your room early if you come in the summer season.

The 60-room **Hotel İsfahan,** Emniyet Caddesi 26, Doğubeyazıt 04410 (tel. 0278/1159 or 2045), is the only really good place right in town. Equipped with a decent dining room, very helpful (if somewhat inexperienced) staff, an elevator, and a Turkish bath, the hotel rents good, clean rooms with private shower for 5,000TL ($7) single, 8,500TL ($11.90) double, and 10,600TL ($14.85) triple.

The alternative is the 62-room **Sim-Er Moteli,** P. K. 13, Doğubeyazıt 04410 (tel. 0278/1601 or 2254), east of town three miles (five kilometers) on Hwy. E-23, the road to Iran. This one is the truck drivers' first choice, as it has all the services of a good highway truck stop. The motel is quite comfortable, and charges 5,500TL ($7.70) for a single room with shower; doubles are 9,100TL ($12.75). Children get a 30% discount on the price of a bed. In the restaurant, a set-price meal costs 2,000TL ($2.80).

RESTAURANTS: The best are in the two aforementioned hotels. Otherwise, the town's main street harbors a few very simple little kebap restaurants.

ISHAK PASHA PALACE: In 1685 a local potentate named Çolak Abdi Pasha began to build himself a fortified palace. He didn't live to see its completion, but his son, Ishak Pasha, did complete the work and take up residence in 1784. The palace (İşak Paşa Sarayı), constructed over a century at this crossroads of cultures, is a wonderful mixture of Suljuk Turkish, Persian, Ottoman Turkish, and Russian styles. It crowns a promontory 4½ miles (7 km) east of town.

Getting There

On Saturday or Sunday you might be able to catch a dolmush going out to the palace, but otherwise the only alternative to a long walk is a taxi. Haggle with a driver, and you should be able to get the round trip, with waiting time, for something like 2,000TL ($2.80) to 3,000TL ($4.20).

Visiting the Palace

The guard here tends to be in residence most of the time, and he will sell you an admission ticket for 200TL (28¢).

The palace's main gateway is massive and powerful. It was once fitted with gold-plated doors, but they were carted off to Moscow by invading Russian troops in 1917.

As you wander through the highly decorated palace rooms, you may notice that the entire complex was equipped with central heating, running water, and sewers.

The view from up here is magnificent. Your eye may fall on a small mosque, and ruins of another fortress, across a valley from the palace. The fortress has been here at this mountain pass for thousands of years; the mosque probably dates only from Ottoman times, perhaps the reign of Selim the Grim (1512–1520). Down on the plain are the ruins of Eski Beyazıt, the ancient city which may have been founded by the Urartians some 3,000 years ago.

MOUNT ARARAT: Gazing at the mountain just after dawn from a vantage-point in Doğubeyazıt, you'll see that Ararat clearly has two peaks, named **Great Ararat** and **Little Ararat**. Numerous expeditions have made their way up the snowy slopes, through savage country inhabited by smugglers, bandits, and wolves, in search of the remains of the Ark. So far there have been tantalizing clues, but no conclusive proof. Should you want to try your luck, you must know that climbers are permitted on the mountain only with written permission from Ankara, and all expeditions must go with an official guide. A platoon of Turkish soldiers is often sent along to protect the party.

But I don't want to make it sound impossible to climb the mountain. It's not. Organized climbing groups do make the ascent, and you can join one, but you must do so well in advance in order for all the arrangements to be made.

5. Van

A vast inland sea covers much of the southeastern corner of Turkey. This is Lake Van, a naturally formed body of water created when a volcano on the western shore blew its top and blocked the course of a river. The lake has never had a natural outlet, and thus its water level is maintained only by evaporation. Like the biblical Dead Sea, Lake Van is highly alkaline. (You can wash your clothes in the soapy-feeling water without adding any soap or detergent. If you swim in the lake, you'll float and bob like a cork, but don't do this if you have sunburn or recent cuts or wounds, as the damaged skin will burn like fire from the alkaline salts.)

On the eastern side of the lake, over 60 miles across the water from the western railhead at Tatvan, lies the very old city of Van (pronounced *vahn*). Though most vestiges of the Ottoman city were destroyed in the cataclysm of

World War I, the great Rock of Van, carved with long cuneiform inscriptions, has stood here for millennia and will no doubt continue to stand for centuries. The modern city has a nice museum, in which you can examine many examples of the fine woven work done in the region, especially kilims and traditional Kurdish tribal furnishings. After seeing the best in the museum, you can shop for similar items in Van's many carpet shops.

But the real reason for journeying to Van is to visit the beautiful 10th-century **Church of the Holy Cross,** on an island called Akdamar lying off the southern shore of the lake, not far from Van.

GETTING THERE: The 260-mile (419-km) trip by **bus** from Erzurum takes seven or eight hours, and costs 3,500TL ($4.90). Coming from Doğubeyazıt by bus, you will pass through Ağrı, Patnos, and Erciş, a distance of 195 miles (315 km), at a fare of 2000TL ($2.80). The other, shorter road, which runs close to the border, is not in good condition and is troubled by highwaymen and smugglers.

From Diyarbakır, there are four buses daily on the seven-hour, 252-mile (406-km) trip, at a cost of 2,500TL ($3.50).

Turkish Airlines, Cumhuriyet Caddesi 196, Van (tel. 061/11-241 or 11-768), flies from Istanbul via Ankara to Van daily except Thursday and Saturday. The airport bus into town costs 350TL (50¢).

There is rail service to Van—of a sort. The **Lake Van Express** *(Van Gölü Ekspresi)* departs Ankara at 6:40 a.m. on Tuesday, Thursday, and Sunday on the long trip to Tatvan, at the western edge of the lake. From Tatvan, passengers board a lake steamer for the four-hour cruise eastward to Van. If the train is on time (which it rarely is), the trip from Ankara to Tatvan takes almost 30 hours; to Van, more than 34 hours.

ORIENTATION: Van is not a big city, but, as with most Turkish cities, modern growth has been planned for, and wide boulevards built for the future make the city look larger than it actually is.

The center of downtown Van is the intersection of **Cumhuriyet Caddesi** and **Alpaslan/Çavuştepe Caddesi.** Hotels, shops, the minibus station, and most other services are a short walk from here. Bus companies have ticket offices near the intersection.

The **Otogar,** however, is on the northern edge of town. Van has two **train stations,** the main passenger station (Şehir İstasyon) not far from the Otogar, and the lakeside station (İskele İstasyon) where the ferry from Tatvan arrives.

The **Tourism Information Office,** Cumhuriyet Caddesi 127 (tel. 061/12-018), is at the southern end of Cumhuriyet Caddesi.

HOTELS: The accommodation situation in Van is good. Several hotels offer very nice rooms and, as always here in the East, prices are refreshingly, surprisingly low.

The newest and finest of Van's hostelries is the **Büyük Urartu Oteli,** Cumhuriyet Caddesi 60, Van 65200 (tel. 061/20-660), owned, operated, and decorated by a Turkish professor of archeology. Situated conveniently on the city's main boulevard, run by an extremely helpful and willing staff, the hotel charges only 9,500TL ($13.30) single, 12,500TL ($17.50) double, for its modern rooms with bath. Try this one first.

Next in line is the very fine, 75-room **Hotel Akdamar,** Kazım Karabekir Caddesi 56, Van 65200 (tel. 061/13-036), on a broad street which runs west off Cumhuriyet Caddesi near the Tourism Information Office. The Akdamar has elevators, a terrace restaurant, a bar, private parking, and modern, comfortable rooms renting for 8,000TL ($11.20) single, 11,200TL ($15.70) double, with bath.

The 52-room **Tekin Oteli**, Küçük Cami Civarı, Van 65200 (tel. 061/13-010), has a prominent sign on its roof, which should guide you easily to it. The location is quiet, the rooms (with private showers) are simple but adequate, and the price is very good: 5,800TL ($8.10) double.

A similar choice is the 48-room **Büyük Asur Oteli**, Cumhuriyet Caddesi 126 (tel. 061/18-792). Room prices here are 5,000TL ($7) single, 6,300TL ($8.80) double, with bath, and the hotel has all the basic services: elevators, restaurant, and parking lot.

The Starvation Budget

For those travelers journeying on a very low budget, Van also has lots of choices.

The fairly large (72 rooms) **Bayram Oteli**, Cumhuriyet Caddesi 1/A, Van 65200 (tel. 061/11-136), is at the very center of all the action. The rooms are somewhat beat-up, but the friendliness of the staff makes up for that. Even at prices of 3,200TL ($4.50) single, 4,800TL ($6.70) double, you get a hostelry with elevators, television lounge, and its own Turkish bath.

Even cheaper? Take a look at the 63-room **Kent Oteli**, Türkiye İş Bankası Arkası, Van 65200 (tel. 061/12-404), where a basic double room with private shower goes for 4,300TL ($6), or 2,800TL ($3.90) for a double room without the shower.

The 48-room **Çaldıran Oteli**, Sihke Caddesi, Van 65200 (tel. 061/12-718), also has doubles with shower for 4,300TL ($6).

The 50-room **Beşkardeşler Oteli**, Cumhuriyet Caddesi 34, Van 65200 (tel. 061/11-116), has bathless rooms only, at rock-bottom prices of 2,750TL ($3.85) single, 3,650TL ($5.10) double, 5,000TL ($7) triple.

RESTAURANTS: Those looking for comfort and style should stick to the dining rooms of the better hotels, where the food will be good, the service fairly careful, and the prices still nice and low. But those out for a bit of adventure, or to save money, can try some of the local places. Cumhuriyet Caddesi holds lots of simple kebap eateries, for instance.

For kebap and many other dishes as well, head for the **Birkoç Restaurant**, Sümerbank Sokak 15 (tel. 11-029), behind the building at Cumhuriyet Caddesi 79. No one would call this place fancy, but the food is tasty, filling, and just incredibly cheap. An entire three-course meal can be had for less than 1,200TL ($1.70).

THE ROCK OF VAN: Archeologists and historians don't know much about the Urartians, a people who occupied this region in the distant, shadowy past almost 3,000 years ago. Among the major clues to the mysteries of Urartian culture and history is the Rock of Van (Van Kalesi), a huge mound of rock about three miles (five kilometers) west of the center of town.

You can walk to the rock, but it will take a while. For faster transport, catch a minibus at the corner of Cumhuriyet and Çavuştepe, or take a taxi.

You arrive at the site to find the mysterious, not very impressive rock rising from the flat lakeshore. On the north side of the rock is a Muslim saint's tomb. Women in traditional dress come and go all day, paying their respects to the holy man.

But what you have come to see are the long inscriptions in cuneiform (signs formed of wedge-shaped cuts), dating from Urartian times, about 800 B.C., on the southern face of the rock. They were cut when this was the fortified strong point of Tushpa, an Urartian city. Tombs carved right into the rock are presently closed to visitors.

VAN MUSEUM: The modern museum has a collection rich in the meager remains of Urartian civilization, including some beautiful golden jewelry, signature seals, and breastplates. Oldest exhibits (pre-Urartian) are from the Early Bronze Age, about 5000 B.C.

The museum is open daily from 9 a.m. to noon and 1:30 to 5:30 p.m.; admission costs 400TL (55¢). You cannot take photographs in the museum.

AN EXCURSION TO AKDAMAR: About 25 miles (40 km) south and west of Van along the shore road is a small-boat dock. From here, at a point about a mile west of the turnoff for the village of Gevaş, boats shuttle across the water to the island of Akdamar, site of the wonderful **Church of the Holy Cross.**

Catch a Gevaş minibus near the Hotel Akdamar in Van, and it will drop you at the dock for a fare of 500TL (70¢). When you reach the dock, which you should try to do fairly early in the day, hop in a boat (they leave about every half hour in high summer) for the short two-mile, 20-minute trip to the island. Round-trip tickets (you can't stay on the island!) cost 700TL ($1). If you arrive off-season, when there are not enough passengers to warrant a boat trip, you can bargain with the boat owner for a special trip, which can cost upward of 10,000TL ($14).

Debark on Akdamar, which is a fairly small island, and you will be only a few yards from one of the masterpieces of Armenian religious architecture, the cruciform church built in 921 by King Gagik Artzruni of Vaspurakan. Though the interior of the church is disappointing, with only a few faded, badly ruined frescoes of saints, the exterior, as always in Armenian buildings, is a joy. Many of the most eventful stories from the Bible are illustrated by delightful high-relief figures carved along the walls.

Look carefully and you'll be able to follow the stories: here are Adam and Eve making their fateful choices in the Garden of Eden; Jonah being swallowed by the great fish; David miraculously subduing Goliath with a stone from his sling; and Abraham ready to sacrifice Isaac, the son of his old age, when God tells him to kill the ram, caught in a nearby bush, instead.

Besides the church, the king built a monastery and a palace for himself, but very little remains of these other buildings.

6. Diyarbakır and Mardin

Diyarbakır, the "Land of the Tribe of Bakr," stands on the banks of the Tigris River. It's surrounded by mighty walls of black stone, and makes an imposing sight.

Set out here alone in gently rolling semi-desert, Diyarbakır has the feel of an oasis (especially in the intense, relentless summer heat), a commercial center where traders come to haggle. It has some light industry and it's also an agricultural town. Believe it or not, one of the principal crops is watermelons. They're sprouted in holes dug near the river, and the roots drink enough from these little artesian wells to swell the fruit to incredible size and weight.

Diyarbakır, like Erzurum, lies at the confluence of trade routes, which of course means that it was also open to frequent attack and conquest by armies which came along the same routes. The first city on this site was founded by the Hurrians around 1500 B.C. and was later occupied by the Urartians, the Assyrians, the Persians, and the armies of Alexander the Great. Even with the advent of the Romans in A.D. 115, Diyarbakır was not to enjoy peace for long. It was subject to raids by various peoples until definitive conquest came with the Arabs in 639. It was they who named it for one of their tribes, the Beni Bakr, who were settled here as a sort of natural garrison.

Though it preserved its Arab name, the city fell to the Seljuks (in 1085) and the Ottomans (in 1515), and was even conquered from the Ottomans several times for short periods.

Though this part of the country was somewhat neglected by investors for years, a new development program has resulted in an economic boom. The Atatürk Dam project, now in the late stages of construction, promises to bring vital irrigation water to the entire region, converting it from semi-desert to a lush breadbasket.

Come to Diyarbakır to see its walls, and to get the flavor of a medieval Arab town, some of which still remains.

GETTING THERE: The **bus** ride to Diyarbakır from Ankara (13 hours) costs 2,000TL ($2.80); from Şanlıurfa, the trip takes 2½ hours at a fare of 2,000TL ($2.80); from Van, it's a six-hour trip costing 3,500TL ($4.90).

Turkish Airlines, İzzet Paşa Caddesi (tel. 831/10-101 or 12-314), in the Demir Oteli in Diyarbakır, operates one flight per day in each direction on the route Istanbul–Ankara–Diyarbakır.

As for train service, I cannot recommend it. But just so you know, the **Kurtalan Express** *(Kurtalan Ekspresi)* leaves Ankara at 6:40 a.m. on Monday, Wednesday, Friday, and Saturday, on the 25-hour journey to Diyarbakır. A first-class ticket costs 3,300TL ($4.60).

ORIENTATION: When you arrive at the airport, bus station, or train station, you'll be at least a mile from the old walled city. Once you arrive downtown, there's no need for elaborate transportation plans, as everything worth seeing is within the walls.

Diyarbakır's Roman town plan, with gates in the walls at the points of the compass, and main streets connecting them from north to south and east to west, is still apparent. But over the centuries other streets have been added, obscuring somewhat the original, elegantly simple layout. However, the main point of reference downtown for the visitor is the **Dağ Kapısı** ("Mountain Gate"), near which are the main commercial streets, with their hotels, restaurants, bus- and air-ticket offices.

The city's **Otogar** is two miles northeast of downtown. To get to the Dağ Kapısı from the Otogar, take a minibus (60TL, 8¢) from in front of the bus station. Taxi drivers may tell you there are no minibuses. Don't believe them.

To buy bus tickets downtown, look for the ticket offices along Kıbrıs Caddesi, near the Dağ Kapısı.

The **train station** (Gar) is at the western end of İstasyon Caddesi. There are minibuses to the Dağ Kapısı from the intersection in front of the station.

The **airport bus** costs 200TL (28¢); a taxi from the airport into town costs roughly three or four times as much. If you're leaving Diyarbakır by air, check in for your flight at the airport at least a half hour before flight time.

Tourism Information

The government's **Tourism Information Office,** Lise Caddesi 24 (tel. 831/11-2173 or 17-840), is in the new city north of the walls. Lise Caddesi runs west from Elazığ Caddesi about three blocks north of the Dağ Kapısı. It may take you a little time to find the office.

HOTELS: Diyarbakır's best hotels are moderate in price and comfort, as Turkish hotels go. Many of them are located on İnönü/İzzet Paşa Caddesi, two blocks south of the Dağ Kapısı, but the old favorite is a block or two northwest of Dağ Kapısı on Ziya Gökalp Caddesi.

The **Turistik Oteli,** Ziya Gökalp Caddesi 7 (tel. 831/12-662), was Diyarbakır's first "luxury" hotel. Though its 39 rooms are not really luxurious or modern, they are larger than most rooms built in recent years, and there is a simple graciousness to this old place which may come partly from its spaciousness, and partly from its tradition of being Diyarbakır's top hotel. In any case, rooms cost 8,900TL ($12.45) single, 15,200TL ($21.30) double, or 19,000TL ($26.60) triple, with private bath. Ask for a room on the back side of the hotel to avoid the annoying noise from the street.

On İnönü/İzzet Paşa Caddesi within the city walls, the traditional first choice for lodgings is the fairly small (39 rooms) **Demir Oteli,** İzzet Paşa Caddesi 8 (tel. 831/12-315), at the corner of Gazi Caddesi two blocks south of the Dağ Kapısı. The Turkish Airlines office is in this building, testifying to its touristic status. Though often busy with tour groups, you may find a room vacant. If you do, it will cost 7,000TL ($9.80) single, 9,000TL ($12.60) double, with bath.

Just a few doors down the street from the Demir stands the **Otel Saraç,** İzzet Paşa Caddesi 16 (tel. 831/12-365), a much simpler, even spartan place with 35 bare guest rooms, each with private shower. Prices here are several dollars lower than at the Demir.

On the opposite side of Gazi Caddesi, İzzet Paşa Caddesi becomes İnönü Caddesi. The large (75 rooms) **Büyük Otel,** İnönü Caddesi 4 (tel. 831/15-832), has a fancy lobby, restaurant, and lounge, but the guest rooms offer only the standard comforts and conveniences, at a slightly higher price than comparable places. Rooms here are priced at 9,500TL ($13.30) single, 13,000TL ($18.20) double, with bath. The hotel is supposedly air-conditioned, but is not all that cool, even so.

The recently renovated **Hotel Derya,** İnönü Caddesi 13 (tel. 831/14-966 or 19-735), across the street from the Büyük, is a good value. Its rooms are almost up to the standard of the aforementioned places, but they cost only 5,000TL ($7) single, 7,500TL ($10.50) double, with shower.

The Starvation Budget

Diyarbakır has numerous extremely cheap hotels, where a double room without running water costs only a dollar or two. But these places tend to be very hot and very drab. However, you can save money, and still sleep in comfort, at the **Dicle Otel,** Kıbrıs Caddesi 3 (tel. 831/23-066), facing the Dağ Kapısı just inside the walls. The Dicle (that's Turkish for "Tigris") is pretty nice looking and comfy, and yet it charges only 4,400TL ($6.15) single, 6,600TL ($9.25) double, for a room with shower.

Even cheaper beds are available at the old-fashioned **Hotel Aslan,** Kıbrıs Caddesi 53 (tel. 831/13-971), on the street just inside the city walls, running west from the Dağ Kapısı. For a room with running water, you pay 3,300TL ($4.60) single, 5,500TL ($7.70) double.

RESTAURANTS: Haute cuisine is not this city's strong point. Even the hotel dining rooms aren't so great. But simple, filling, inexpensive food is easy enough to find. A short stroll near the Dağ Kapısı reveals half a dozen kebap places where a full meal need cost only 700TL ($1) to 1,400TL ($1.95).

Equally simple and cheap restaurants are to be found on Kıbrıs Caddesi, the street skirting the inside of the city walls, west from the Dağ Kapısı. For instance, the **Babaman Lokantası,** Kıbrıs Caddesi (tel. 15-887), has the familiar steam tables with many ready-food dishes, and they also grill up kebaps in the evening. The dining room is plain, but there's a terrace dining area for use in good weather. Dig in and eat four courses and you still won't pay more than 1,800TL ($2.50).

TOURING THE WALLS: Diyarbakır's massive walls have 72 towers, four principal gates, a citadel (İç Kale), and are almost four miles (six kilometers) in circumference, so inspection of them requires some planning. Along some portions of the walls you can walk on top.

Many visitors choose to tour the walls in a *fayton,* one of those quaint old horse-drawn carriages. The standard price for a tour is about 4,000TL ($5.60), which is pretty expensive. Bargain and see if you can get a lower price.

Highlights of a tour along the walls are the four ancient gates, the **Dağ Kapısı** (also called the **Harput Kapısı** (north), the **Mardin Kapısı** (south), the **Yenikapı** (east), and the **Urfa Kapısı** (west). The walls as they stand date from early Byzantine times (A.D. 330–500).

THE GREAT MOSQUE: The predominant architectural style among Diyarbakır's old buildings is distinctly Arabic. Mosques tend to be rectangular, in the Syrian style, without the characteristic grand portals of the Seljuks or domes of the Ottomans. The stonework has the alternating pattern of light and dark courses familiar in classical Arabic buildings.

The largest and most interesting mosque is the **Great Mosque** (Ulu Cami), built in 1091 and extensively restored in 1155. The mosque's founder was, surprisingly, the Persian Seljuk Sultan Malik Şah. The **Mesudiye Medresesi,** a seminary attached to the mosque, lies across the mosque's large courtyard. It's now used for offices of religious affairs.

THE MUSEUM: There's a brand-new museum abuilding in Diyarbakır, north of the Dağ Kapısı on the right-hand side of Ziya Gökalp Caddesi in the fairgrounds (Fuar Sahası). Ask at your hotel for details on the progress of construction, and whether or not the museum has opened.

AN EXCURSION TO MARDİN: The most interesting day trip you can take from Diyarbakır is to Mardin, a curious old city perched on the side of a mountain overlooking a flat and fertile plain which positively broils in the summer sun. Mardin has little to recommend in the way of hotels and restaurants, but several of its historic buildings are worth a look.

Mardin has a small but significant population of Assyrian Christians, an Orthodox church with a patriarch who resided in Mardin for years, but whose official residence is now Damascus. In the barren hills to the east of the town lie numerous age-old Assyrian monasteries, one of which you can visit easily.

Getting There

Mardin is 62 miles (100 km) south of Diyarbakır. Minibuses (500TL, 70¢) leave frequently from the city's southern gate, the Mardin Kapısı, on the 1¾-hour trip.

Orientation

The minibus arrives at Mardin's bus station, which is at the western end of the town's one long main street named, appropriately, **Birinci Cadde** (First Street). Birinci Cadde is about 1½ miles long. City buses (40TL, 6¢) and Şehiriçi (intracity) dolmushes (50TL, 7¢) run back and forth along the street, making transportation quick, easy, and cheap.

Less than a mile east of the bus station is the town's main square, **Cumhuriyet Meydanı,** a dusty and unimpressive lot used partly for parking and partly for impromptu soccer matches. Dominating the "skyline" here is the 50-room **Hotel Bayraktar** (tel. 1338 or 1645), Mardin's best. Rooms here have showers and rent for 3,500TL ($4.90) double. This is the only half-comfortable place in town, and is certainly far from being luxurious. It's all there is.

The restaurant of the Bayraktar is where you should go for lunch, also. There is no Tourism Information Office in Mardin.

A Walking Tour

Walking is the best way to see Mardin, as all of its significant buildings are up or down the steep hillside off Birinci Cadde. Actually, walking is the *only* way to see the sights. In summer, walking here is very hot work.

Walk east from Cumhuriyet Meydanı to the tiny Hotel Başak Palas on the left-hand side. Turn left (north) up the stairs by the hotel to reach Mardin's most impressive building, the **Sultan İsa Medresesi,** built in 1385. Its magnificent doorway is the building's prime feature; there is little to see on the inside, which is a private residence in any case.

To the left of the doorway, in a building adjoining the medrese, is the small, quaint **Mardin Museum** (tel. 1664). Look for the flagpole and sign. You may have to make some noise to rouse the attendant, who will let you in for free anytime between 8:30 a.m. and 5:30 p.m. daily—if he's around.

Mardin's Arab-style **Great Mosque** (Ulu Cami) was built by Seljuk Turks from Iraq in the 1000s. The stone building withstood the tumult of centuries pretty well until, in 1832, during a Kurdish rebellion, it was blown up. Some of it has been rebuilt. Look for it just down the slope from Cumhuriyet Meydanı.

Another notable old building is the **Kasım Paşa Medresesi,** which dates from the 1400s. It's near the western end of town, down the slope from Birinci Cadde. Ask for directions as there are no signs.

Deyrul Zafaran

Of the Assyrian monasteries in this region, the most accessible is that of **Mar Hanania,** more often called by its Arabic sobriquet of **Deyrul Zafaran,** the "Saffron Monastery." The tawny-yellow fortress-like building lies about four miles (six kilometers) east of Cumhuriyet Meydanı, reachable by a paved, if curvy, road.

Talk to a taxi driver in town and strike a bargain on a price for the round-trip journey, plus about a 45-minute wait at the monastery. The price should be about 2,000TL ($2.80). You can visit the monastery any day of the week without prior arrangement, but try not to come at lunchtime.

The hills east of Mardin have been inhabited by Christian ascetics since the 400s. Within a century after the first monks arrived, Jacob Baradeus, bishop of Edessa (now the Turkish city of Şanlıurfa), got into a bitter theological wrangle with the bishop of Constantinople. The controversy, over the exact nature of the divinity of Christ, turned on this point: did Christ have both a divine and a human nature, as the bishop of Constantinople held, or did he have only a divine nature, as Baradeus said? Constantinople was more powerful than Edessa, and Baradeus lost the argument, so he promptly set up his own church based on the single-nature (Monophysite) beliefs. His followers were known as Jacobites, and many of them fled the control of Constantinople to settle in these barren hills. Today their descendants are known as the Syrian Orthodox church.

The monastery is still inhabited and working, now mostly as an orphanage for a handful of local lads. The Syrian patriarch's suite of rooms is kept in readiness for a visit, though he has not dropped by for decades.

The monastery was founded on this spot in 792. As you enter beneath a plaque bearing an inscription in Syriac, a black-robed, bushy-bearded priest will greet you, then call one of the orphan boys to give you the standard tour, which includes a look at an extremely ancient **underground room** with a stone ceiling. It may have been used first by Zoroastrians. Also on the tour is a look at the tombs of the various prelates who have headed the monastery through the centuries.

The high point of the tour is a visit to the small, quaint but harmonious **chapel,** with a throne for the patriarch, another for the reigning metropolitan (bishop), a carved stone altar, and many charming primitive paintings and woven pieces.

At the end of the tour, the guide will refuse your tip once or twice (offer about $1), but custom demands that you persist. Finally he'll accept.

7. Şanlıurfa and Gaziantep

Şanlıurfa, more commonly called Urfa, was once called Edessa. It got that name from Alexander the Great, who granted it in honor of a fondly remembered town in his native Macedonia. That was several centuries before Christ, but Alexander's town was not the first one on the site.

The earliest settlement here may date as far back as 1500 B.C., when some people set up camp, perhaps in a cave. The Babylonians called them Hurri, a name which has its root in the Babylonian word for cave. Well, there is still a cave here, and it's now revered as the birthplace of Abraham, so we may have a history of occupation and reverence spanning 3,500 years. The Hurrites knew about chariots, the technological miracle of the age, and they used these versatile weapons to build a great empire with this city as its capital. Ever since then Urfa has been the most important town in the region, and often the seat of kings, princes, and bishops.

After the Hurrites came the Hittites, whose real power center was nearby Carcemish (of which little remains). Assyrians took over from the Hittites, and then Alexander took over from them. After Alexander, his successors, the Seleucids, gained control, but they were superceded by the Aramean people who held onto Edessa, just barely, until the coming of the Romans some four centuries later. The Arameans spoke Aramaic, the language of Jesus, which is interesting to note because the Edessans adopted Christianity around the year 200, before just about everyone else. Some historians think they did this because they liked being contrary, a people apart, not subject to control from outside. The Edessans naturally used Aramaic in their services, and the Syrian Orthodox church (the modern continuation of the ancient Edessan church) still uses the language of Jesus in its services today.

Most of the Syrian Christians hereabouts are in or near Mardin, which at one time was the official seat of the bishop of Edessa, otherwise known as the Syrian Orthodox patriarch.

The checkered history of Edessa is one of religious strife, controversy, and conquest until the Arabs arrived in the mid-600s. For 300 years things were pretty quiet, but then armies marched through again. The First Crusade, led by Baldwin of Boulogne, established a European-style feudal state, the County of Edessa, with Baldwin as count. It wasn't very important, but when it fell to the "Saracens" in 1144, the pope used the occasion to call up the Second Crusade. The Crusaders never got within 1,000 miles of Edessa, preferring to cause mischief elsewhere.

Not even Muslim princes could agree on who should have this city, and until the Ottomans took over in 1637, the city saw little peace.

Such is not the case today. Urfa is a sleepy town of moderate size. A huge fortress sits atop a craggy hill, looming above the town. At its foot, half a dozen mosques crowd around the cave where Abraham is said to have entered this world. Next to them, surrounded by more mosques and medreses, a murky pool teems with fat carp thought somehow to be sacred. Though you will enjoy all of these sights, perhaps the most fascinating part of Urfa is its wonderful, almost medieval bazaar, a real picture out of Turkey's colorful past.

While you're in Urfa you may want to take an excursion south to Harran, a town in which, according to the Bible, Abraham stayed several millennia ago, and which is still made up of very biblical-looking beehive houses built of mud.

GETTING THERE: The 118-mile (190-km) trip from Diyarbakır takes 2½ or 3 hours and costs 1,500TL ($2.10). From Mardin, the three-hour, 109-mile (175-km) trip is along a highway crowded with oil tankers; bus fare is 1,500TL ($2.10). There is no train or air service to Urfa.

ORIENTATION: The city's **Otogar** is on the highway next to the dry bed of a river. A municipal bus can bring you into town, or if your luggage is light, you can walk the mile over the hill to the Belediye (City Hall), near which you'll find the better hotels.

From the Belediye it's a mile to the cave of Abraham, the mosques, the bazaar, and the fortress along Urfa's one main street, named **Atatürk Bulvarı** or **Sarayönü Caddesi** near the Belediye, and **Divan Caddesi** near the bazaar.

The **Tourism Information Office,** Asfalt Caddesi 3/B (tel. 8711/2467) is only two blocks from the Belediye, just off Sarayönü Caddesi. It's usually open all day every day, including Sunday, except for a daily break for lunch.

HOTELS: Urfa has two decent touristic hotels, several more modest places, and a good number of rock-bottom lodgings.

Urfa's best hotel is without doubt the 54-room **Hotel Harran,** Atatürk Bulvarı (tel. 8711/4918, 4743, or 2860), across the main street from the Belediye. Each room here has a noisy and breezy evaporative air conditioner which, even in spite of its noisy gale, is a comfort in Urfa's debilitating summer heat. All rooms also have private baths, and some have little refrigerators and even TV sets. The hotel's terrace restaurant, on the back side, is quite good and moderately priced. To relax after a hot day's hiking in dusty Harran, there's a Turkish bath. For all this you pay 12,000TL ($16.80) single, 15,000TL ($21) double.

Almost next door, on the south side, is the 53-room **Turban Urfa Oteli,** Atatürk Bulvarı (tel. 8711/3520), an element in the government-supported chain. The staff here seems less than solicitous, but the rooms are comfortable, with telephones, twin beds, and private showers. Some of the guest rooms, as well as the lobby, restaurant, and bar, are air-conditioned. For 7,350TL ($10.30) single, 9,750TL ($13.65) double, you get an air-conditioned room with bath, breakfast included. If you don't need the air conditioning, you'll pay 14% less.

Much less fancy, and slightly cheaper, are the rooms at the **Hotel Kapaklı,** Sarayönü Caddesi (tel. 8711/1430 or 2016), near the Tourism Information Office at the corner with Asfalt Caddesi. The better rooms here have private baths and evaportive air conditioners, and cost 6,750TL ($9.45) double. Cheaper rooms have only washbasins, for 4,000TL ($5.60) double.

The Starvation Budget
Across the street from the Turban Urfa Oteli is the modest **Otel 11 Nisan,** Sarayönü Caddesi 141 (tel. 8711/1089), a small family-run place with simple rooms renting for 2,850TL ($4) double, without bath.

Just a few doors down the street, the similar **Hotel Güven,** Sarayönü Caddesi (tel. 8711/1700), charges just slightly more for similar rooms without bath.

RESTAURANTS: In Urfa, those in the know looking for a good meal head for the third-floor terrace restaurant of the **Hotel Harran,** a nice open-air dining area with a view, friendly and fairly efficient service, good food, and moderate prices. I had shish kebap, a salad, and a bottle of cold beer for 3,500TL ($4.90), which is expensive as far as Urfa goes, but fine value nonetheless.

Otherwise Urfa's eateries are on the order of the very modest and cheap **Güney Lokantası,** Köprübaşı Çarşısı 3/D (tel. 2237), more or less behind the Turban Urfa Oteli on a narrow market street. Despite the best efforts of the ceiling fan, the kitchen heats up the dining room even more than normal for Urfa. But the food is tasty, the drinks are cold, and an entire meal of tas kebap (mutton-and-vegetable stew), beans, bread, and soft drink costs an incredibly low 650TL (90¢).

If you find yourself down by Abraham's Cave, next to the pool with the carp, try the shady little **Göl Restaurant and Çay Evi,** in the park. No alcoholic drinks are served, but instead you can order tea, a soft drink, or a full lunch, which will run about 950TL ($1.35).

SEEING THE SIGHTS: Urfa has a nice little **museum,** by a park about a third of a mile north of the Belediye, but it's closed for renovations. Other than the museum, all of Urfa's sights are at the southern end of the main street, near Abraham's Cave. You can walk to them all, and the entire tour will take only a few hours.

The Bazaar

Walking from the Belediye down the main street, called Divan Caddesi along its southern extent, introduces you to the more modern part of Urfa's timeless bazaar. But when you get to a place where you must turn right to continue along the thoroughfare, the bazaar gets really interesting.

Soon you'll see a large stone building on the left. This is the **Gümrük Hanı,** or Customs Caravanserai. Adjoining it is Urfa's **Covered Bazaar** (Kapalı Çarşı), perhaps the only covered market in Turkey where the merchants preserve so well the Ottoman style of doing business.

Once you've taken a look at these major buildings, just wander in the bazaar. You can't go too far wrong. Each little street and alley leads to more interesting scenes: knife makers, tailors, tinsmiths, potters, dealers in livestock and used apparel, stationers, dealers in dry goods—the variety is endless.

Abraham's Cave

The bus stop here is called **Dergah,** "Prayer place," which is what the cave has been for, well, about 3,500 years. The buildings surrounding the modest cave (Hazreti İbrahim'in Doğum Mağarası, "Holy Abraham's Birth Cave") are religious schools, mosques, and charitable foundations established over the centuries. You can enter the cave (there are separate entrances for men and women), but please remember that this is a sacred spot for Muslims, a place of prayer. Be modestly dressed, and don't take photographs. Admission is free, though donations are accepted.

The Sacred Pool

Just a few steps west of the cave is **Gölbaşı,** "Lakeside." While the pool with the sacred carp is hardly a lake (except in arid Urfa), it is certainly a pleasant and verdant spot in this otherwise parched landscape. Surrounding the pool are several significant religious buildings, including the **Rızvaniye** and **Abdürrahman Mosques.** The Abdürrahman Camii and Medrese is a 17th-century building with a square 12th-century minaret. Several of its rooms are open to visitors.

Citadel

Some historians and archeologists believe that the Hurrians, those earliest settlers here, built a fortress on this hill. The theory makes sense. Everyone since them has wanted to capture the fortress and, once they have, they improved and strengthened its defenses only to be overwhelmed by the forces of the next conqueror.

The citadel (kale) is thus large, mighty, and imposing. I would recommend that you climb up to explore it only during a cooler part of the day, as the flight of steps up the hillside is very long. At the top of the stairs is a pair of columns bearing the inscrutable name of **Throne of Nimrod** (Nemrud'un Tahtı), in reference to a biblical figure.

EXCURSION TO HARRAN: There is a curious thrill in visiting a place so directly connected with the Bible as Harran, where Abraham supposedly spent several years while en route from Mesopotamia, where he was raised, to the land of Israel. Though the story of his passing through may not jibe exactly with the legend of his birth in Urfa's cave, such are the problems with legendary figures. Harran is still bewitching, a clutter of beehive mud houses set here and there around the base of a small hill rising from an otherwise utterly flat plain. On the hill are some massive but much-destroyed ruins. The beehive houses, by the way, are still occupied by farming families, who may even invite you in for a look.

Getting There

If you have your own car, there's no problem in getting to Harran. Head out of town following the signs to **Akçakale,** the border post on the way to Syria. After driving 23 miles (37 km), turn left (east), and drive another 6 miles (10 km) to **Altınbaşak,** which is the modern Turkish name for the place, though most people still call it Harran.

Without a car, you go by taxi. The round-trip excursion takes three or four hours, depending on how long you want to explore the ruins and take photos. The distance from Urfa to the village is 31 miles (50 km). Taxi drivers get about 11,000TL ($15.40) per car for the entire trip, waiting time included.

Exploring the Ruins

As you approach the town you'll see the low hill, surrounded by a ruined city wall. The major building here, badly ruined, is the **Great Mosque** erected by the last of the Arab Umayyad caliphs, Marwan II, in the 8th century.

Go over the top of the hill and there is much more to see, especially the **fortress,** a much better-preserved structure, rising above a cluster of beehive houses.

When you get out of your car, village children will run from anywhere within sight of you and gather around for a close look at the weird foreigners, laughing and jostling. Some will ask for coins, ballpoint pens, cigarettes, candy, or even the empty plastic water bottles you may have in your car. You needn't give anything. In fact, giving usually increases the level and frequency of demand.

GAZİANTEP: Named Aintab by its former Arab occupants, Gaziantep today is not really a tourist town, for there's not much to see or do here. Rather, tourists tend to stop for the night if they're driving through, knowing that the city has a few comfortable hotels. Then there are the pistachios.

Yes! Gaziantep is the pistachio-nut capital of Turkey, and devotees of this delicacy will enjoy hearing that huge bags of their favorite treat can be bought here at bargain prices. A pound of nuts, in the shell, costs about $1. Ask for *Şam fıstığı* (pronounced "*shahm* fuss-tuh"), "Damascus Peanuts".

Getting There

The easiest way to get to Gaziantep is by **bus**. Here are some times and prices: Adana, 3½ to 4 hours, 1,000TL ($1.40) to 1,500TL ($2.10); Antakya, 3½ hours, 1,500TL ($2.10); Diyarbakır, 5 hours, 2,000TL ($2.80); Mardin, 5½ hours, 2,000TL ($2.80) to 3,000TL ($4.20); Şanlıurfa, 2½ hours, 1,000TL ($1.40).

As for train service, there is the **Taurus Express** *(Toros Ekspresi),* departing Ankara at 8:50 p.m. on Tuesday, Thursday, and Sunday, making the run via Adana to Gaziantep in about 23 hours, usually hauling sleeping cars and a diner. A first-class seat costs 2,800TL ($3.90). If there are no sleeping cars, you can usually get a couchette *(kuşet)* bunk.

Gaziantep has an airport, but as of this writing there is no scheduled service to it.

Orientation

The heart of downtown Gaziantep, right next to the provincial government headquarters (Hükümet Konağı) and near most of the city's hotels, is the intersection of **Atatürk Bulvarı/Suburcu Caddesi** and **Hürriyet/İstasyon Caddesi.**

From the **Otogar** (bus terminal), a mile and a half from downtown, take a "Devlet Hastanesi" minibus (60TL, 9¢). Ask to get off at the **Konak** (provincial government headquarters). If you miss the stop, don't worry; the last stop, at the Government Hospital, is just a few blocks farther along Hürriyet Caddesi, and it's actually nearer the best hotels.

From the **Gar** (railway station), catch a "Devlet Hastanesi" minibus from the large intersection in front of the station.

There is no official Tourism Information Office in town, but the provincial authorities maintain a **Tourism Directorate** (İl Kültür ve Turizm Müdürlüğü) on Atatürk Bulvarı; it's not geared to dealing with foreign tourists, but they may be able to help if you have a problem.

Hotels

Most tourists passing through Gaziantep put up at the **Hotel Kaleli,** Hürriyet Caddesi, Güzelce Sokak 50 (tel. 851/13-417 or 12-728), almost across the street from the Government Hospital (Devlet Hastanesi). The weary travelers lend this comfortable place an oldtime roadhouse atmosphere, swapping stories of adventure in the lounge or the rooftop restaurant. The rooms are comfortable and mostly quiet, with thoughtful provisions for cross-ventilation in this sultry climate. Prices are 8,500TL ($11.90) single, 10,500TL ($14.70) double, or 18,000TL ($25.20) triple in a suite, all with private bath or shower.

Just down the street is the **Hotel Türk,** Hürriyet Caddesi 27 (tel. 851/19-480), where fairly simple rooms with bath cost 5,910TL ($8.25) single, 7,400TL ($10.35) double.

The city's other hotels are right near the intersection of Hürriyet Caddesi and Atatürk Bulvarı. The **Hotel Seç,** Atatürk Bulvarı 4/B (tel. 851/15-272), is right at the famous intersection, offering a choice between rooms with bath and rooms without. With the private facilities the price is 5,300TL ($7.40) double; without the bath you pay 3,500TL ($4.90). Watch out for traffic noise.

A few steps farther along Atatürk Bulvarı are several more hotels, including the bright and modern **Hotel Veliç**, Atatürk Bulvarı 23 (tel. 851/22-341 or 11-726). All of the rooms here have private bath and prices of 6,000TL ($8.40) double.

The **Hotel Güney**, Atatürk Bulvarı 10 (tel. 851/16-886), has quite presentable double rooms with bath for slightly more, 6,400TL ($8.95).

Restaurants

The place to go is that same intersection of Hürriyet Caddesi and Atatürk Bulvarı. On Hürriyet, facing the open plaza, is the **Keyvan Bey Restaurant,** Hürriyet Caddesi (tel. 12-651), on the upper floor, with an outdoor terrace and full meals with a main course of kebap for only 1,500TL ($2.10).

The **Burç Restaurant**, Suburcu Caddesi (tel. 13-012), faces the plaza on the other side of the intersection (Suburcu Caddesi is the continuation of Atatürk Bulvarı). The glass-enclosed dining room overlooks the plaza from the second floor, and lunch or dinner, with the view, costs about 2,000TL ($2.80).

Gaziantep's Sights

Gaziantep does have a few sights of interest. You can walk if you have an hour or two. Otherwise, catch a bus or dolmush heading down the hill on İstasyon Caddesi from the downtown intersection and get off at the *müze* (museum).

The **Gaziantep Museum** (tel. 11-171) is open from 8:30 a.m. to noon and 1 to 5:30 p.m., closed Monday; admission costs 400TL (36¢), half price on Saturday and Sunday. Exhibits here include everything from mastodon bones to Turkish carpets, with Hittite and Roman artworks thrown in.

From the museum, cross İstasyon Caddesi and look for the sign pointing the way to the **Kale (Citadel)**, a ten-minute walk through a residential and tradesmen's quarter. First built by Justinian around A.D. 500, it was reconstructed and enlarged by the Seljuk Turks 600 years later.

8. Nemrut Dağı

Between the southeastern cities of Malatya and Adıyaman, Nemrut Dağı **(Mount Nimrod)** rises 6,500 feet toward the sky. Resting on its summit are twin temples, one facing the rising sun, the other the setting sun. Sitting in mute testimony to the megalomaniac dreams of an ancient petty king are gigantic statues of the gods. Their huge limestone bodies sit stiffly upright. Their heads rest on the ground before them, observing the celestial movements.

Nemrut Dağı is certainly among the most fascinating and dramatic sights in Turkey, and no one who visits here can ever forget it. The temples atop the mountain are surprisingly accessible, with daily minibus tours operating from Adıyaman and also from the village of Kahta, closer to the mountain road. When you plan your trip to Nemrut Dağı, note that the mountaintop is covered in snow, and therefore inaccessible, for much of the year. In spring and fall, even if there is no snow, the weather at the summit is freezing cold, and perhaps very windy, and you must be prepared for this with winter clothing. In high summer, when the sun bakes you in Adıyaman and Kahta, you will still feel chilly when you reach the mountaintop. Please heed this warning, and no matter how hot it is at the base of the mountain, take warm clothing with you to the top, and don't try to make the ascent except from late May till mid-October. At any time other than mid-June to mid-September be prepared for *freezing* weather on the summit.

GETTING THERE: The only way to reach Nemrut is by road, and the same goes for Adıyaman and Kahta. Turkish Airlines does run flights five days a week to Malatya, but you must then take a bus from Malatya to Kahta, a 115-mile

(186-km), three-hour journey costing 1,700TL ($2.40). The trip from Diyarbakır takes about the same amount of time, for about the same fare.

For travel between Adıyaman and Kahta, there are minibuses shuttling back and forth throughout the day at a fare of 400TL (55¢).

ORIENTATION: You can make your base in either **Adıyaman,** a fairly uninteresting provincial capital with two suitable hotels, or in **Kahta,** a smaller town with a few decent hotels. From the standpoint of hotel comfort it doesn't matter which town you choose. Most people prefer Kahta because it's where the road to the summit begins. The distance between Adıyaman and Kahta is 22 miles (35 km); from Kahta to the summit of Nemrut, 44 miles (70 km).

There is a **Tourism Information Office** (tel. 8781/1008) in Adıyaman next door to the post office ("PTT") on the main street, which is also the highway through town. Kahta does not have its own tourism office.

HOTELS: There are fewer than half a dozen suitable hotels in the area. Two are in Adıyaman, three more are in Kahta, and one is on the slopes of Nemrut itself.

In Adıyaman

The 43-room **Motel Antiochos,** Atatürk Bulvarı, Adıyaman 02100 (tel. 8781/1240 or 1184), on the main highway, is on the west side of town, as you enter from Malatya, Adana, or Gaziantep. Despite its name it is more of a hotel than a motel, with a restaurant and simple rooms with bath going for 8,500TL ($11.90) per night.

At the eastern end of town, nearer to Kahta, you'll find the **Motel Arsemia,** Atatürk Bulvarı 146, Adıyaman 02100 (tel. 8781/2112 or 3131), where doubles with shower rent for 7,500TL ($10.50). The "motel" has a restaurant, and is fairly near Adıyaman's bus and dolmush station.

In Kahta

Unfortunately, tour sharks hang out at most of Kahta's hotels and will try to book you on a minibus tour as soon as you approach a hotel. The problem with this is that you may end up paying a good deal more than necessary. Take my advice: settle into your hotel; then ask around about tours and prices before saying "yes" to anyone. Price guidelines are given below.

The best place in town is actually half a mile out of town, to the west. It's the tidy **Hotel Nemrut Tur,** Kahta 02400 (tel. 1459 or 1863), and because it's the best place in town, it's often filled by package-tour groups. Should you be lucky enough to find a vacant room, you can enjoy the shady terrace restaurant and the small swimming pool for 4,500TL ($6.30) single, 7,000TL ($9.80) double, with bath.

The alternative is the small, 28-room **Hotel Merhaba,** Kahta 02400 (tel. 1098 or 1139), right downtown in Kahta—follow the signs or ask anyone. It has a restaurant, and rents its small rooms with bath for 6,500TL ($9.10) double, or 4,000TL ($5.60) single.

There's also the modest **Hotel Kommagene,** P. K. 4, Kahta 02400 (tel. 1092), west of town at the junction with the road to Nemrut Dağı. The hotel is actually a large house converted to a sort of pension. It's a friendly place with a terrace and a restaurant, charging 3,500TL ($4.90) single, 6,000TL ($8.40) double, with bath.

On Nemrut Dağı

If you have your own car, consider staying at the new **Zeus Motel,** on the slopes of Nemrut, but contactable at an office in Kahta: Atatürk Bulvarı 43 (tel.

1919 or 4775). The motel is fairly simple, with some rooms containing up to four beds, but the price is only 5,000TL ($7) *per person* for bed and breakfast. Though the motel boasts that it provides minibus service from Kahta to the motel and from the motel to the summit, you should check on the scheduling carefully. You probably don't want to sit around for an hour or two waiting to go.

RESTAURANTS: Your hotel is the best place to have meals, unless you want to try one of the rough-and-ready eateries such as the **Kent Restaurant** on the highway in downtown Kahta, where you can easily have lunch for a dollar or less.

AN EXPEDITION TO NEMRUT DAĞI: Your visit to Nemrut will require at least an overnight in this area, and preferably two, as the trip up the mountain and down takes the better part of a day. Before heading out, though, perhaps you'd like to know how this strange sight came to be here.

A Bit of History

Alexander the Great conquered the entire Middle East, and after him his generals set up various kingdoms in parts of the disintegrating empire. In this region the Seleucids had control, but began to weaken during the 1st century B.C. in the face of Roman pressure. With the support of Rome, the Seleucid governor of this area declared his independence from the Seleucids and set up his own little kingdom here at the foot of Nemrut Dağı. This was Mithridates I Callinicus.

Mithridates built his capital at Arsameia, the ruins of which lie near the present-day village of Eski Kahta on the road to Nemrut. The new king quickly had genealogists come up with a royal lineage for himself, going back to the founder of the Seleucid Empire on the one hand, and the Persian imperial family on the other. Then he married a princess from Parthia, the kingdom southeast of the Caspian Sea which was the major power to the east.

The fun begins after Mithridates' death in 64 B.C., when the crown passed to his son, Antiochus I Epiphanes (64–32 B.C.). Antiochus signed a nonaggression treaty with Rome, thereby protecting his western border. His mother was of the Parthian royal family, so he did not have to worry about an attack on his eastern border. And sitting pretty on fertile lands in the middle, he grew fat and rich. So did his delusions of grandeur.

Having concluded that he was descended from the greatest monarchs in the world, Antiochus decided he must be divine, and that he deserved a proper monument. He ordered the building of the twin temples at the summit of Nemrut Dağı, and also caused a huge pile of crushed rock—in effect, an artificial mountain peak—to be placed between them. He may be buried beneath the stones. No one knows.

In any case, Antiochus' dreams of grandeur got him into trouble, for in 38 B.C., having forgotten the way the world really works, he thumbed his nose at Rome over some matter of state and the Romans replaced him with another puppet. Thus the great and golden age of the Kingdom of Commagene lasted for merely 26 years, those of the reign of Antiochus I Epiphanes. By the year A.D. 72 the little kingdom was an integral part of the Roman Empire.

The great statues on the mountaintop sat alone in silence, forgotten by the world, until 1881, when an Ottoman geologist on a surveying mission discovered them. They remained a geologist's curiosity until excavation finally began in 1953. Much of it was carried out under the auspices of the American School of Oriental Research.

Getting There

It takes over two hours to drive the 44 miles (70 km) from Kahta to the summit along the rough road. Add another two or three hours for visiting the various sights along the way, and lingering at the summit, plus the two hours for the trip down, and the excursion up Nemrut takes seven or eight hours—in effect, a full day.

Many visitors follow the custom of arising at 2 a.m. and clambering into a minibus for the ride in darkness to the summit, where they watch the sunrise. Or they start up the mountain in late afternoon, stopping at points of interest along the way, then watch the sunset at the summit, and bang down the rocky road in the dark. I prefer to go both ways in daylight. Outside of the hottest summer months, you'd be well advised to visit the summit only in mid-afternoon, during the warmest part of the day.

Going by Car: With your own car, be sure to fill the fuel tank completely, and pack some snacks or a full picnic lunch, and a bottle of water—you'll be thankful for these provisions. As for the fuel, though the distances are not great, you will be driving much of the way in lower gears, and your car will use much more fuel climbing a mountain than on a highway.

Another point to reckon with is finding your way. Sometimes the minibus drivers or their cohorts take down the directional signs, making it more difficult for tourists on their own to find their way to the top. I'll give you exact directions so you won't get lost.

Going by Minibus: Minibus drivers usually offer a choice of the short tour and the long tour. For the short tour, they charge anywhere from 17,000TL ($23.80) to 20,000TL ($28) for the hire of the entire minibus, then take you from Kahta directly to the summit. After an hour's wait there, they bring you right back down.

The long tour, for which hire of the entire minibus costs about 5,000TL ($7) more, includes stops at the ruins of Arsameia (Antiochus' capital city), a Mameluke fortress named Yeni Kale, and the Commagene burial ground at Karakuş. A minibus can hold about a dozen people, so the price per person should range from a low of 1,500TL ($2.10) for a full minibus on the short tour to 5,000TL ($7) per person for a half-full minibus on the long tour.

On the Road

If the signs are placed as they should be along the road, drivers should follow them to these intermediate points to the summit: Karakuş, Cendere, Eski Kahta, Yeni Kale, Damlacık, Kuştepe, Tüten Ocak, Narince, and Karadut. You can follow signs for Gerger for about the first 31 miles (50 km), but then you must turn left toward Karadut, whereas the road to Gerger goes straight. When in doubt, follow my directions:

Karakuş and Yeni Kale: The road to Nemrut begins west of Kahta next to the Hotel Kommagene. Watch your odometer, and after 6.2 miles (10 km), look to the left to see the **Commagene tombs** at Karakuş. This is the burial place for the women of the royal family. Columns rise above the graves, one of them topped by a headless black eagle (*karakuş* means "black bird").

At a point 9.3 miles (15 km) from Kahta the road forks; follow the right fork.

Just short of 12 miles (19 km) from Kahta, you cross an arched Roman bridge dating from around A.D. 200, built with twin columns at either end. Only three of the original four columns have survived.

Some 15 miles (24 km) from Kahta lies the little village of Eski Kahta and, looming above it, **Yeni Kale,** a Mameluke fortress constructed in the 1300s. You can climb around the ruins if you like.

By Yeni Kale the road forks left to a dead end in the village of Eski Kahta, or right toward Gerger and the summit of the mountain. Follow the right fork through a dramatic gorge, and half a mile up the road, on the left, is the turnoff for Arsameia, the ruined capital of Commagene.

Arsameia: Paths lead uphill from the parking lot to the hilltop site with its ruined foundations, past several steles with bas-relief figures carved on them. On one large stele, Mithridates I Callinicus, founder of the kingdom, shakes hands with his "peer," the god Heracles. An inscription in Greek explains what good friends they were. Near the stone is a tunnel heading deep into the earth.

Onward and Upward: From Arsameia the road passes through several villages. About 4.5 miles (7 km) beyond the village of Narince, turn left for the summit; the road straight ahead goes to Gerger.

Three miles past the turn is the village of **Karadut,** near which the road is paved in stone blocks for the final 6.8 miles (11 km) to the summit.

At the Summit: You arrive at a parking lot, from which you must hike over rough, stony ground for about a half mile (15 minutes) to reach the western temple. Here sits Antiochus himself, with his "friends" the immortal gods of Greece and Rome. The statues on the western side have been more badly damaged by earthquakes than have those on the far, eastern side, so be sure to take the trouble to clamber around the huge mound of stones. The eastern-temple statues have Greek inscriptions on their backs.

The gods present in each temple are these (from left to right): Apollo and Fortuna, with Zeus in the middle; then Antiochus, and finally Heracles.

The view up here at the summit is simply spectacular on a clear day, and the air is fresh, light, and clean. You will want to linger for a while if you've brought warm clothing. If not, you'll feel chilly in a matter of minutes, and may want to head right back down.

GETTING ALONG IN TURKISH

1. Speaking Turkish
2. Menu Translations and Restaurant Tips

THE INFORMATION THAT FOLLOWS is all meant to make things easier for you as you travel throughout Turkey. German, English, and French are spoken by many Turks, and workers who have been in Europe may know Dutch or a Scandinavian language as well. No one will expect you to know Turkish, but will be delighted if you have learned a few words and phrases. In price bargaining, I have found that prices arrived at completely in Turkish tend to be lower, so practice your numbers.

1. Speaking Turkish

Turkish is written phonetically. If you give each letter its sound—never combine two or more into diphthongs as in English—you should have little trouble with pronunciation. The main snags for foreigners are the six letters that do not appear in English and the two that are pronounced differently. A letter with a cedilla under it is pronounced like its English equivalent with an "h" after it. Turkish "ç," therefore, is like our "ch," and "ş" like "sh," as in "church," "should." Turkish has two "i's," one with a dot, one without. The dotted one is pronounced like our "e," the undotted one pronounced "uh." The "ö" and "ü" are like the same sounds in German, made with pursed lips. The Turkish "c" is exactly the same as English "j," while the Turkish "j" is like the French "j," softer, more like an English "zh." Finally, the funny-looking "soft "ğ"—with a curved line over it—is usually not pronounced at all. Your best bet is to ignore it altogether.

Here is a useful glossary of common words and phrases. If you have the chance, and if you're going to do much traveling in Turkey, you should consider buying *Turkish For Travellers,* by Berlitz. This handy phrasebook covers virtually every common situation you're liable to get into, and is available in most good bookstores.

Hello	**Merhaba**	*mehr*-hah-bah
How are you?	**Nasılsınız?**	*nah*-suhl-sun-uz
Very well	**Çok iyiyim**	"choke" *ee*-yum

Good-bye	Allahaısmarladık	ah-*lahs*-mahr-lah-duhk
Bon voyage	Güle güle	gew-*lay* gew-*lay*
Yes, No	Evet, Hayır	*eh*-veht, "higher"
Please	Lütfen	*lewt*-fehn
Thank you	Teşekkür ederim	tesh-eh-*kewr* eh-dehr-im
Excuse me	Affedersiniz	*ahf*-feh-*dehr*-si-niz
You're welcome	Bir şey değil	beer shey day-*eel*
Please have some (one) . . .	Buyrunuz	*booy*-roo-nooz
What's this?	Bu ne?	*boo* nay?
Where is . . . ?	. . . Nerede?	*neh*-reh-deh
the station	İstasyon	ees-tahs-*yohn*
the bus station	Otogar	*oht*-toh-gahr
a hotel	Bir otel	beer oh-*tehl*
a restaurant	Bir lokanta	beer loh-*kahn*-tah
the toilet	Tuvalet	too-vah-*leht*
someone who speaks English	İngilizce bilen bir kimse	een-geel-*eez*-jeh beel-ehn beer keem-seh
Left, Right	Sol, Sağ	sohl, saah
To the right	Sağa	sah-*ah*
To the left	Sola	sohl-*ah*
Straight ahead	Doğru	doh-*roo*
Here	Burada	*boo*-rah-dah
Over here	Şurada	*shoo*-rah-dah
Over there	Örada	*ohr*-ah-dah
Near, Far	Yakın, Uzak	yah-kuhn, oo-*zahk*
Give me . . .	. . . bana veriniz	bah-*nah* vehr-rin-eez
I would like . . .	. . . istiyorum	ees-tee-*yohr*-oom
a menu	bir yemek listesi	beer yeh-*mehk* lees-teh-see
a meal	bir yemek	beer yeh-*mehk*
breakfast	kahvaltı	kah-vahl-*tuh*
lunch	öğle yemeği	ewy-*leh* yem-meh-yee
dinner	akşam yemeği	ahk-*shahm* yem-meh-yee
the check	hesap	heh-*sahp*
the price list	fiat listesi	fee-*yaht* lees-teh-see
a room	bir oda	beer oh-*dah*
for one, two	bir, iki kişilik	*beer*, ee-*kee* kee-shee-leek
with . . . beds	. . . yataklı	yah-tahk-*luh*
twin beds	çift yatak	*cheeft* yah-tahk
a double bed	geniş yatak	geh-*neesh* yah-tahk
a shower	bir duş	beer *doosh*
a bathtub	bir gömme banyo	beer gewm-*meh* bahn-yoh

without bath	banyosuz	bahn-yoh-*sooz*
for one night	bir gece için	*beer* geh-jeh ee-chin
It's very noisy	Çok gürültülü	"choke" gew-rewl-tew-lew
What does it cost?	Kaç para?	*kahch* pah-rah
Something cheaper	Bir şey daha ucuz	beer shay dah-*hah* oo-jooz
Something more expensive	Bir şey daha pahalı	beer shay dah-*hah* pah-hah-luh
Service charge	Servis ücreti	sehr-*vees* ewj-reh-tee
Tax	Vergi	*vehr*-gee
Very expensive	Çok pahalı	"choke" pah-hah-luh
How?	Nasıl?	*nah*-suhl
How long? (time)	Ne kadar zaman?	*neh* kah-dahr zah-mahn
When, Which?	Ne zaman, Hangi?	*nay* zah-mahn, *hahn*-gee
When does it leave?	Ne zaman kalkar?	*nay* zah-mahn kal-kahr
When does it arrive?	Ne zaman geliyor?	*nay* zah-mahn gehl-ee-yohr
. . . hours, . . . minutes	. . . saat, . . . dakika	saa-*aht*, dah-kee-kah
Eight o'clock	Saat sekiz	saa-*aht* seh-*keez*
Before, After	Önce, Sonra	*ewn*-jeh, *sohn*-rah
Now, Later	Şimdi, Sonra	*shim*-dee, *sohn*-rah
Yesterday	Dün	dewn
Today	Bugün	*boo*-gewn
Tomorrow	Yarın	*yahr*-uhn
Ticket	Bilet	bee-*leht*
Reserved seat	Numaralı yer	noo-mahr-ah-*luh* yehr
First, second class	Birinci, ikinci mevki	beer-*een*-jee, ee-*kin*-jee mehv-kee
Train	Tren	trehn
Railroad	Demiryolu	deh-*meer*-yohl-oo
Railroad station	Gar, İstasyon	gahr, ees-tahs-*yohn*
Sleeping car	Yataklı vagon	yah-tahk-*luh* vahg-ohn
Dining car	Yemekli vagon	yeh-mehk-*lee* vahg-ohn
Bus, Bus station	Otobüs, Otogar	oh-toh-*bews*, oh-toh-gahr
Airport, Airplane	Havaalanı, Uçak	hah-*vah*-ahl-ahn-uh, oo-*chahk*
Baggage checkroom	Emanetçi	eh-mahn-*eht*-chee
Timetable	Tarife	tah-ree-*feh*
Cheap, Expensive	Ucuz, Pahalı	oo-*jooz*, pah-hah-*luh*
Hot, Cold	Sıcak, Soğuk	suh-*jahk*, soh-*ook*

Good, Bad	İyi, Fena	ee-*ee*, feh-*nah*
Big, Small	Büyük, Küçük	bew-*yewk*, kew-*chewk*
Old, New	Eski, Yeni	ehs-*kee*, yeh-*nee*
Open, Closed	Açık, Kapalı	ah-*chuhk*, kah-pah-*luh*
Money	Para	*pah*-rah
Small change	Bozuk para	boh-*zook* pah-rah
Do you have?	Var mı?	*vahr* muh
There is none	Yok	"yoke"
Cigarettes, Matches	Sigara, Kibrit	see-*gahr*-ah, kee-*breet*
With a filter	Filtreli	*feel*-tray-*lee*
Map	Harita	hahr-ee-*tah*
Laundry	Çamaşır	chah-mah-*shuhr*
Dry cleaning	Kuru temizleme	koo-*roo* teh-meez-leh-meh
Turkish bath	Hamam	hah-*mahm*
Shower	Duş	doosh
Soap	Sabun	sah-*boon*
Towel	Havlu	hahv-*loo*
Not	Değil	day-*eel*
And	Ve	veh
Or	Veya	ve-yah
Pretty	Güzel	gew-*zehl*
Gorgeous	Şahane	shah-ha-*neh*

1	**Bir** (beer)	**9**	**Dokuz** (doh-*kooz*)	**60**	**Altmış** (ahlt-*mush*)
2	**İki** (ee-*kee*)	**10**	**On** (ohn)	**70**	**Yetmiş** (yeht-*mish*)
3	**Üç** (ewtch)	**11**	**On bir** (ohn beer)	**80**	**Seksen** (sehk-*sehn*)
4	**Dört** ("dirt")	**12**	**On iki** (ohn ee-*kee*)	**90**	**Doksan** (dohk-*sahn*)
5	**Beş** (besh)	**20**	**Yirmi** (heer-*mee*)	**100**	**Yüz** (yewz)
6	**Altı** (ahl-*tuh*)	**30**	**Otuz** (oh-*tooz*)	**1,000**	**Bin** (bin)
7	**Yedi** (yeh-*dee*)	**40**	**Kırk** ("kirk")	half	**Yarım** (*yahr*-um)
8	**Sekiz** (seh-*keez*)	**50**	**Elli** (ehl-*lee*)	half	**Buçuk** (boo-*chook*)

Note: "Buçuk" is never used alone, but always with a number, as "Dört buçuk," 4½; "yarım" is used in all other situations, as "yarım porsiyon," a half portion, or "yarım veriniz," "give me half (of that)."

Gün	Day	**Ay**	Month
Pazartesi	Monday	**Yıl, sene**	Year
Salı	Tuesday	**Ocak**	January
Çarşamba	Wednesday	**Şubat**	February
Perşembe	Thursday	**Mart**	March
Cuma	Friday	**Nisan**	April
Cumartesi	Saturday	**Mayıs**	May
Pazar	Sunday	**Haziran**	June
Hafta	Week	**Temmuz**	July

Ağustos	August	Ekim	October
Eylül	September	Kasım	November
		Aralık	December

2. Menu Translations and Restaurant Tips
SOUPS—ÇORBALAR

Balık çorbası	Fish soup	Mercimek çorbası	Lentil (pea)
Domates çorbası	Tomato soup		soup
Düğün çorbası	Mincemeat, egg, and lemon soup	Paça	Sheep-trotter soup
		Sebze çorbası	Vegetable soup
Et suyu (yumurtalı)	Broth (with egg)	Şehriye çorbası	Vermicelli (noodle) soup
Haşlama	Boiled meat in broth	Yayla çorbası	Yogurt-and-barley
İşkembe çorbası	Tripe (stomach) soup		soup

MEATS—ETLER

Böbrek	Kidney	Köfte	Spiced grilled-meat patties
Bonfile	Small filet steak	Kuzu	Lamb, mutton
Çerkez tavuğu	Chicken, crushed walnut and oil sauce	Macar gulyas	Hungarian goulash
		Pastırma	Turkish pastrami
Ciğer	Liver	Pirzola	Chop, usually lamb
Dana	Veal	Şatobriyan	Chateaubriand
Domuz, jambon	Pork, ham	Sığır	Beef
Karışık et ızgara	Mixed grill (lamb)	Şinitzel	Wienerschnitzel (breaded veal)
Koç yumurtası	Ram's "eggs" (testicles)	Tavuk, piliç	Chicken

KEBAPS—KEBAPLAR

Adana kebap	Spicy grilled rissole	Halep İşi kebap	Grilled rissoles, onions, and spices
Bursa kebap	Sliced grilled lamb, tomato sauce, butter, and yogurt	İskender kebap	Mixed lamb kebap plate
		Kağıt kebap	Lamb and vegetables cooked in paper
Çöp kebap	Diced skewered lamb	Orman kebap	Roast lamb with onions
Döner kebap	Lamb grilled on vertical spit	Patlıcan kebap	Stewed meat and eggplant
Güveç	Meat and vegetables cooked in crock	Şiş kebap (kuşbaşı)	Skewered lamb

Tandır kebap	Roast lamb	**Urfa kebap**	Lamb stew with
Tas kebap	Meat and vegetable stew		onions

Note: Kebaps are served three ways: as chunks of meat, as ground-meat patties, or as sliced meat. The meat is almost always lamb, and in the ground-meat dishes savory spices are added. Ingredients are usually the same—it's the preparation that's different. Adana kebap is heavily spiced, though they let you put the red pepper on by yourself. Yogurt can be ordered with kebaps. Many kebaps are served with pide bread, under the meat or separately.

FISH—BALIKLAR

Alabalık	Trout	**Lüfer**	Bosphorus bluefish
Barbunya	Red mullet	**Mercan**	Red coral fish
Dil balığı	Sole	**Midye**	Mussels
Hamsi	Anchovy (fresh)	**Palamut**	Tunny, bonito
İstakoz	Lobster	**Pisi**	Plaice
Kalkan	Turbot	**Sardalya**	Sardines
Karagöz	Black bream	**Tarama**	Roe, red caviar
Karides	Shrimp	**Trança**	Aegean fish
Kefal	Grey mullet	**Uskumru**	Mackerel
Kılıç	Swordfish	**Yengeç**	Crab
Levrek	Sea bass		

Note: Prices for fish are sometimes marked in profit percentages of wholesale price. Make sure you know what you're paying. Often you can bargain for a good price. Fish are very seasonal, and very expensive out of season.

SALADS—SALATALAR

Amerikan salatası	Russian(!) salad	**Marul**	A sweet, delicious Romaine lettuce
Beyin salatası	Sheep's brain salad	**Patlıcan salatası**	Eggplant salad (purée)
Çoban salatası	Chopped mixed salad	**Rus salatası**	Russian salad
Domates salatalık salatası	Tomato-and-cucumber salad	**Söğüş**	Plain sliced vegetables
		Turşu	Pickled vegetables
Karışık salata	Mixed salad	**Yeşil salata**	Green salad

Note: Salads are ordered "sirkeli" (with vinegar) or "limonlu" (with lemon juice), and if you don't like hot peppers, "bibersiz."

VEGETABLES—SEBZELER

Ayşe kadın fasulye	French beans with meat	Karnabahar	Cauliflower
Bamya	Okra	Kuru fasulye	White beans
Barbunye	Red beans	Lahana	Cabbage
Bezelye	Peas	Patates	Potatoes
Biber	Peppers	Pilav	Rice
Domates	Tomatoes	Salata	Lettuce
Havuç	Carrots	Salatalık, hıyar	Cucumber
İç pilav	Rice with pine nuts and currants	Soğan	Onions
		Taze fasulye	String beans
		Turp	Radish
Ispanak	Spinach	Türlü fırın sebze	Assorted baked vegetables
Kabak	Squash		

FRUITS—MEYVE

Armut	Pear	Kiraz	Cherries
Ayva	Quince	Mandalin	Tangerine
Çilek	Strawberries	Muz	Banana
Elma	Apple	Nar	Pomegranate
Greyfurut	Grapefruit	Portakal	Orange
İncir	Figs	Şeftali	Peach
Karpuz	Watermelon	Turunç	Seville orange
Kavun	Melon	Üzüm	Grapes
Kayısı	Apricots	Vişne	Morello (sour) cherries

SIDE DISHES

Biber dolması	Stuffed green peppers	Makarna, spaket	Macaroni, spaghetti
Cacık	Yogurt with cucumber and garlic	Menemen	Spicy tomato slices with eggs
İç pilav	Rice cooked in broth with currants, liver, pine nuts	Musakka	Ground meat & vegetable pie
		Peynirli börek	Pastry with goat's cheese
İmam Bayıldı	Stuffed eggplant, served cold	Pilaki, Piyaz	White beans and onions in olive oil (cold)
Kabak dolması	Stuffed squash		
Kadın budu köfte	Batter-fried meat and rice rissoles	Sigara böreği	Fried pastry stuffed with sheep's cheese
Karnıyarık	Stuffed eggplant, served hot	Su böreği	Pastry (hot or cold) filled with cheese or mincemeat
Kıymalı börek	Pastry with ground meat	Yaprak dolması	Stuffed vine leaves
Lahana dolması	Stuffed cabbage		

Note: Dolmas (or sarmas) are served either hot with meat stuffing or cold with rice stuffing and olive oil. Specify which you want by saying "etli" (hot) or "zeytinyağlı" (cold). Börek is a general term for flaky pastry stuffed with meat, sausage, cheese, etc., usually served hot.

DESSERTS—TATLILAR

Aşure	Sweet pudding with walnuts, raisins, and peas	**Keşkül**	Milk, almond, and pistachio pudding
Baklava	Sweet many-layered pie, nut stuffing	**Komposto**	Stewed fruit
Bülbül yuvası	Shredded wheat with pistachios and syrup	**Krem karamel**	Caramel custard
		Krem şokolade	Chocolate pudding
Burma kadayıf	Shredded wheat bun stuffed with pistachios, in syrup	**Muhallebi**	Milk, rice flour, and rosewater pudding
		Peynir tatlısı	Cheesecake
Dondurma	Ice cream	**Samsa tatlısı**	Pastry in syrup
Ekmek kadayıfı	Crumpet in syrup	**Sütlaç**	Rice pudding
		Sütlaç fırın	Baked rice pudding (cold)
Güllaç	Flaky pastry with pistachios and milk	**Tavuk göğsü**	Milk, rice flour, and chicken pudding
Helva	Halvah		
Hurma tatlısı	Semolina cake in syrup	**Tel kadayıf**	Shredded wheat in syrup
Kabak tatlısı	Candied squash	**Yoğurt tatlısı**	Yogurt and egg pudding
Kadın göbeği	Doughnut in syrup		
Kazandibi	Baked "Tavuk göğsü"	**Zerde**	Sweet of saffron and rice

Note: Baklava is made with different things: pistachios, walnuts, or clotted cream (kaymak). Most Turkish desserts are smothered in syrup; best to look before you order.

BEVERAGES—İÇKİLER

Ayran	Buttermilk-like yogurt drink	**Limonata**	Lemonade
		Maden sodası	Mineral soda
Bira, beyaz/siya	Beer, light/dark	**Maden suyu**	Mineral water (naturally carbonated)
Boza	Fermented wheat (millet) drink	**Rakı**	Arrack, anisette
Çay	Tea	**Sahlep**	Hot milk and tapioca-root drink
Kahve	Coffee		
Türk kahvesi	Turkish coffee	**Şarap**	Wine
Amerikan kahvesi	American coffee	**Beyaz**	White
Fransız kahvesi	Coffee and milk	**Kırmızı**	Red
Kanyak	Brandy	**Roze**	Rosé
Köpüklü	Sparkling wine	**Su**	Water

Süt	Milk	**Viski**	Whiskey
Vermut	Vermouth	**Votka**	Vodka

CONDIMENTS AND OTHERS

Bal	Honey	**Pasta**	Pastry
Beyaz peynir	White sheep's milk	**Peynir**	Cheese
	cheese	**Pide**	Flat bread; pizza
Bisküvi	Biscuit	**Reçel**	Jam, preserves
Buz	Ice	**Sarmısak**	Garlic
Ekmek	Bread	**Şeker**	Sugar; candy
Hardal	Mustard	**Sirke**	Vinegar
Kara biber	Black pepper	**Siyah biber**	Black pepper
Kasar peynir	Mild yellow cheese	**Tereyağı**	Butter
Ketçap	Ketchup	**Tuz**	Salt
Limon	Lemon	**Yoğurt**	Yogurt
Lokum	Turkish Delight		

COOKING TERMS

Buğlama	Steamed	**Pişkin**	Well done (same as iyi
Etli	With meat		pişmiş)
Ezme, pure	Purée	**Rosto**	Roasted
Fırın	Baked	**Salçalı**	With savory tomato
Haşlama	Boiled		sauce
İyi pişmiş	Well done (said of	**Sıcak**	Hot
	grilled meats)	**Soğuk**	Cold
Izgara	Charcoal grilled	**Terbiyelı, soslu**	With sauce
Kıymalı	With ground meat	**Yoğurtlu**	With yogurt
Kızartma	Broiled	**Yumurtalı**	With eggs
Peynirlı	With cheese		

Note: The suffix -lı (or -lu, -lü) means "with," so "pilavlı" is "with rice." The -siz (or -suz, -süz) suffix indicates "without," so "bibersiz" means "without peppers."

SHOPPING: BARGAINING IN THE BAZAARS

1. Customs, Antiquities, and Bargaining
2. An Alphabetical Guide

ISTANBUL'S GRAND BAZAAR for centuries has excited the imagination of every traveler who has come to the city. But the bazaar is not unique. Almost every town of any size has a similar, if smaller, covered market, and those that don't have the same shops on small, uncovered streets. Most of the fabulous bargains, such as priceless old icons bought for a song, are gone, but what remains is more suitable to our budget range. Notice I said "most." There are still some people who come away with surprises, like a woman I met who brought back a ring decorated with what she thought were imitation stones, only to find that they were real and that the ring was worth five times what she had paid for it. But really, some of the things made and sold in Turkey today offer surprises just as big.

1. Customs, Antiquities, and Bargaining

CUSTOMS: When the time comes for you to leave Turkey, you may be asked to open your luggage for inspection by Customs officials. The regulations say that you may take $1,000 worth of clothes and souvenirs out of the country without having to show proof that you bought the items with legally exchanged foreign currency; if you show your bank-exchange slips, you're allowed to export more. If you want to export a lot of carpets, you must have receipts for them and an attestation from the local museum officials that none of the carpets is an antique.

In practice these regulations are not enforced uniformly. Most tourists are treated with the utmost leniency by Customs officials, who do not check their bags either on entering or departing, but every now and then a man will require you to open your bags, will find a carpet, will demand that you show proof that it's not an "antique" (without defining the meaning of that term), and will give you considerable trouble about taking it out of the country. He is not looking for a bribe. He is not a rug expert, he is asked to enforce very unspecific regulations, and he may have had a bad day, and that's why all the trouble occurs. In the unlikely event that this should happen to you, the best course is this: Under no circumstances lose your temper; discuss it quietly and politely, saying that you know the rug to be only 20 or 30 years old, that it was cheap, that you really want a nice souvenir of your Turkish vacation in your home. If he is adamant, talk to the representative of the airline you're flying or the ship or bus you're taking to see if they can help. Above all, be patient: the official is only doing his duty as he sees it, and he's also human—an appeal to his kinder sympathies will usually have some effect.

If you want to avoid any slight chance of hassles at the border by mailing goods out of Turkey, you will have to find a friendly post office. They are rare. The small one in the Grand Bazaar is said to be helpful to tourists, but you must meet the regulations by having your item well packaged and sewn into a cloth sack for shipping—but don't pack it all up until after an official has inspected it. The main international parcel-post office in Karaköy/Tophane is an impossible place. You may be told to take your package there for mailing. Don't bother. If you're really in a bind about mailing, ask your hotel clerk or a travel agent to recommend a Customs broker and shipping agent who can ship your things. This will cost some money, but will end your worries.

ANTIQUITIES: A special warning is in order on the subject of genuine antiquities. This doesn't mean century-old antiques, but articles out of Turkey's Hittite, Greek, Roman, and Seljuk heritage. Things of this sort cannot, under any circumstances, be bought, sold, possessed, or taken out of the country. Old coins and little old oil lamps are supposedly included in this ban, as are Greek amphorae, statuary, and the like. The former are sold everywhere at very low prices, but even so are officially antiques and if found in your bags will be confiscated.

BARGAINING: In Turkey, as in most countries of the Middle East, this is an art as well as a social custom. Bargaining changes time directly into money, for if you pay the "first price" in any shop that goes by bargaining, you'll be paying much more than the shopkeeper really expects. Don't look upon it as a battle. It is a skilled art, and your proficiency will be rewarded by extra savings.

Here are some pointers: First, never be in a hurry. Get to know a shopkeeper and his shop. He'll expect you to drink tea, coffee, or a soft drink with him, and talk. Then move on to another shop and repeat the process before buying. I make it a rule never to buy in the first shop I enter—you can always come back later in the day. By visiting several shops you get a good idea of the quality, range, and going price of the items you're interested in, and you must know these things to bargain effectively. Along with this knowledge of the market, you must combine an attitude of indifference. Show the shopkeeper you know what you're talking about, don't allow yourself to be talked into buying something, and never show too much enthusiasm for what he has to sell, particularly the item you want to buy.

A session in a shop might go like this: You enter a leather clothes shop casually, looking at the items displayed. The shopkeeper immediately asks you in English what sort of thing you want to buy. Instead of blurting out, "A jacket!" you act as though you might not want to buy anything at all. He orders a drink, according to your preference. You sit down and chat a while, about his relatives in California, the latest space effort, etc. He gets his assistant to show you long coats, vests, skirts, suits, and jackets. There is no talk of price. You look at the stitching, check the leather for blemishes, feel its softness. You're not impressed (or so you look, even if you are). The shopkeeper, seeing that you know more or less what you're doing, has already lowered his estimate of the markup he can ask for. He'll slip in a few good prices to see how you react. You ignore him, still examining the goods. Finally you break your silence and ask about colors, different leathers, different styles. Try a few things on. Then you ask for the price of an item you don't especially want. If you know that market, you'll be able to tell whether he's overcharging you or not.

Last of all you tackle the item you want to buy, working him down to the price that you want, not the one he wants. If you think it's too much, or if you honestly want to look around some more, as you should, tell him you'll think about it and perhaps come back later. This will usually cause him to knock a few more liras off the price. If it's still too high, thank him and leave the shop, walk around, look at some other things in other shops, and, if you really want the item, return. Offer to pay a little more than your last price and he'll probably cut as much off his demand, and you'll end up with a compromise that suits you both. There's nothing wrong with going through this whole process and then not buying. Shopkeepers get more of this than they do quick sales. They'll respect you for your skill as a bargainer, someone who buys only what he wants at a suitable price.

This technique applies to any bargaining you do in the Grand Bazaar and in most other markets. Keepers of classy shops not in the market areas may bargain, but if they're not going to, they'll tell you so. Apropos of this, I must mention that an acquaintance of mine in the bazaar complained recently to me that customers tried to bargain even when he made it clear he wouldn't. "I give them a good price right off," he said, "and hope to save time for both of us. Look, I'm a modern businessman interested in selling volume, not robbing a foreign customer." Well, the hard part, of course, is to know who it is worth bargaining with, and who not. The only fail-safe way to decide what an item is worth to you. If you see a pot and think "I'd buy that for $10," and the shopkeeper offers it to you for $8, you've done well. To avoid confusion, know the market price and shop around.

2. An Alphabetical Guide

ALABASTER: The best place to buy is at the factory in Avanos, near Ürgüp in Cappadocia. Every imaginable item is made from this soft stone, and in this town the prices are rock-bottom. But alabaster is a standard tourist item and can be found anywhere there's a souvenir shop. Look for flaws (hold the piece up to the light), for bad workmanship, like a hollowed-out piece being unevenly hollowed out, and for pleasing color and pattern. Competition is stiff in this market, so you can get good prices. Remember that you'll have to carry what you buy, and that the stone breaks if dropped in shipment. A standard-size vase should cost about 3,500TL ($4.90) in the Grand Bazaar, cheaper in Avanos.

ANTIQUES: Fancy antiques (furniture, clocks, china, etc.) are found mostly in Istanbul. The Grand Bazaar, especially the Old Bazaar, has many treasures and many more fakes. The Zincirli Han, a small old "inn" of the bazaar, has lots of shops visited mostly by local buyers—others don't know about it yet. From the Nuruosmaniye gate of the bazaar, turn right onto the second street inside the bazaar (Terzibaşı) and follow it straight past the quaint sandwich kiosk in the middle of the street. Just before you get to the gate out of the bazaar, turn right into the Han. Try also the predominantly copper and metal-working streets of Çadırcılar Caddesi, along the west wall of the Bazaar. A good street for antiques in the new city is Asmalımescit Caddesi, which runs between the American Consulate and İstiklal Caddesi. The most expensive shops are near the Hilton on Cumhuriyet Caddesi, or near Tünel Square on İstiklal.

The "precious junk" (hurdacılar) section of the city is great for browsing.

It's near the Galata Tower in Beyoğlu. From Tünel Square at the end of İstiklal, follow the main road around the corner and down the hill, but when it curves to the right to enter Şişhane Square, keep going straight on İlk Belediye Sokak. The junk shops are a few blocks down, with the biggest concentration in a courtyard on the right-hand side of the street.

BOOKS, OLD: Again Istanbul is the best place to look. The shops which sell old books do not specialize in antique books, but used books, among which there are some finds. First try the couple of shops on Galipdede Caddesi, the one which connects Tünel Square with the Galata Tower, where many of the books from the libraries of old Pera have come to rest. The shopkeepers speak some English. In the Old Book Bazaar, called Sahaflar in Turkish, across Çadırcılar Caddesi from the Grand Bazaar, most of the old books will be in Turkish—in the Arabic script. English and European books tend to be more recent.

CARPETS AND KİLİMS: If you've always wanted an Oriental carpet, you might be able to fulfill your wish in Turkey. There are rug shops in all of the big cities, and individual weavers in small towns. Ankara is a good place to get rugs at bargain prices, as is the town of Milas, south of İzmir near Bodrum. The biggest selection of styles and prices is in the Grand Bazaar. Turkish designs tend to be geometrical, sort of like American Indian; the flowery carpet designs are Persian.

It's best to read up on carpets before buying, because a carpet is a relatively big purchase. Here are some hints for buying: Watch for running dyes, both natural and chemical. To test, moisten a corner of your handkerchief and rub it vigorously on a patch of color. A certain amount will come off, but if it's a lot, beware. Feel the rug, top and bottom, for softness. If the bottom is very fuzzy, the rug is probably brand-new. Now look at the top. Bend the rug and look at the color at the base of the fibers. If it's a lot deeper than on the surface, the rug's an older one. All-silk rugs are the most expensive (synthetic-fiber imitations exist), then silk-and-wool, and plain wool rugs are the cheapest. Don't recoil from old rugs, even those that have been used for a hundred years. There's usually another hundred years' use in them; they've been tested and found good.

Rugs come in several sizes. The smallest are no more than one-foot-square seat covers which you should get for $5 or $6. Next are the yastıks, or covers for long Turkish pillows. Saddlebags are similar in size, and cost a slight bit more. These are a foot or more wide and several feet long, and go for about $15 to $40, the latter price for best-quality pieces. Prayer rugs are just big enough to kneel on comfortably; you can pick one up for around $60 to $100, more if it's silk and very nice. Then there's the throw-rug size, several feet wide and four or more feet long. According to design (and therefore scarcity), age, conditions, and exact size, these run for $90 to $300, with imported Persian masterpieces for as much as $500. Finally, large room-size rugs start at $750 or $800 and go up from there.

Kilims are Turkish village rugs that might be called "hairless." They have no pile on them, just warp and woof. These are sometimes cheaper than carpets and, if not so valuable, just as decorative. The most important thing with these is getting one with designs and colors you like. Quality varies, but not as widely as with rugs. Check to see if the dyes run a lot; make sure it's woven tightly and won't come apart after a year's wear. Prices for a three- by five-foot kilim (not an antique) should be in the $80 range, $250 or slightly more for room size. There are selections of these in the big cities, but if you make a point of looking for kilims in the smaller towns and villages that you visit, you'll buy the local patterns right at the source, for a saving of about 25%.

A standard tourist item in the carpet trade is the goat-hair rug. These are very popular because, though inexpensive, the long goat hair has a feeling of luxury about it. Those that have bands of color in them you can expect to look the same after washing, but those that have a pattern woven in—usually solid-color rugs—will come out of the wash minus the pattern. Color bands are part of the basic rug; a woven pattern is painstakingly worked in to make the rug good for sale, but doesn't last, and it's too much trouble to reknit the pattern yourself. The longest hair sheds, so pick a rug with hair of medium length. A small rug is $20 in Istanbul, Ankara, and most other places. Rugs made of Angora goat hair (*tiftik* in Turkish) are twice as much.

CERAMICS: Turkish tiles have been famous for centuries. A visit to the Çinili Kiosk in Istanbul gives you an idea of what the art achieved in the past. Compare the old ones to the ones made within the last years in Kütahya, Turkey's tile center, and you'll see that the art has declined. Today's Kütahya-ware, if not perfection, is still quite nice and not at all expensive. It's not worth going to the village unless you're a dealer. The place's fame has gotten to it, and the shops on the main street are just as expensive as those in Ankara, İzmir, or Istanbul. The range of items in the Grand Bazaar runs from square tiles through Turkish coffee sets, beer mugs, and vases to large decorative plates.

CLOTH: Several items of interest are on sale everywhere. The plain white cotton cloths hand-printed with black motifs are fun for covering tables. There are three qualities, depending on the fineness of the cloth. Pick one of several designs, for a few dollars per item. These cloths are always made of two pieces, with a seam down the middle; watch for more seams than that—sometimes bad pieces are cut and pieced, giving you more seams and a poorer quality cloth. The colorful Gaziantep cloth, with geometric designs and a loose weave, can be found in most cities and towns, and costs about $4 or $5 for a small table-size square. My favorite shop for cloth is in the Grand Bazaar. Walking from the Şark Kahvesi coffeehouse at the end of Fesçiler Caddesi, go down Yağcılar Caddesi; the second street on the right is Kavaflar Caddesi, and the shop is near the intersection of these two streets, on the left as you look down Kavaflar.

COINS, OLD: Unless you're an expert and know a $100 prize from a 10¢ fake, you'll just pick these up as oddities. Every jewelry shop in the Grand Bazaar has a trayful in the window, usually mixed in with contemporary Deutschmarks, French francs, and a Kennedy half dollar or two. Old men sell these from their trays on the streets of most cities and big towns. Base-metal coins, even the oldest, are judged on condition and size alone. If it's a nice-looking coin, it's worth more. Most are $1 or less, the better ones go for a dollar or two, and silver coins are, of course, more expensive. Most of the silver coins are Ottoman.

COPPER: All shapes and sizes, for a myriad of uses. The most popular items are large, flat trays to use as coffee tables, but you'll also find cups, bowls, pitchers, and so forth. The older pieces usually have better designs, heavier gauge metal, and sometimes even dates written in old Turkish characters pounded into the piece. For pots and bowls, those with gentler curves are the older ones; the angular ones are new. I bought a heavy old yogurt pot, about the size of a small saucepan, for less than $10 and found out (the Customs man told me!) that it was 250 years old; no trouble getting it out of the country. Another clue to age is the little spots of tin which fill dents in a tray or bowl. All copper vessels must be coated with tin for use in cooking or serving since copper is poisonous, and those with the tin spots are the ones made some time ago, used a while, and then cleaned of the tin for sale. Brand-new pieces may be "antiqued" with tin spots, though. Small cups and pots run to $5 to $10; bigger ones, $10 to $20. Trays are expensive if they're very big, heavy, and old.

Samovars are among my favorite items on sale here. Most of them were made in Russia and brought across Turkey's border to Erzurum, where Istanbul and Ankara dealers go to pick out lots for their shops. They come in several sizes, the biggest ones, surprisingly, being among the least expensive—no one wants to cart them home. You'll be most interested in the smallest size (not the toy ones). A small samovar in good condition (few dents), with most of its original fittings (make sure a new bottom or top piece has not been put on; the handles should be hinged, not stationary) and several "seals" or metal die stamps made on the surface for prizes won by the design in competitions—such a samovar should be about $35 to $50 on Çadırcılar Caddesi next to the Grand Bazaar or in the Saman Pazarı (market near the Citadel) in Ankara. In the Grand Bazaar this samovar will cost twice as much.

There are many accessories you can buy to go with these, including a cap for the chimney, an extension of the chimney to increase the draft for the fire inside, a copper tea pot (though the original pots were always of china), a bowl to catch the inevitable drip, and a copper tray to put under the whole set. These accessory items can jack the price up, though you'll get them for a lump sum lower than if you buy them one by one. The next size bigger in samovars is about 50% more on Çadırcılar. These prices do not apply to the Grand Bazaar, where shops will ask a lot more, admittedly for good merchandise, and get it from rich tourists. Beware of fakes—well-made new samovars "aged" with stamps to look old—unless it doesn't matter to you.

Copper prices seem to run in direct proportion to the size of the town in which you buy them. Highest prices are in Istanbul, lowest in villages (except very touristy ones).

EMBROIDERY: A great variety of embroidery items is sold everywhere in Turkey. Prices vary according to fineness and amount of workmanship, sometimes according to age. Remember that these are difficult if not impossible to clean.

INLAID WORK: Much of what you'll see is actually not Turkish work but stuff imported from Syria. The work can be good, but you have to inspect each individual box to find the best one. A medium-size cigarette box of pretty good quality will run $9; a chess board with inlaid work, $30 or $40. This is a standard souvenir item sold in most tourist centers.

JEWELRY: One of the first things you'll spot in the jewelry shops of the Old Bazaar is the "silver" jewelry. Some of this old Ottoman work is silver, but most of it is tin—only as much of a "fraud" as pewter is. Shopkeepers won't sell it to you as silver; don't buy it as such. It's a standard item, with good selections in the Grand Bazaar and in most cities. Small things like earrings and rings run $3 to $5; large necklaces, $8 to $16; bracelets, slightly less.

Gold and silver jewelry is much cheaper here than at home because you pay for the weight of the metal rather than for the workmanship. Since these metals have a general market price, and since most shops stock about the same items, be sure to look in a few shops to see which one has the best buys.

LEATHER AND SUEDE: Most visitors come to Turkey expecting to fit themselves out in leather for substantial savings. There are three standard grades of quality in all leather made in Turkey. You won't find this marked on a label or burned into the skin—you have to decide for yourself whether or not you're getting the top-quality stuff the shopkeeper proclaims it to be. Although most shops will offer to custom-make any garments you have in mind—will even copy a photograph or drawing—and most shopkeepers will offer to send your purchases to you, I have had sad experiences in this matter, and have heard of enough other disappointments that I feel I must recommend that you not buy things to order, or have them sent. To avoid the disappointment of having to take ordered items which don't turn out to be what you expected (or perhaps what the shopkeeper promised), or if waiting for months for coats that will never be sent, find something on the racks that you like, pay for it, get a receipt, and take it with you. Remember that if you order something, the shopkeeper holds all the cards: he knows Customs laws, currency laws, and how to hang you up in these regulations if he wants to force you to take an order.

The place to buy leather is Istanbul, though İzmir is building up a healthy trade in its market as well. The competition in the Grand Bazaar is so stiff the prices are at rock-bottom, but in such a condition some shops have to sacrifice quality in return for price. The cheapest is not often the best. The shops with the best-quality goods are on İstiklal and Cumhuriyet Caddesis; prices are the highest here too, but you get what you pay for. Beware of small shops on these two streets which have empty racks (meaning they do mostly made-to-order business) and which charge "bargain" prices—it's usually not a bargain you get, but a gyp. If you shop in Beyoğlu, expect to pay more to get more.

Here's a general guideline on good-quality leather and suede items. The prices given are from the Grand Bazaar, and for not-quite-first-quality goods; for the prices of İstiklal Caddesi shops offering first-quality goods, add about 25%: men's jackets and sport coats, $35 to $55; vests, $20 to $25; men's full-length overcoats in leather, unlined, $100 to $200; women's skirts, $35 to $60; full-length suede coats, $90 to $150; full-length leather coats are about the same price. These are current (during an inflationary period), reasonable prices that any Grand Bazaar merchant should not shun. You'll find things for less, and for more.

Istanbul holds lots of unorthodox leather articles as well. The warm sheepskin coats with the skin side out and the wool worn as a lining run from $100 to $150, depending on quality. These things are often virgin, and smell like the barnyard they came from. You can have them cleaned. Can you stand them until you do?

A last note on leather jackets and coats: Tailors here sometimes cut the sleeves too small in diameter, or the backs too narrow. Be sure of the fit before you buy.

MEERSCHAUM: You think of pipes when you think of this soft white stone. Turkey produces the world's finest meerschaum, and some of the best, and cheapest, pipes. There are also cigarette holders with meerschaum tips and imitation amber mouthpieces, and trinkets carved from stone. The best place to buy is Eskisehir, where the pipes are produced, but any town of any size will sell them to tourists. Here are some things to look for: Meerschaum is valued for pipes because of its porousness—it makes the pipes smoke dry. Weigh several pipes in your hand and pick the one that's lightest for size. Look at the bowl to see if it has been hollowed out well, so that the walls are the same thickness all around, and not too thin. If you want one of the fancy carved pipes, keep in mind that carving can cover up flaws in the stone. A small problem: The stem of the pipe is attached to the bowl by means of threaded tubes of bone or plastic which screw into one another. This is fine, for the bone expands with heat at the same rate as the meerschaum. But the Turkish glue often runs when hot, so you may have to reglue the socket.

Pipes come in literally all shapes and sizes, and vary accordingly when it comes to price. A plain-bowled pipe of a normal, good size, well made of good stone, runs about $8 to $15.

NARGHILES: A romantic remnant of the charm of the East, narghiles, or water pipes, are still used a great deal in Turkey. Few men buy their own, but rather rent them for the afternoon or evening in a tea house, for a few liras. If you're interested in smoking one for pleasure, your cheapest buys are from the shops which sell new chrome-plated pipes to tea houses; these cost about $12 or $15 apiece. Walk down Uzun Çarşı Caddesi, which runs between the Grand Bazaar and the Rüstem Paşa Mosque in Eminönü, to find a few of these wholesale shops, a few minutes' walk down the street near the university walls. In the Grand Bazaar and in souvenir shops in other towns, antique pipes used by rich gentlemen are sold as curiosities. Whereas a new chrome pipe might cost only about $15, the older ones will run as high as $100, with many items spread over the whole range in between. Remember to pick up a few of the specially shaped, extremely strong "plugs" of tobacco to burn in the pipe.

NOW, SAVE MONEY ON ALL YOUR TRAVELS!
Join Arthur Frommer's $25-A-Day Travel Club™

Saving money while traveling is never a simple matter, which is why, over 25 years ago, the **$25-A-Day Travel Club** was formed. Actually, the idea came from readers of the Arthur Frommer Publications who felt that such an organization could bring financial benefits, continuing travel information, and a sense of community to economy-minded travelers all over the world.

In keeping with the money-saving concept, the annual membership fee is low—$18 (U.S. residents) or $20 U.S. (Canadian, Mexican, and foreign residents)—and is immediately exceeded by the value of your benefits which include:

(1) The latest edition of any TWO of the books listed on the following pages.

(2) An annual subscription to an 8-page quarterly newspaper *The Wonderful World of Budget Travel* which keeps you up-to-date on fastbreaking developments in low-cost travel in all parts of the world—bringing you the kind of information you'd have to pay over $25 a year to obtain elsewhere. This consumer-conscious publication also includes the following columns:

Hospitality Exchange—members all over the world who are willing to provide hospitality to other members as they pass through their home cities.

Share-a-Trip—requests from members for travel companions who can share costs and help avoid the burdensome single supplement.

Readers Ask . . . Readers Reply—travel questions from members to which other members reply with authentic firsthand information.

(3) A copy of *Arthur Frommer's Guide to New York.*

(4) Your personal membership card which entitles you to purchase through the Club all Arthur Frommer Publications for a third to a half off their regular retail prices during the term of your membership.

So why not join this hardy band of international budgeteers NOW and participate in its exchange of information and hospitality? Simply send $18 (U.S. residents) or $20 U.S. (Canadian, Mexican, and other foreign residents) along with your name and address to: $25-A-Day Travel Club, Inc., Gulf + Western Building, One Gulf + Western Plaza, New York, NY 10023. Remember to specify which *two* of the books in section (1) above you wish to receive in your initial package of member's benefits. Or tear out the next page, check off any two of the books listed on either side, and send it to us with your membership fee.

Date_____

FROMMER BOOKS
PRENTICE HALL PRESS
ONE GULF + WESTERN PLAZA
NEW YORK, NY 10023

Friends:

Please send me the books checked below:

FROMMER'S $-A-DAY GUIDES™

(In-depth guides to sightseeing and low-cost tourist accommodations and facilities.)

☐ Europe on $25 a Day $12.95
☐ Australia on $25 a Day $10.95
☐ Eastern Europe on $25 a Day $10.95
☐ England on $35 a Day.............. $10.95
☐ Greece on $25 a Day............... $10.95
☐ Hawaii on $50 a Day................ $10.95
☐ India on $15 & $25 a Day........... $9.95
☐ Ireland on $30 a Day............... $10.95
☐ Israel on $30 & $35 a Day $10.95
☐ Mexico on $20 a Day $10.95

☐ New Zealand on $25 a Day.......... $10.95
☐ New York on $45 a Day............. $9.95
☐ Scandinavia on $50 a Day........... $10.95
☐ Scotland and Wales on $35 a Day..... $10.95
☐ South America on $30 a Day $10.95
☐ Spain and Morocco (plus the Canary
     Is.) on $40 a Day $10.95
☐ Turkey on $25 a Day............... $10.95
☐ Washington, D.C., on $40 a Day $10.95

FROMMER'S DOLLARWISE GUIDES™

(Guides to sightseeing and tourist accommodations and facilities from budget to deluxe, with emphasis on the medium-priced.)

☐ Alaska........................... $12.95
☐ Austria & Hungary $11.95
☐ Belgium, Holland, Luxembourg $11.95
☐ Egypt............................ $11.95
☐ England & Scotland $11.95
☐ France........................... $11.95
☐ Germany......................... $11.95
☐ Italy............................. $11.95
☐ Japan & Hong Kong $12.95
☐ Portugal (incl. Madeira & the Azores) . $11.95
☐ South Pacific..................... $12.95
☐ Switzerland & Liechtenstein $11.95
☐ Bermuda & The Bahamas........... $10.95
☐ Canada $12.95
☐ Caribbean $12.95

☐ Cruises (incl. Alaska, Carib, Mex,
     Hawaii, Panama, Canada, & US) $12.95
☐ California & Las Vegas $11.95
☐ Florida........................... $10.95
☐ Mid-Atlantic States $12.95
☐ New England...................... $11.95
☐ New York State $11.95
☐ Northwest........................ $11.95
☐ Skiing in Europe $12.95
☐ Skiing USA—East $10.95
☐ Skiing USA—West $10.95
☐ Southeast & New Orleans........... $11.95
☐ Southwest........................ $11.95
☐ Texas $11.95

TURN PAGE FOR ADDITIONAL BOOKS AND ORDER FORM.